I met the girl
under full-bloomed cherry blossoms,
and my fate has begun to change.

4

Naoshi Arakawa

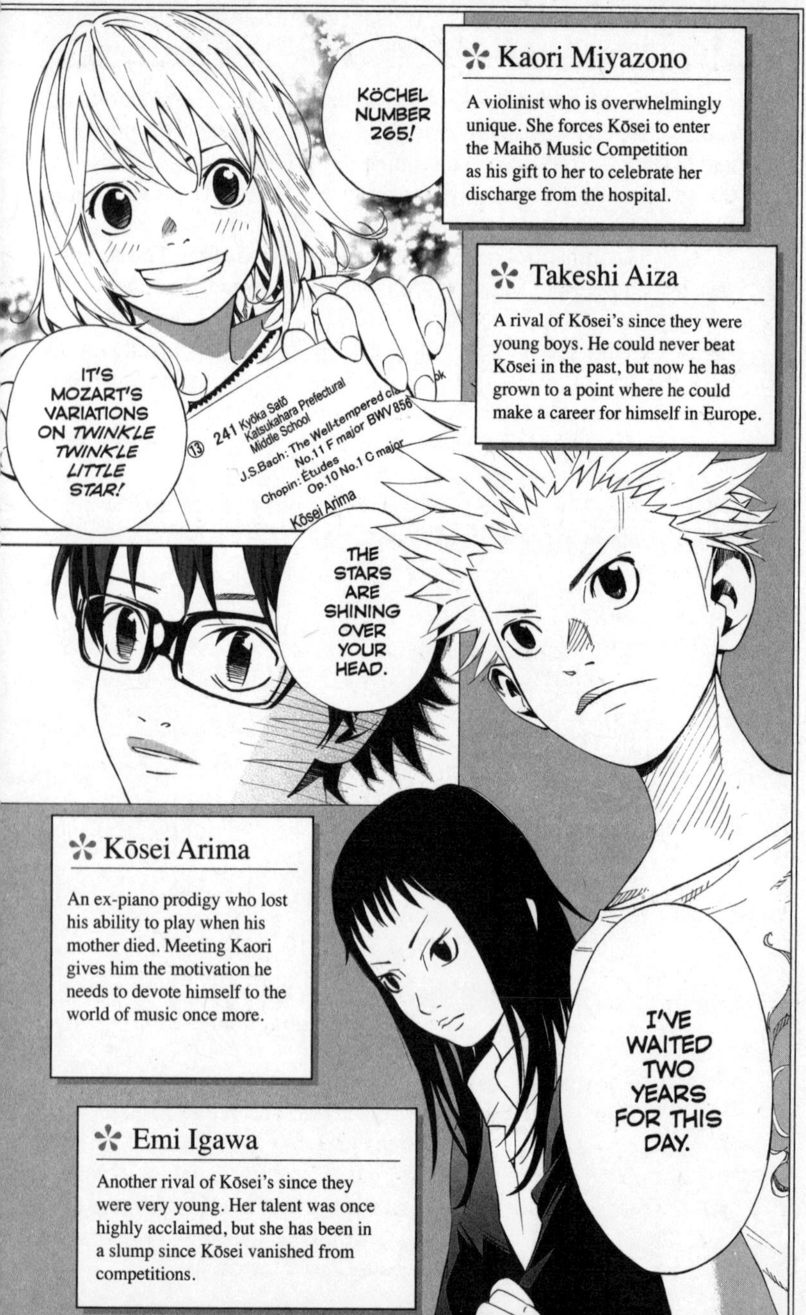
KÖCHEL NUMBER 265!
IT'S MOZART'S VARIATIONS ON *TWINKLE TWINKLE LITTLE STAR!*
13 241 Kyōka Satō
Katsukahara Prefectural Middle School
J.S.Bach: The Well-tempered
No.11 F major BWV856
Chopin: Études
Op.10 No.1 C major
Kōsei Arima
THE STARS ARE SHINING OVER YOUR HEAD.
I'VE WAITED TWO YEARS FOR THIS DAY.

Kaori Miyazono

A violinist who is overwhelmingly unique. She forces Kōsei to enter the Maihō Music Competition as his gift to her to celebrate her discharge from the hospital.

Takeshi Aiza

A rival of Kōsei's since they were young boys. He could never beat Kōsei in the past, but now he has grown to a point where he could make a career for himself in Europe.

Kōsei Arima

An ex-piano prodigy who lost his ability to play when his mother died. Meeting Kaori gives him the motivation he needs to devote himself to the world of music once more.

Emi Igawa

Another rival of Kōsei's since they were very young. Her talent was once highly acclaimed, but she has been in a slump since Kōsei vanished from competitions.

❊ STORY & CHARACTERS ❊

In the autumn of Kōsei Arima's 12th year, his mother died, causing him to lose the ability to play the piano. He lost his purpose, and his days lost all color, continuing on in a drab monotone. But in the spring when he was 14, his encounter with the exceptionally quirky violinist Kaori Miyazono started to change his fate.

Kaori had advanced to the second round of the Tōwa Music Competition, and she ordered Kōsei to provide her piano accompaniment. However, since his mother's death, Kōsei had become unable to hear the music when he focused too intently on his performance. At the competition, although Kōsei had learned to play the accompaniment precisely, he suddenly lost track and grew confused. In response, Kaori, knowing full well that it could mean disqualification, stopped playing and urged him on.

"Again." That one word gave the boy courage, and he delivered a performance that won him a hearty round of applause from the entire audience.

YOU'RE JUST YOU.

The seasons moved onward, to the last summer of Kōsei's middle school career. His classmates Watari and Tsubaki fought valiantly to win their various summer tournaments, but were defeated. At Kaori's request, Kōsei entered the Maihō Music Competition alone. Rivals who knew Kōsei way back when lay in wait, eager to defeat their long-time foe! The favorite to win, Takeshi Aiza, gave a masterful performance, and another rival, Emi Igawa, proudly faced the piano.

contents

Chapter 13: Surge

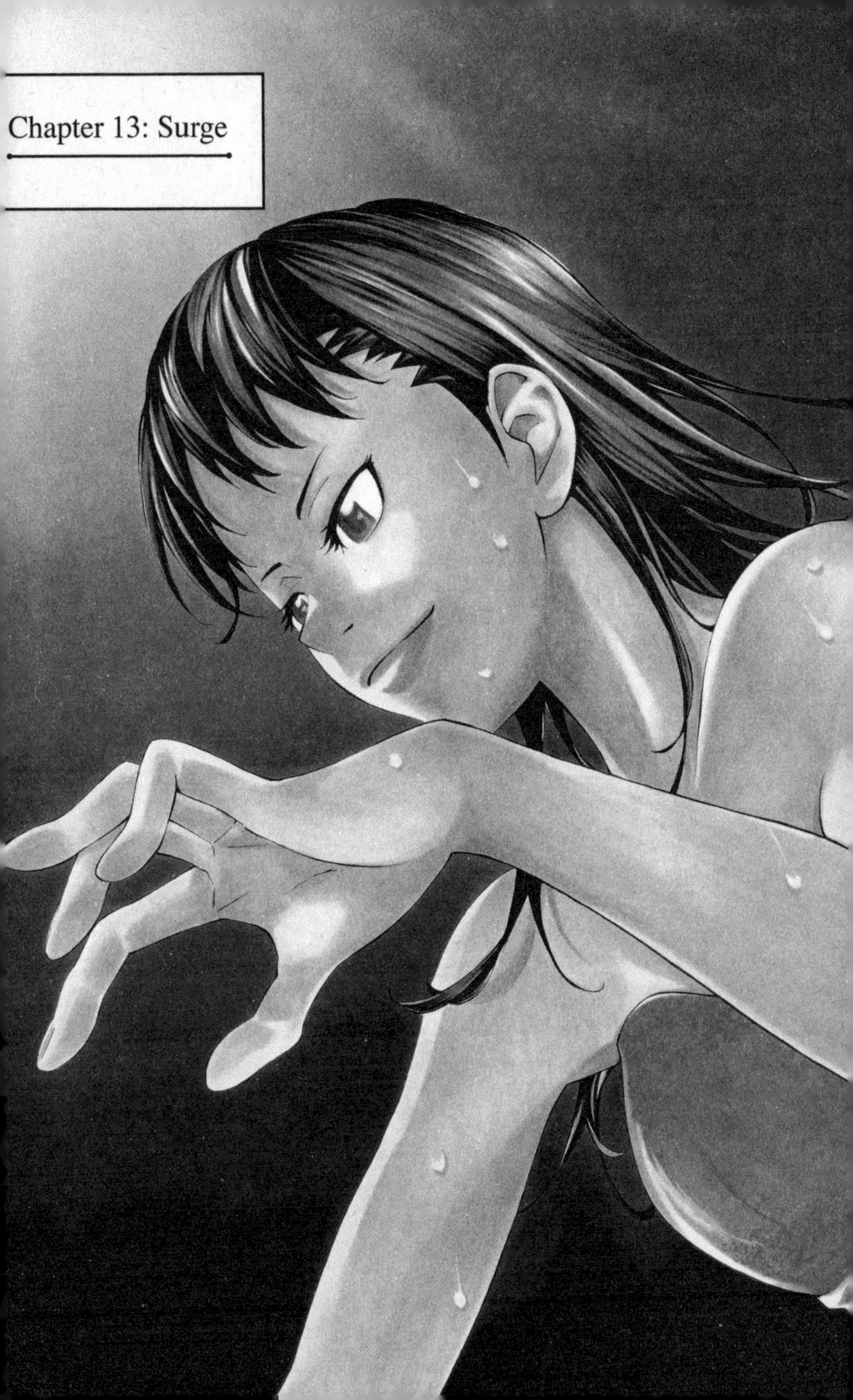

Your Lie in April

I met the girl under full-bloomed cherry blossoms, and my fate has begun to change.

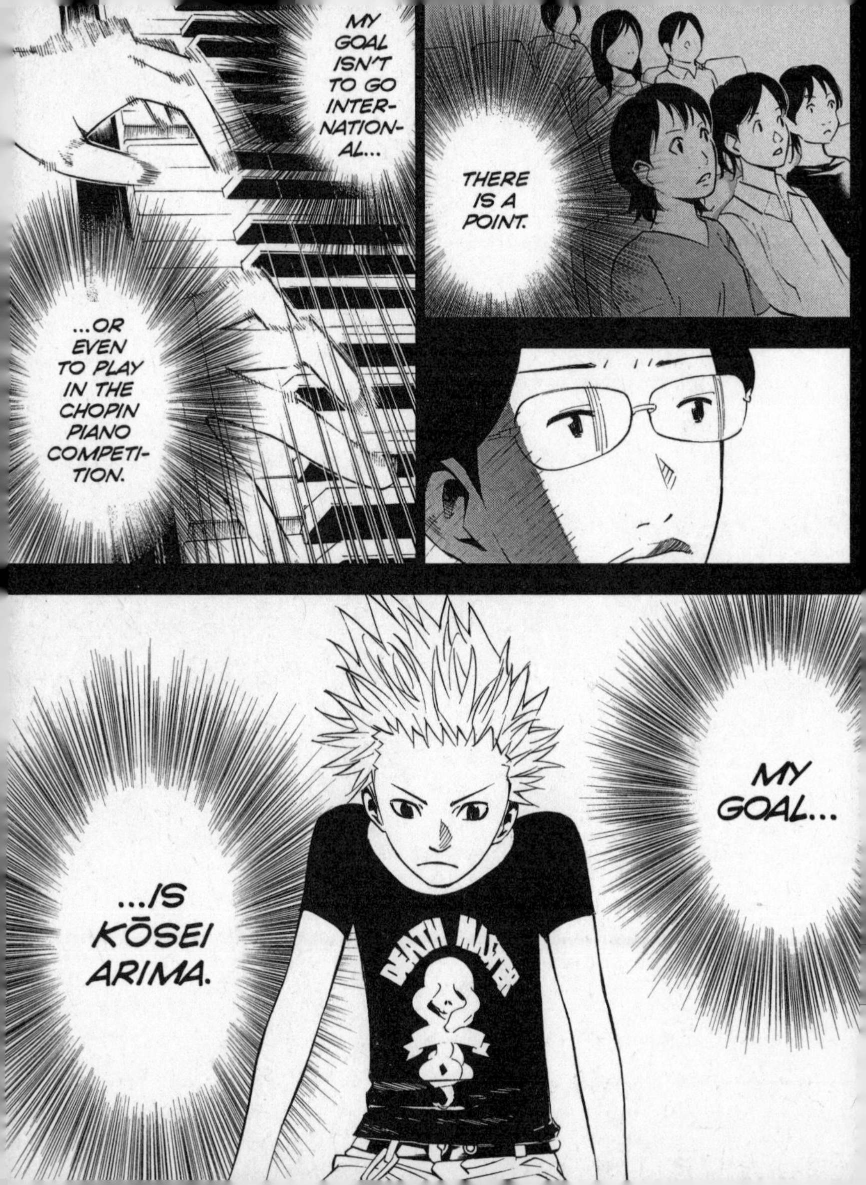
THERE IS A POINT.
MY GOAL ISN'T TO GO INTERNATIONAL...
...OR EVEN TO PLAY IN THE CHOPIN PIANO COMPETITION.
MY GOAL...
DEATH MASTER
...IS KŌSEI ARIMA.

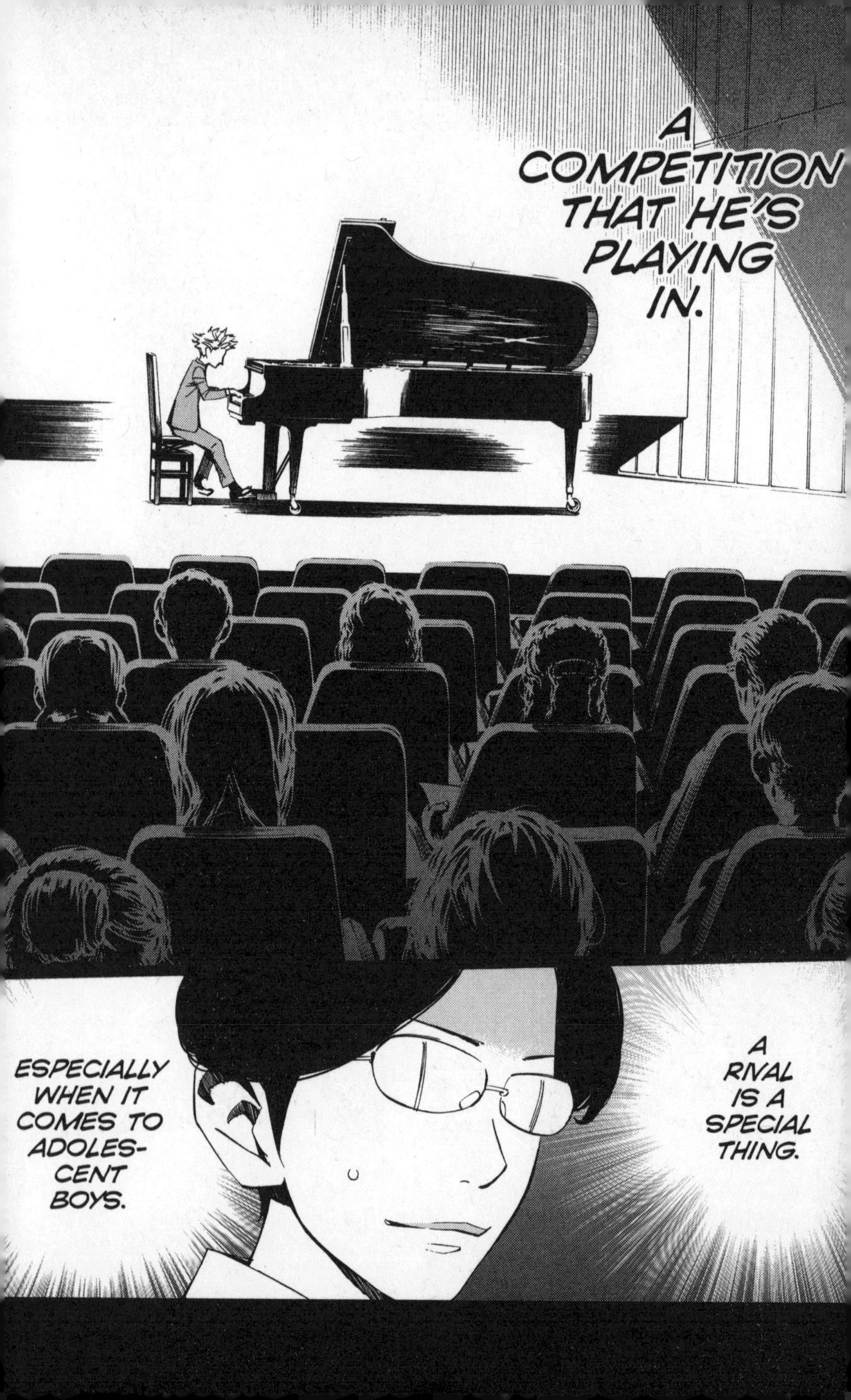
A COMPETITION THAT HE'S PLAYING IN.
A RIVAL IS A SPECIAL THING.
ESPECIALLY WHEN IT COMES TO ADOLESCENT BOYS.

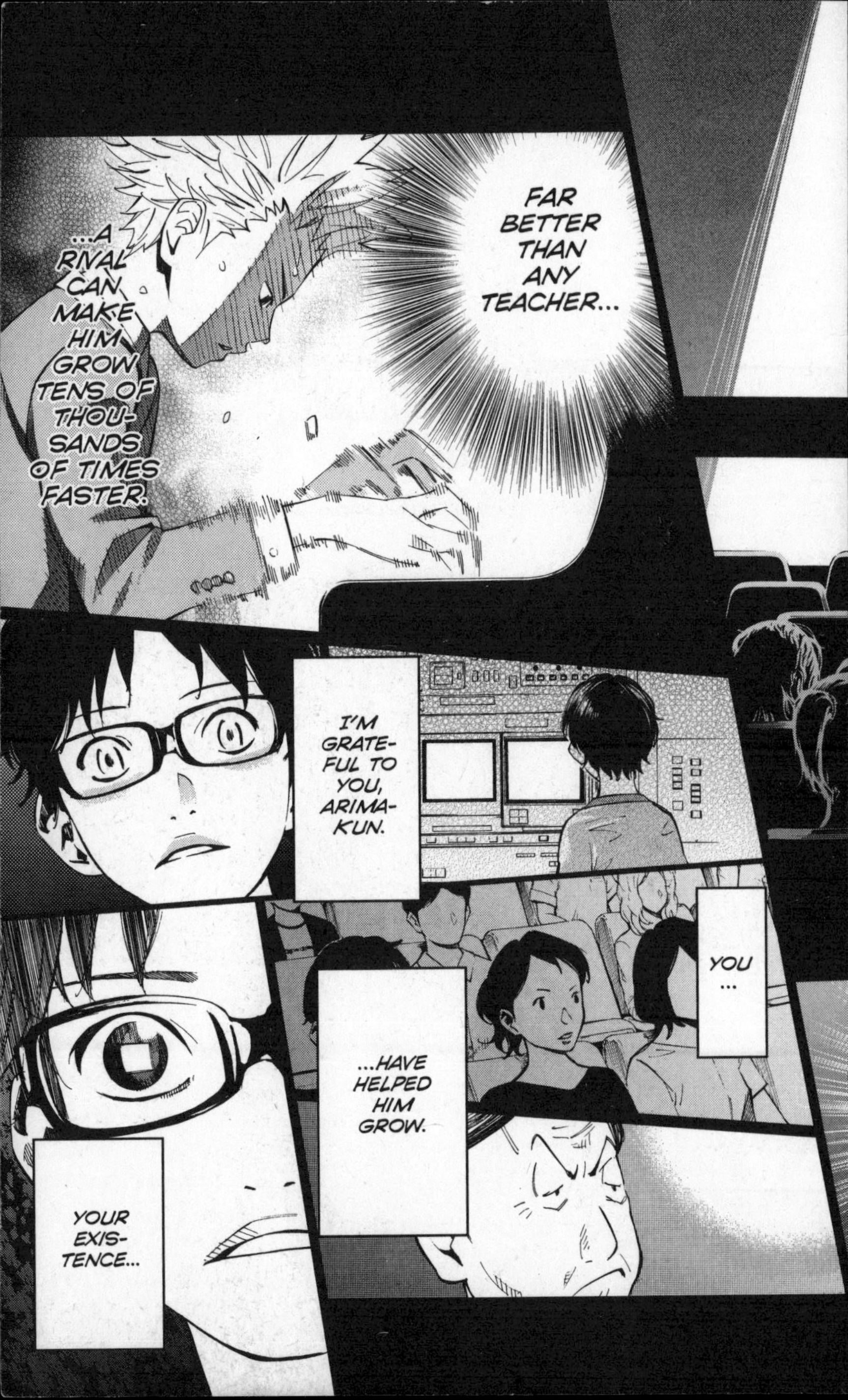
FAR BETTER THAN ANY TEACHER...
...A RIVAL CAN MAKE HIM GROW TENS OF THOU-SANDS OF TIMES FASTER.
I'M GRATE-FUL TO YOU, ARIMA-KUN.
YOU ...
...HAVE HELPED HIM GROW.
YOUR EXIS-TENCE...

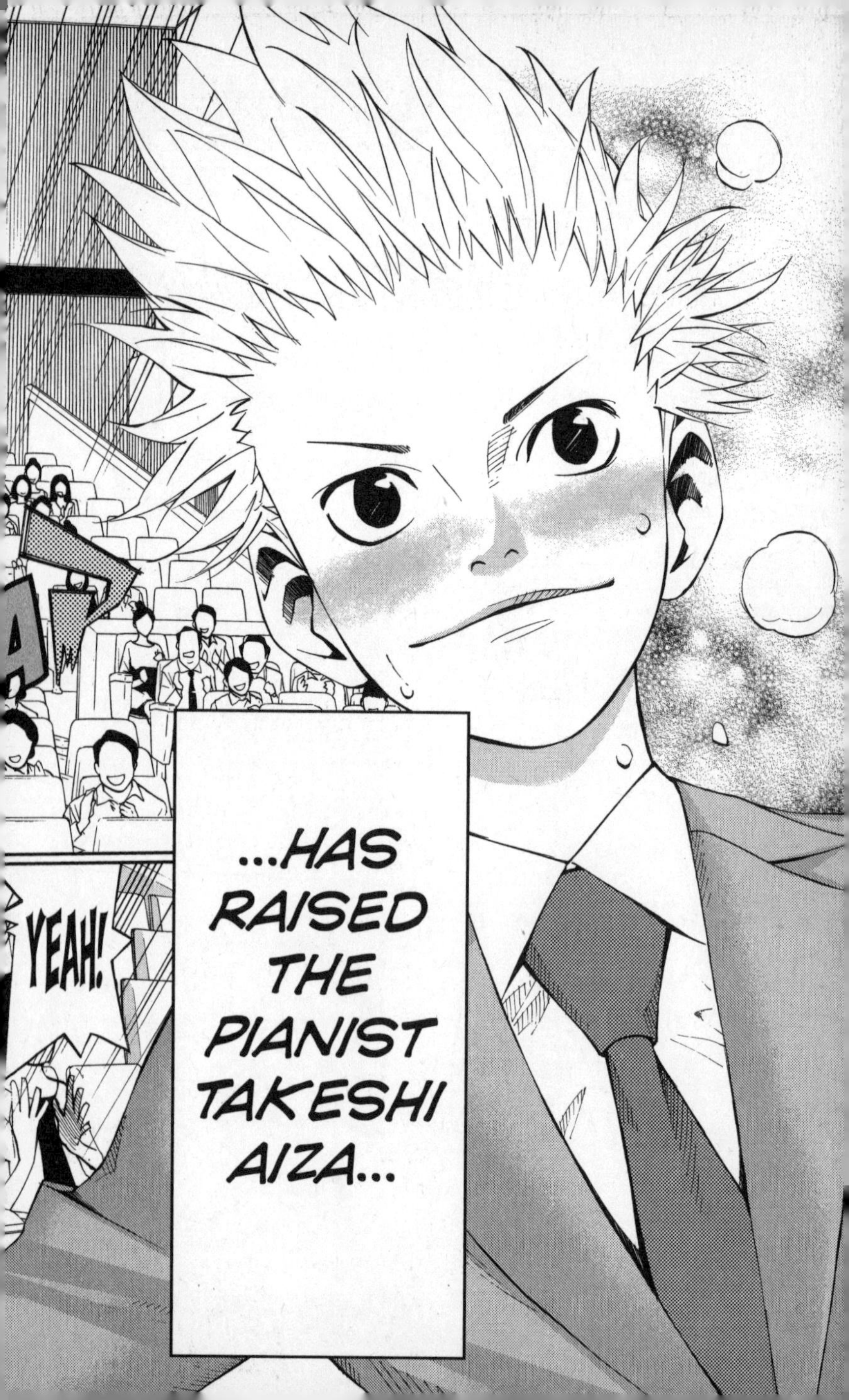
...HAS RAISED THE PIANIST TAKESHI AIZA...
YEAH!

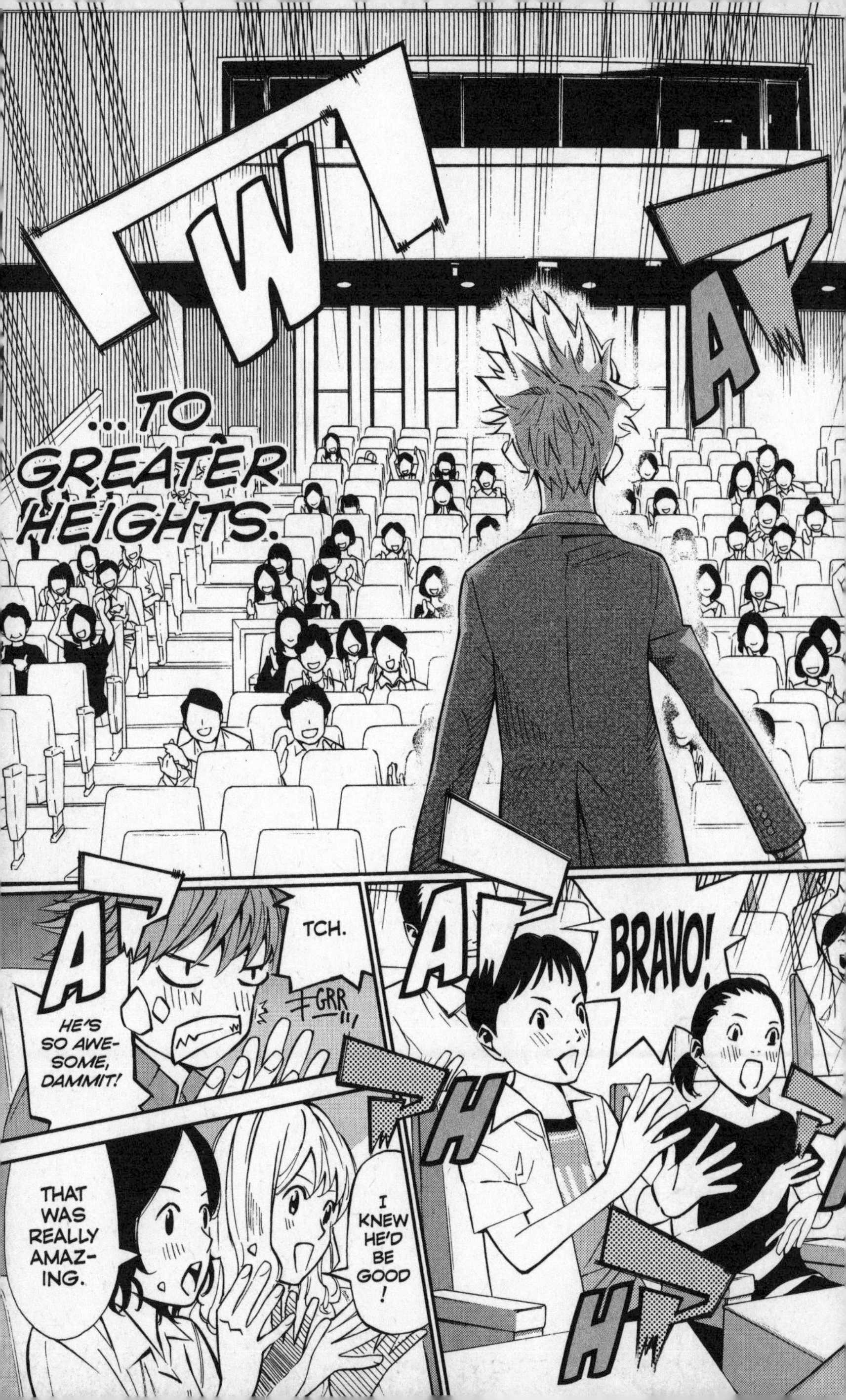
WA
...TO GREATER HEIGHTS.
A
BRAVO!
H
H
A
TCH.
GRR
HE'S SO AWE-SOME, DAMMIT!
I KNEW HE'D BE GOOD!
THAT WAS REALLY AMAZ-ING.

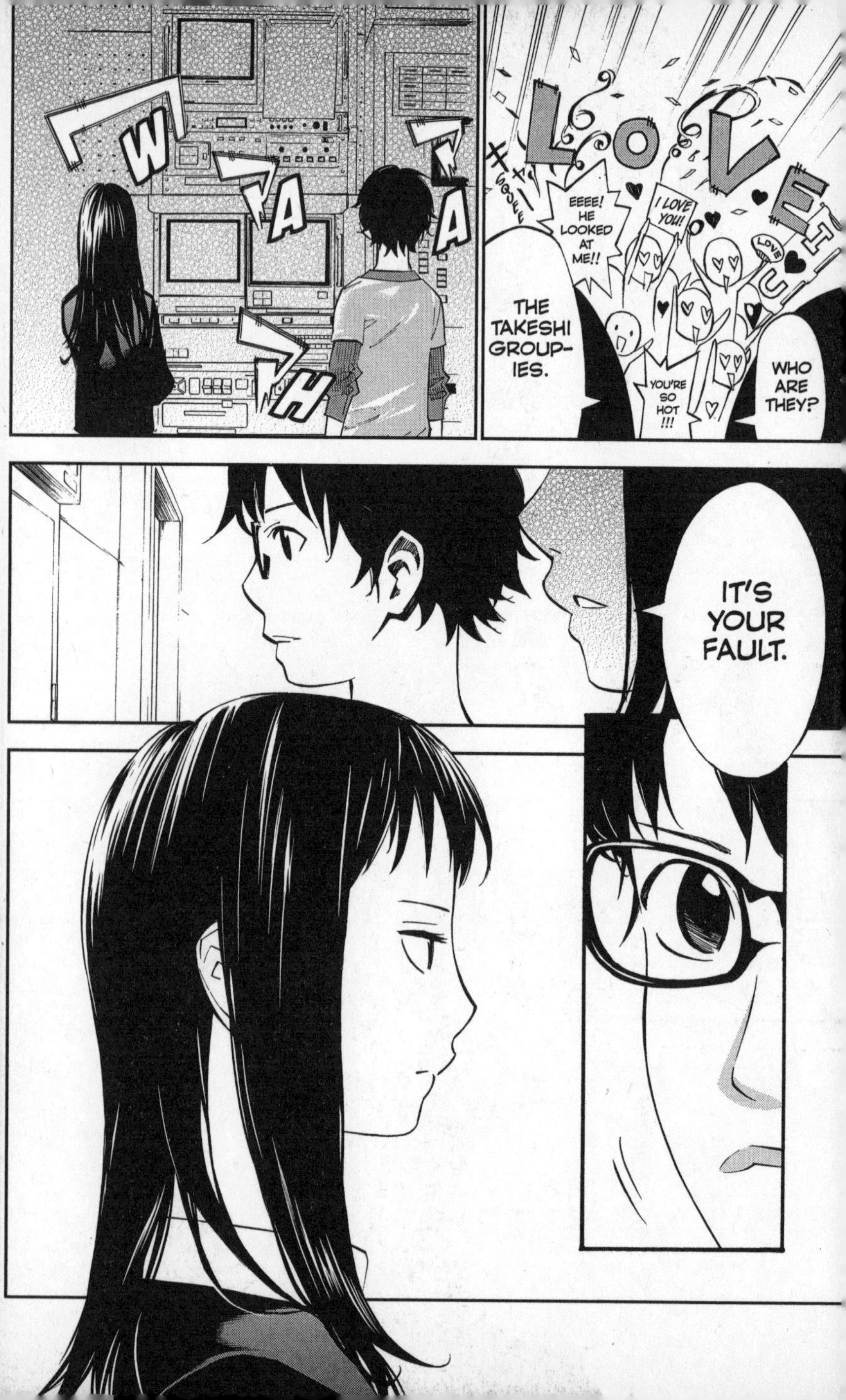
LOVE
I LOVE YOU!
EEEE! HE LOOKED AT ME!!
LOVE
YOU'RE SO HOT!!!
WHO ARE THEY?
THE TAKESHI GROUP-IES.
WAAH
IT'S YOUR FAULT.

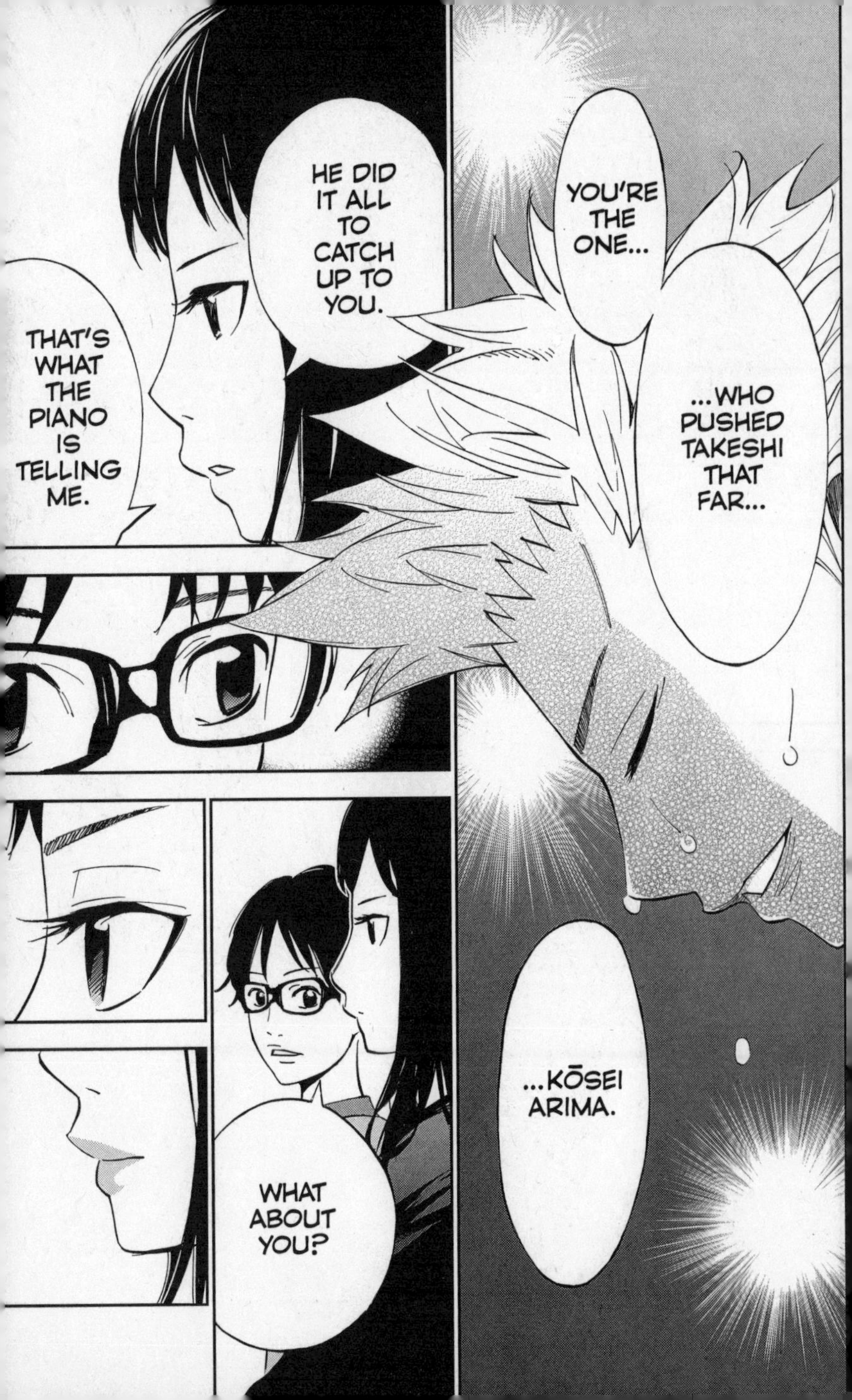
YOU'RE THE ONE...
...WHO PUSHED TAKESHI THAT FAR...
...KŌSEI ARIMA.
HE DID IT ALL TO CATCH UP TO YOU.
THAT'S WHAT THE PIANO IS TELLING ME.
WHAT ABOUT YOU?

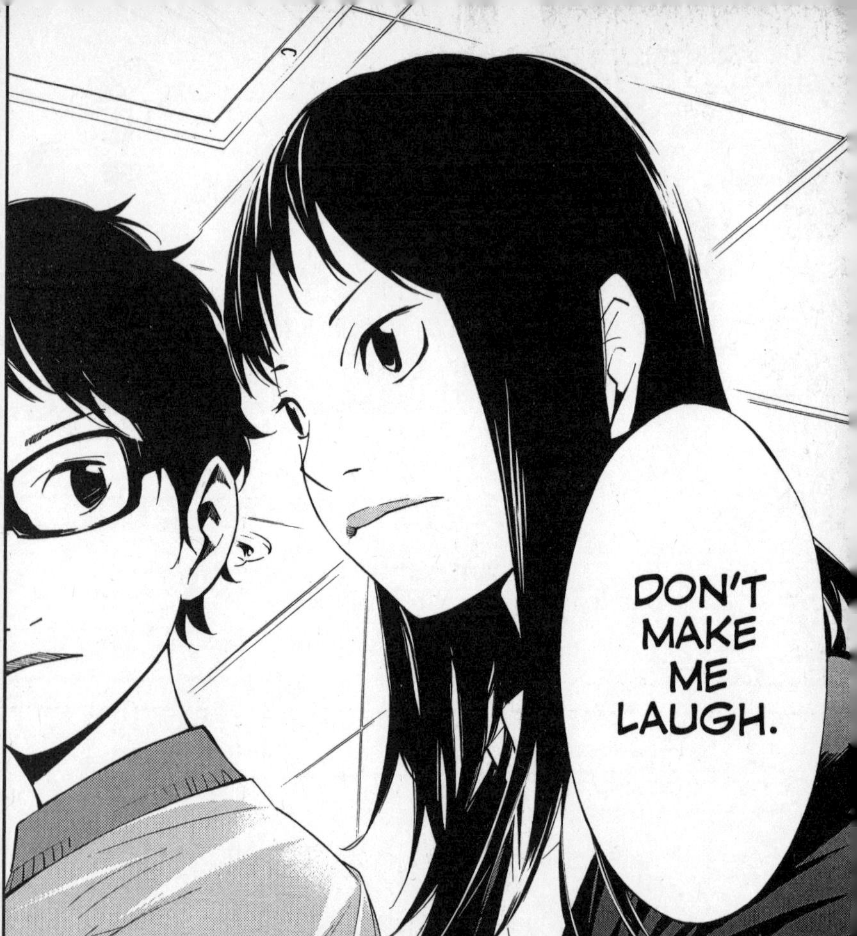
DON'T MAKE ME LAUGH.

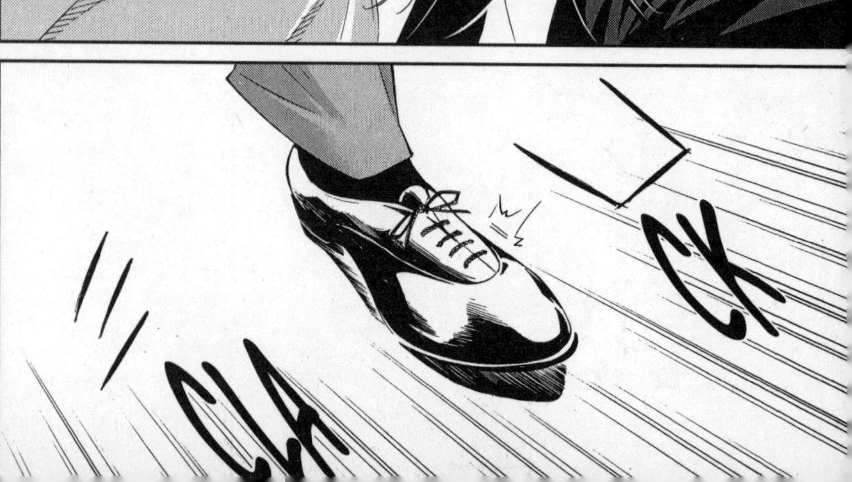
CLA
CK

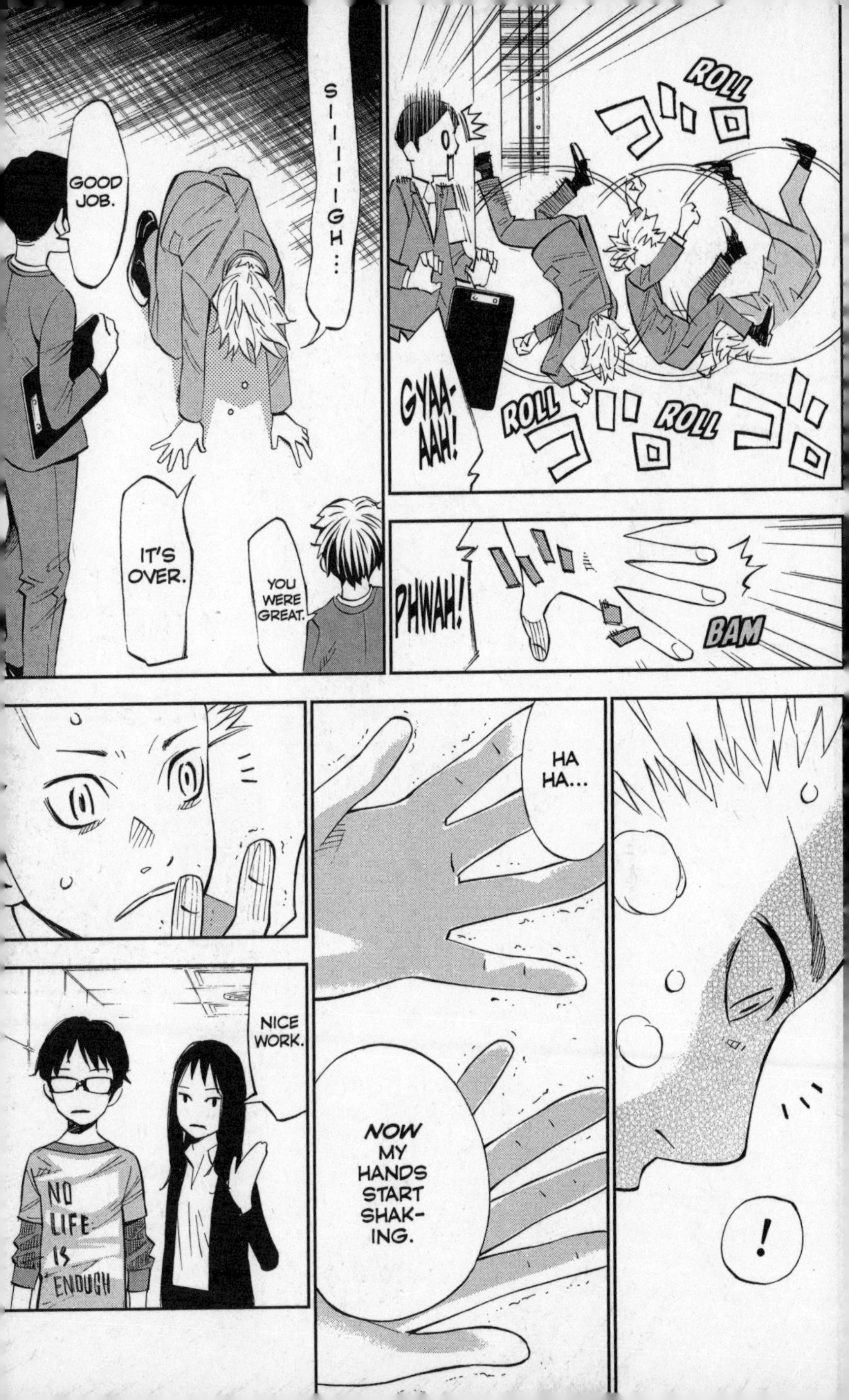
ROLL
ROLL
ROLL
GYAA-AAH!
BAM
PHWAH!
S I I I I G H...
GOOD JOB.
YOU WERE GREAT.
IT'S OVER.
!
HA HA...
NOW MY HANDS START SHAK-ING.
NICE WORK.
NO LIFE IS ENOUGH

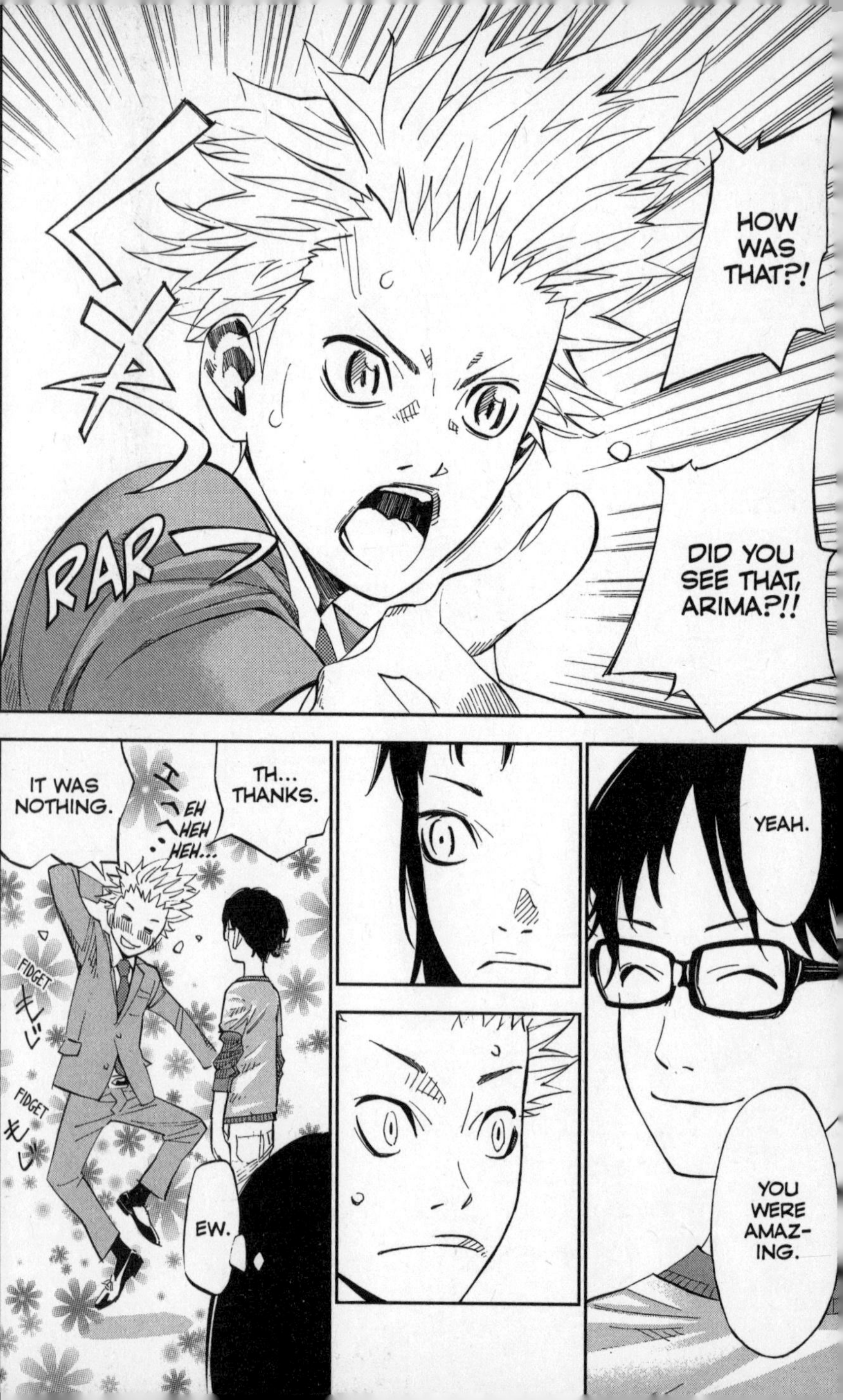
HOW WAS THAT?!
DID YOU SEE THAT, ARIMA?!!
RAR
YEAH.
YOU WERE AMAZ-ING.
TH... THANKS.
EH HEH HEH...
IT WAS NOTHING.
FIDGET
FIDGET
EW.

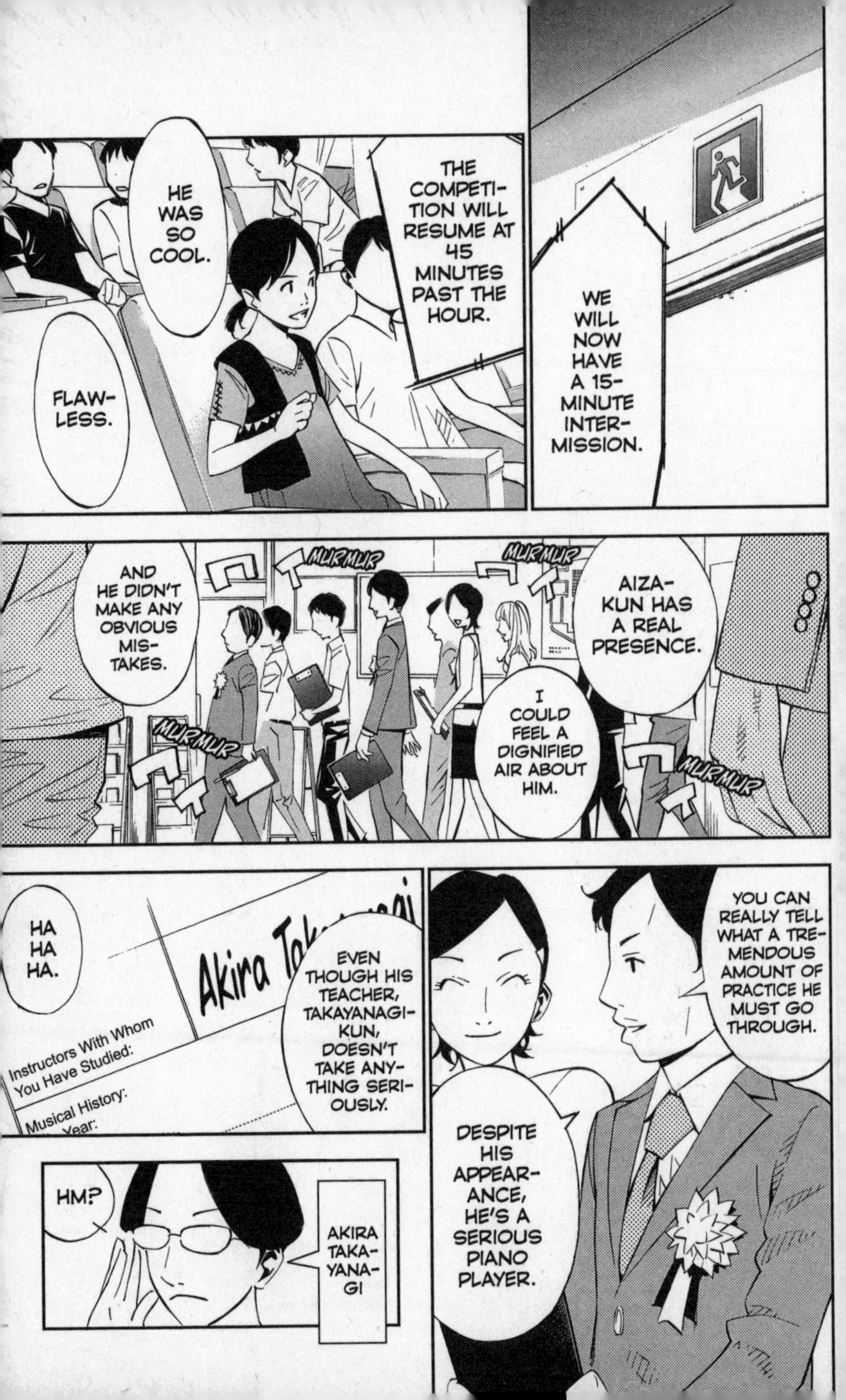
WE WILL NOW HAVE A 15-MINUTE INTERMISSION.
THE COMPETITION WILL RESUME AT 45 MINUTES PAST THE HOUR.
HE WAS SO COOL.
FLAWLESS.
MURMUR
MURMUR
AIZA-KUN HAS A REAL PRESENCE.
I COULD FEEL A DIGNIFIED AIR ABOUT HIM.
AND HE DIDN'T MAKE ANY OBVIOUS MISTAKES.
MURMUR
MURMUR
YOU CAN REALLY TELL WHAT A TREMENDOUS AMOUNT OF PRACTICE HE MUST GO THROUGH.
DESPITE HIS APPEARANCE, HE'S A SERIOUS PIANO PLAYER.
EVEN THOUGH HIS TEACHER, TAKAYANAGI-KUN, DOESN'T TAKE ANYTHING SERIOUSLY.
HA HA HA.
Instructors With Whom You Have Studied:
Musical History:
Year:
AKIRA TAKAYANAGI
HM?

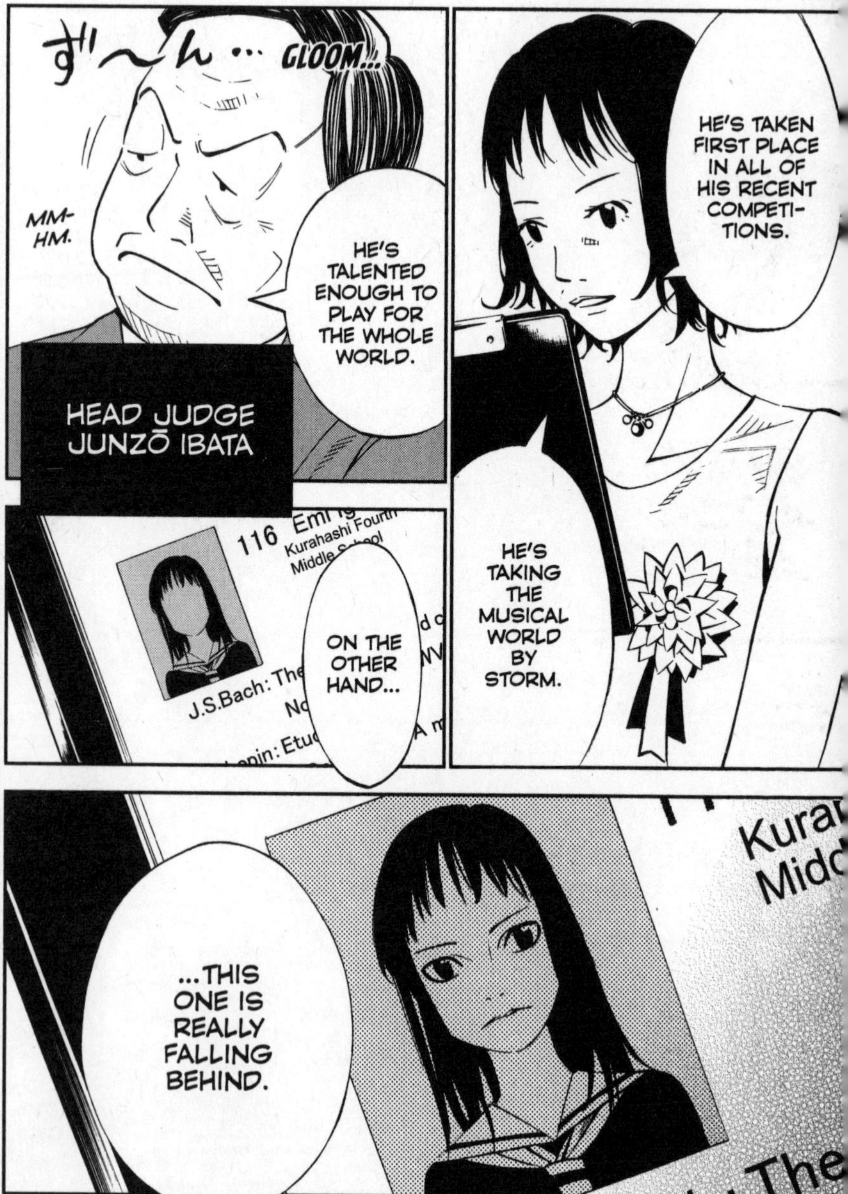
HE'S TAKEN FIRST PLACE IN ALL OF HIS RECENT COMPETI-TIONS.
HE'S TAKING THE MUSICAL WORLD BY STORM.
ず〜ん… GLOOM...
HE'S TALENTED ENOUGH TO PLAY FOR THE WHOLE WORLD.
MM-HM.
HEAD JUDGE JUNZŌ IBATA
116
Kurahashi Fourth Middle School
J.S.Bach: The
ON THE OTHER HAND...
...THIS ONE IS REALLY FALLING BEHIND.

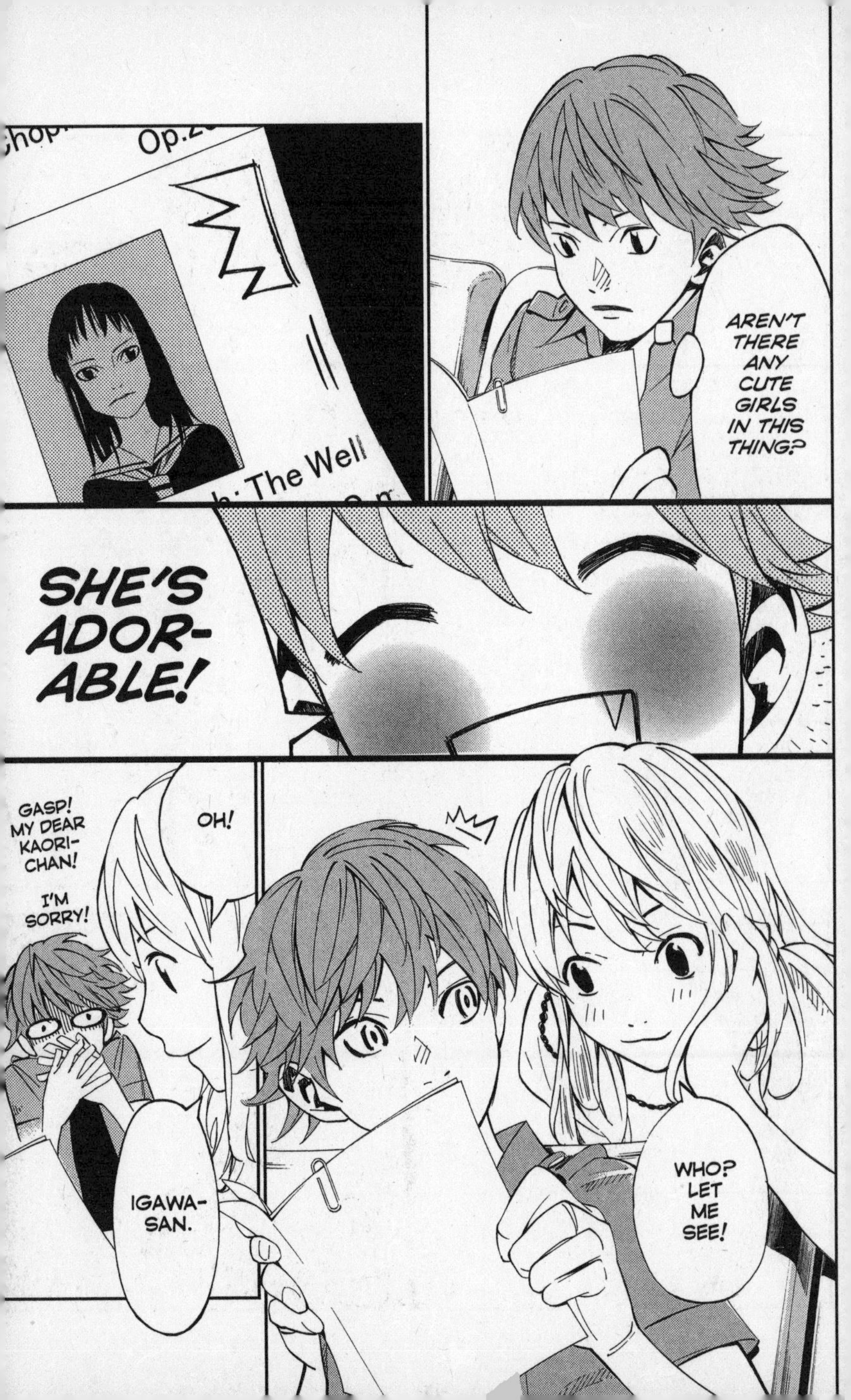
AREN'T THERE ANY CUTE GIRLS IN THIS THING?
Op.2
The Well
SHE'S ADOR-ABLE!
WHO? LET ME SEE!
OH!
GASP! MY DEAR KAORI-CHAN!
I'M SORRY!
IGAWA-SAN.

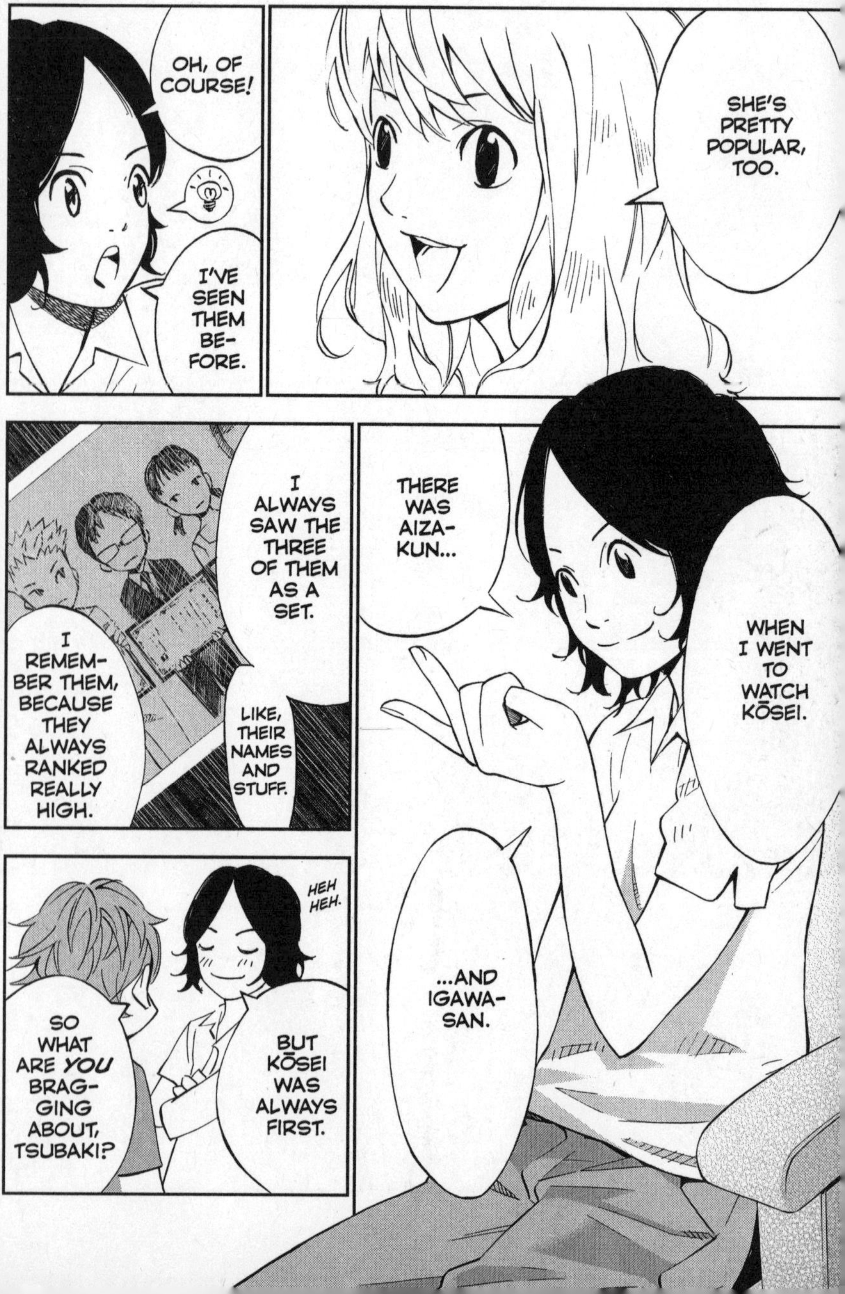
SHE'S PRETTY POPULAR, TOO.
OH, OF COURSE!
I'VE SEEN THEM BEFORE.
WHEN I WENT TO WATCH KŌSEI.
THERE WAS AIZA-KUN...
...AND IGAWA-SAN.
I ALWAYS SAW THE THREE OF THEM AS A SET.
LIKE, THEIR NAMES AND STUFF.
I REMEMBER THEM, BECAUSE THEY ALWAYS RANKED REALLY HIGH.
HEH HEH.
BUT KŌSEI WAS ALWAYS FIRST.
SO WHAT ARE *YOU* BRAGGING ABOUT, TSUBAKI?

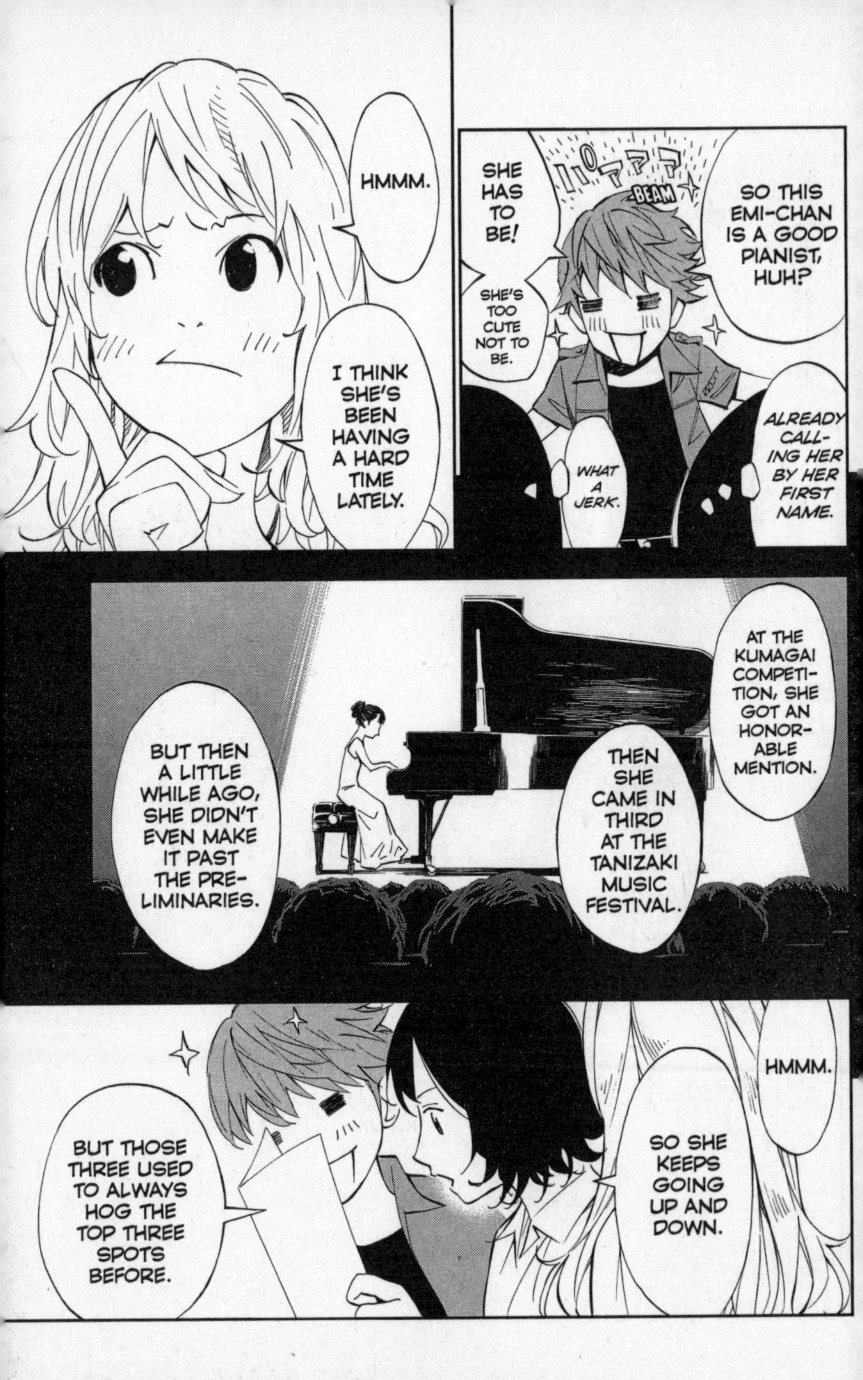
SO THIS EMI-CHAN IS A GOOD PIANIST, HUH?
BEAM
SHE HAS TO BE!
SHE'S TOO CUTE NOT TO BE.
ALREADY CALLING HER BY HER FIRST NAME.
WHAT A JERK.
HMMM.
I THINK SHE'S BEEN HAVING A HARD TIME LATELY.
AT THE KUMAGAI COMPETITION, SHE GOT AN HONORABLE MENTION.
THEN SHE CAME IN THIRD AT THE TANIZAKI MUSIC FESTIVAL.
BUT THEN A LITTLE WHILE AGO, SHE DIDN'T EVEN MAKE IT PAST THE PRELIMINARIES.
HMMM.
SO SHE KEEPS GOING UP AND DOWN.
BUT THOSE THREE USED TO ALWAYS HOG THE TOP THREE SPOTS BEFORE.

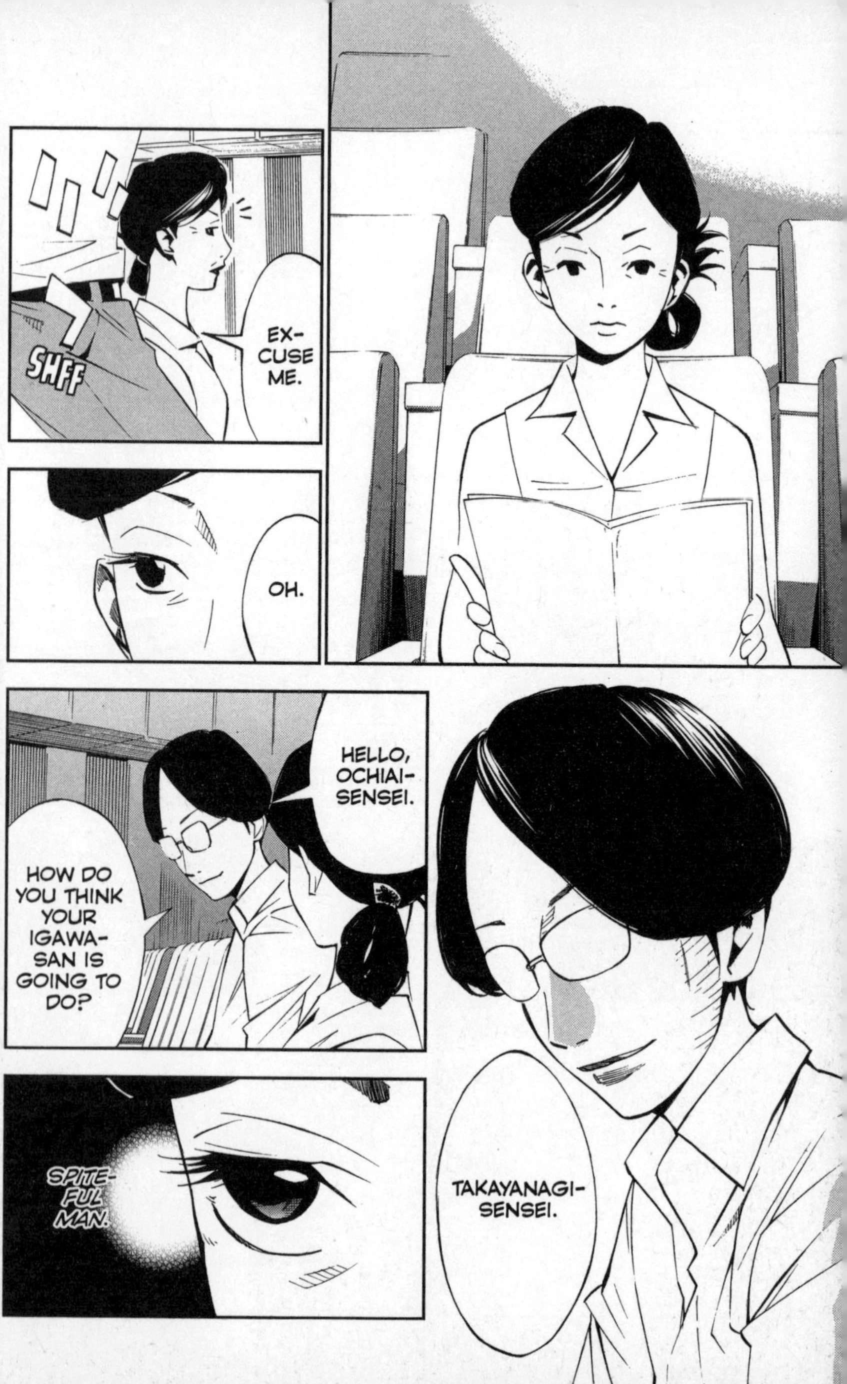
EX-CUSE ME.
SHFF
OH.
TAKAYANAGI-SENSEI.
HELLO, OCHIAI-SENSEI.
HOW DO YOU THINK YOUR IGAWA-SAN IS GOING TO DO?
SPITE-FUL MAN.

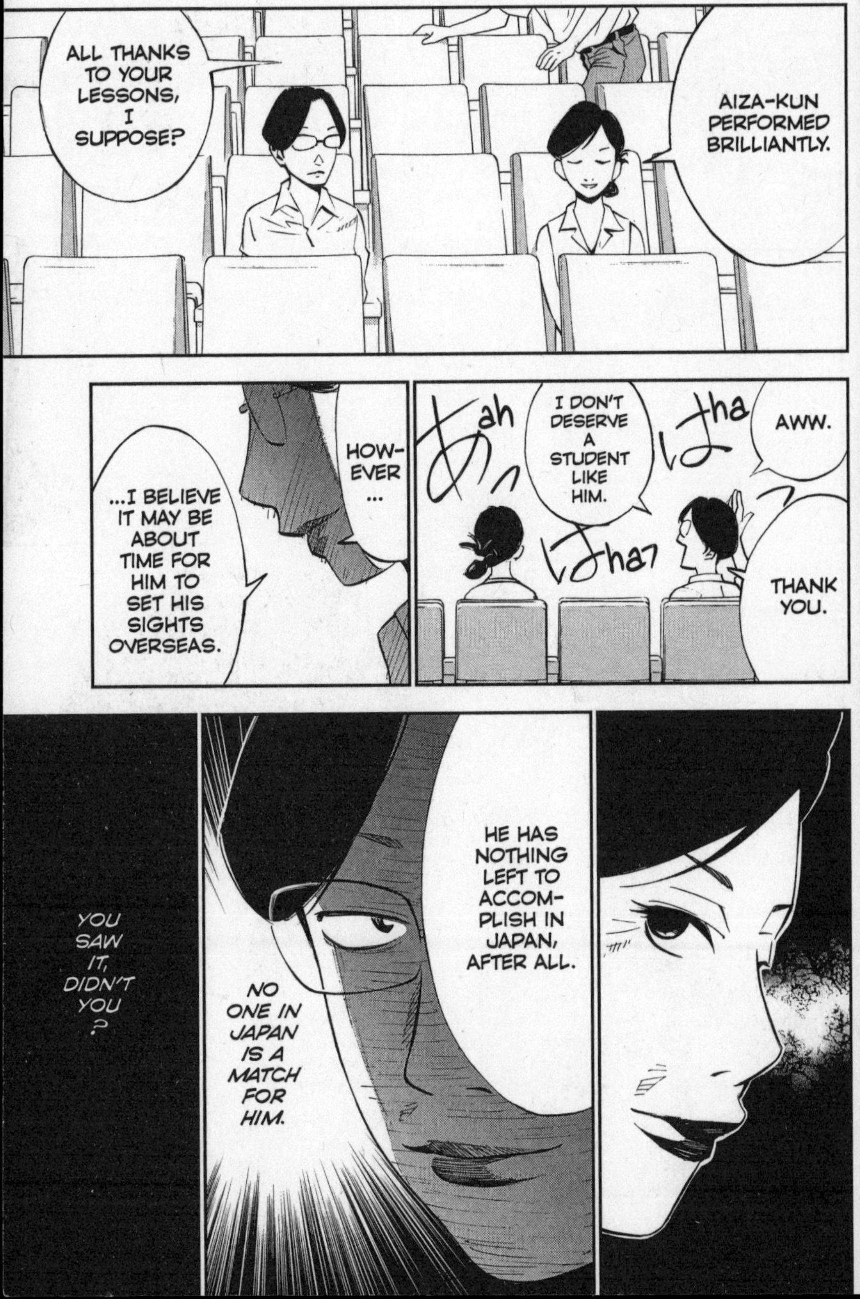
AIZA-KUN PERFORMED BRILLIANTLY.
ALL THANKS TO YOUR LESSONS, I SUPPOSE?
AWW.
ha
I DON'T DESERVE A STUDENT LIKE HIM.
ah
ha
THANK YOU.
HOW-EVER...
...I BELIEVE IT MAY BE ABOUT TIME FOR HIM TO SET HIS SIGHTS OVERSEAS.
HE HAS NOTHING LEFT TO ACCOMPLISH IN JAPAN, AFTER ALL.
NO ONE IN JAPAN IS A MATCH FOR HIM.
YOU SAW IT, DIDN'T YOU?

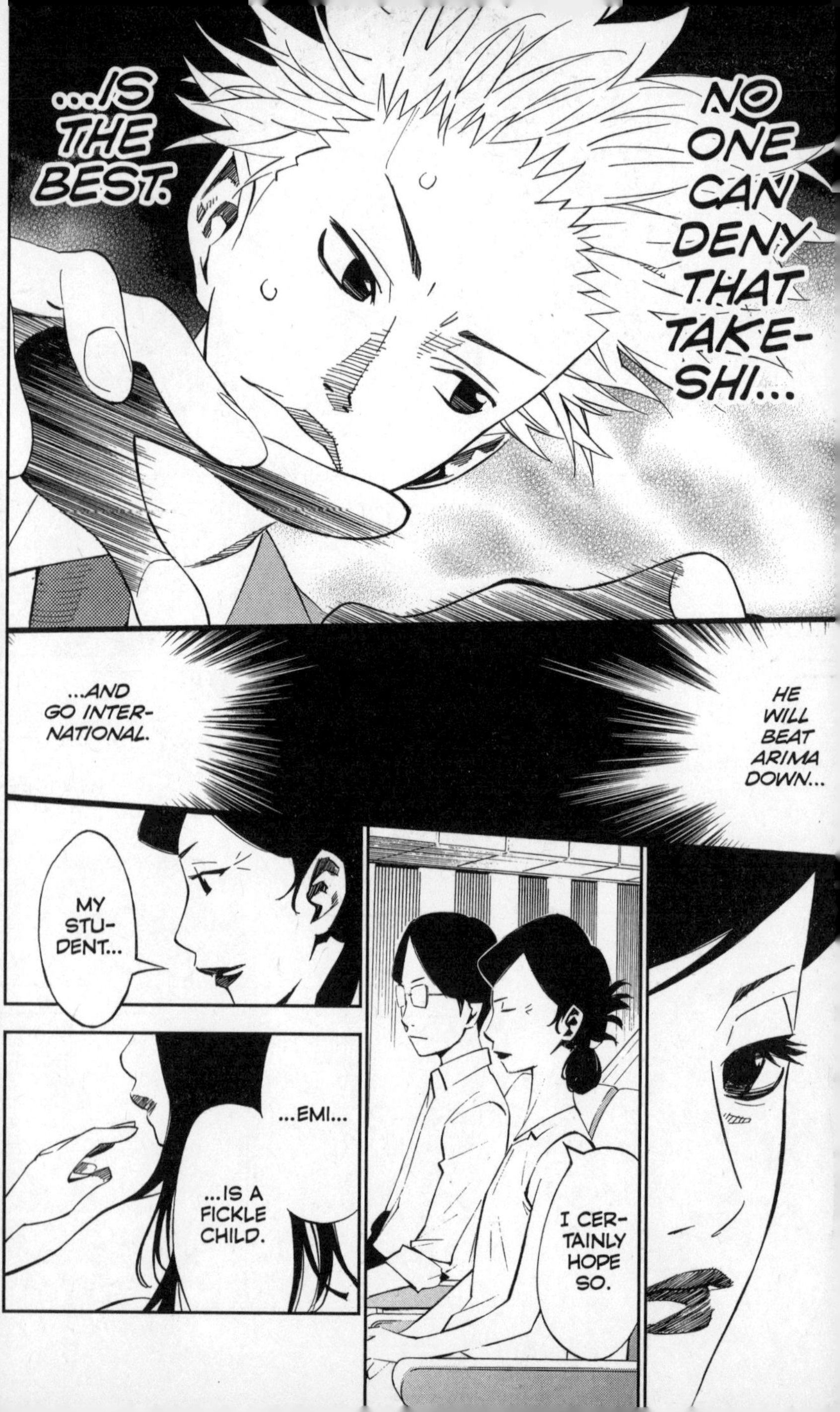
NO ONE CAN DENY THAT TAKE-SHI...
...IS THE BEST.
HE WILL BEAT ARIMA DOWN...
...AND GO INTER-NATIONAL.
I CER-TAINLY HOPE SO.
MY STU-DENT...
...EMI...
...IS A FICKLE CHILD.

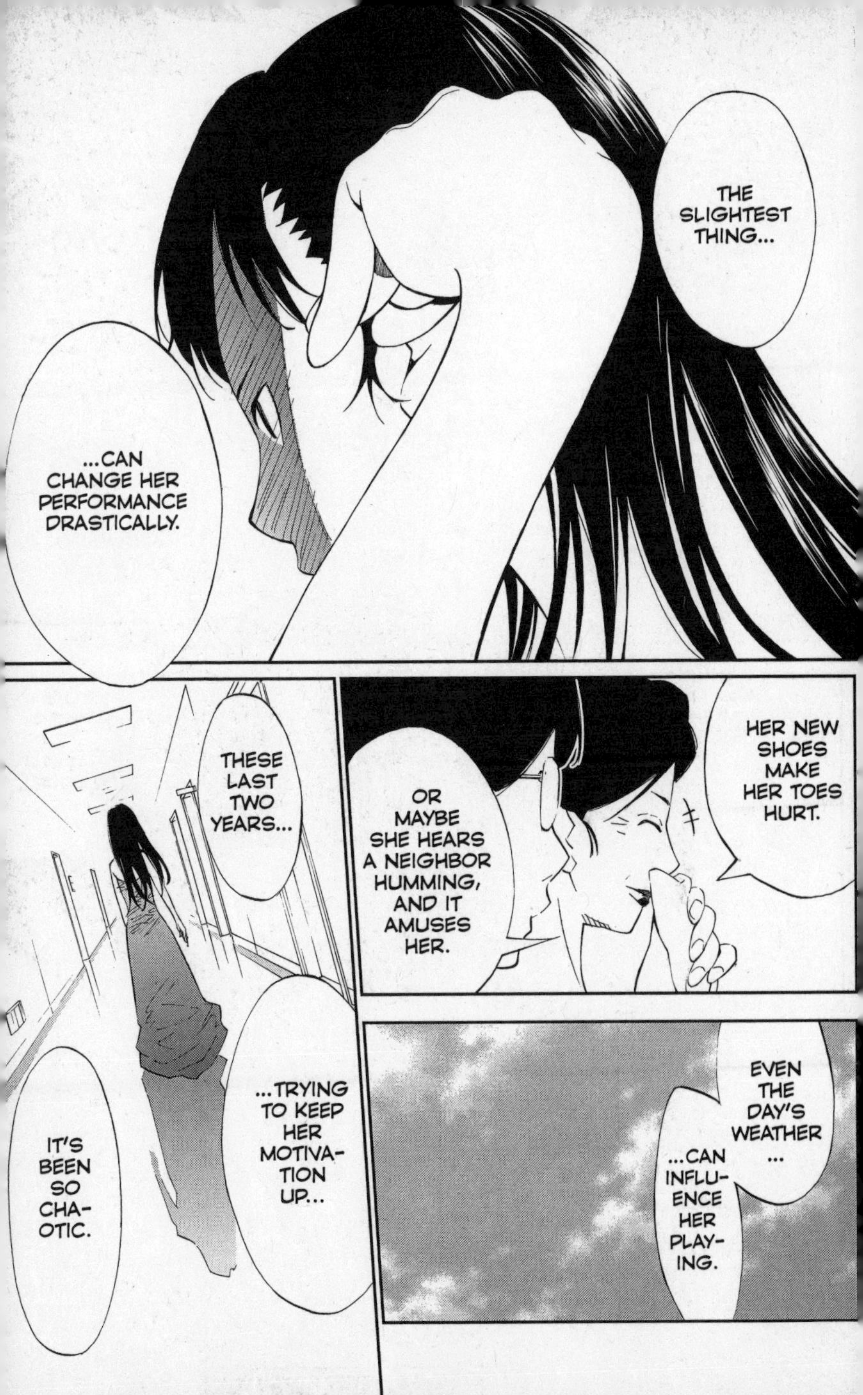
THE SLIGHTEST THING...
...CAN CHANGE HER PERFORMANCE DRASTICALLY.
HER NEW SHOES MAKE HER TOES HURT.
OR MAYBE SHE HEARS A NEIGHBOR HUMMING, AND IT AMUSES HER.
EVEN THE DAY'S WEATHER...
...CAN INFLU-ENCE HER PLAY-ING.
THESE LAST TWO YEARS...
...TRYING TO KEEP HER MOTIVA-TION UP...
IT'S BEEN SO CHA-OTIC.

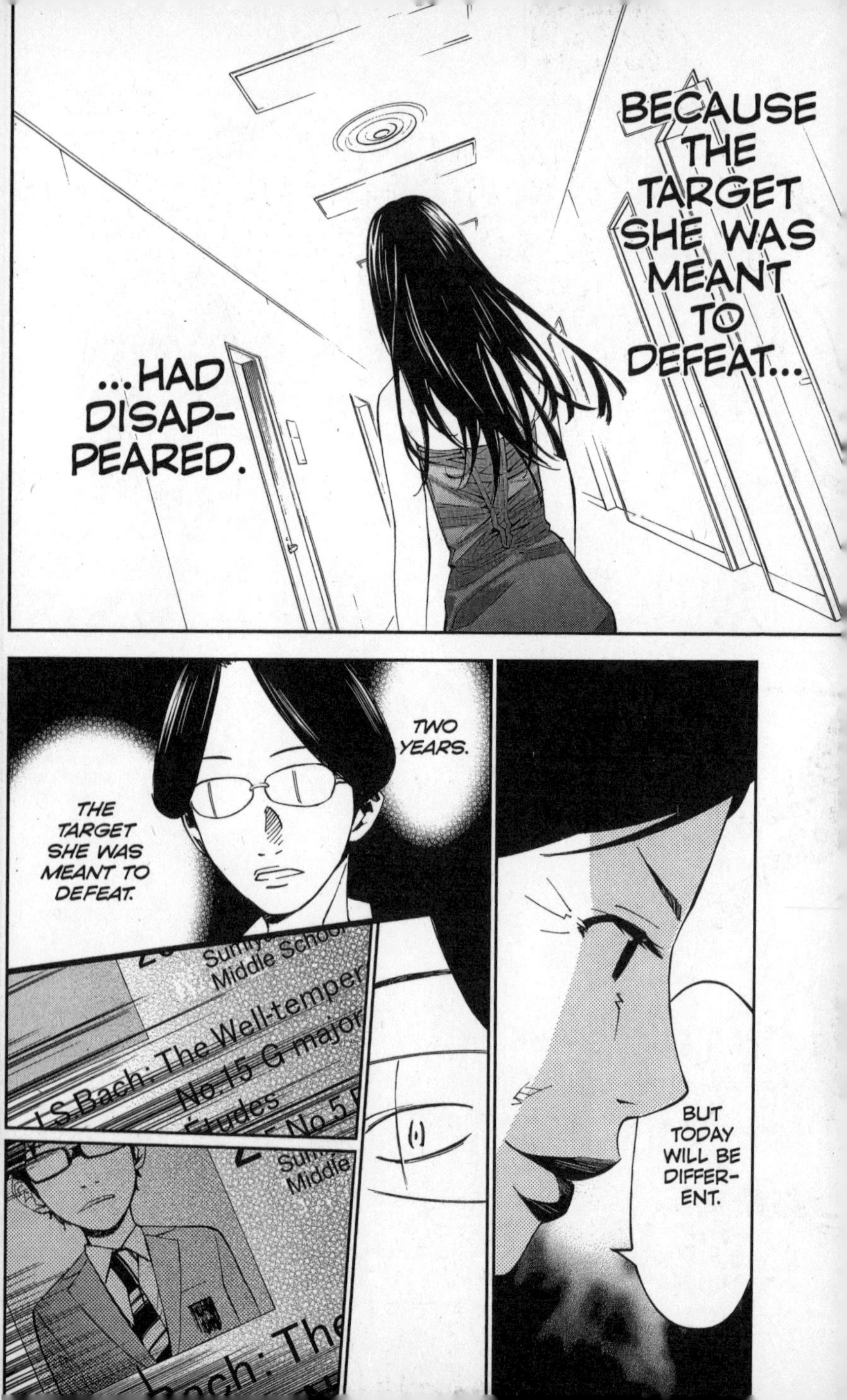
BECAUSE THE TARGET SHE WAS MEANT TO DEFEAT...
...HAD DISAP-PEARED.
BUT TODAY WILL BE DIFFER-ENT.
TWO YEARS.
THE TARGET SHE WAS MEANT TO DEFEAT.
Middle School
J.S.Bach: The Well-temper
No.15 G major
Études
Middle
Bach: The

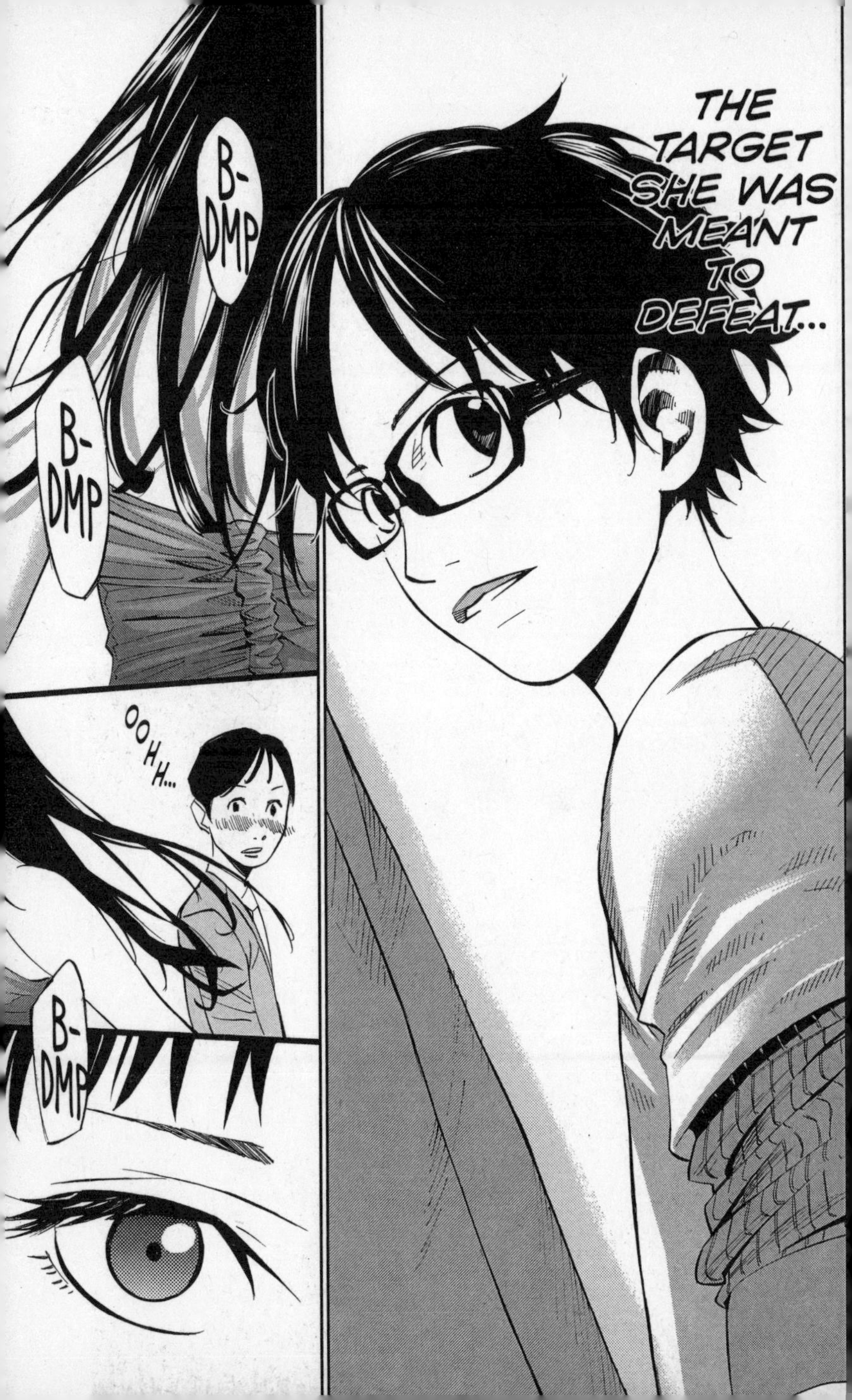
THE TARGET SHE WAS MEANT TO DEFEAT...
B-DMP
B-DMP
OOHH...
B-DMP

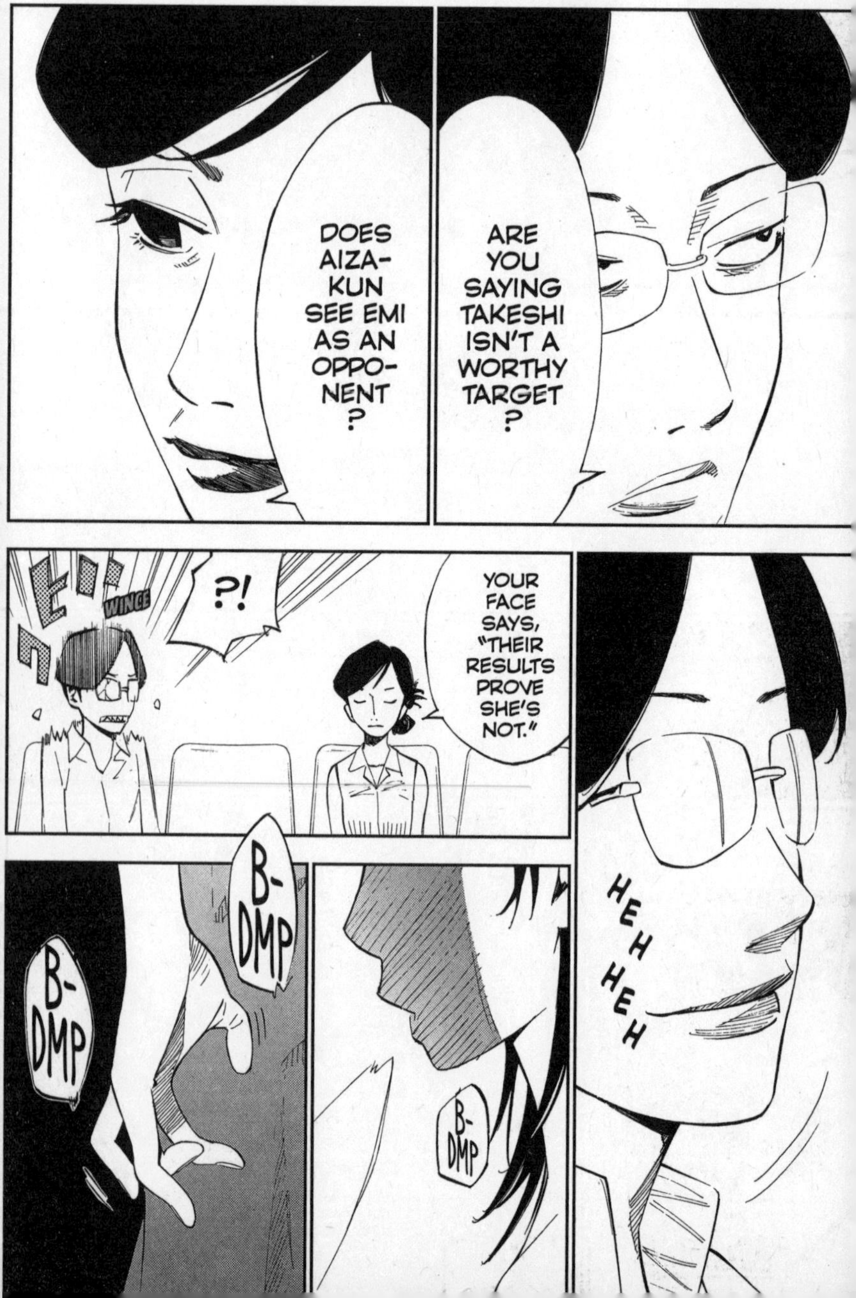
ARE YOU SAYING TAKESHI ISN'T A WORTHY TARGET?
DOES AIZA-KUN SEE EMI AS AN OPPONENT?
HEH HEH HEH
YOUR FACE SAYS, "THEIR RESULTS PROVE SHE'S NOT."
?!
WINCE
B-DMP
B-DMP
B-DMP

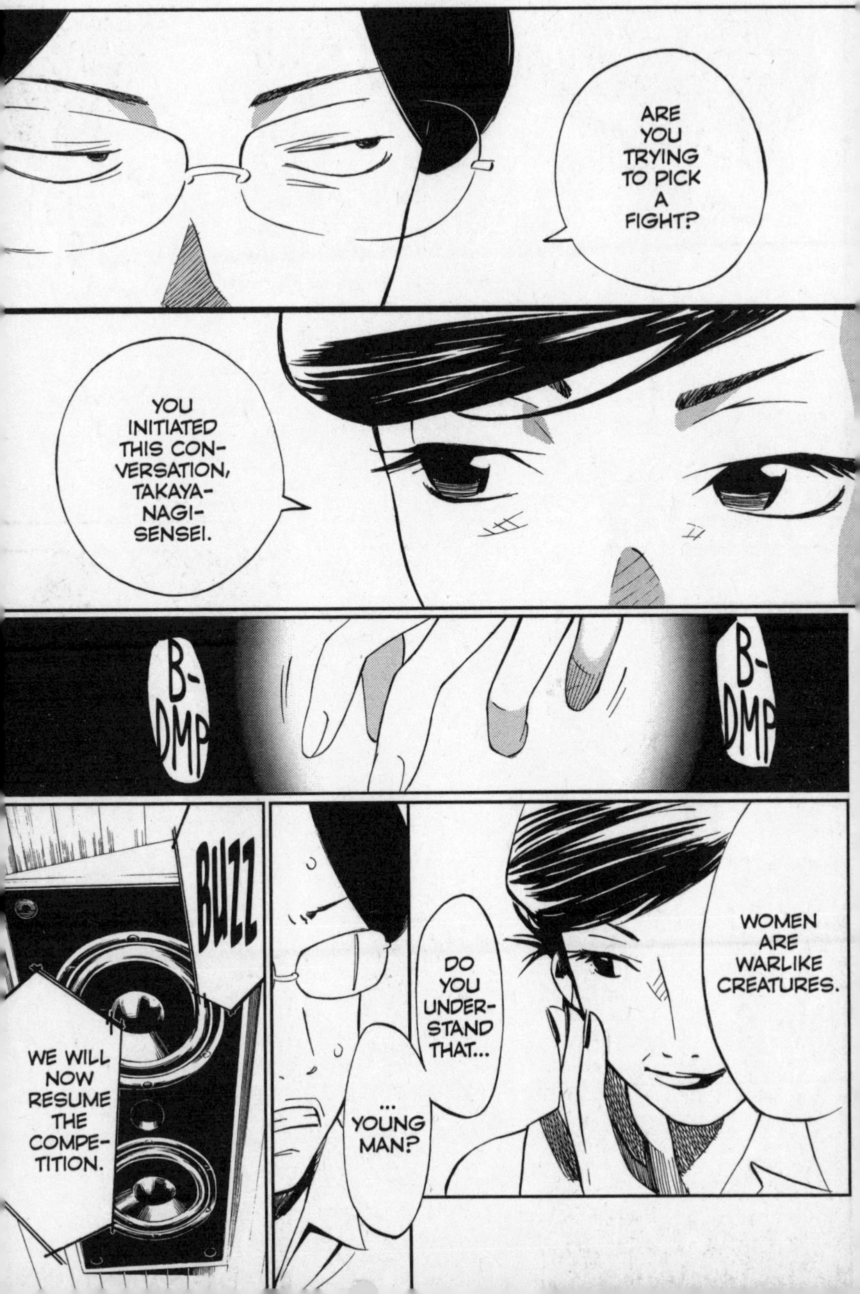
ARE YOU TRYING TO PICK A FIGHT?
YOU INITIATED THIS CON-VERSATION, TAKAYA-NAGI-SENSEI.
B-DMP
B-DMP
WOMEN ARE WARLIKE CREATURES.
DO YOU UNDER-STAND THAT...
...YOUNG MAN?
BUZZ
WE WILL NOW RESUME THE COMPE-TITION.

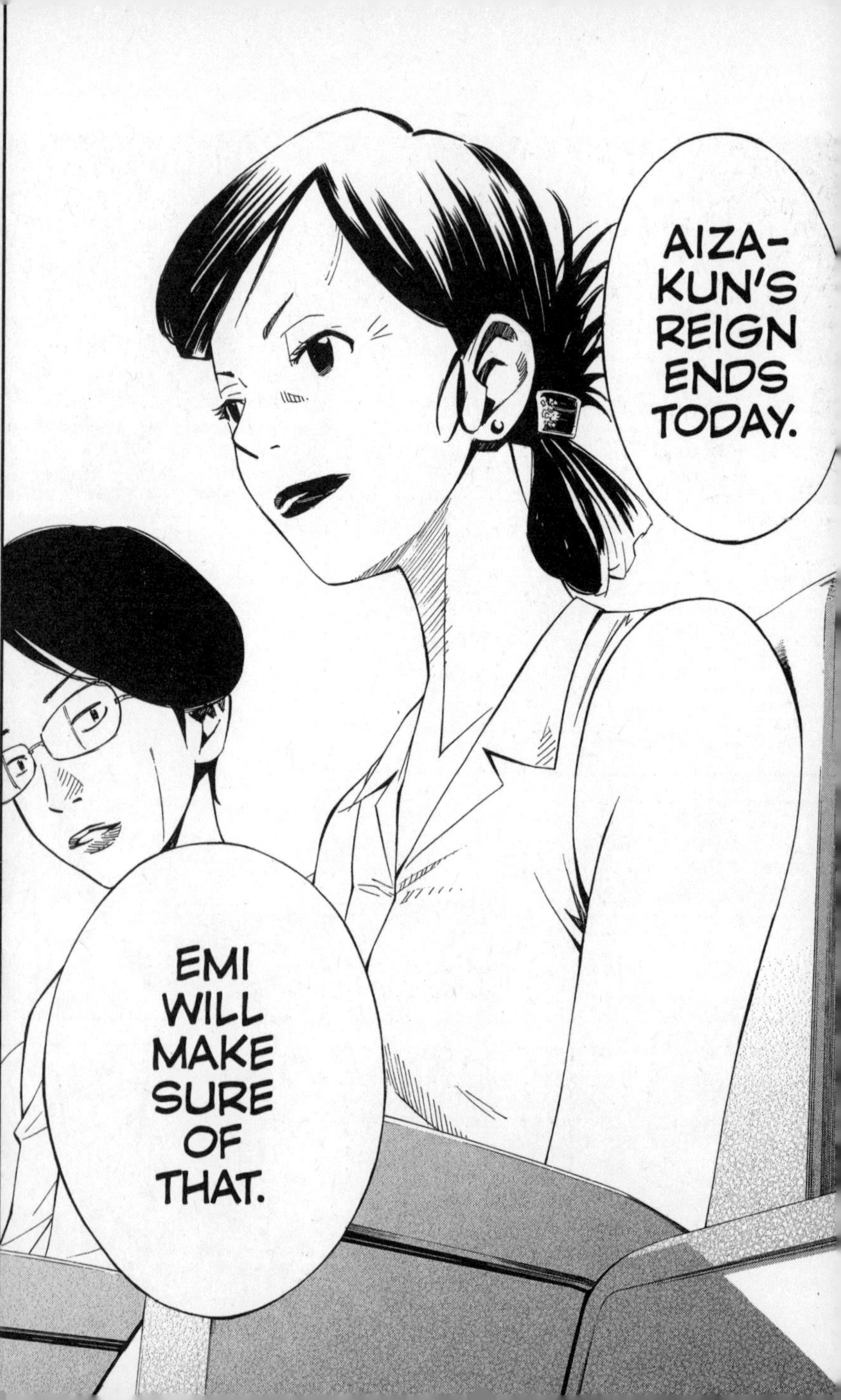
AIZA-KUN'S REIGN ENDS TODAY.
EMI WILL MAKE SURE OF THAT.

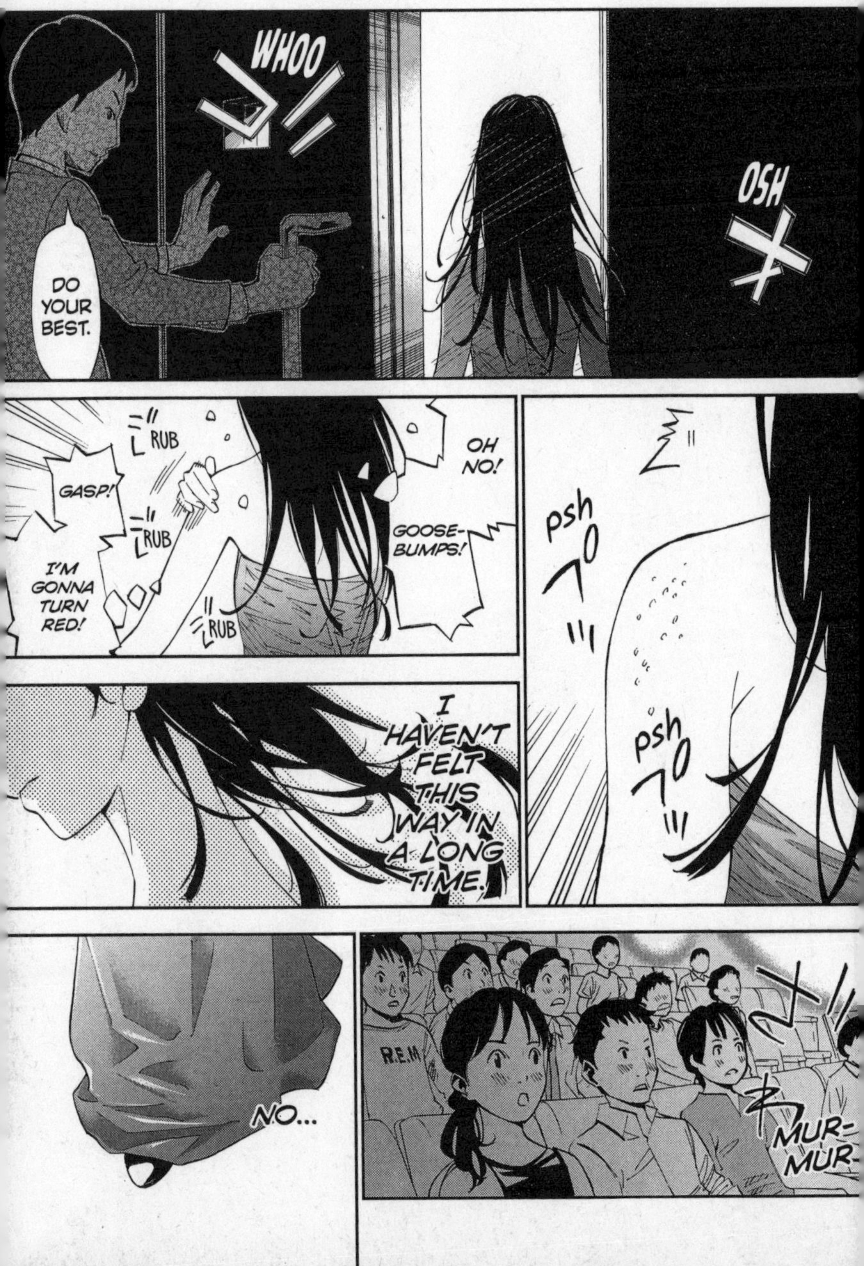
OSH
WHOO
DO YOUR BEST.
psh
psh
OH NO!
RUB
GOOSE-BUMPS!
GASP!
RUB
I'M GONNA TURN RED!
RUB
I HAVEN'T FELT THIS WAY IN A LONG TIME.
MUR-MUR-
NO...

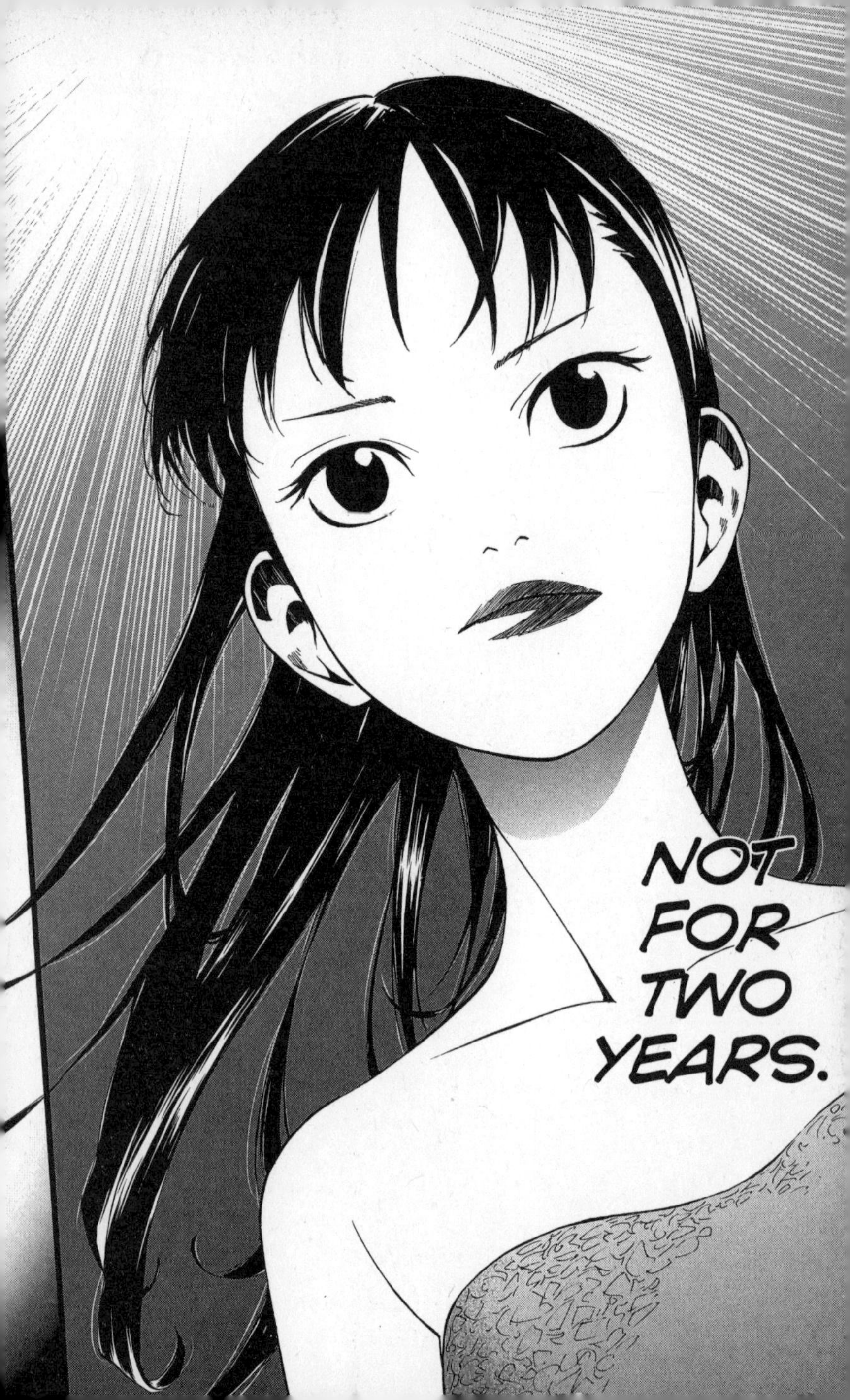
NOT FOR TWO YEARS.

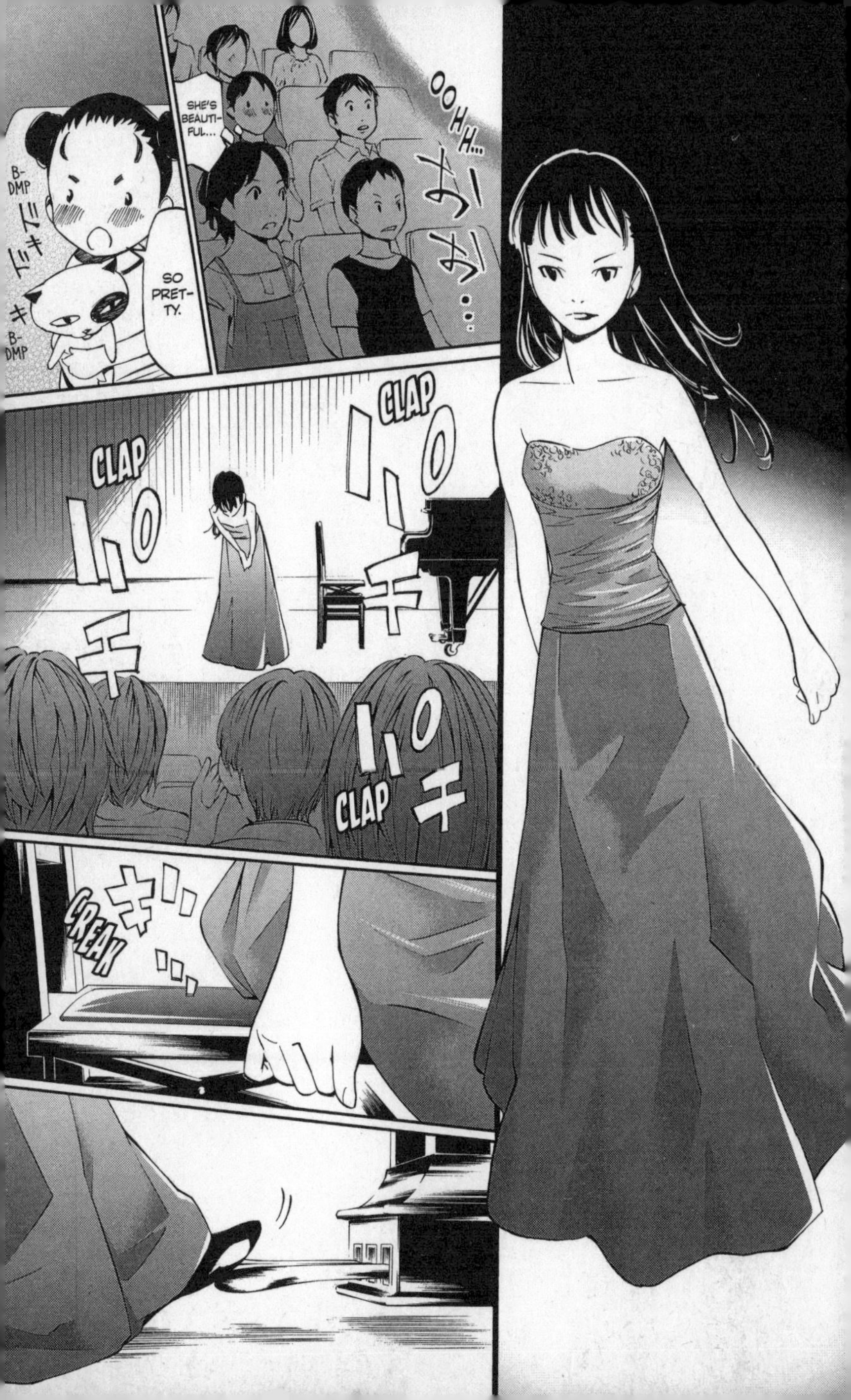
OOHHH...
おーお…
SHE'S BEAUTIFUL...
SO PRETTY.
B-DMP
ドキ
B-DMP
ドキ
CLAP
パチ
CLAP
パチ
CLAP
パチ
CREAK
ギ…

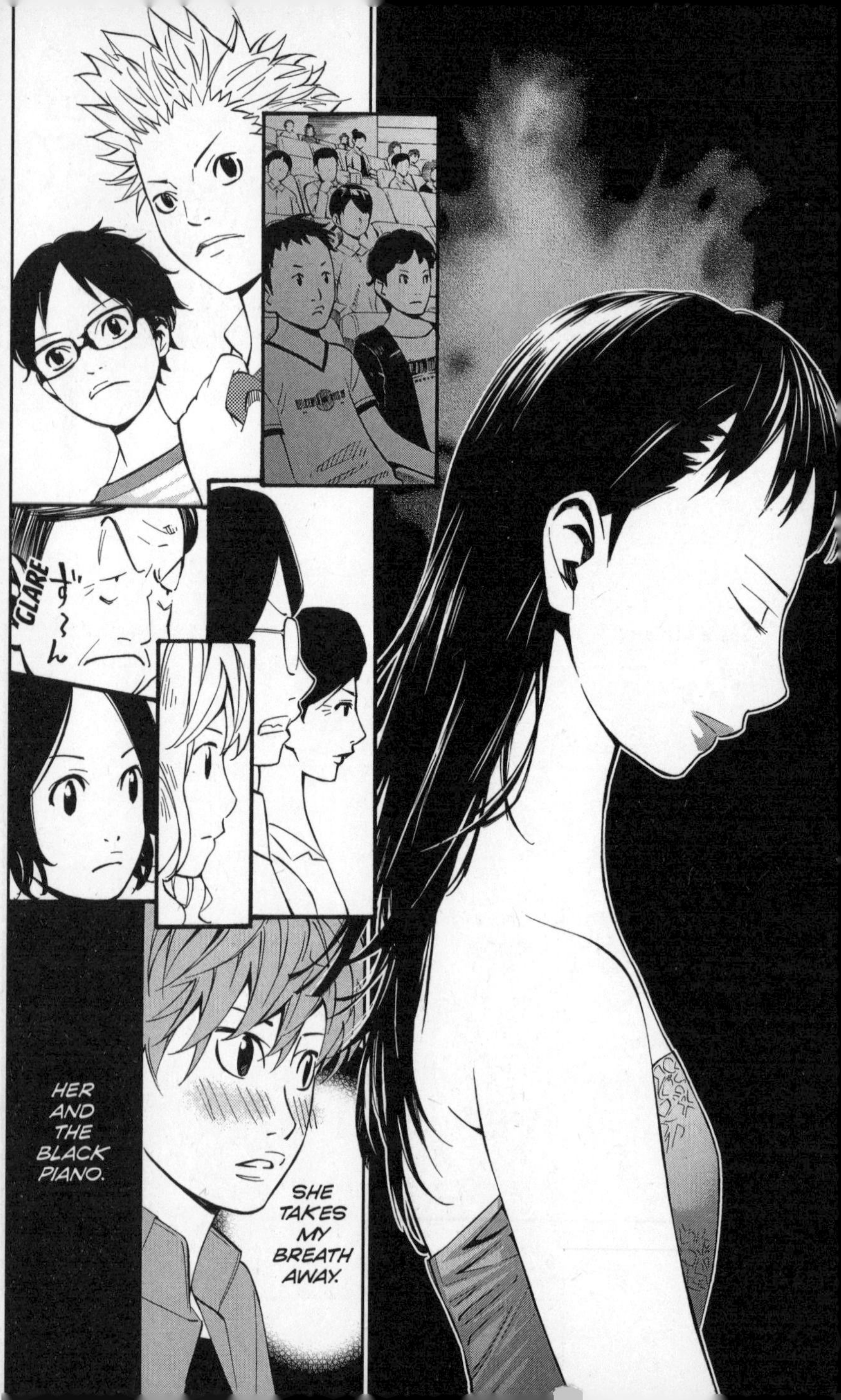
ず～ん
GLARE
HER AND THE BLACK PIANO.
SHE TAKES MY BREATH AWAY.

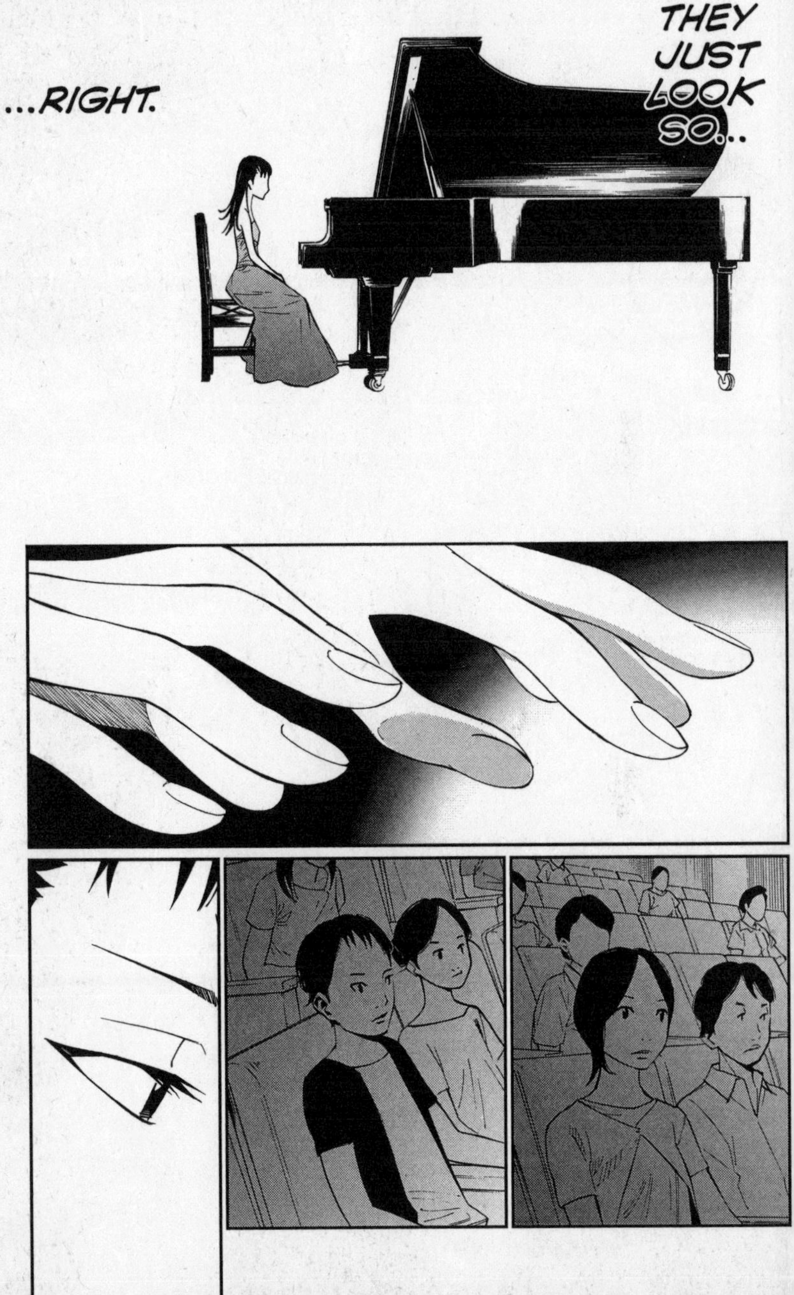
THEY JUST LOOK SO...
...RIGHT.

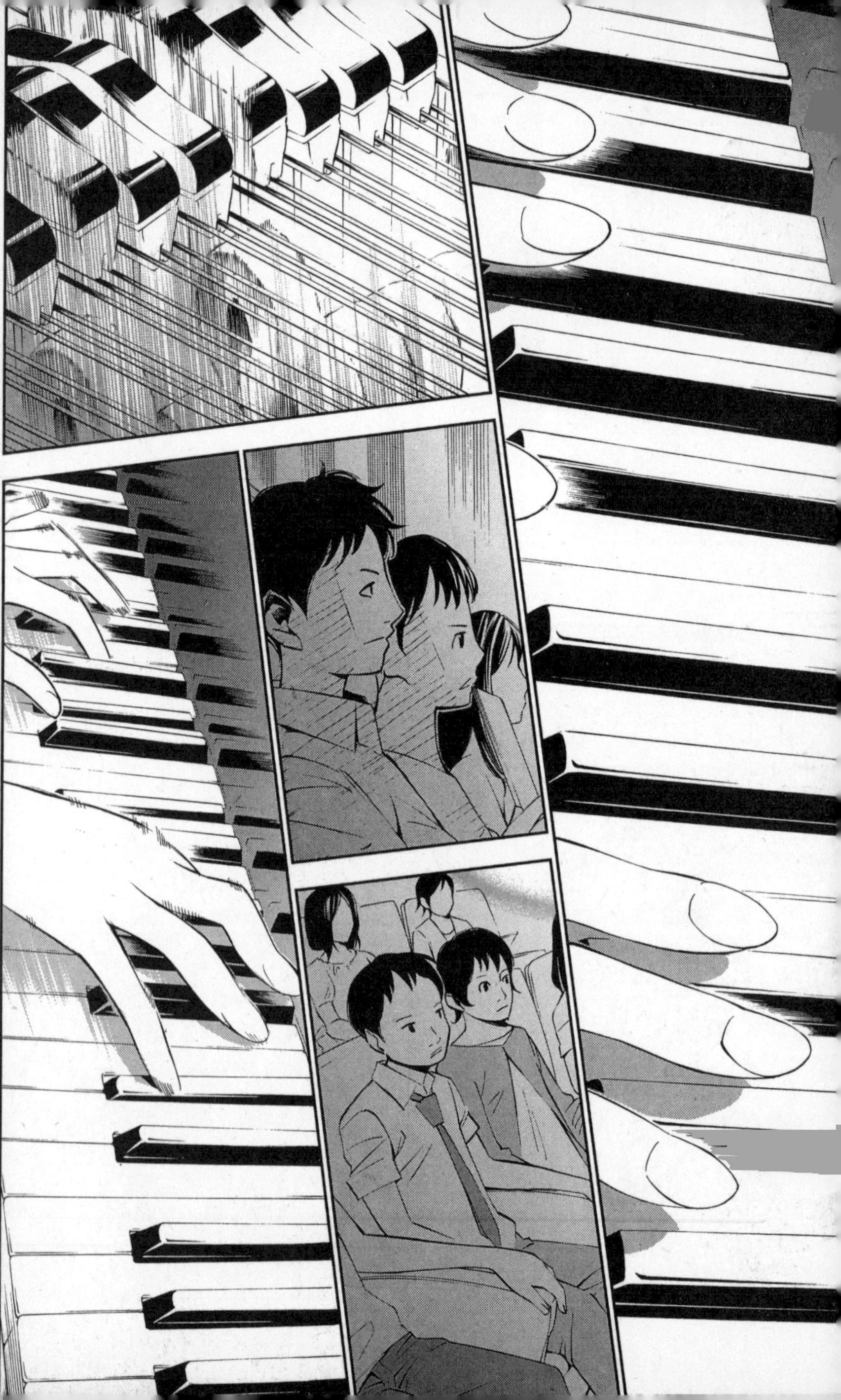

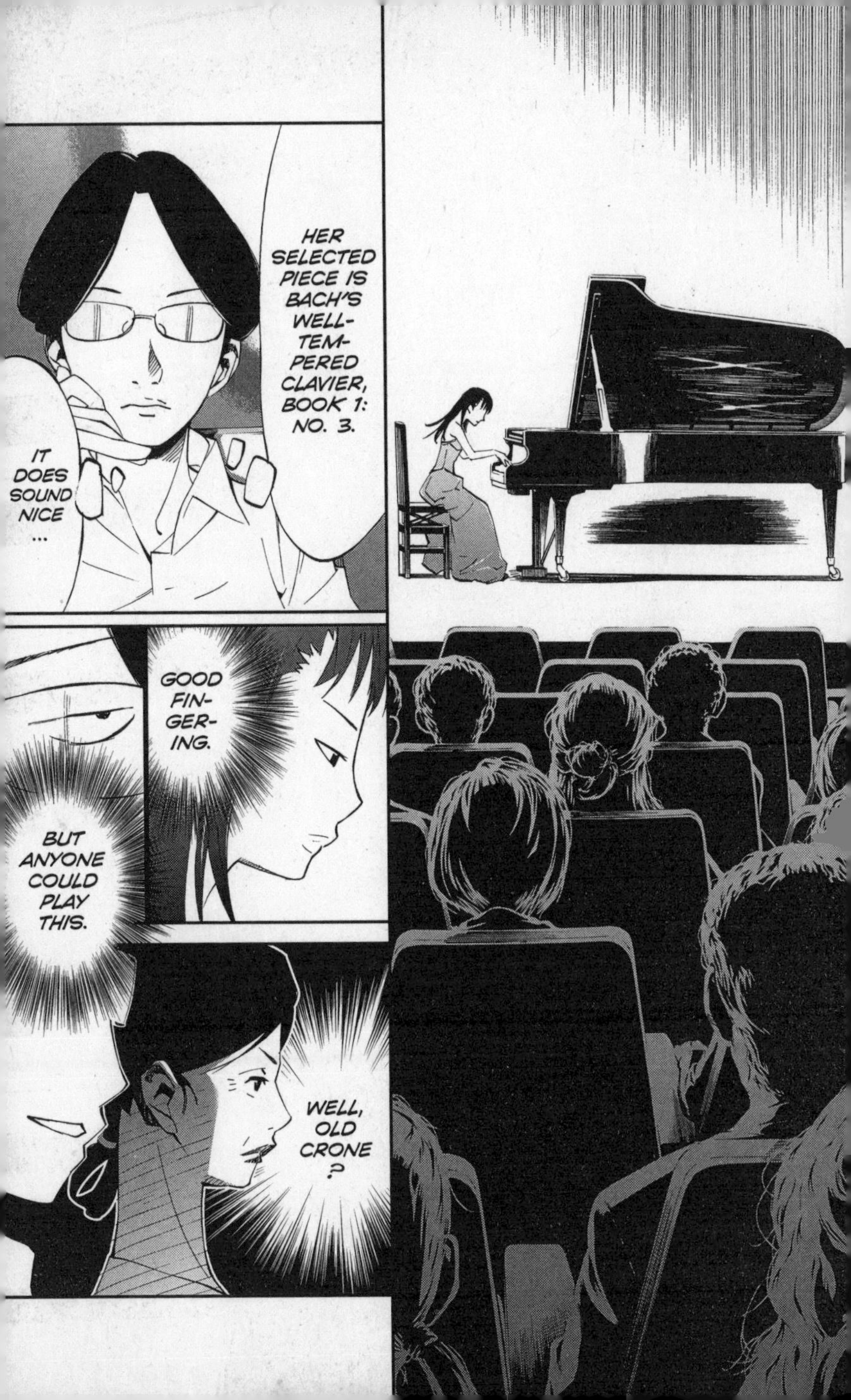
HER SELECTED PIECE IS BACH'S WELL-TEMPERED CLAVIER, BOOK 1: NO. 3.
IT DOES SOUND NICE ...
GOOD FINGERING.
BUT ANYONE COULD PLAY THIS.
WELL, OLD CRONE ?

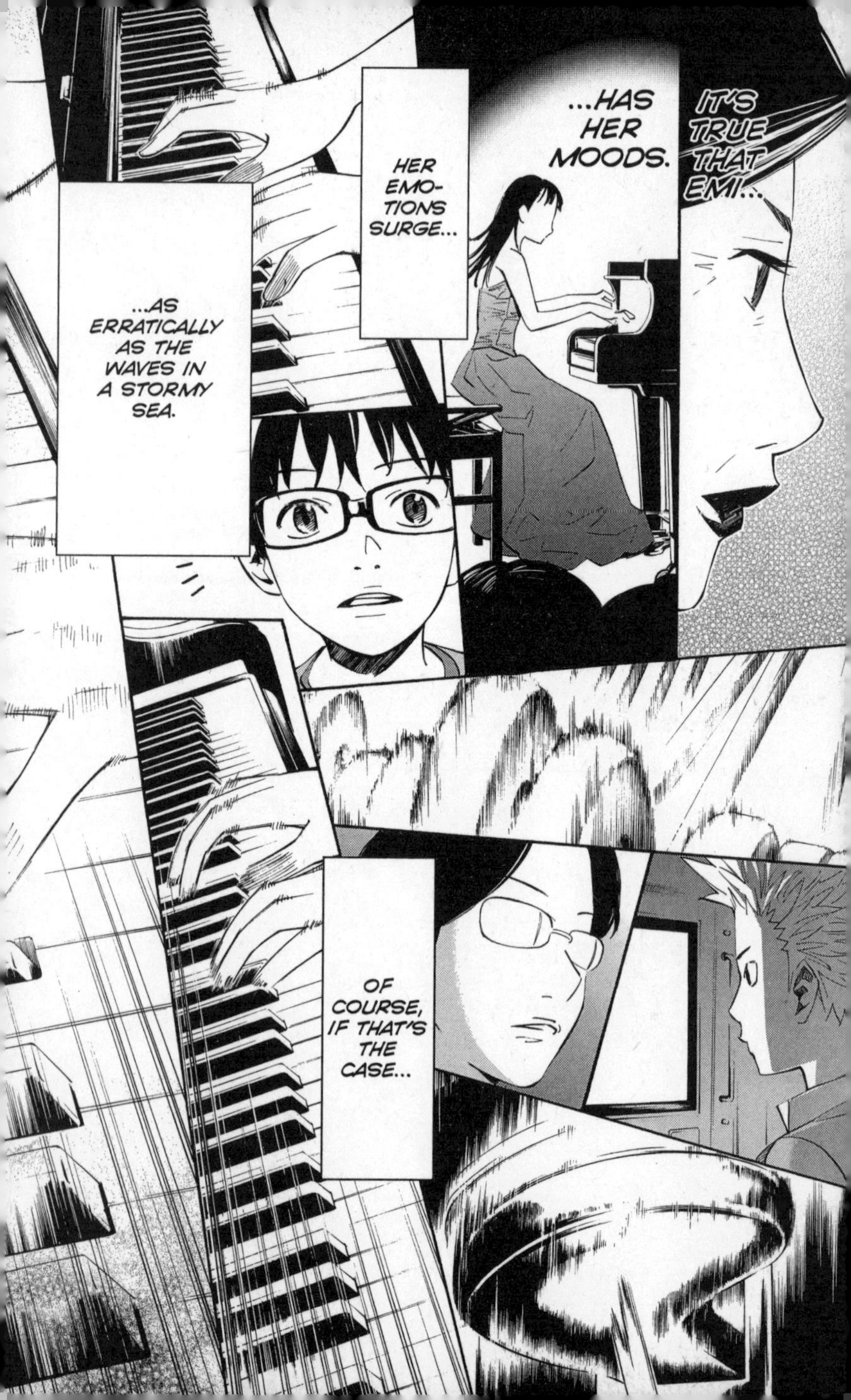
IT'S TRUE THAT EMI...
...HAS HER MOODS.
HER EMO-TIONS SURGE...
...AS ERRATICALLY AS THE WAVES IN A STORMY SEA.
OF COURSE, IF THAT'S THE CASE...

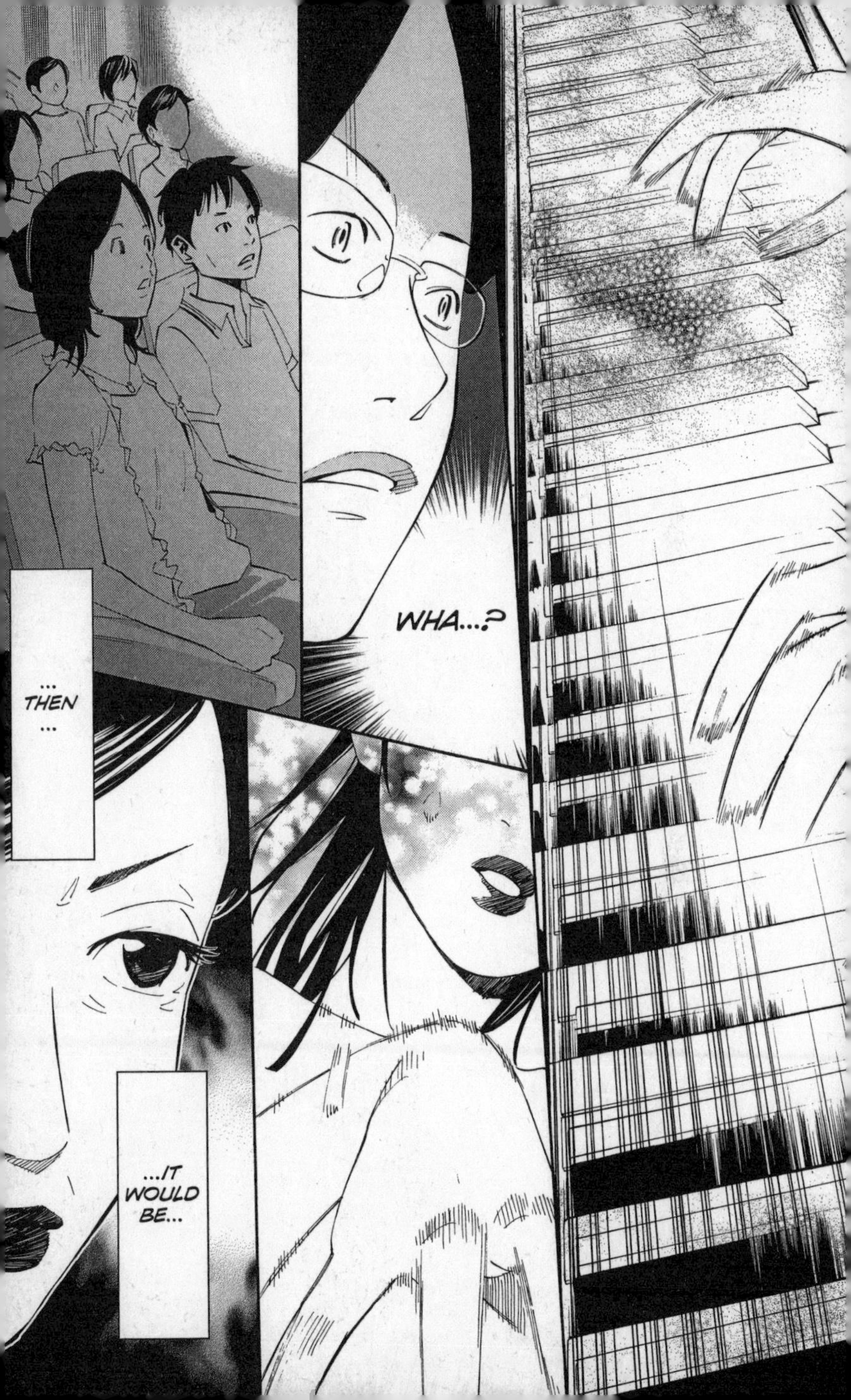
WHA...?
...THEN...
...IT WOULD BE...

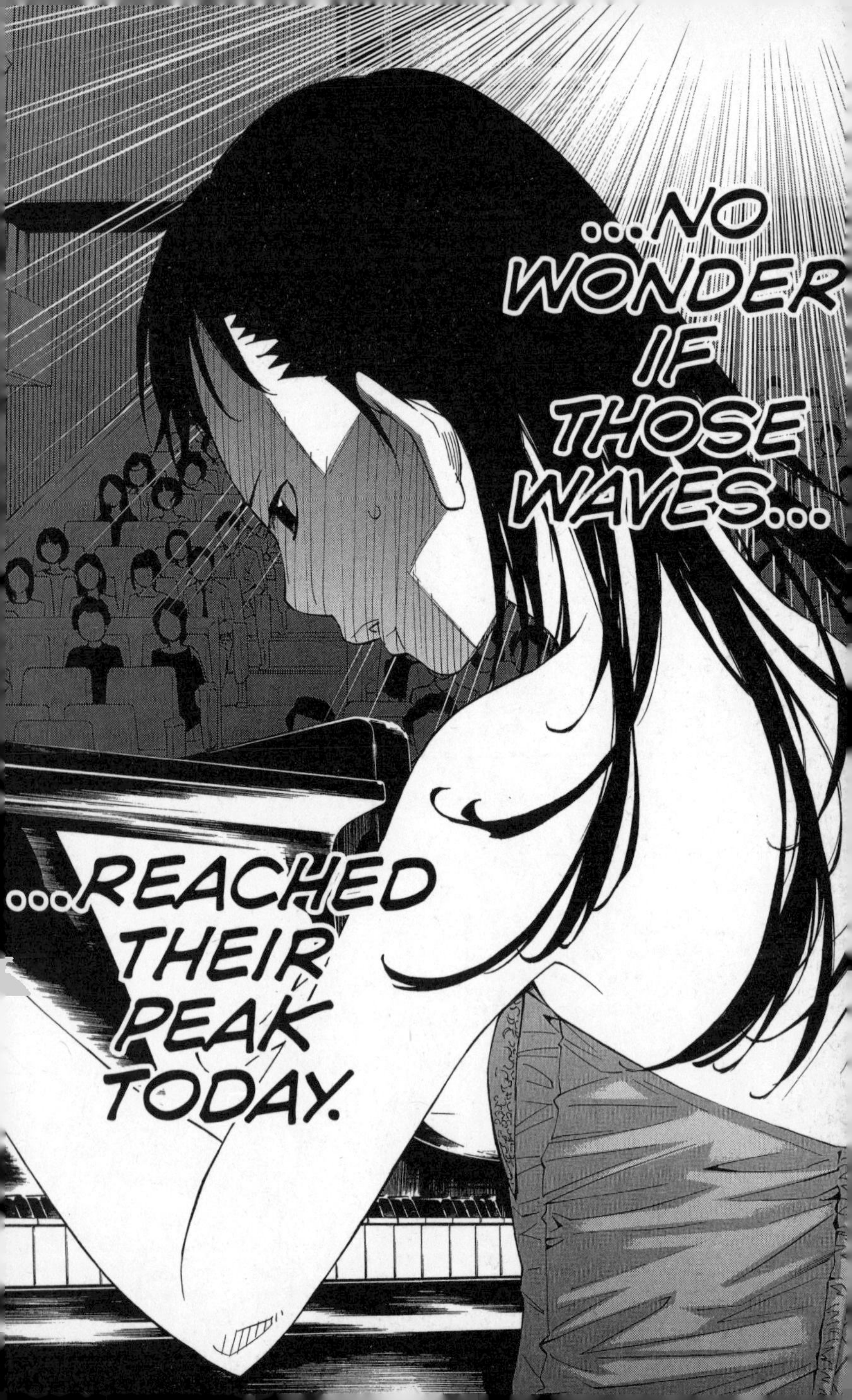
...NO WONDER IF THOSE WAVES...
...REACHED THEIR PEAK TODAY.

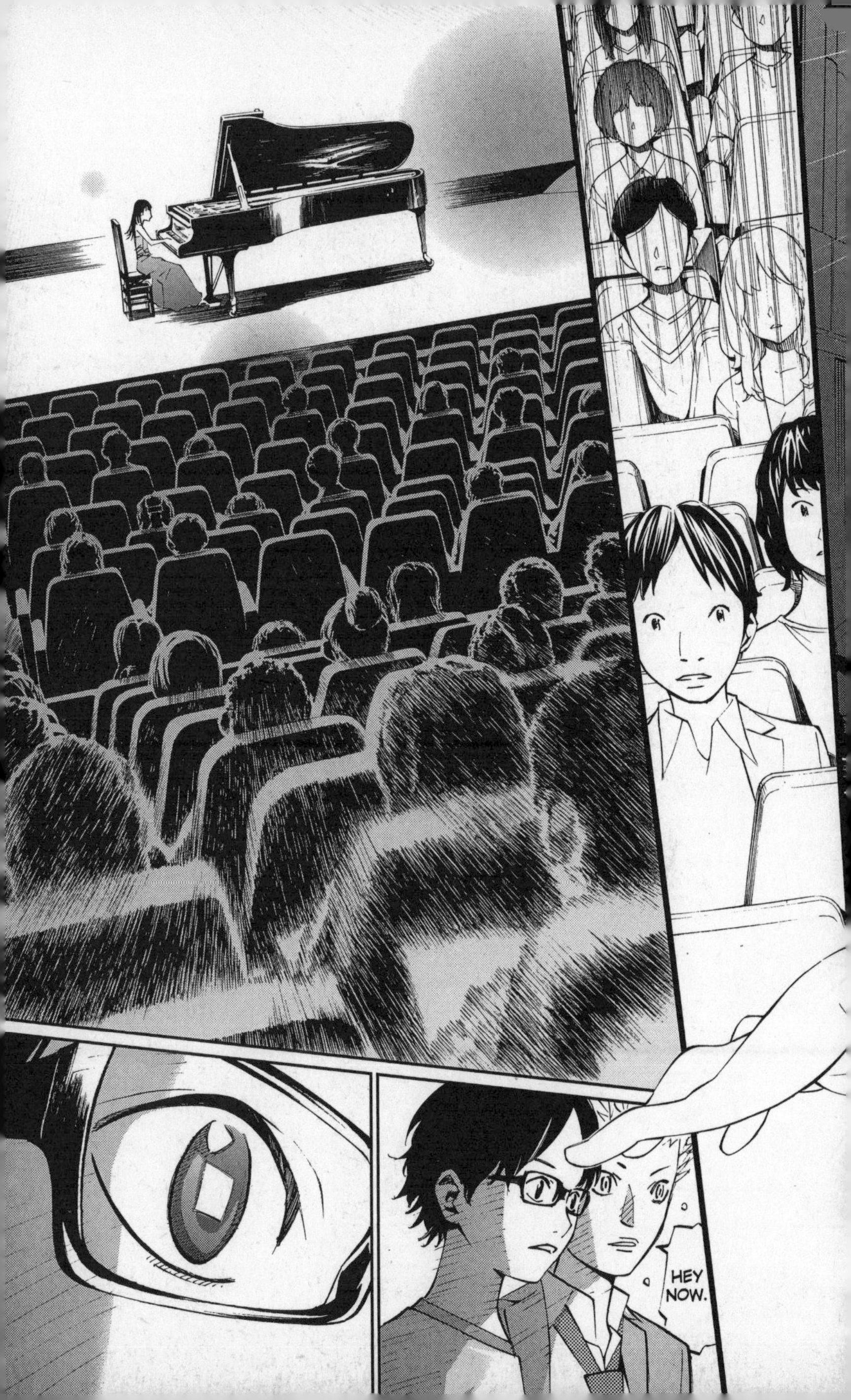
HEY NOW.

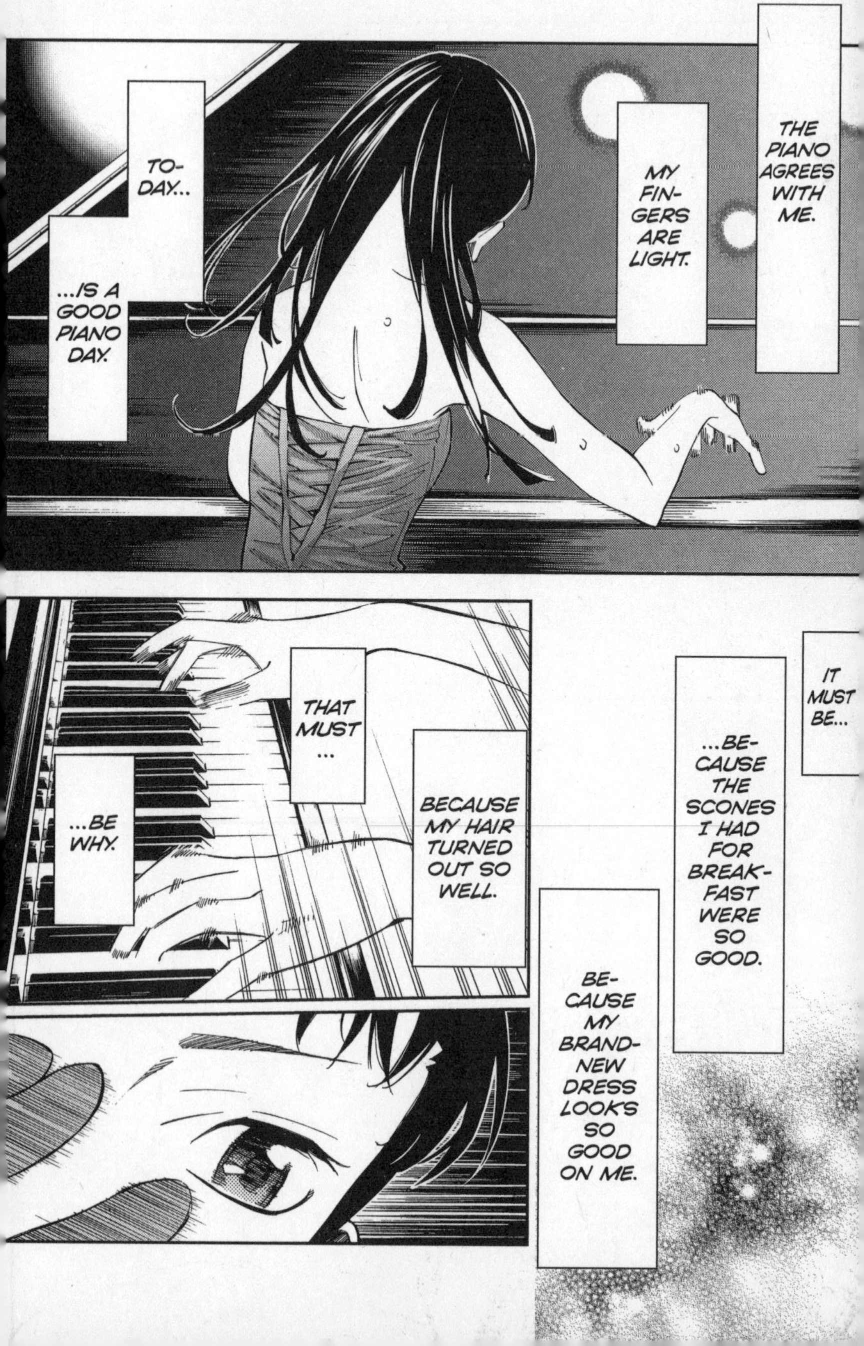
THE PIANO AGREES WITH ME.
MY FINGERS ARE LIGHT.
TODAY...
...IS A GOOD PIANO DAY.
IT MUST BE...
...BECAUSE THE SCONES I HAD FOR BREAKFAST WERE SO GOOD.
BECAUSE MY BRAND-NEW DRESS LOOKS SO GOOD ON ME.
BECAUSE MY HAIR TURNED OUT SO WELL.
THAT MUST...
...BE WHY.

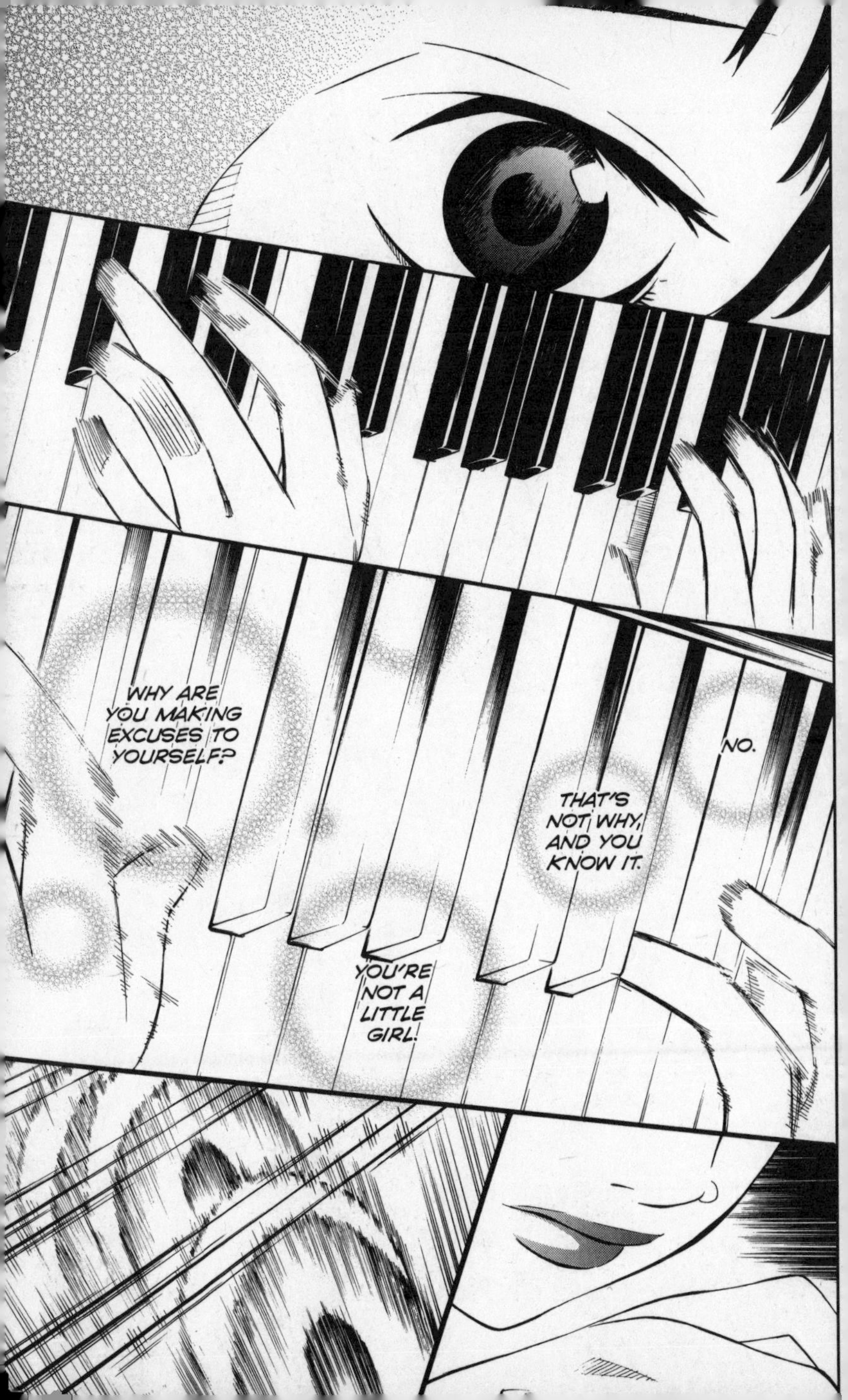
NO.
THAT'S NOT WHY, AND YOU KNOW IT.
YOU'RE NOT A LITTLE GIRL!
WHY ARE YOU MAKING EXCUSES TO YOURSELF?

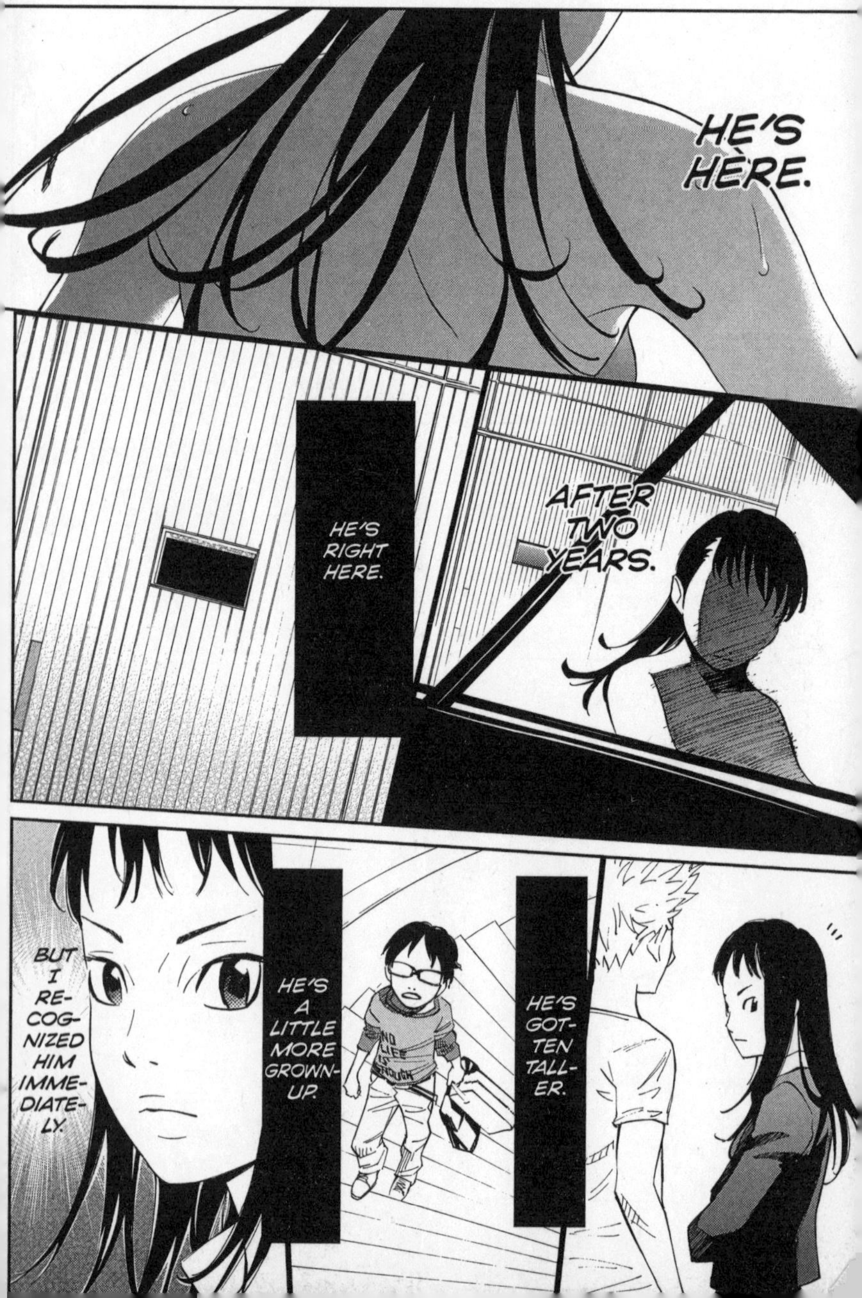
HE'S HERE.
AFTER TWO YEARS.
HE'S RIGHT HERE.
HE'S GOTTEN TALLER.
HE'S A LITTLE MORE GROWN-UP.
BUT I RECOGNIZED HIM IMMEDIATELY.

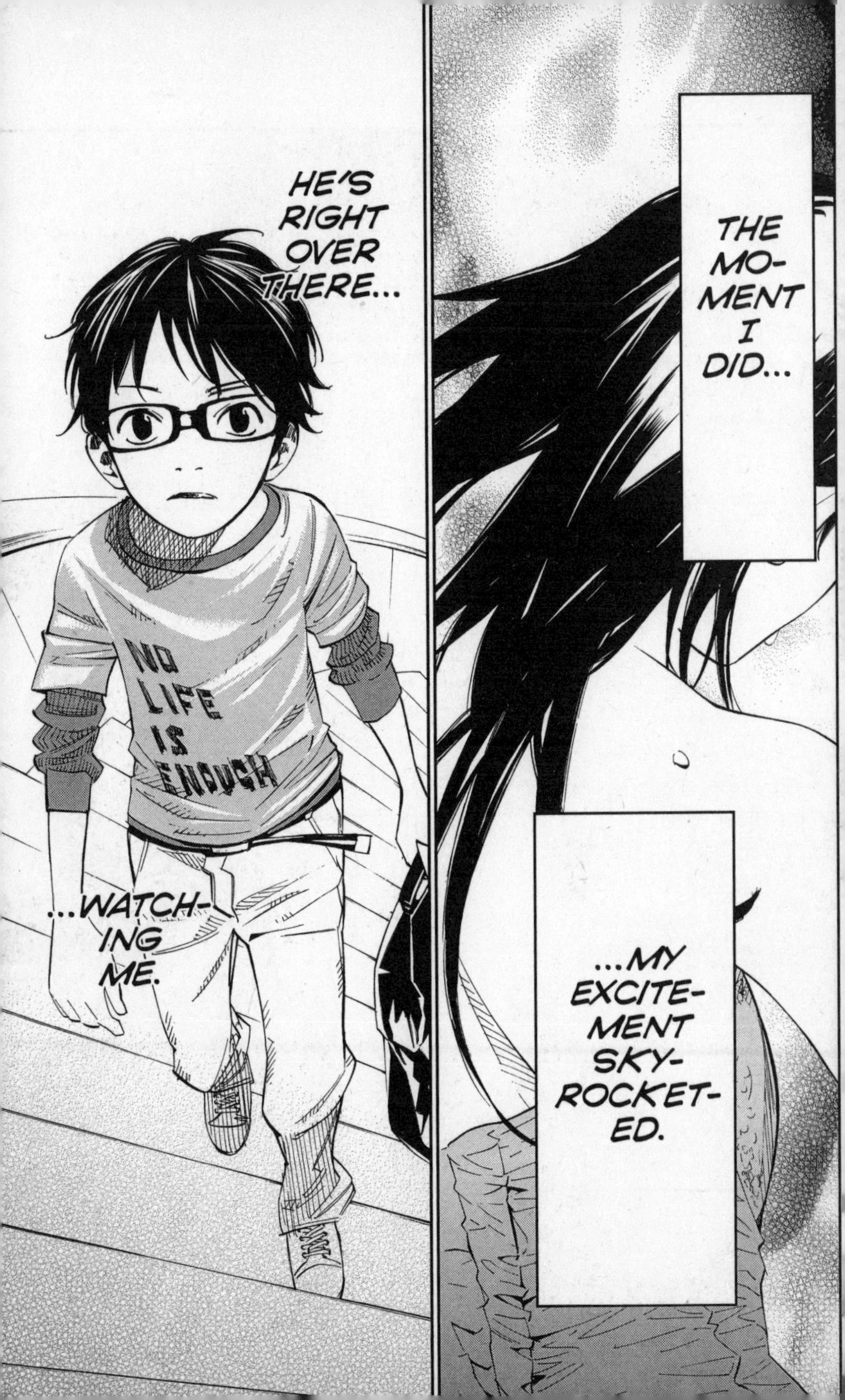
THE MO-MENT I DID...
...MY EXCITE-MENT SKY-ROCKET-ED.
HE'S RIGHT OVER THERE...
...WATCH-ING ME.

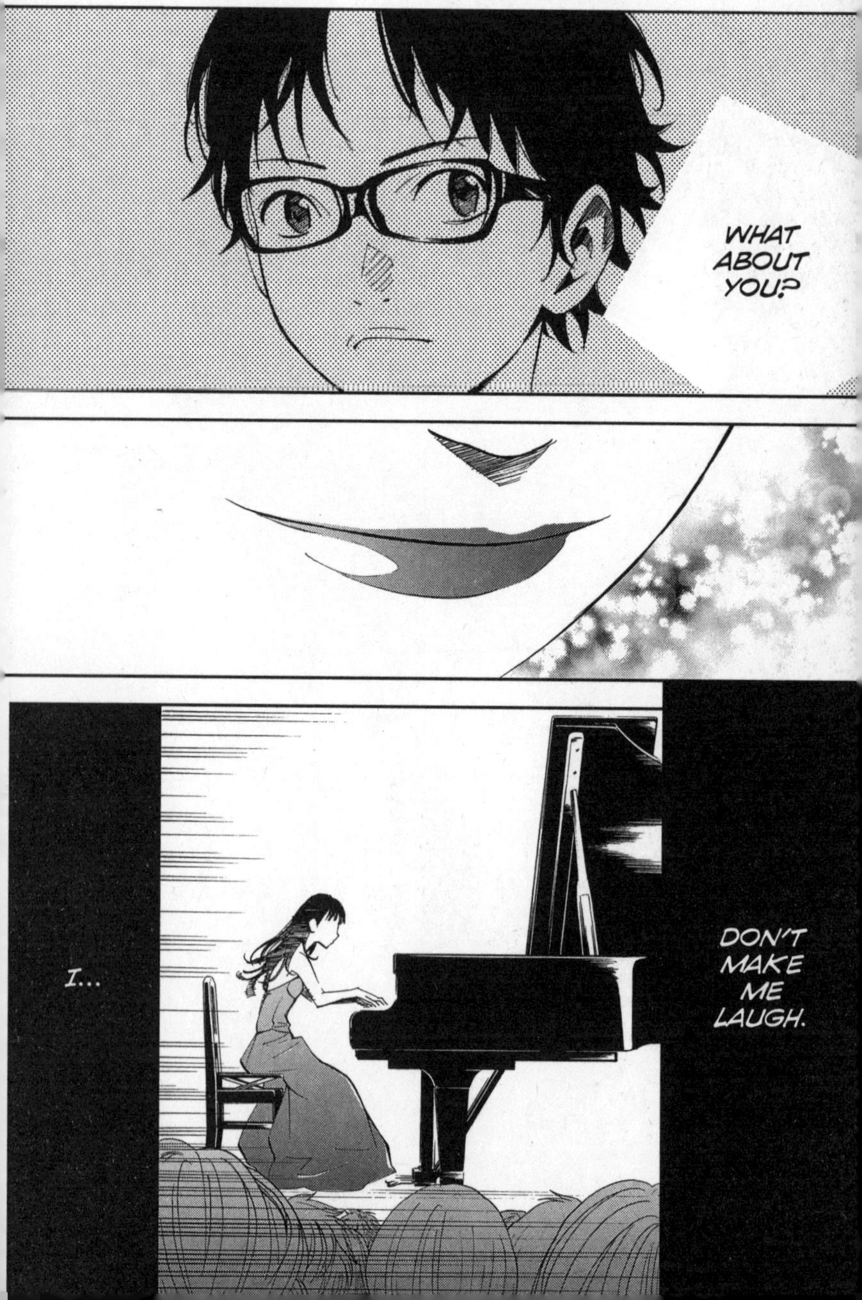
WHAT ABOUT YOU?
DON'T MAKE ME LAUGH.
I...

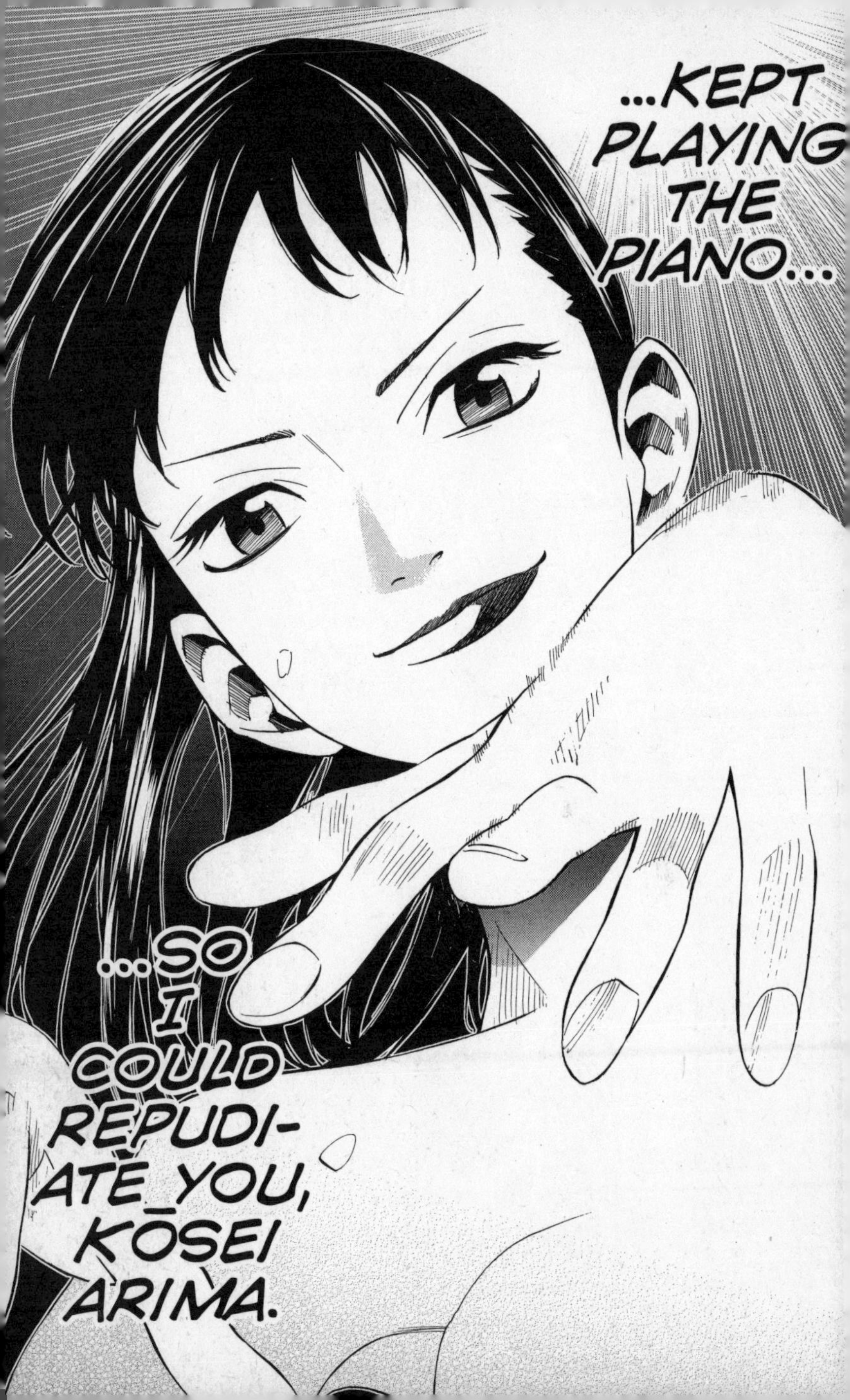
...KEPT PLAYING THE PIANO...
...SO I COULD REPUDI-ATE YOU, KŌSEI ARIMA.

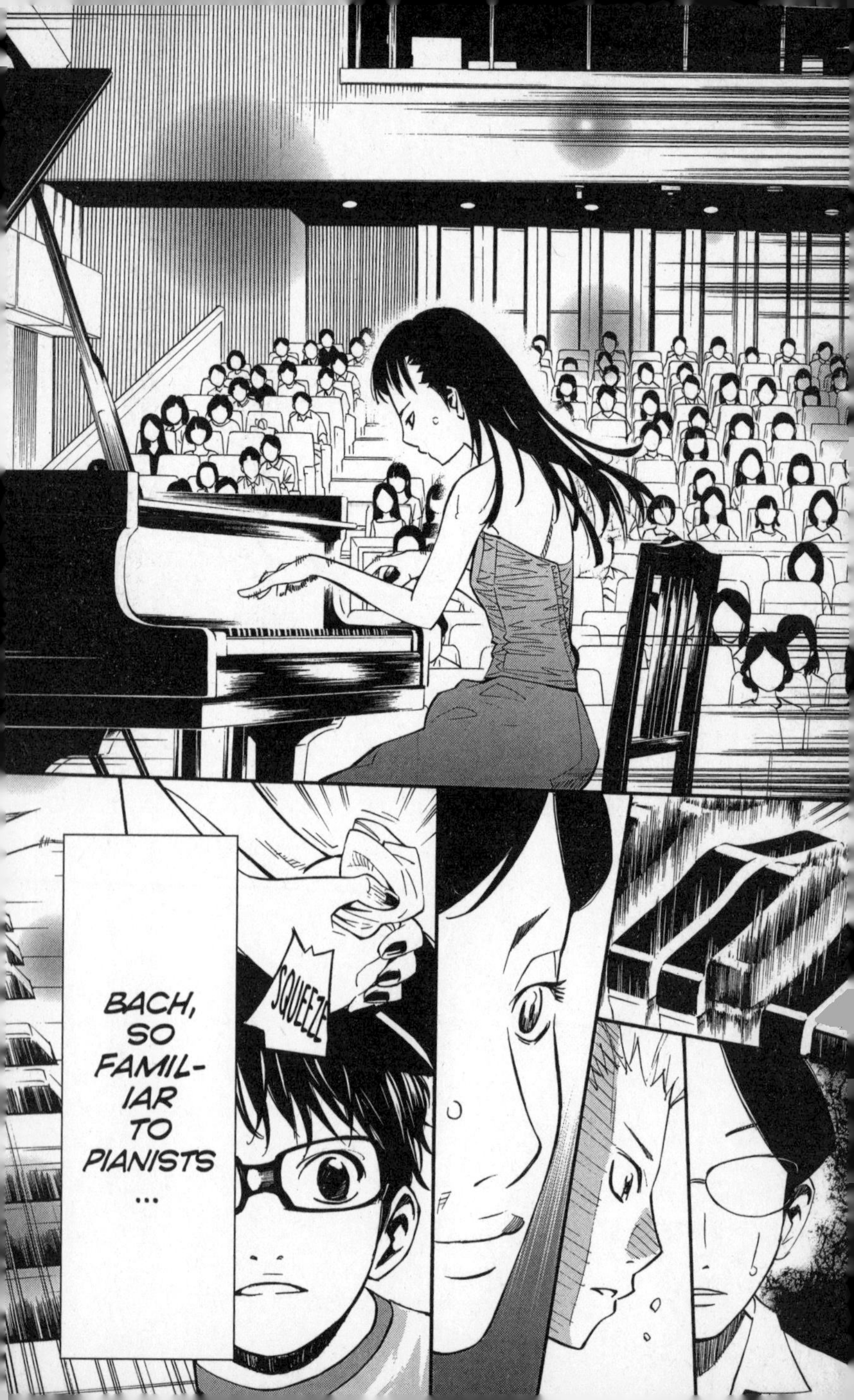
SQUEEZE
BACH, SO FAMILIAR TO PIANISTS...

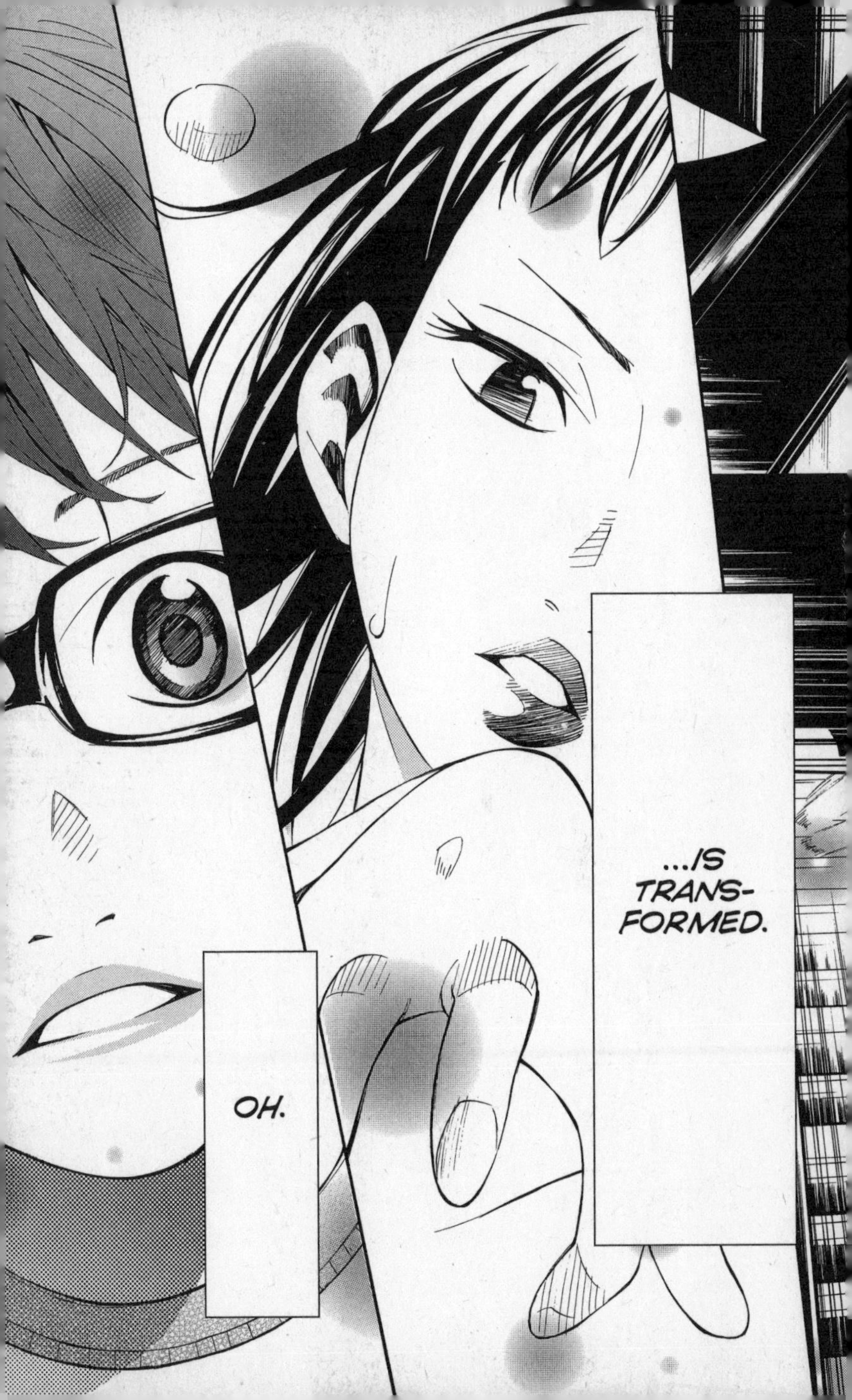
...IS TRANS-FORMED.
OH.

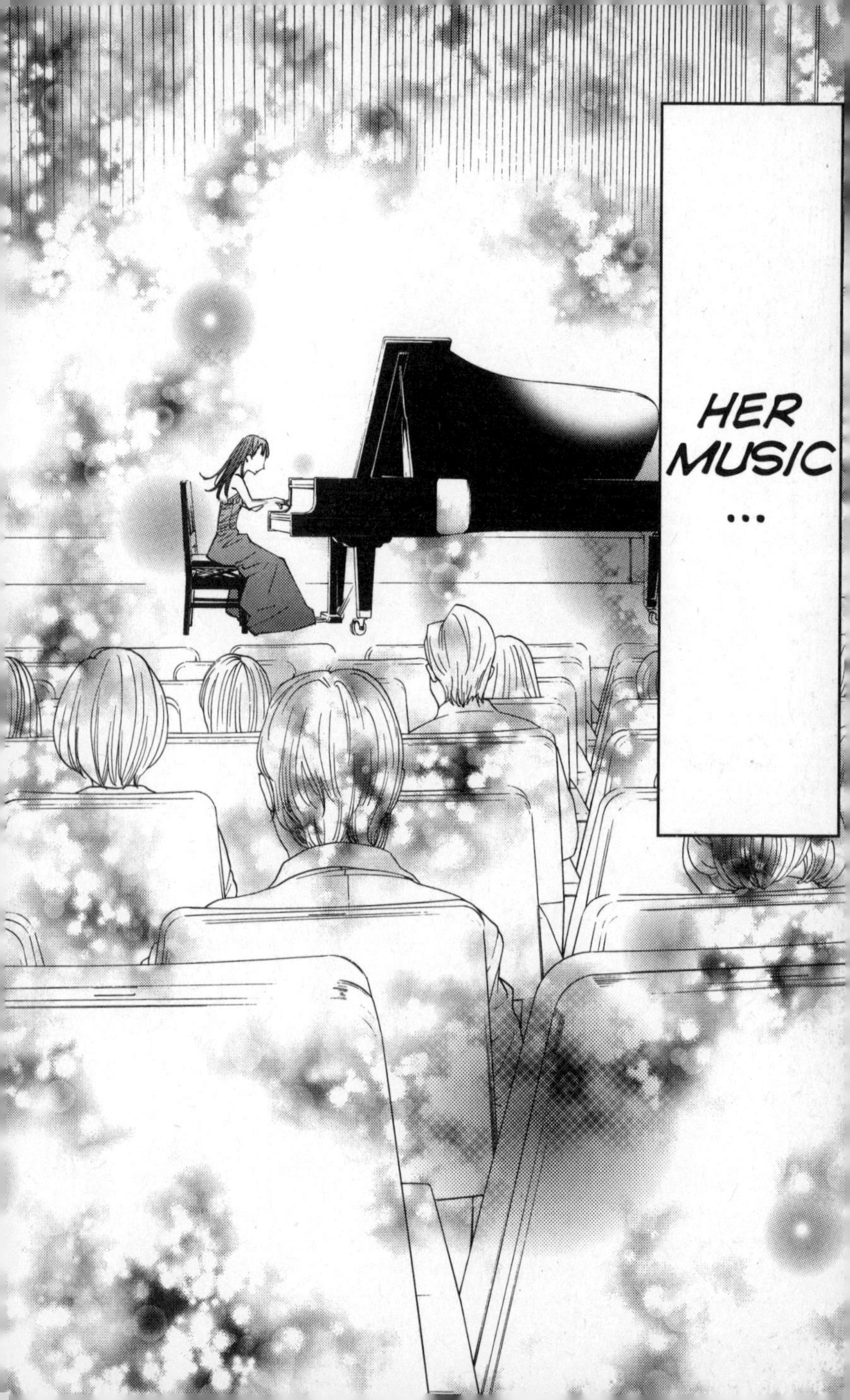
HER MUSIC ...

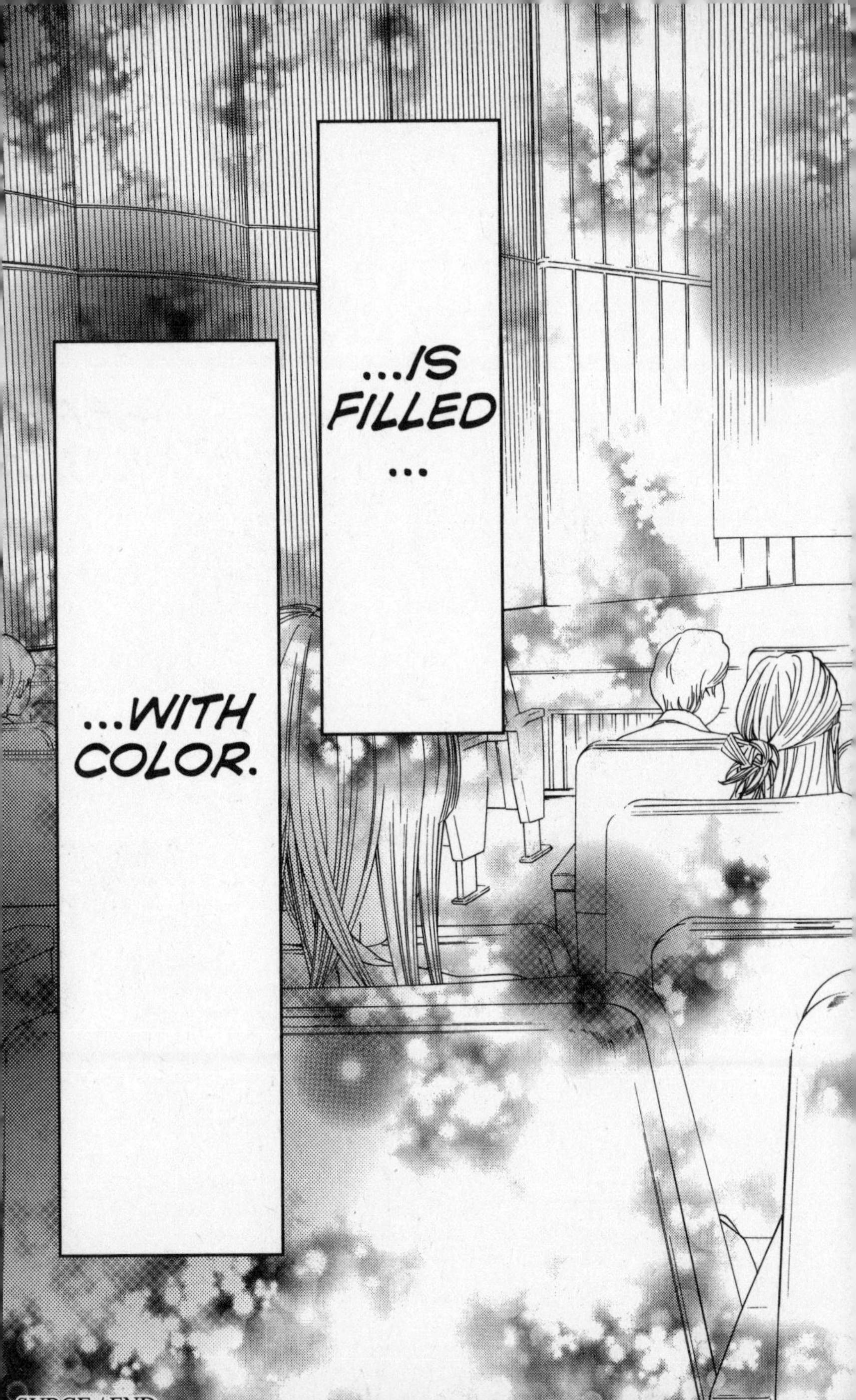
...IS FILLED ...
...WITH COLOR.
SURGE / END

YOUR LIE IN APRIL FEATURED MUSIC

JOHANN SEBASTIAN BACH'S WELL-TEMPERED CLAVIER, BOOK 1: PRELUDE AND FUGUE NO. 3 IN C-SHARP MAJOR BWV 848

The Prelude, which reminds one of twinkling, sparkling lights, was originally written in 1720 for Bach's oldest son, who was nine years old at the time, as a piece for the Klavierbüchlein. The pure joy of life, like that of an energetic child at play, is what gives this piece its charm. When it is combined with the active, rhythmical fugue, the pianist must move her fingers quickly and precisely in order to bring out the beauty of this piece.

The composition is in C-sharp Major, which means that all seven notes in the scale have a sharp attached. Normally, because C-sharp and D-flat are the same note, this piece would be considered as having been written in D-flat Major. The D-flat key would have only required five flats, as opposed to seven... However, Bach attempted to write it with sharps. In that respect, we can see the energy in this piece, as it constantly strives to go higher.

(Pianist Masanori Sugano, lecturer at Tokyo University of the Arts and Musashino Academia Musicae)

Watch it on YouTube (Search "Monthly Shonen Magazine Your Lie in April Featured Music")

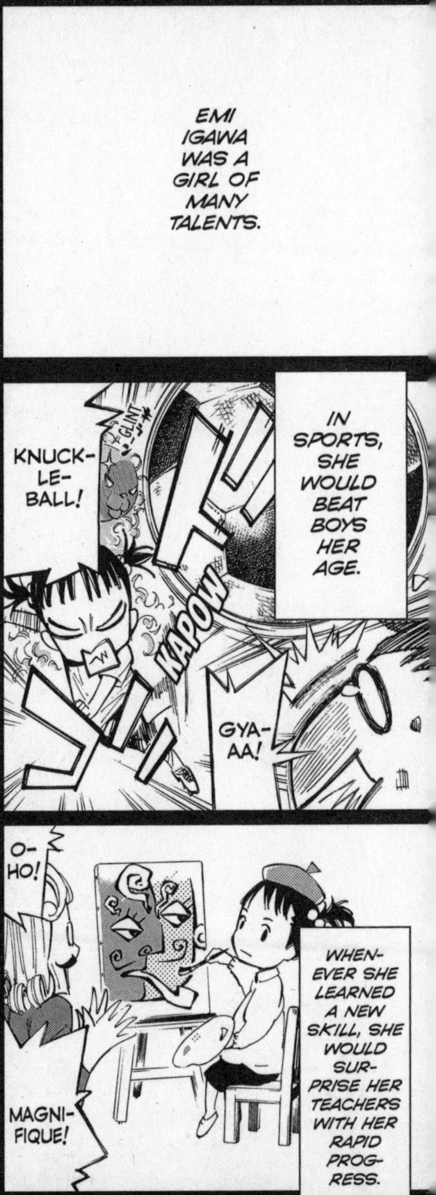
EMI IGAWA WAS A GIRL OF MANY TALENTS.
IN SPORTS, SHE WOULD BEAT BOYS HER AGE.
KNUCKLE-BALL!
GLINT
KAPOW
GYAA-AA!
WHEN-EVER SHE LEARNED A NEW SKILL, SHE WOULD SUR-PRISE HER TEACHERS WITH HER RAPID PROG-RESS.
O-HO!
MAGNI-FIQUE!
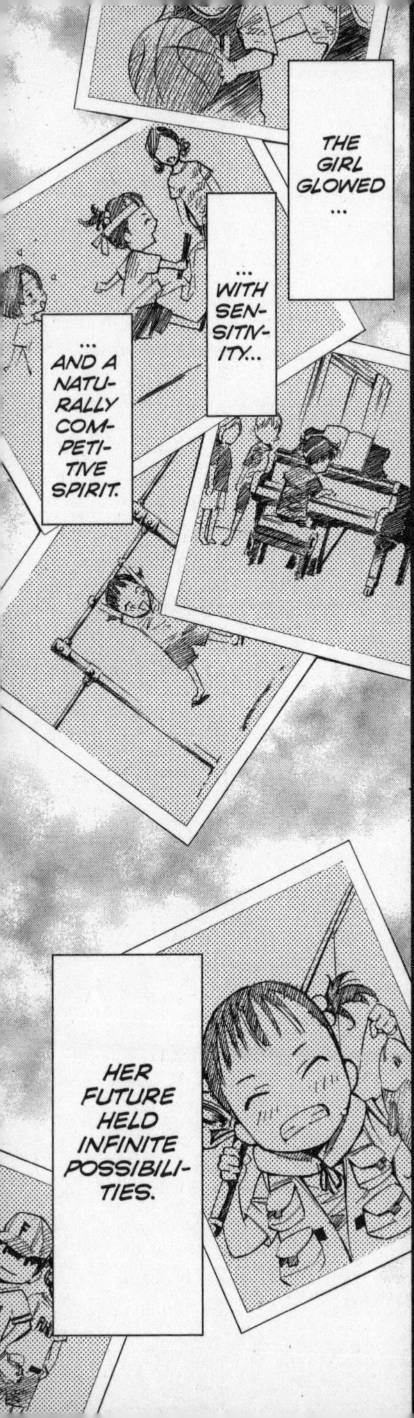
THE GIRL GLOWED ...
... WITH SEN-SITIV-ITY...
... AND A NATU-RALLY COM-PETI-TIVE SPIRIT.
HER FUTURE HELD INFINITE POSSIBILI-TIES.

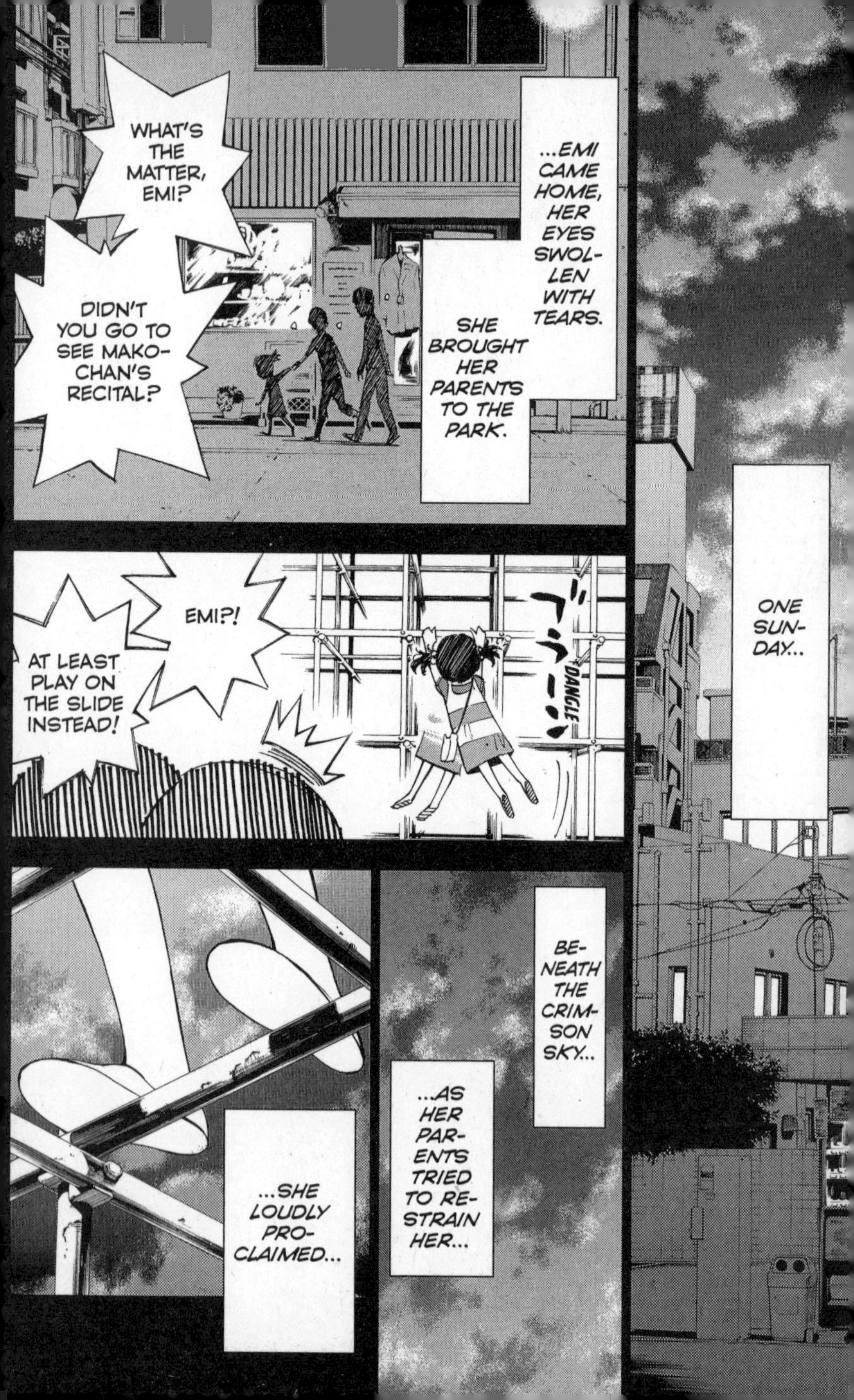
ONE SUNDAY...
...EMI CAME HOME, HER EYES SWOLLEN WITH TEARS.
WHAT'S THE MATTER, EMI?
DIDN'T YOU GO TO SEE MAKO-CHAN'S RECITAL?
SHE BROUGHT HER PARENTS TO THE PARK.
DANGLE
EMI?!
AT LEAST PLAY ON THE SLIDE INSTEAD!
BENEATH THE CRIMSON SKY...
...AS HER PARENTS TRIED TO RESTRAIN HER...
...SHE LOUDLY PROCLAIMED...

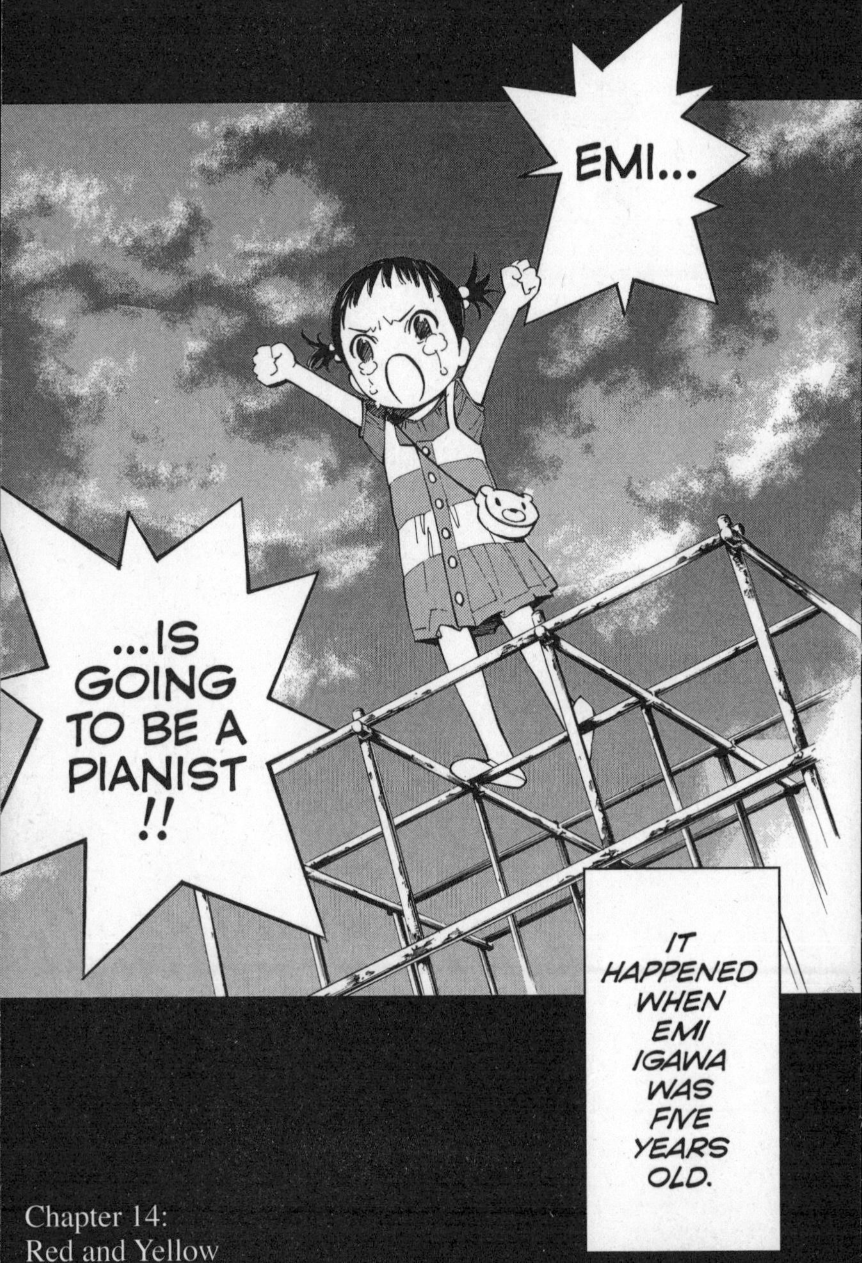
EMI...
...IS GOING TO BE A PIANIST!!
IT HAPPENED WHEN EMI IGAWA WAS FIVE YEARS OLD.

Chapter 14: Red and Yellow

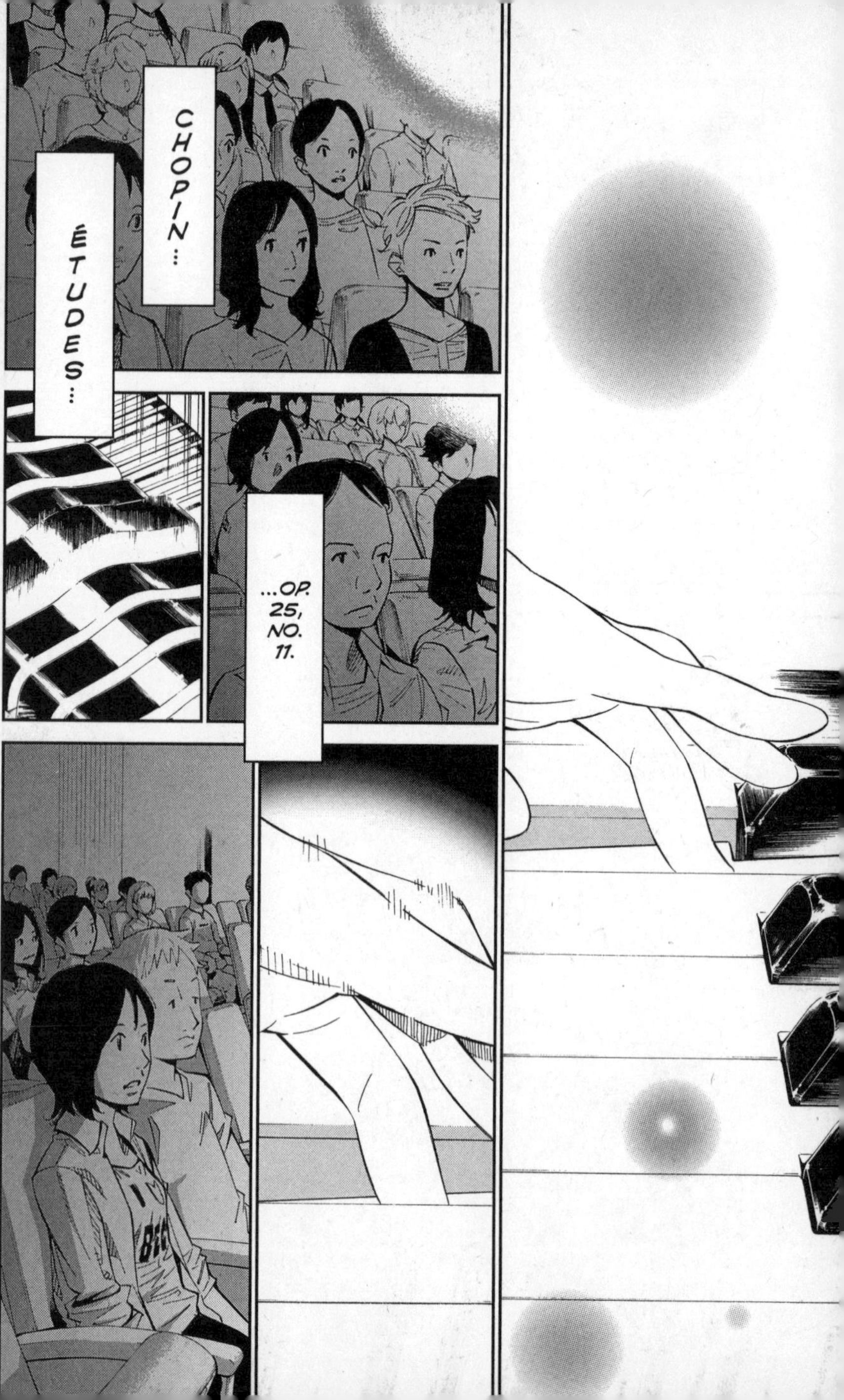
CHOPIN…
ÉTUDES…
…OP. 25, NO. 11.

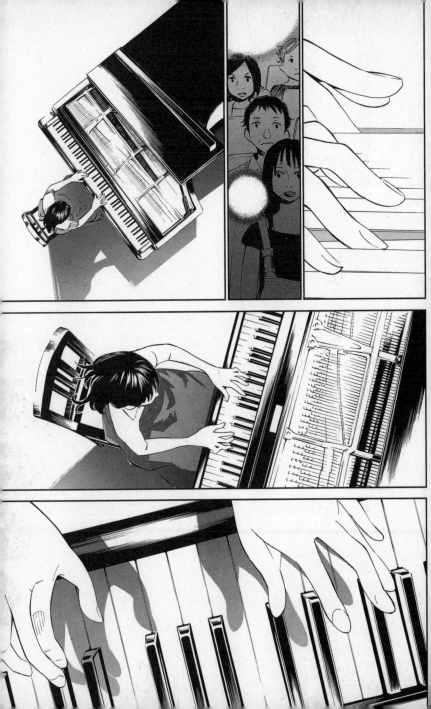

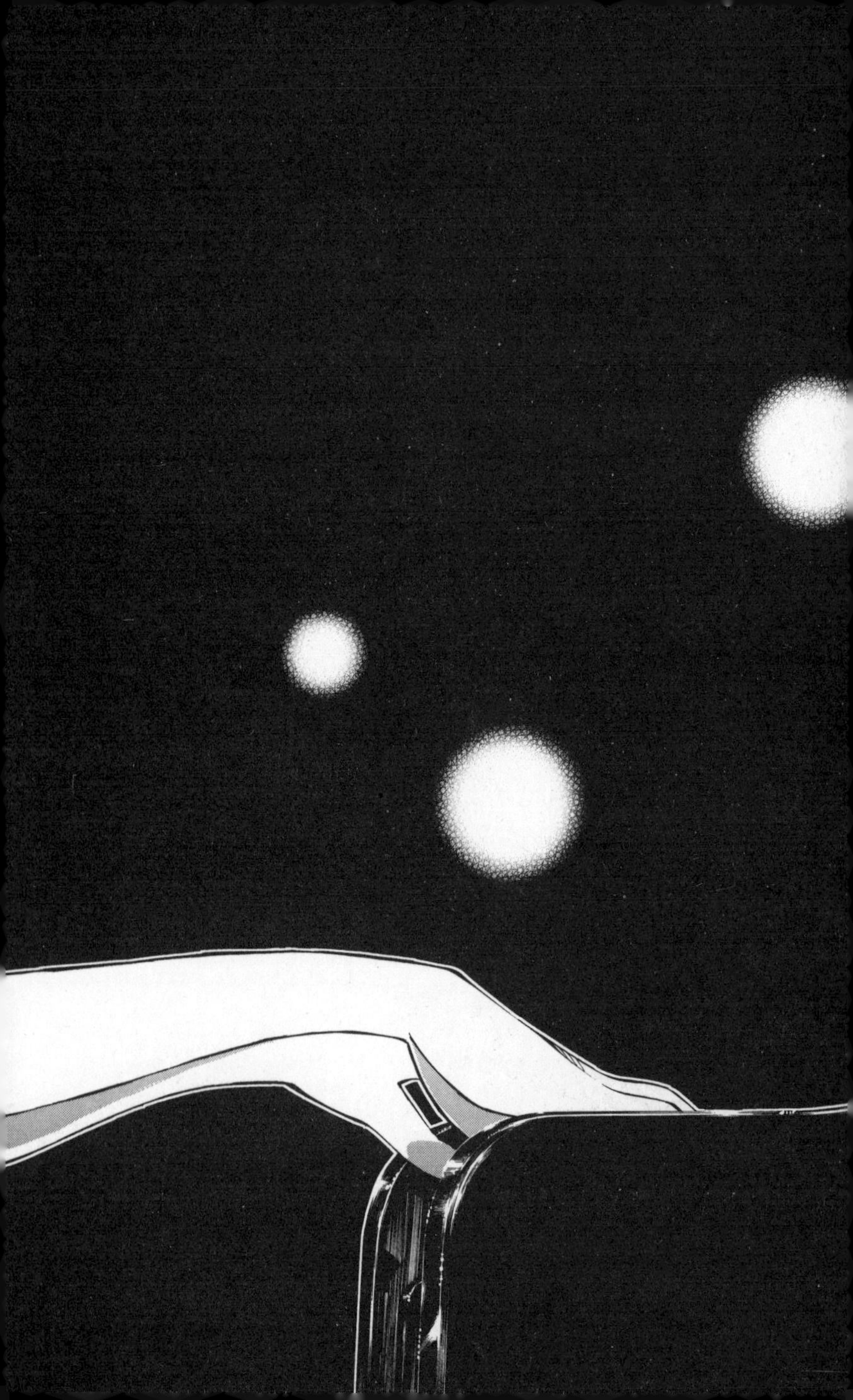

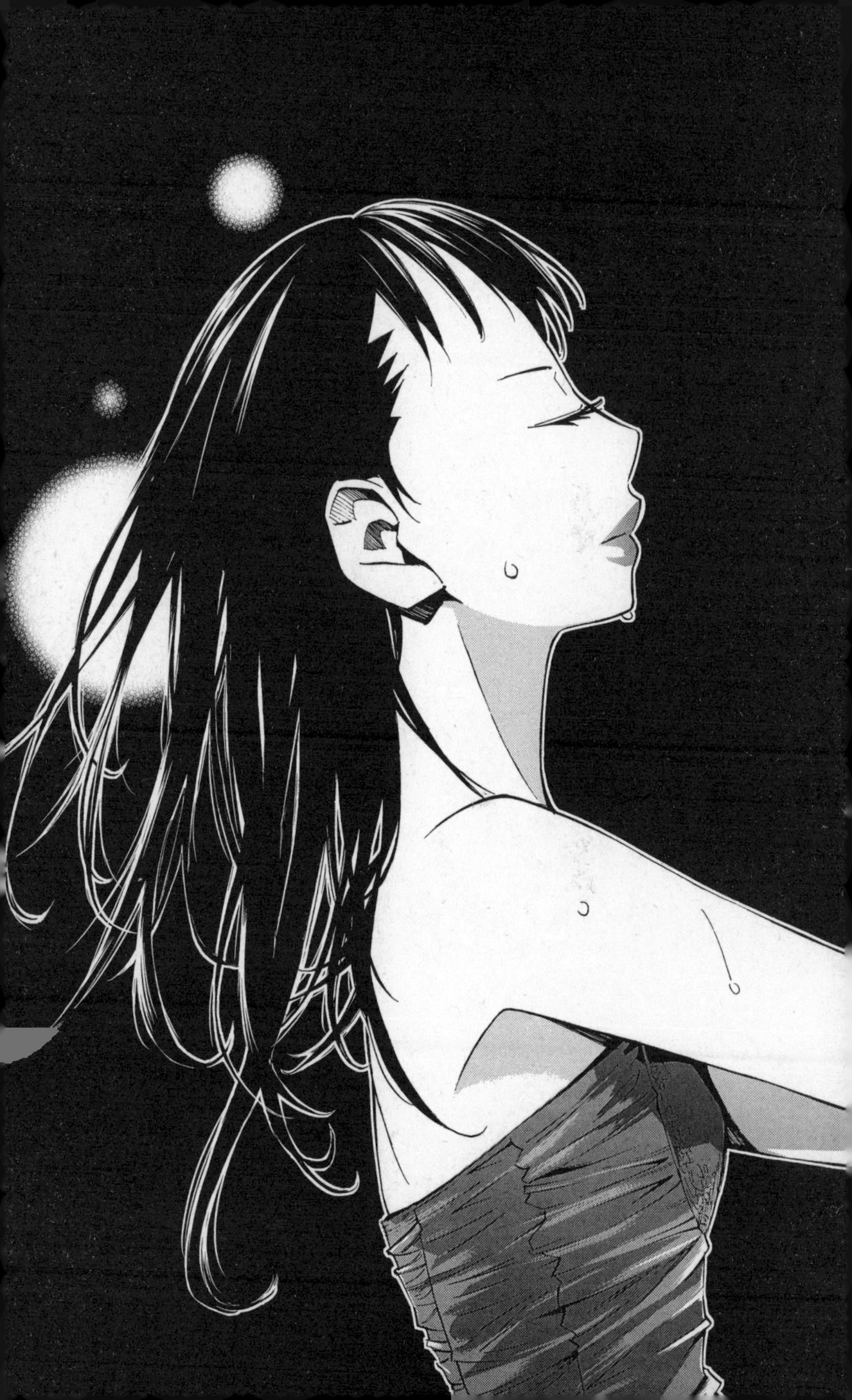

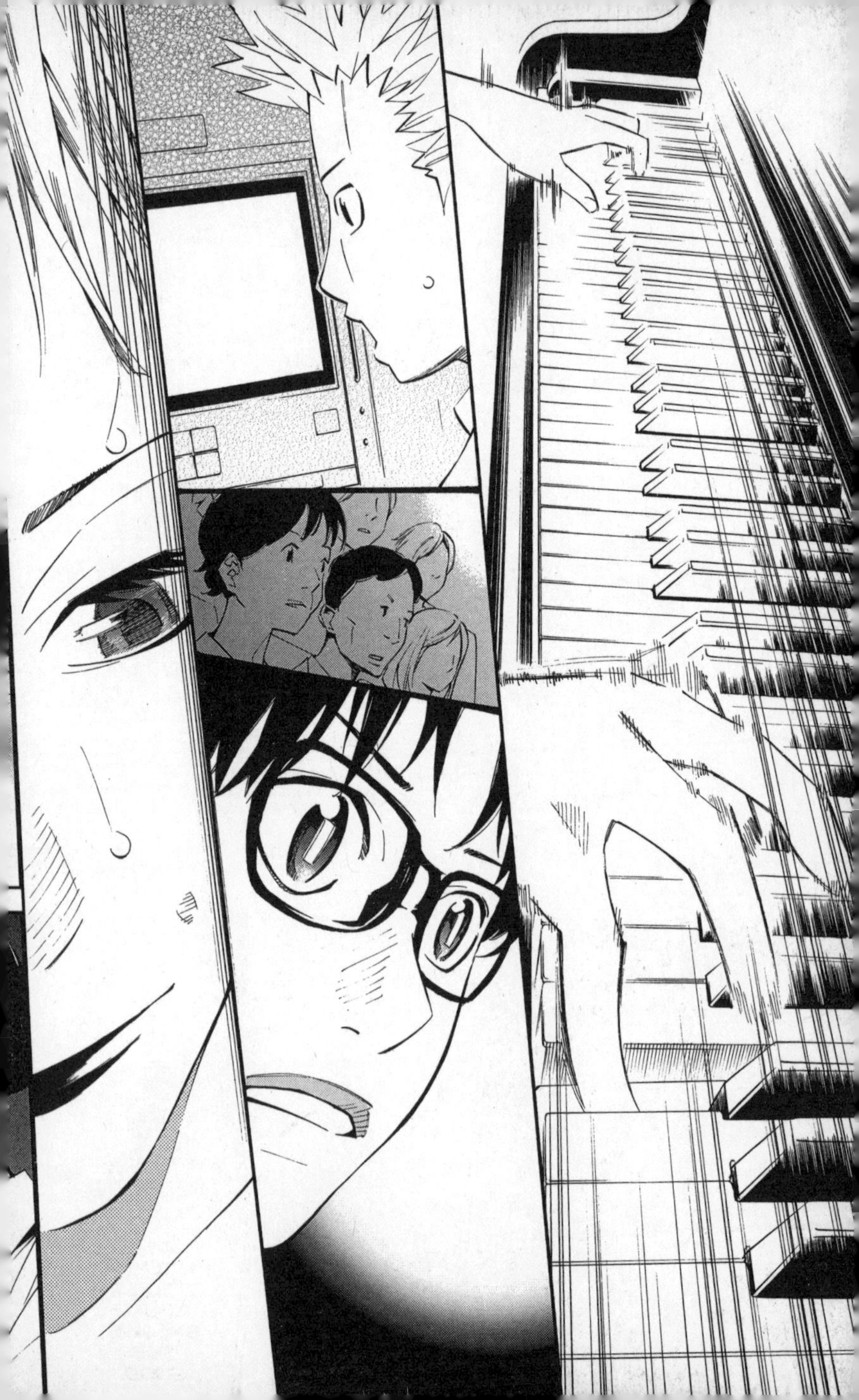

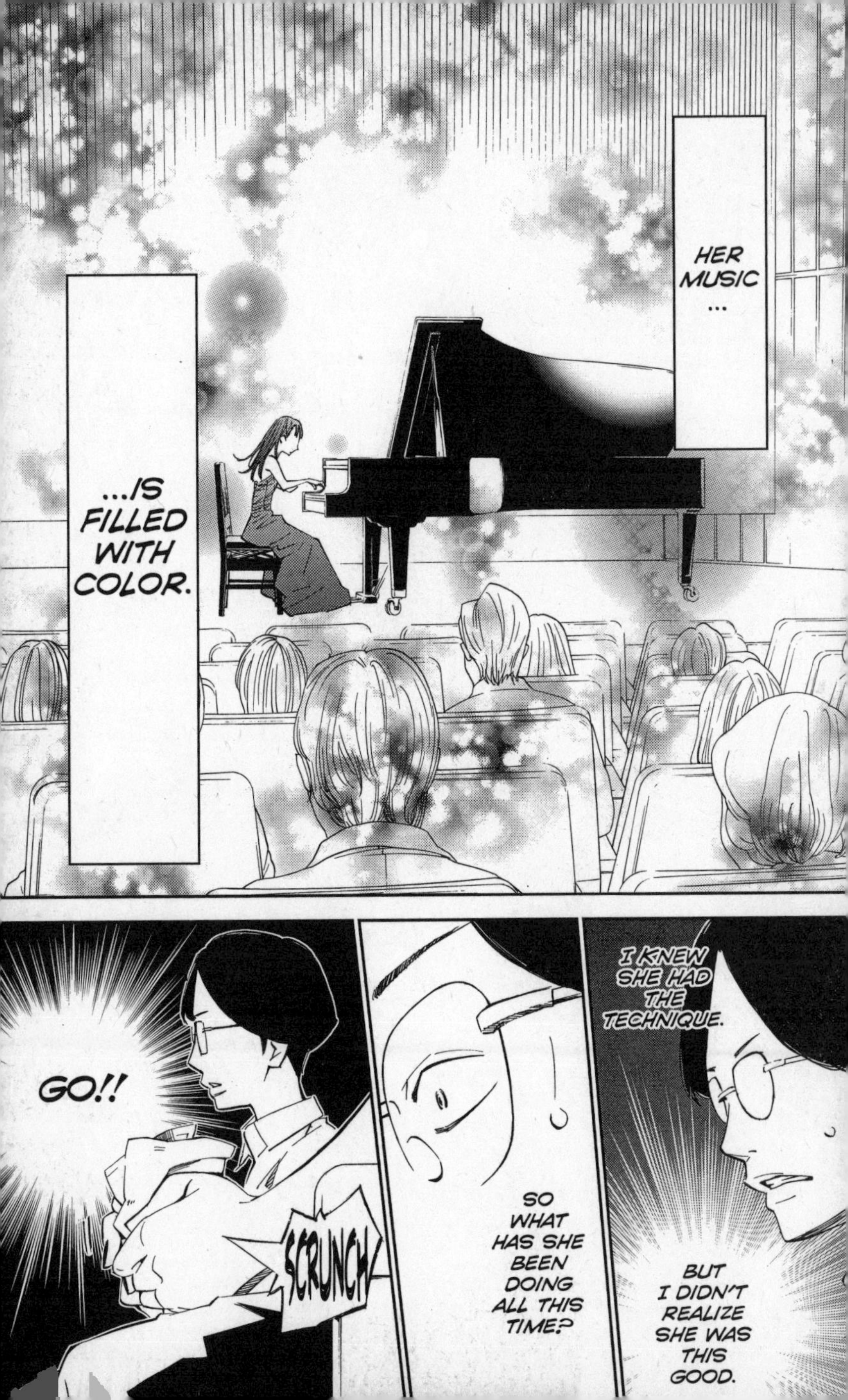
HER MUSIC ...
...IS FILLED WITH COLOR.
I KNEW SHE HAD THE TECHNIQUE.
BUT I DIDN'T REALIZE SHE WAS THIS GOOD.
SO WHAT HAS SHE BEEN DOING ALL THIS TIME?
GO!!
SCRUNCH

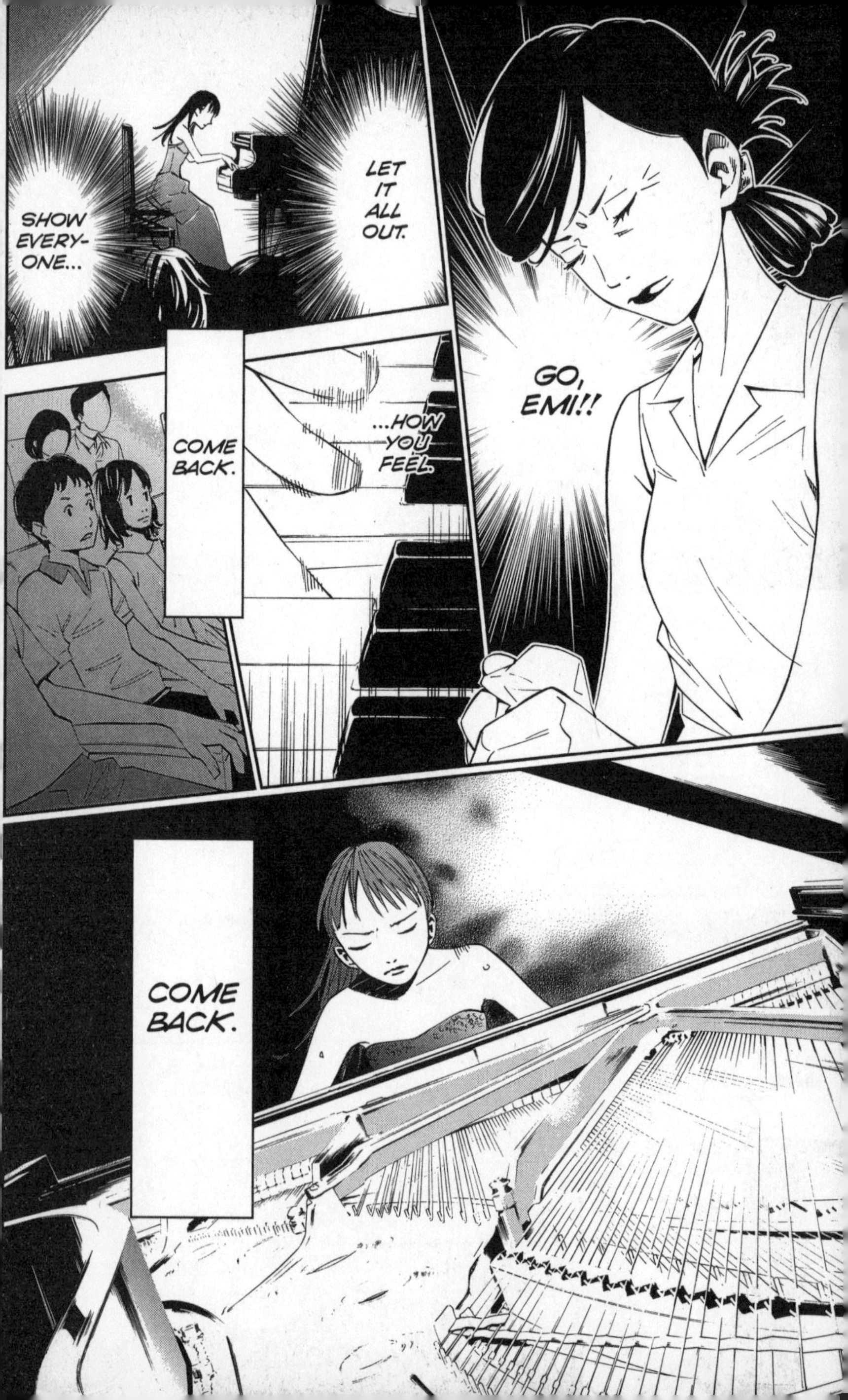
GO, EMI!!
LET IT ALL OUT.
SHOW EVERY-ONE...
...HOW YOU FEEL.
COME BACK.
COME BACK.

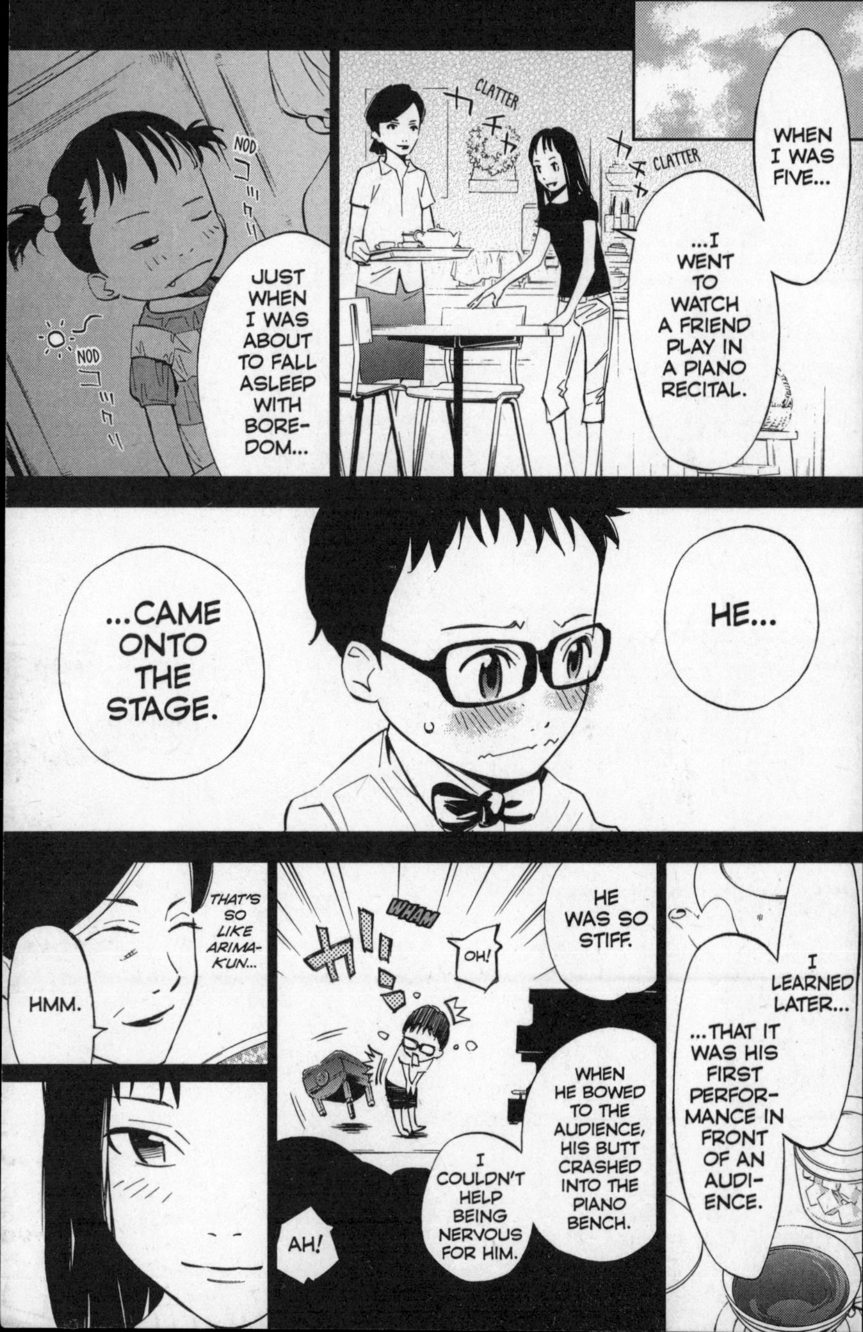
WHEN I WAS FIVE...
...I WENT TO WATCH A FRIEND PLAY IN A PIANO RECITAL.
CLATTER
CLATTER
NOD
NOD
JUST WHEN I WAS ABOUT TO FALL ASLEEP WITH BORE-DOM...
HE...
...CAME ONTO THE STAGE.
I LEARNED LATER...
...THAT IT WAS HIS FIRST PERFOR-MANCE IN FRONT OF AN AUDI-ENCE.
HE WAS SO STIFF.
OH!
WHAM
WHEN HE BOWED TO THE AUDIENCE, HIS BUTT CRASHED INTO THE PIANO BENCH.
I COULDN'T HELP BEING NERVOUS FOR HIM.
AH!
THAT'S SO LIKE ARIMA-KUN...
HMM.

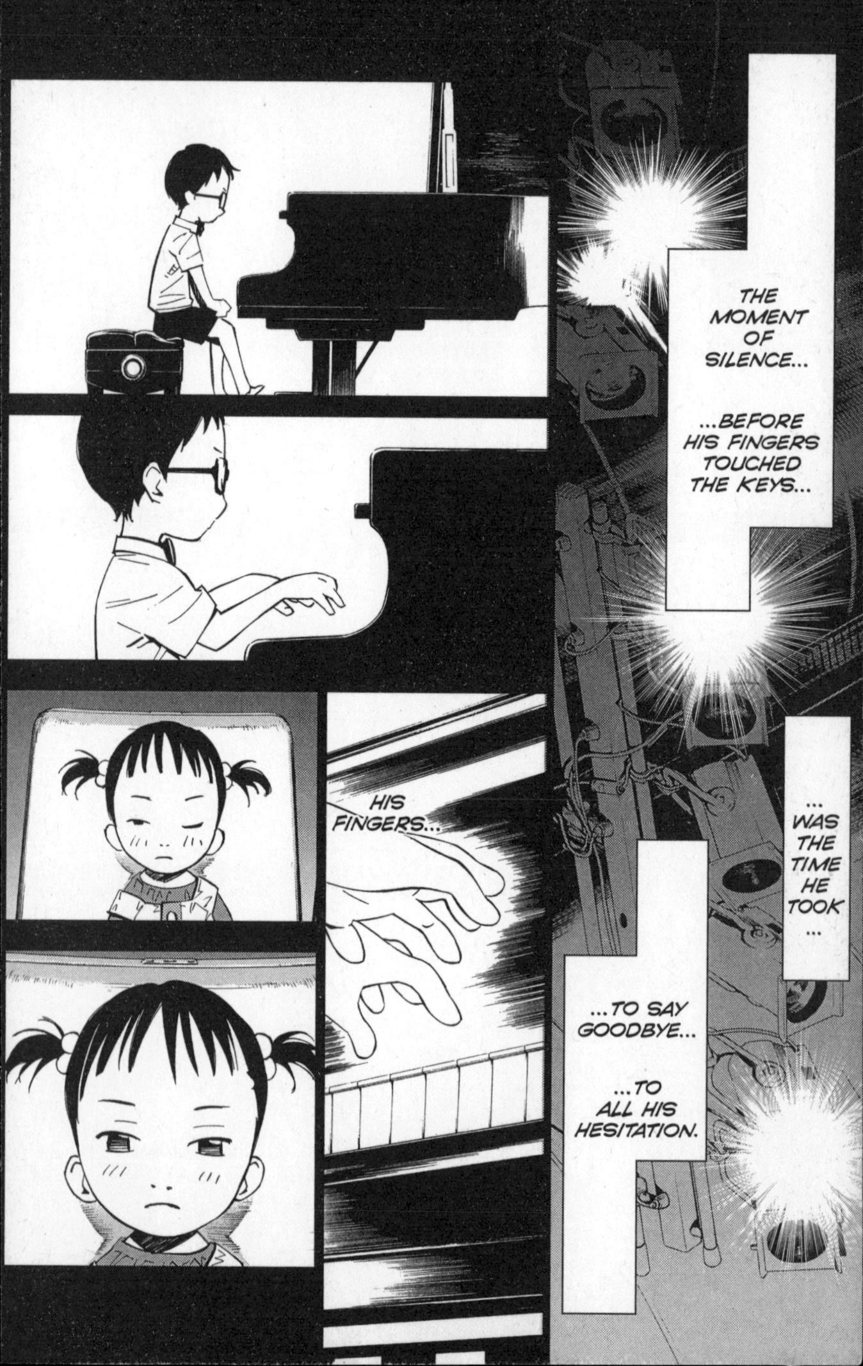
THE MOMENT OF SILENCE...
...BEFORE HIS FINGERS TOUCHED THE KEYS...
...WAS THE TIME HE TOOK...
...TO SAY GOODBYE...
...TO ALL HIS HESITATION.
HIS FINGERS...

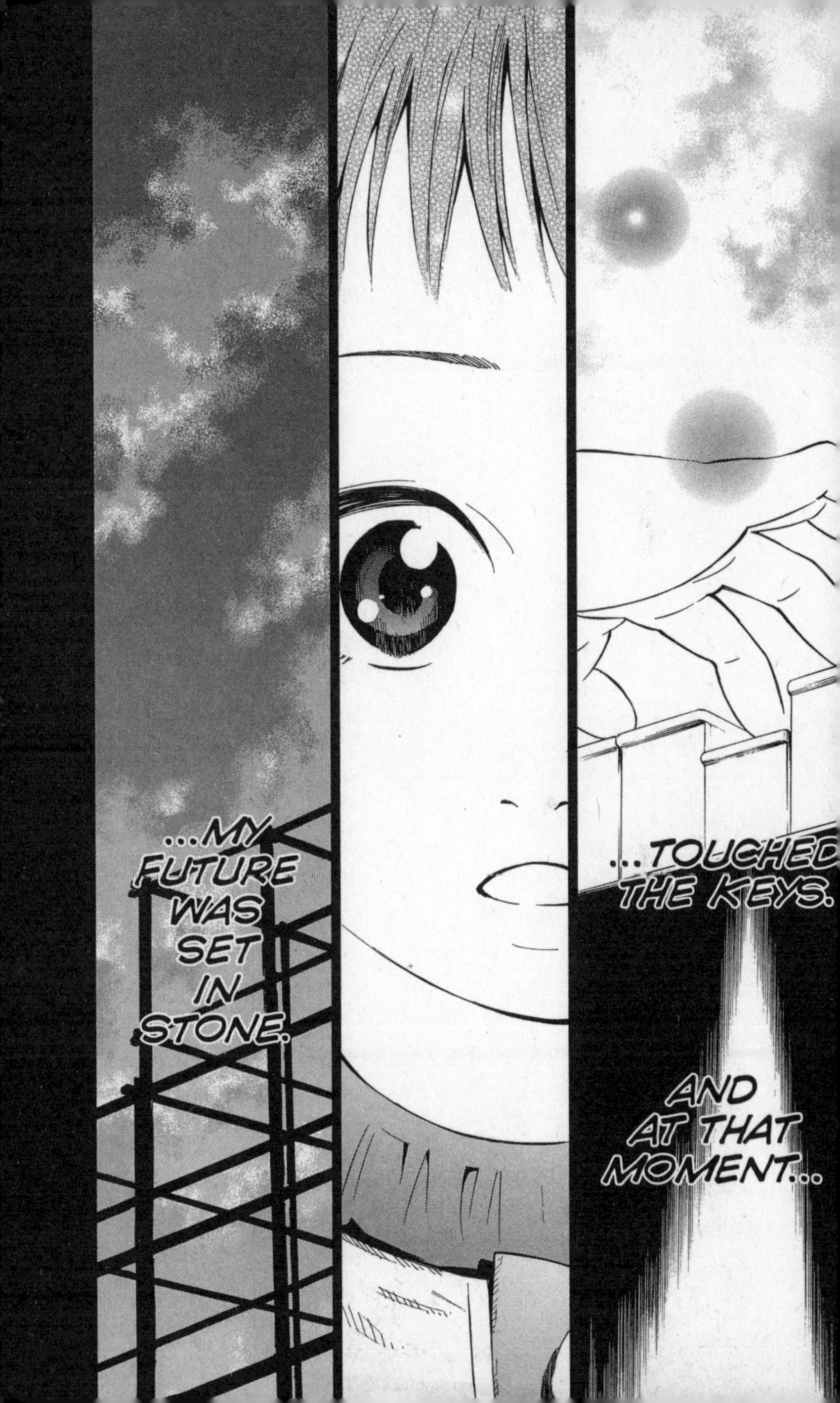
...TOUCHED THE KEYS.
AND AT THAT MOMENT...
...MY FUTURE WAS SET IN STONE.

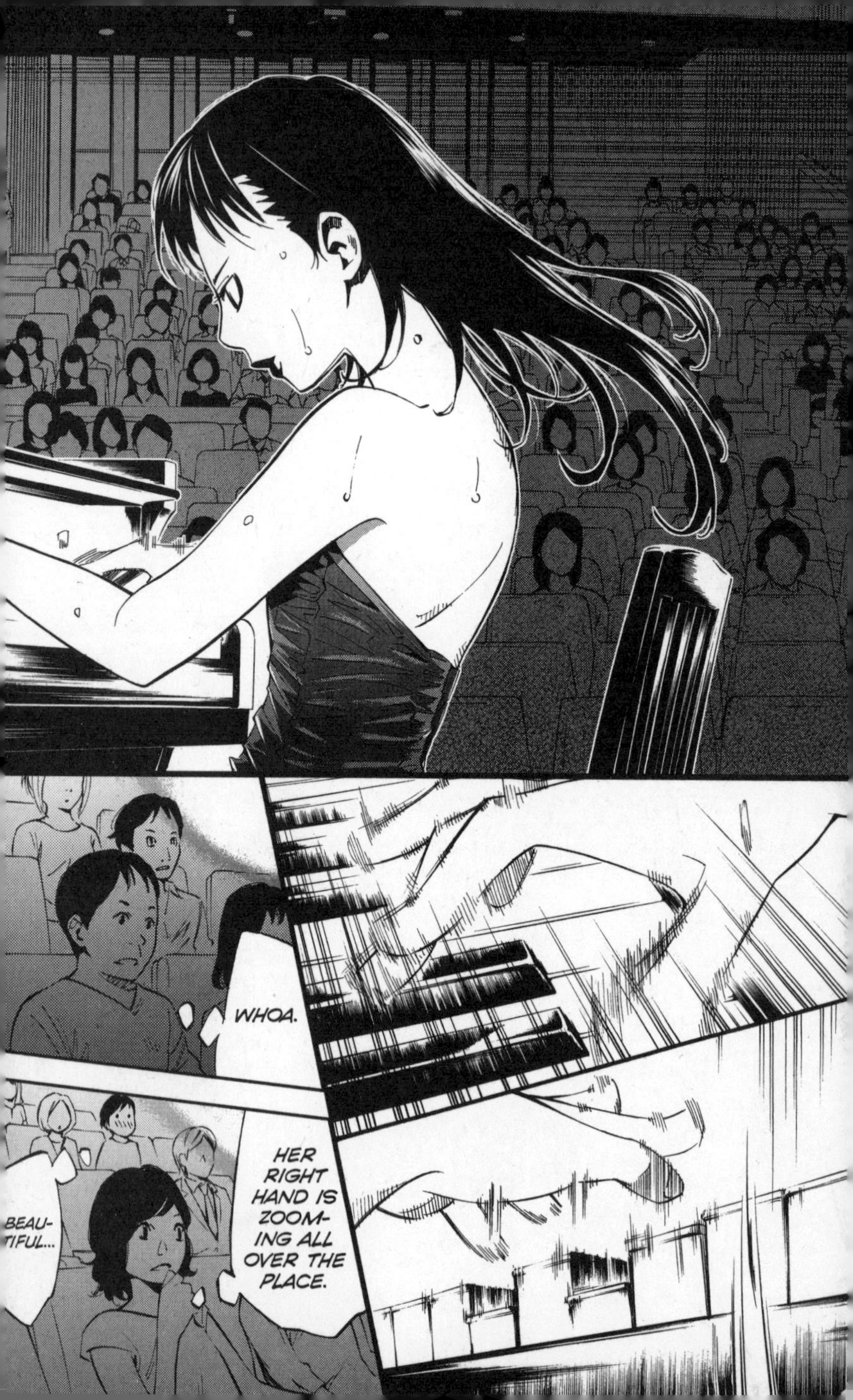
WHOA.
HER RIGHT HAND IS ZOOMING ALL OVER THE PLACE.
BEAUTIFUL...

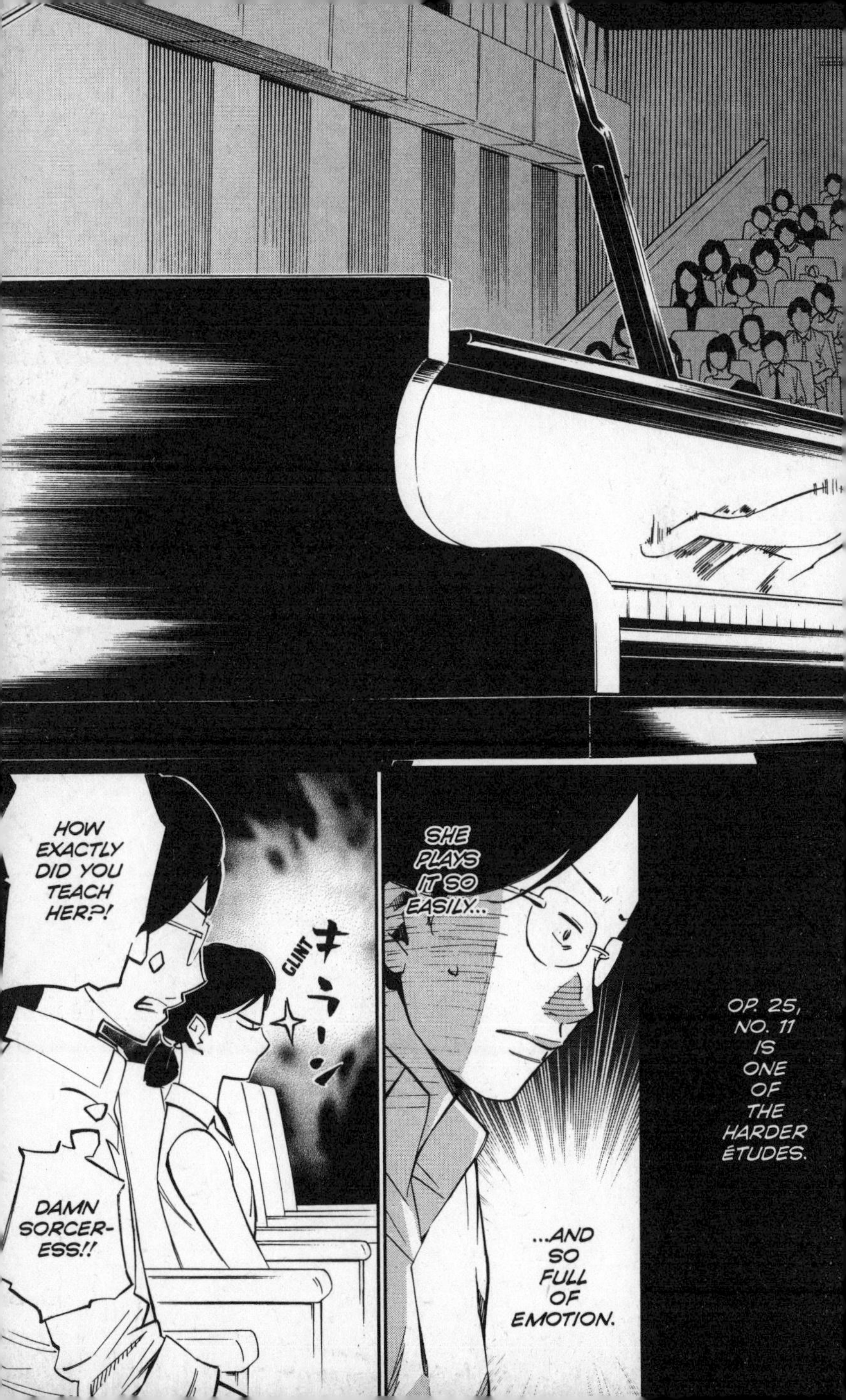
OP. 25, NO. 11 IS ONE OF THE HARDER ÉTUDES.
SHE PLAYS IT SO EASILY...
...AND SO FULL OF EMOTION.
HOW EXACTLY DID YOU TEACH HER?!
GLINT
キラーン
DAMN SORCER-ESS!!

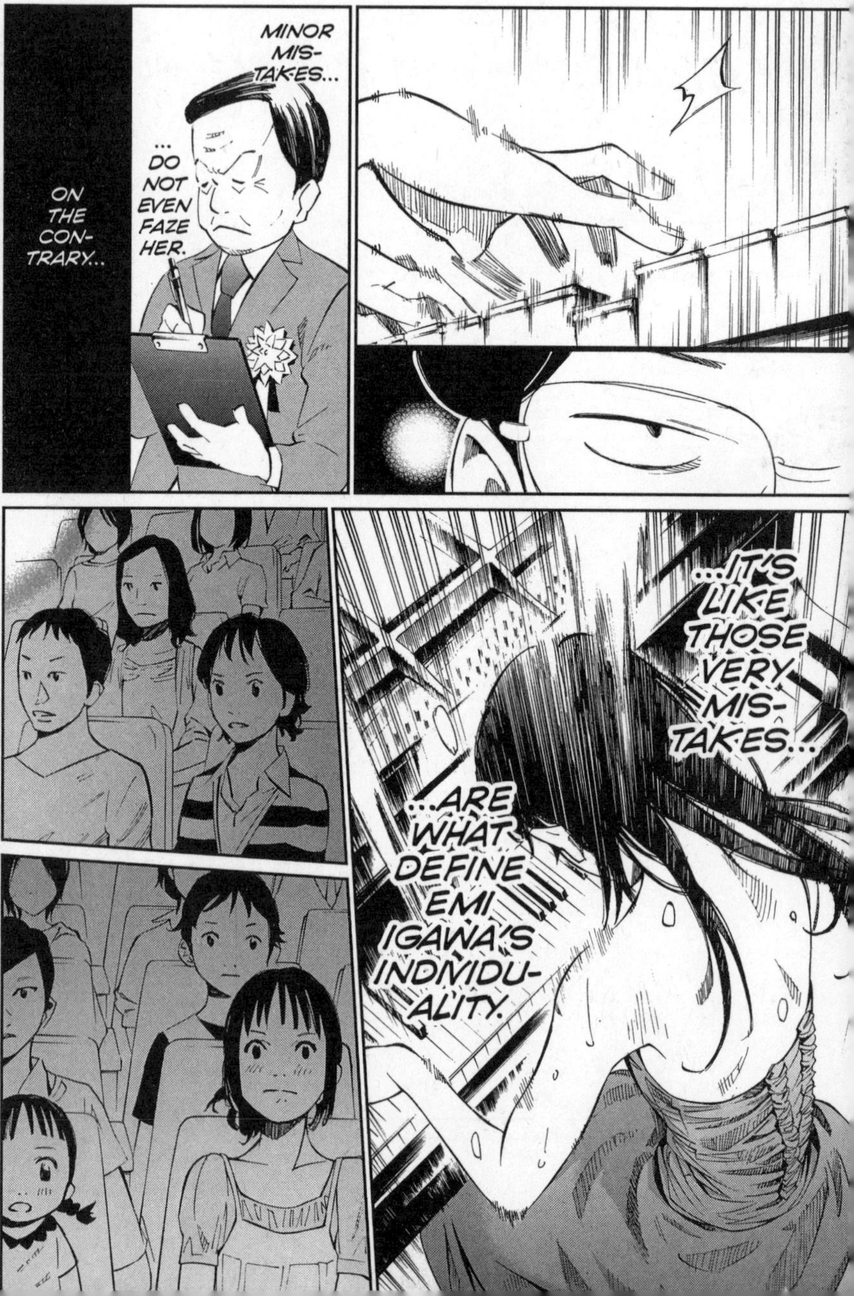
MINOR MISTAKES...
...DO NOT EVEN FAZE HER.
ON THE CONTRARY...
...IT'S LIKE THOSE VERY MISTAKES...
...ARE WHAT DEFINE EMI IGAWA'S INDIVIDUALITY.

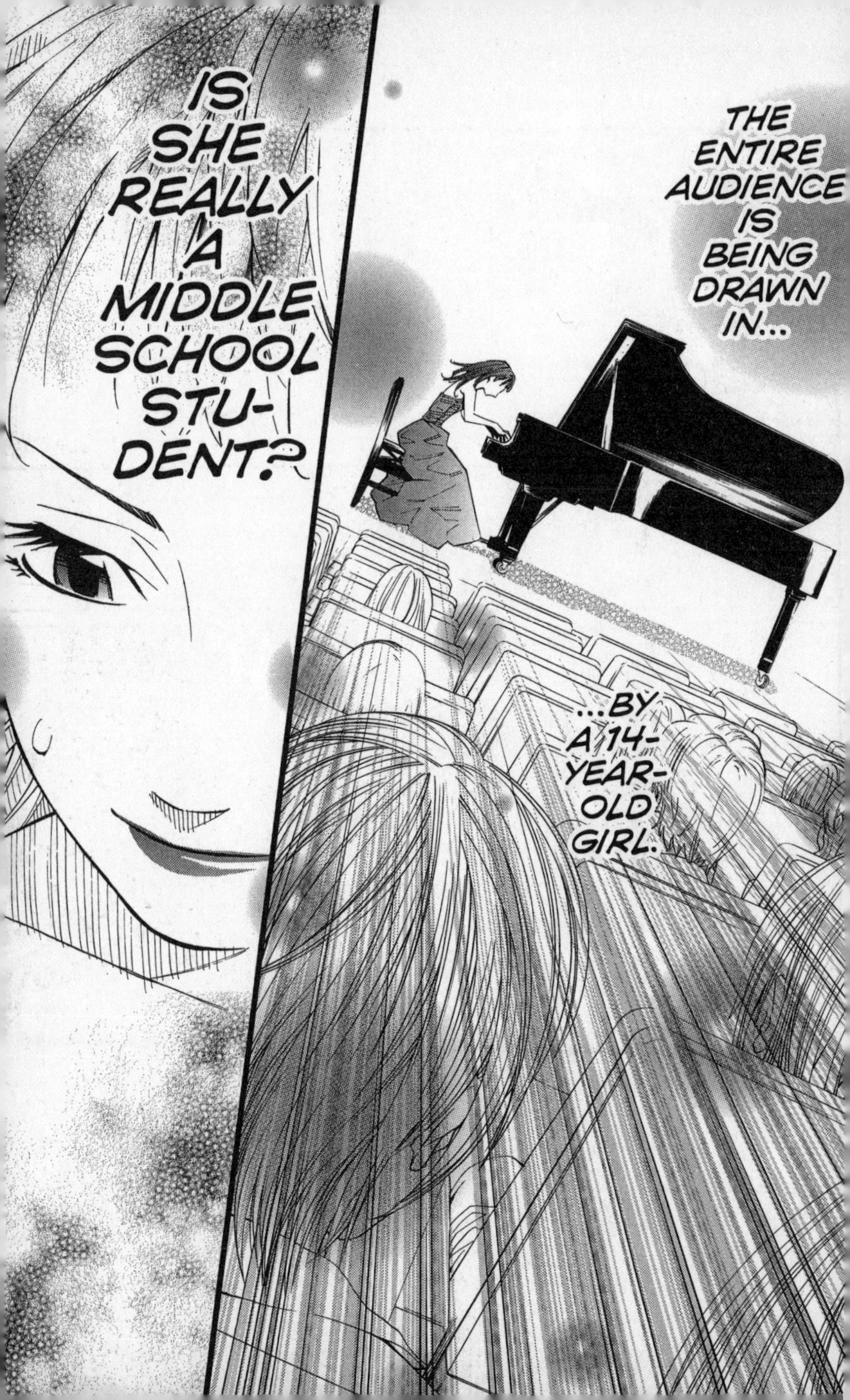
THE ENTIRE AUDIENCE IS BEING DRAWN IN...
...BY A 14-YEAR-OLD GIRL.
IS SHE REALLY A MIDDLE SCHOOL STU-DENT?

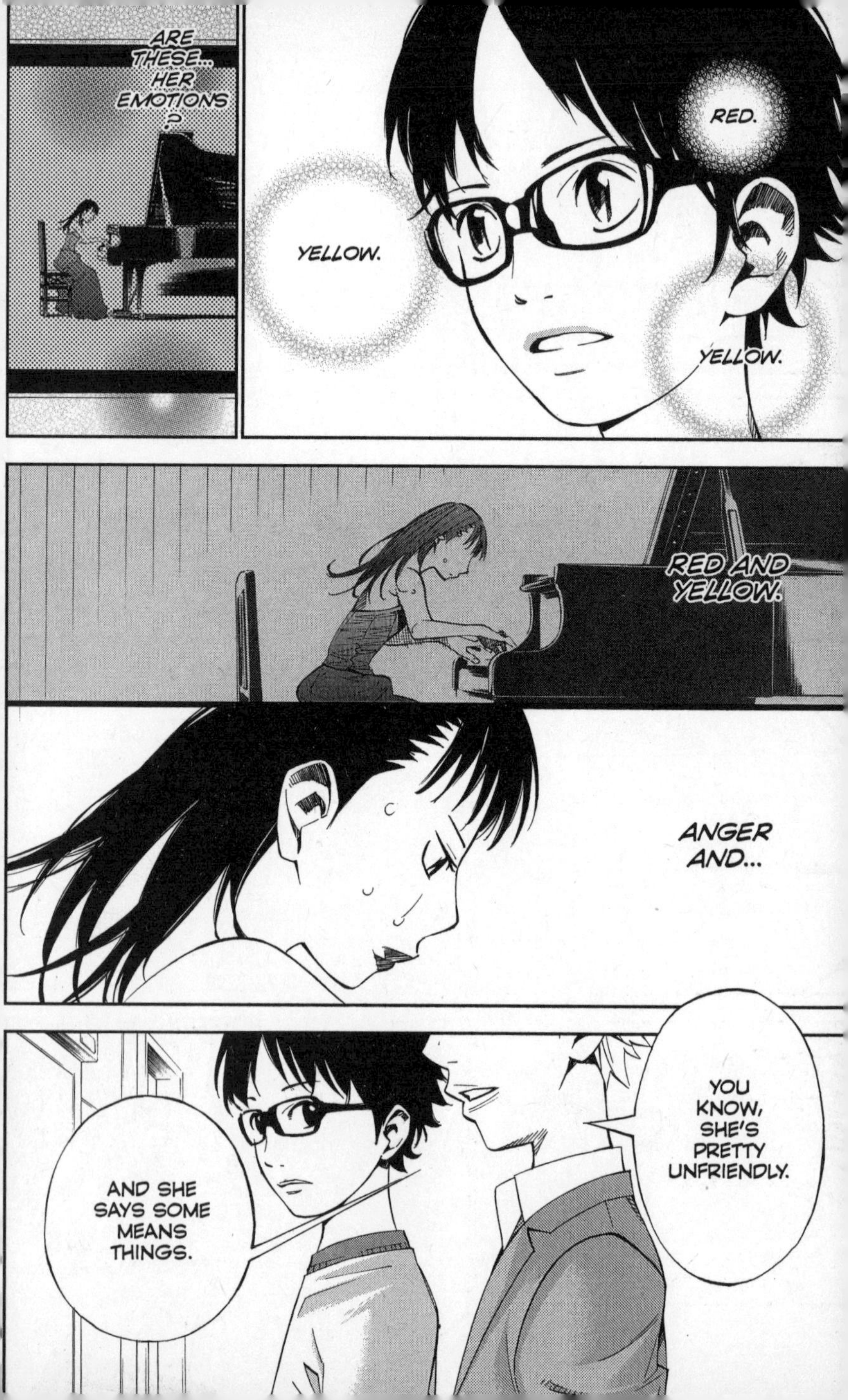
RED.
YELLOW.
YELLOW.
ARE THESE... HER EMOTIONS?
RED AND YELLOW.
ANGER AND...
YOU KNOW, SHE'S PRETTY UNFRIENDLY.
AND SHE SAYS SOME MEANS THINGS.

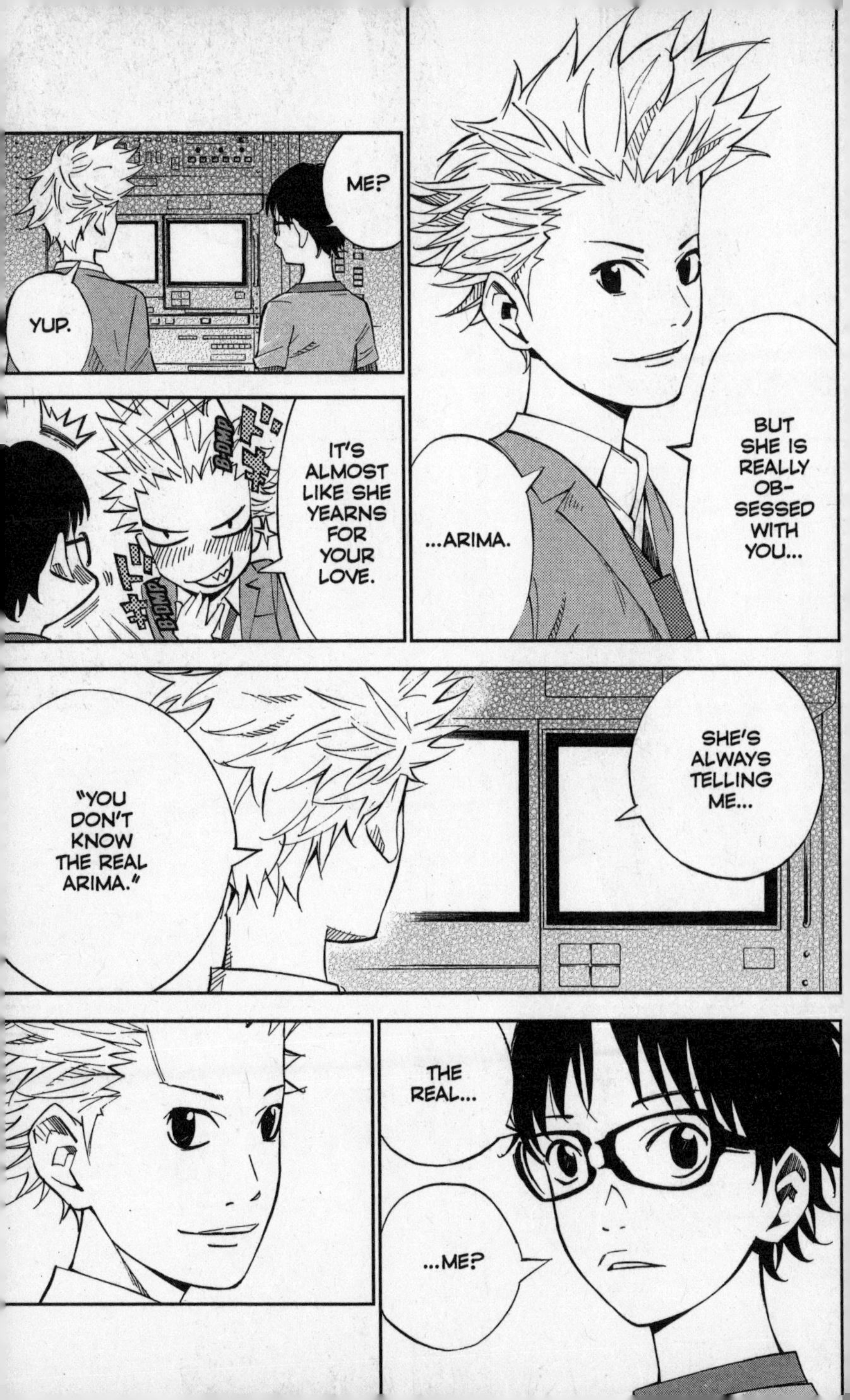
BUT SHE IS REALLY OB- SESSED WITH YOU...
...ARIMA.
ME?
YUP.
IT'S ALMOST LIKE SHE YEARNS FOR YOUR LOVE.
B-DOMP
B-DOMP
SHE'S ALWAYS TELLING ME...
"YOU DON'T KNOW THE REAL ARIMA."
THE REAL...
...ME?

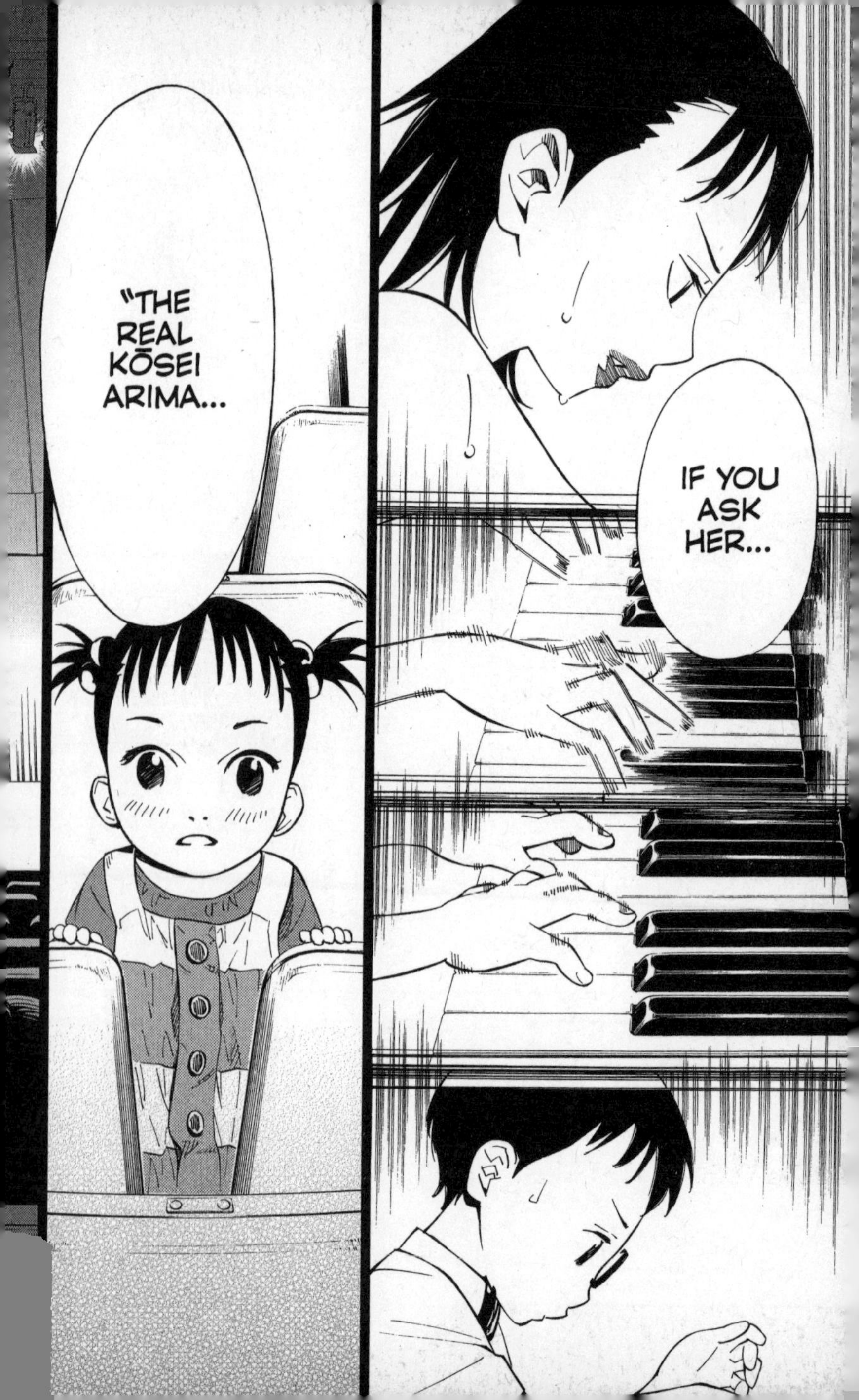
IF YOU ASK HER...
"THE REAL KŌSEI ARIMA...

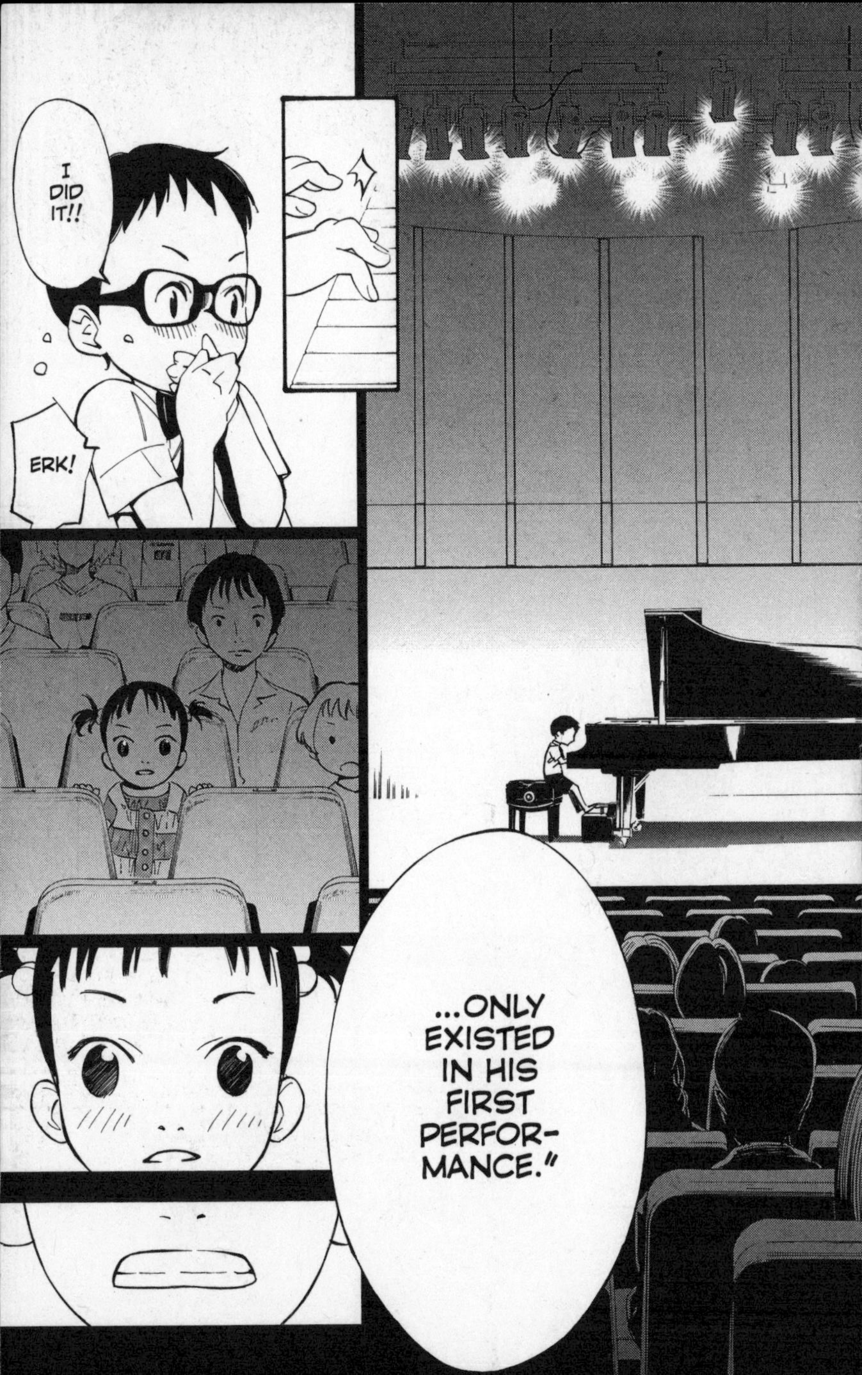
I DID IT!!
ERK!
...ONLY EXISTED IN HIS FIRST PERFORMANCE."

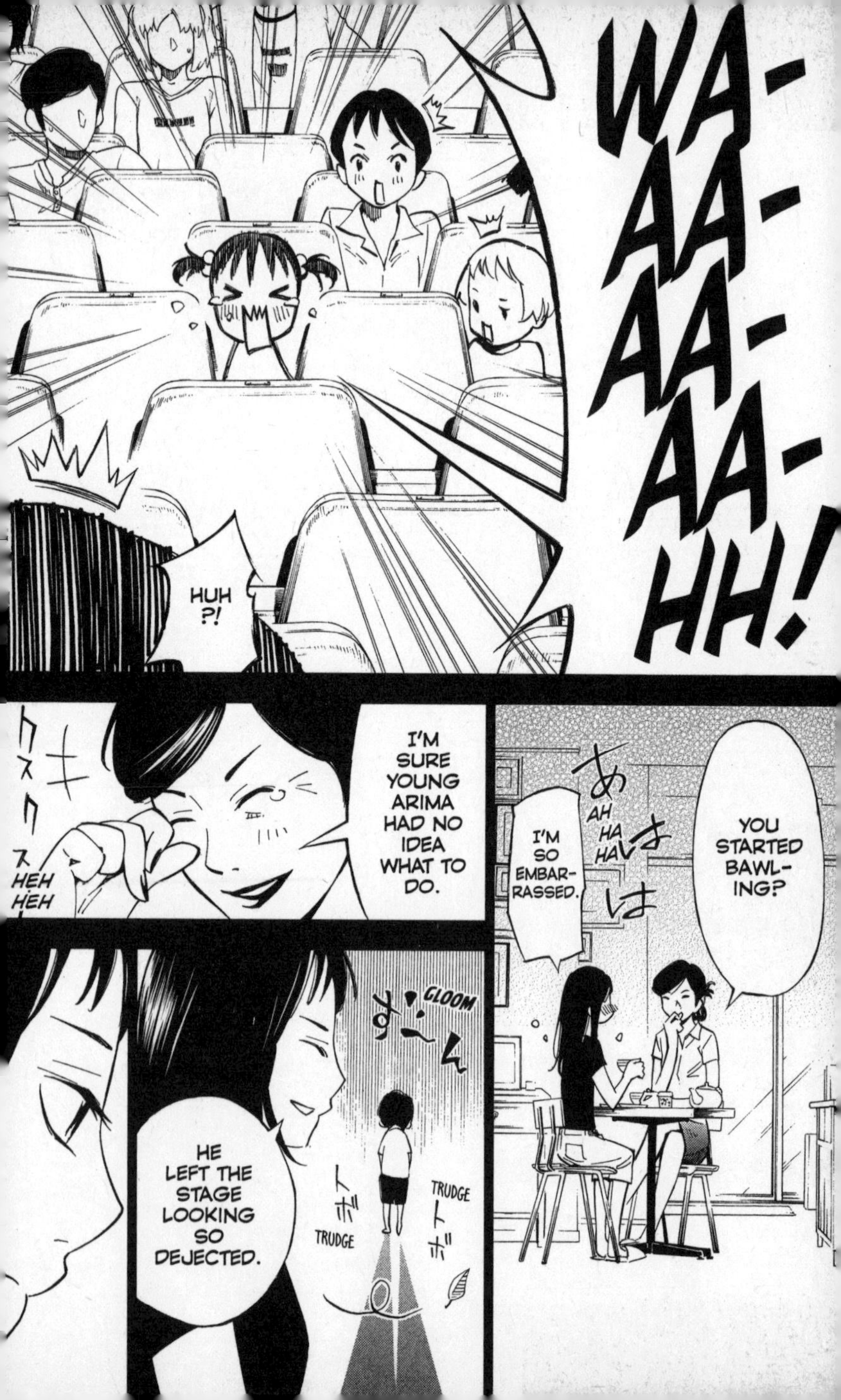
WA-AA-AA-AA-HH!
HUH?!
YOU STARTED BAWL-ING?
あはは
AH HA HA
I'M SO EMBAR-RASSED.
I'M SURE YOUNG ARIMA HAD NO IDEA WHAT TO DO.
クスクス
HEH HEH
すーん
GLOOM
HE LEFT THE STAGE LOOKING SO DEJECTED.
トボ
TRUDGE
トボ
TRUDGE

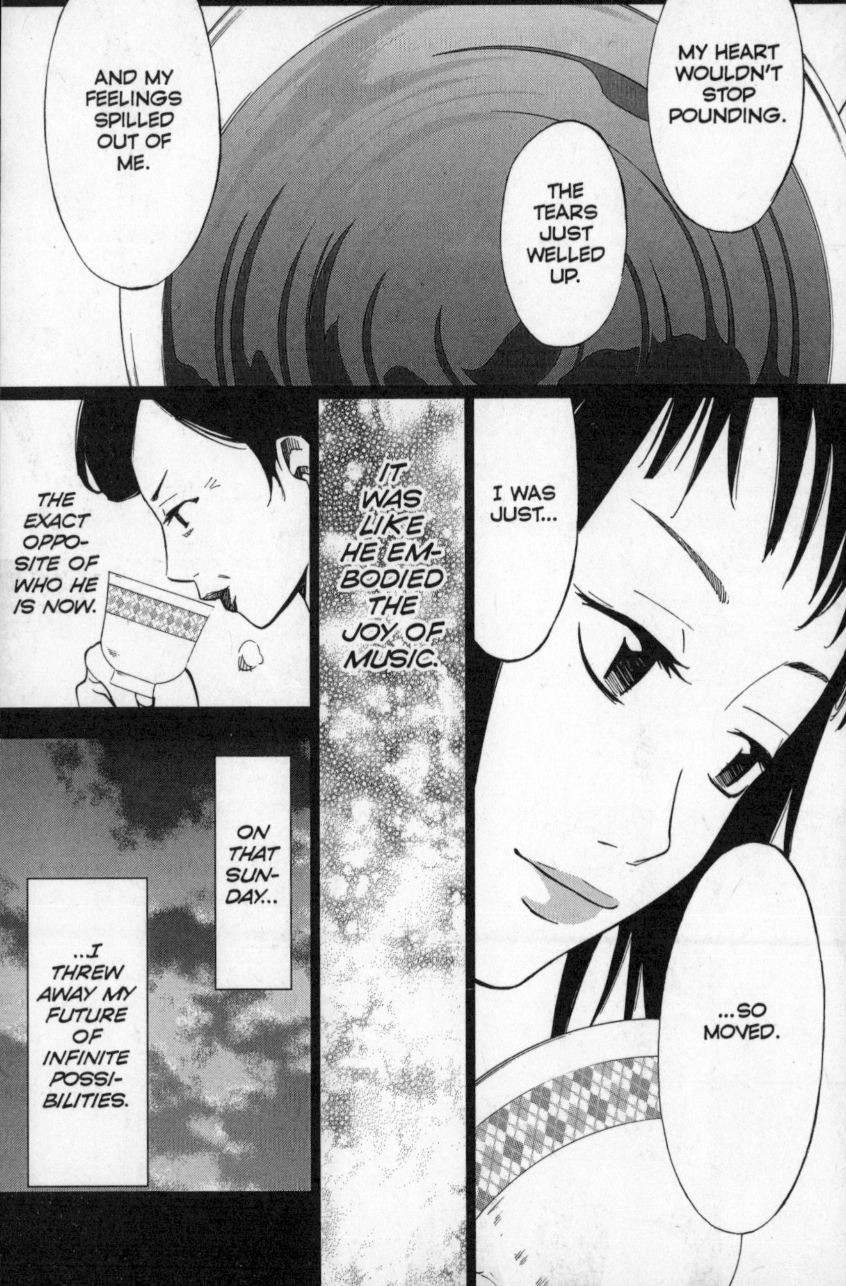
MY HEART WOULDN'T STOP POUNDING.
THE TEARS JUST WELLED UP.
AND MY FEELINGS SPILLED OUT OF ME.
I WAS JUST...
...SO MOVED.
IT WAS LIKE HE EMBODIED THE JOY OF MUSIC.
THE EXACT OPPOSITE OF WHO HE IS NOW.
ON THAT SUNDAY...
...I THREW AWAY MY FUTURE OF INFINITE POSSIBILITIES.

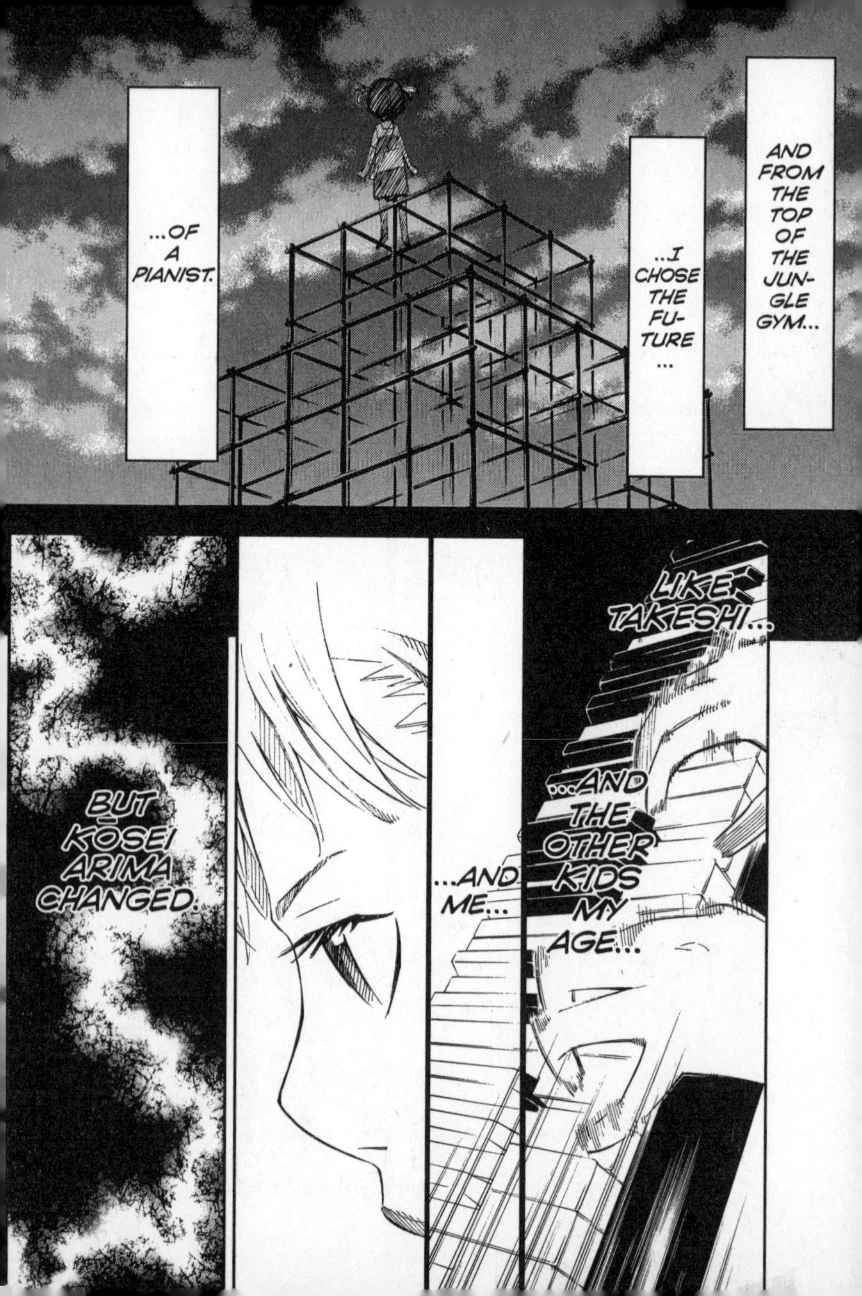
AND FROM THE TOP OF THE JUN-GLE GYM...
...I CHOSE THE FU-TURE...
...OF A PIANIST.
LIKE TAKESHI...
...AND THE OTHER KIDS MY AGE...
...AND ME...
BUT KŌSEI ARIMA CHANGED.

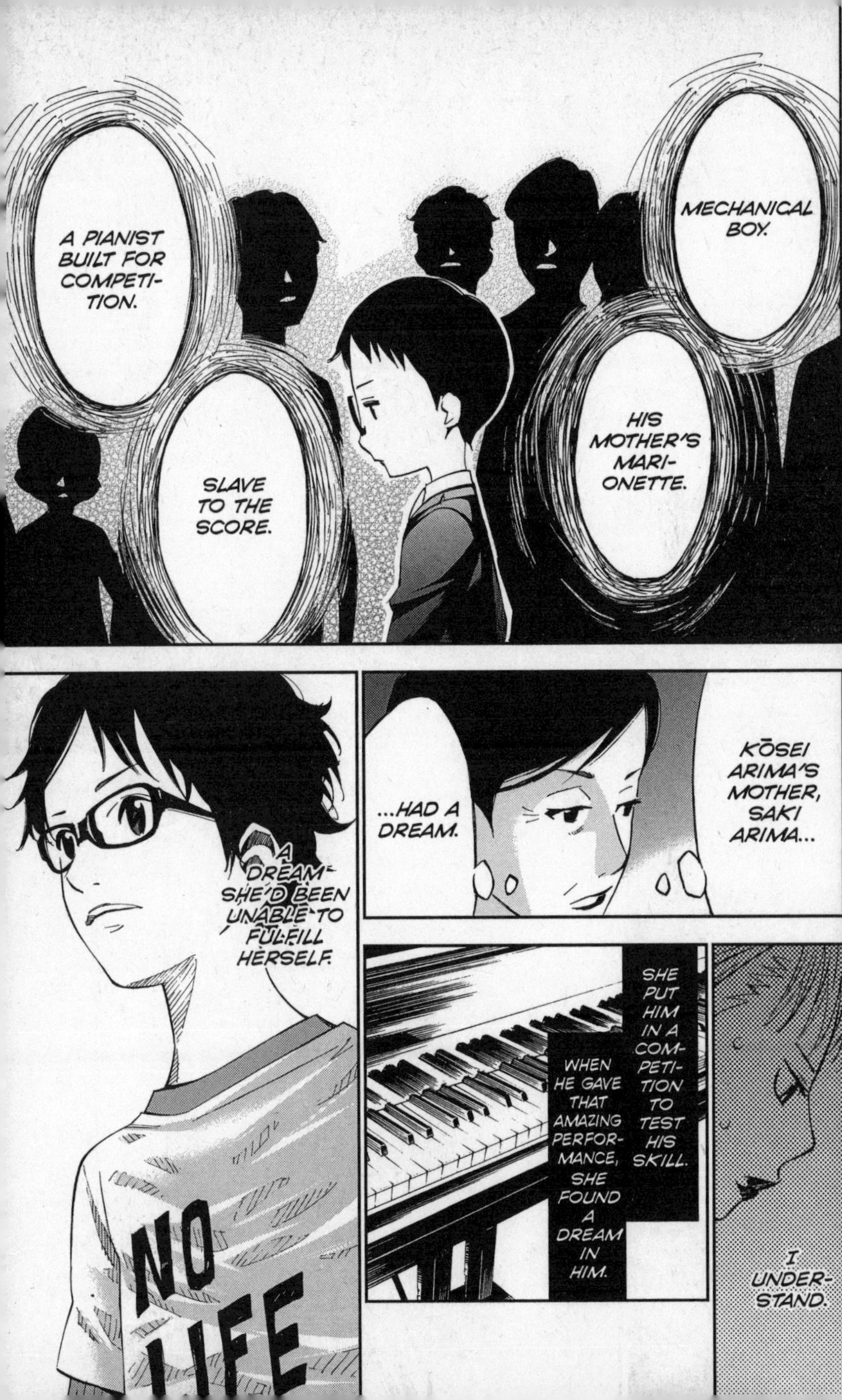
MECHANICAL BOY.
HIS MOTHER'S MARIONETTE.
A PIANIST BUILT FOR COMPETITION.
SLAVE TO THE SCORE.
KŌSEI ARIMA'S MOTHER, SAKI ARIMA...
...HAD A DREAM.
I UNDERSTAND.
SHE PUT HIM IN A COMPETITION TO TEST HIS SKILL.
WHEN HE GAVE THAT AMAZING PERFORMANCE, SHE FOUND A DREAM IN HIM.
A DREAM SHE'D BEEN UNABLE TO FULFILL HERSELF.
NO LIFE

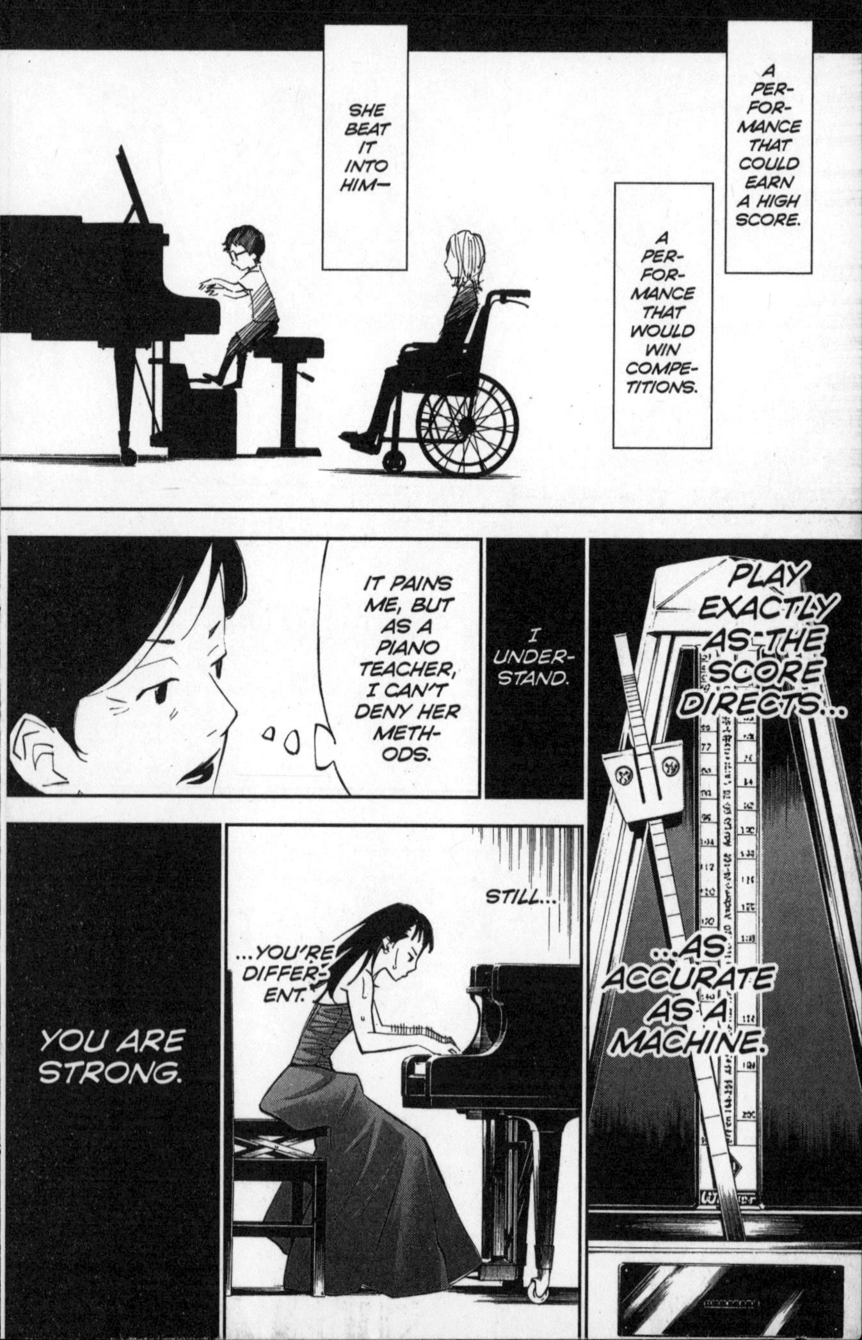
A PERFORMANCE THAT COULD EARN A HIGH SCORE.
A PERFORMANCE THAT WOULD WIN COMPETITIONS.
SHE BEAT IT INTO HIM—
PLAY EXACTLY AS THE SCORE DIRECTS...
...AS ACCURATE AS A MACHINE.
I UNDERSTAND.
IT PAINS ME, BUT AS A PIANO TEACHER, I CAN'T DENY HER METHODS.
STILL...
...YOU'RE DIFFERENT.
YOU ARE STRONG.

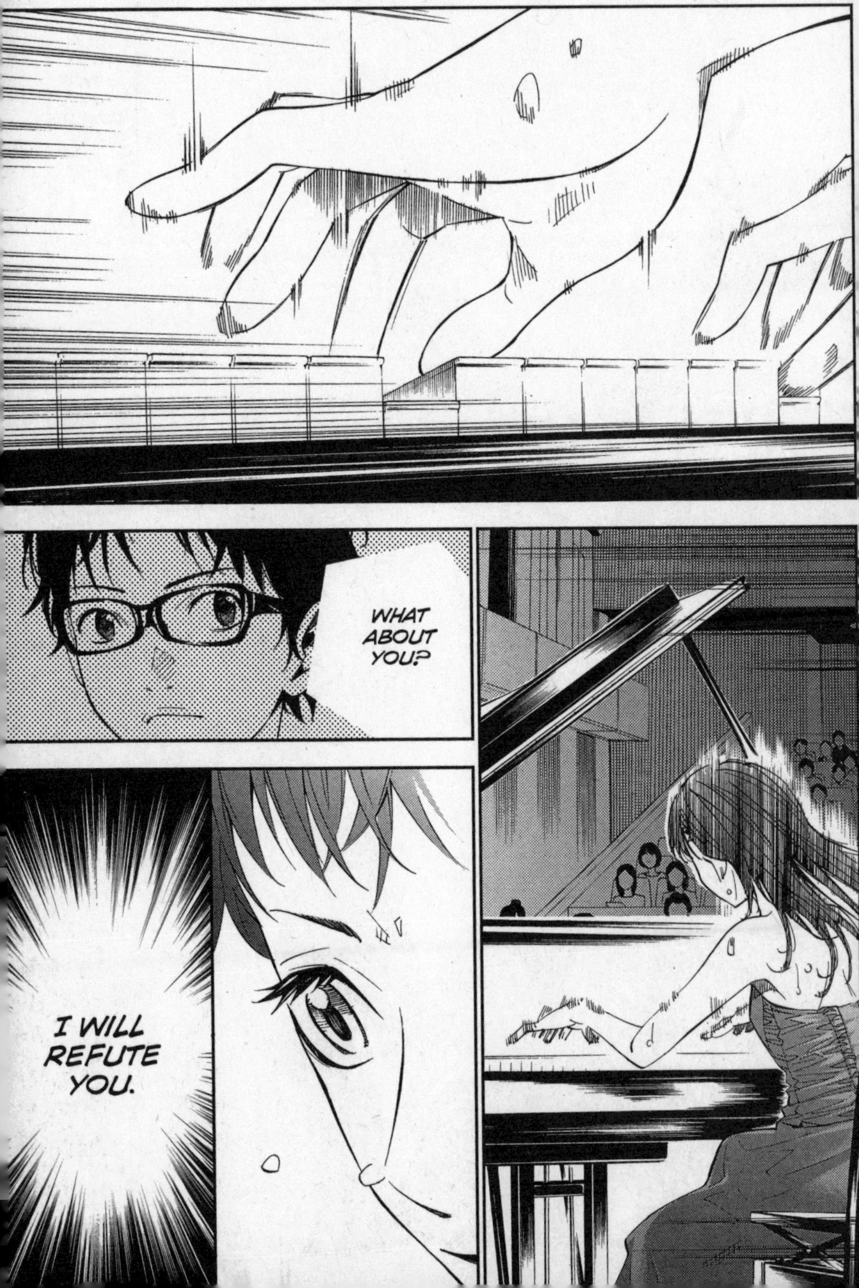
WHAT ABOUT YOU?
I WILL REFUTE YOU.

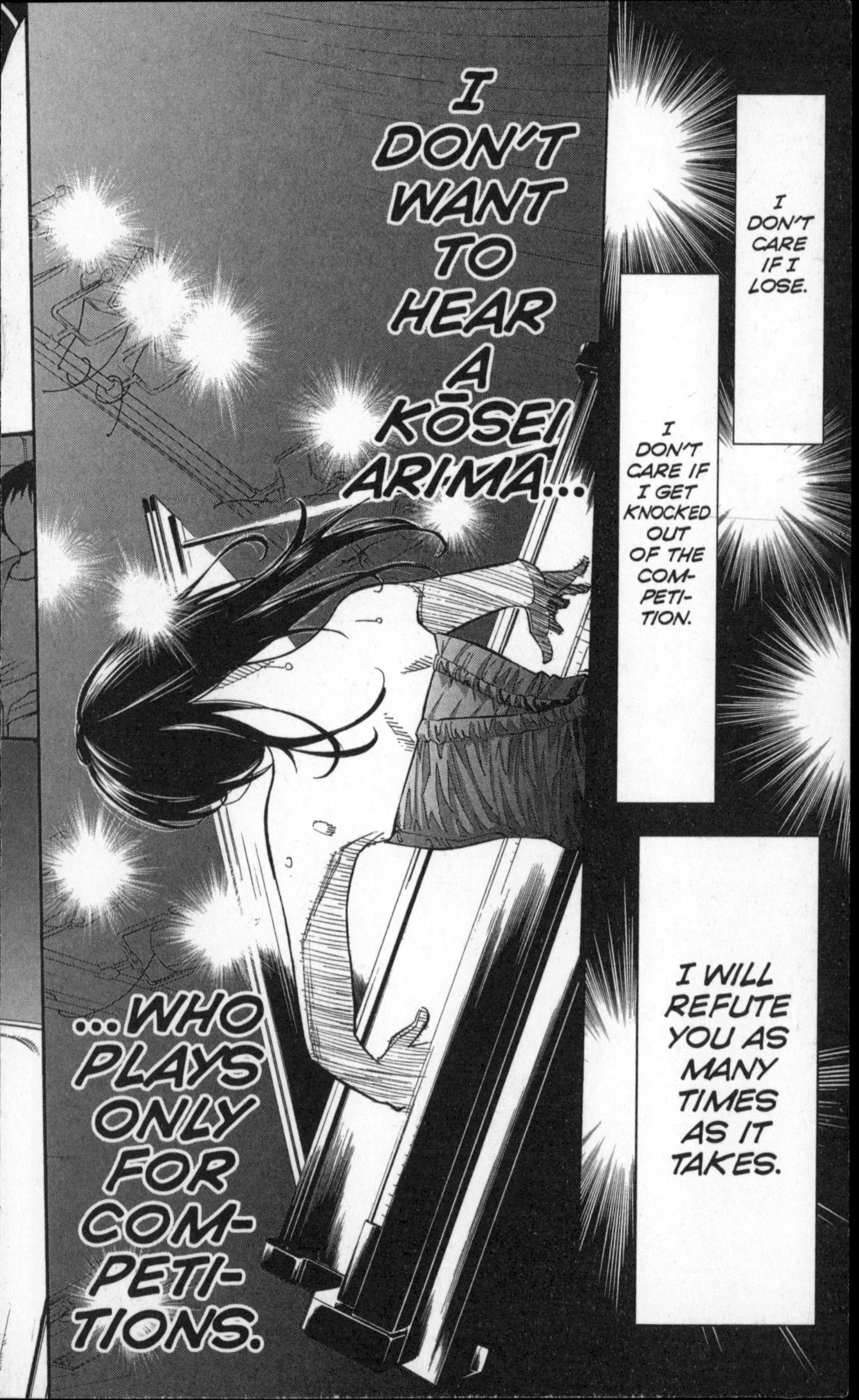
I DON'T CARE IF I LOSE.
I DON'T CARE IF I GET KNOCKED OUT OF THE COM-PETI-TION.
I DON'T WANT TO HEAR A KŌSEI ARIMA...
I WILL REFUTE YOU AS MANY TIMES AS IT TAKES.
...WHO PLAYS ONLY FOR COM-PETI-TIONS.

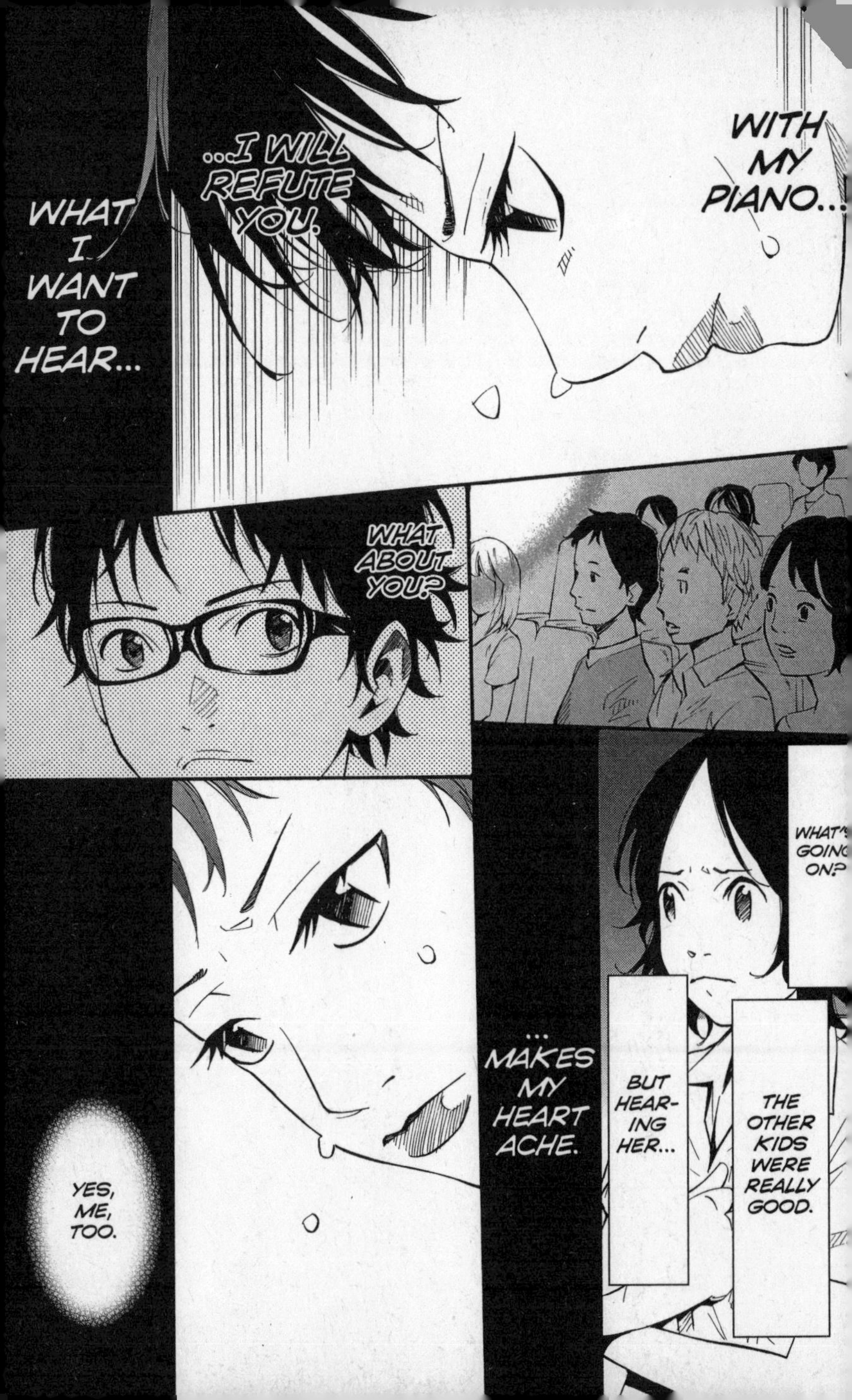

WITH MY PIANO...
...I WILL REFUTE YOU.
WHAT I WANT TO HEAR...
WHAT ABOUT YOU?
WHAT'S GOING ON?
THE OTHER KIDS WERE REALLY GOOD.
BUT HEAR-ING HER...
...MAKES MY HEART ACHE.
YES, ME, TOO.

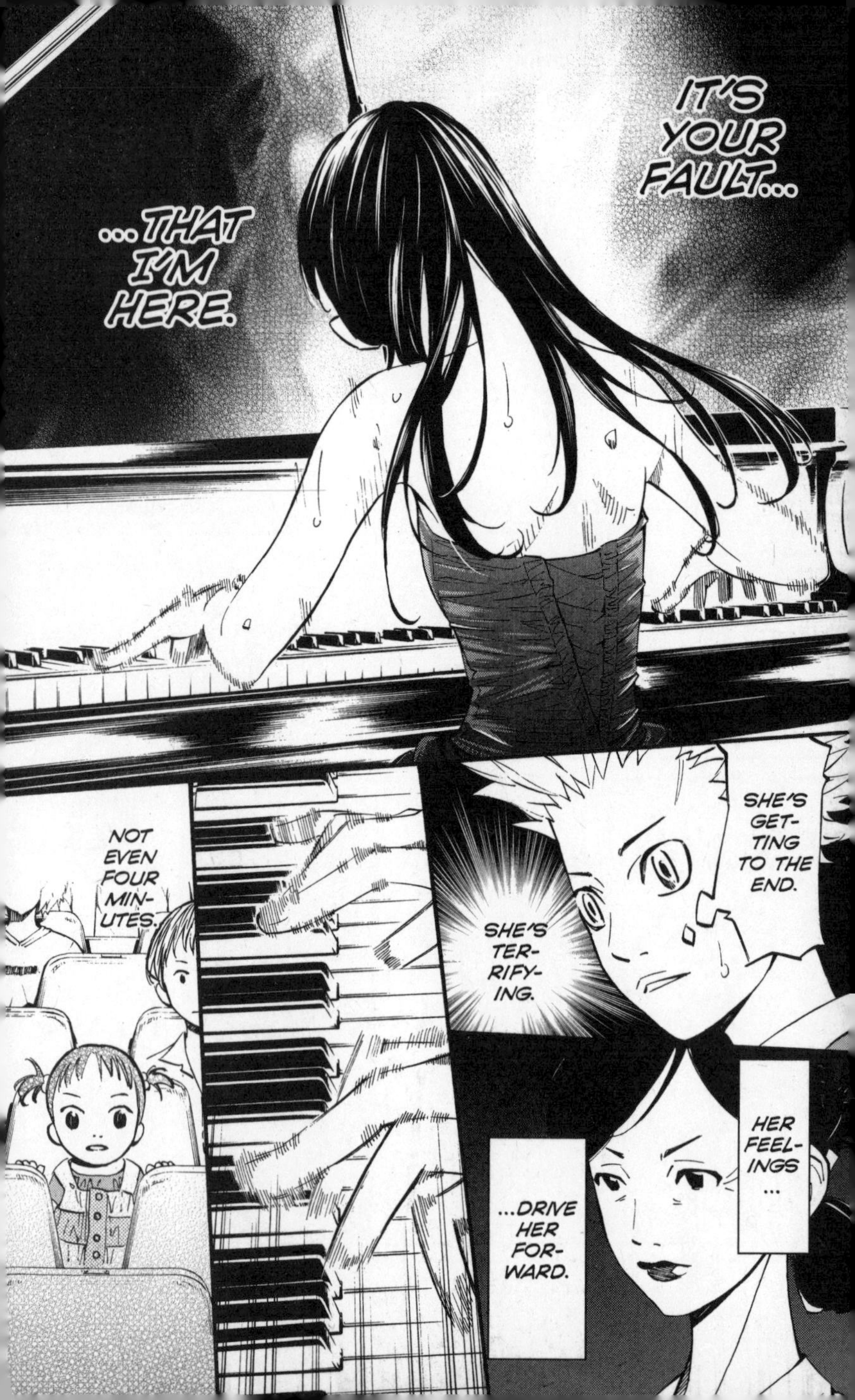
IT'S YOUR FAULT...
...THAT I'M HERE.
SHE'S GET-TING TO THE END.
SHE'S TER-RIFY-ING.
HER FEEL-INGS ...
...DRIVE HER FOR-WARD.
NOT EVEN FOUR MIN-UTES.

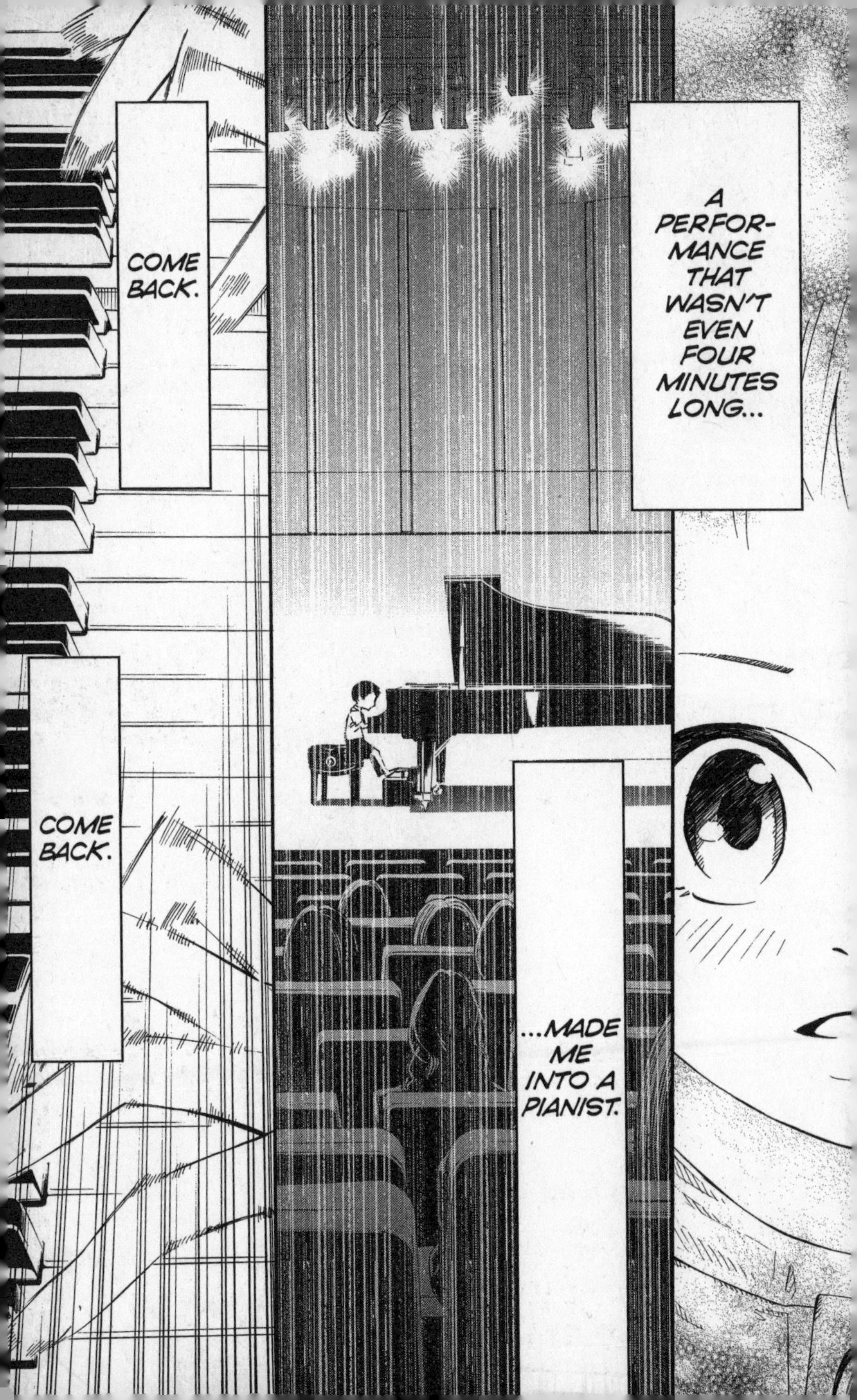
A PERFORMANCE THAT WASN'T EVEN FOUR MINUTES LONG...
...MADE ME INTO A PIANIST.
COME BACK.
COME BACK.

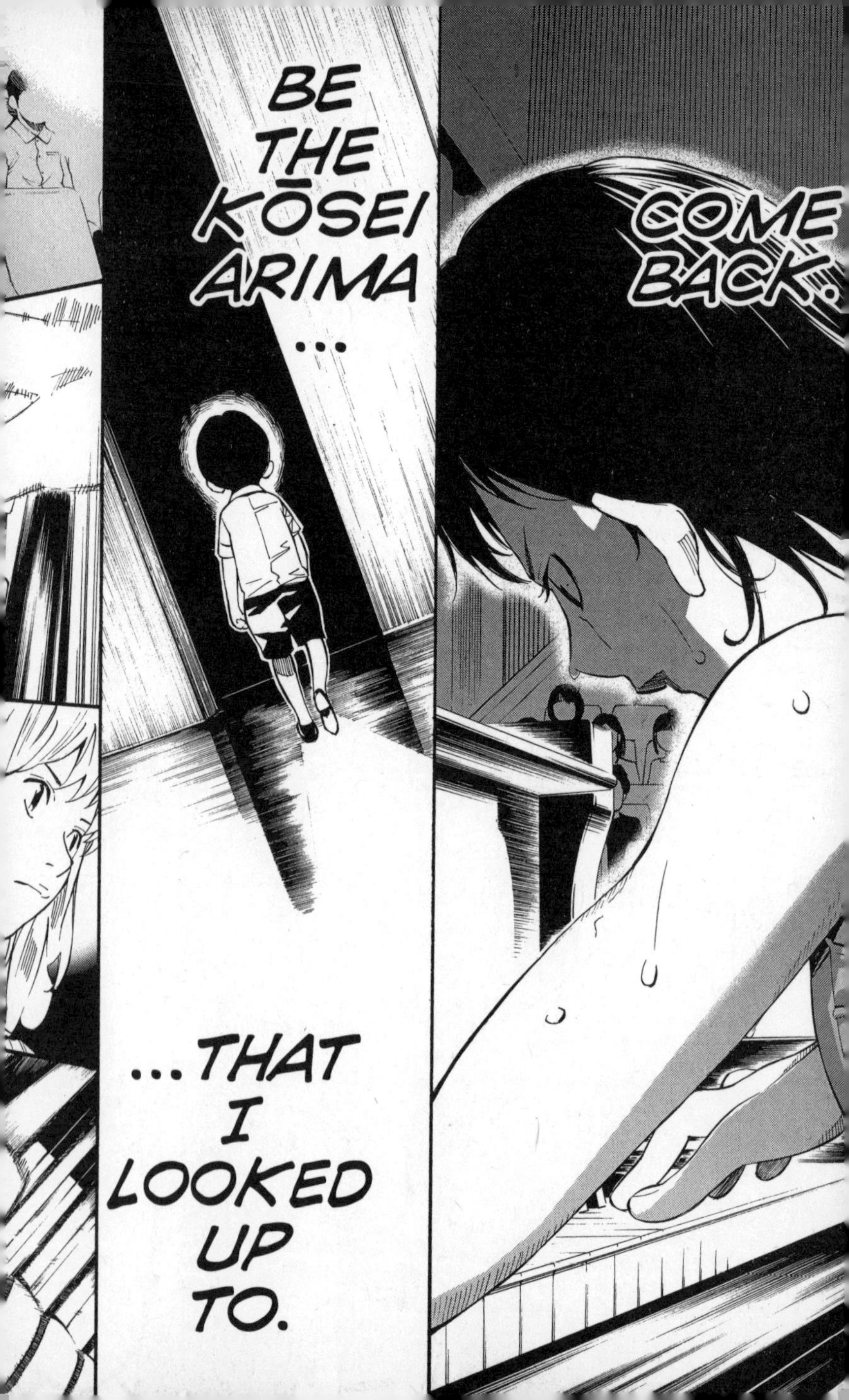
COME BACK.
BE THE KŌSEI ARIMA...
...THAT I LOOKED UP TO.

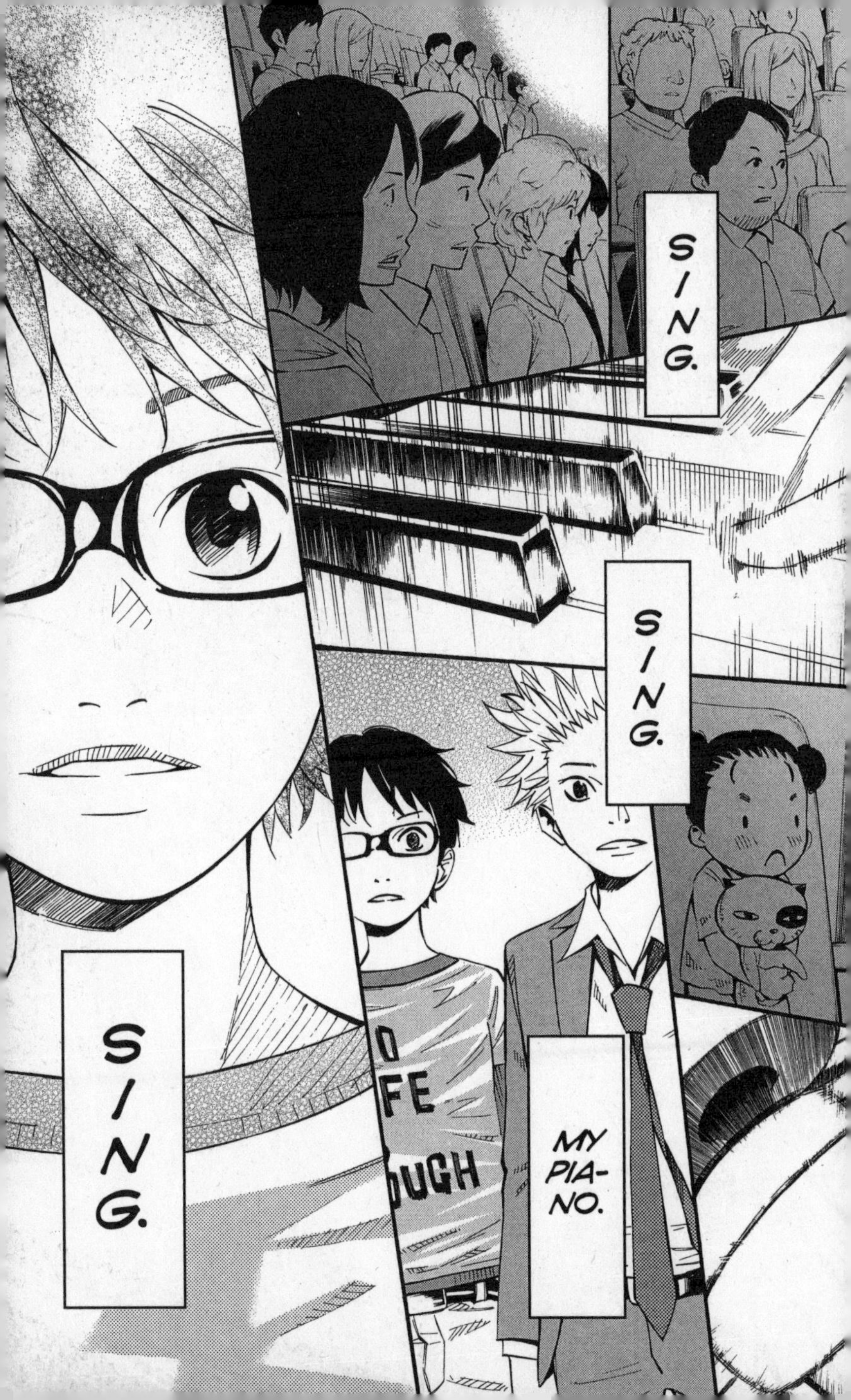
SING.
SING.
MY PIA-NO.
SING.

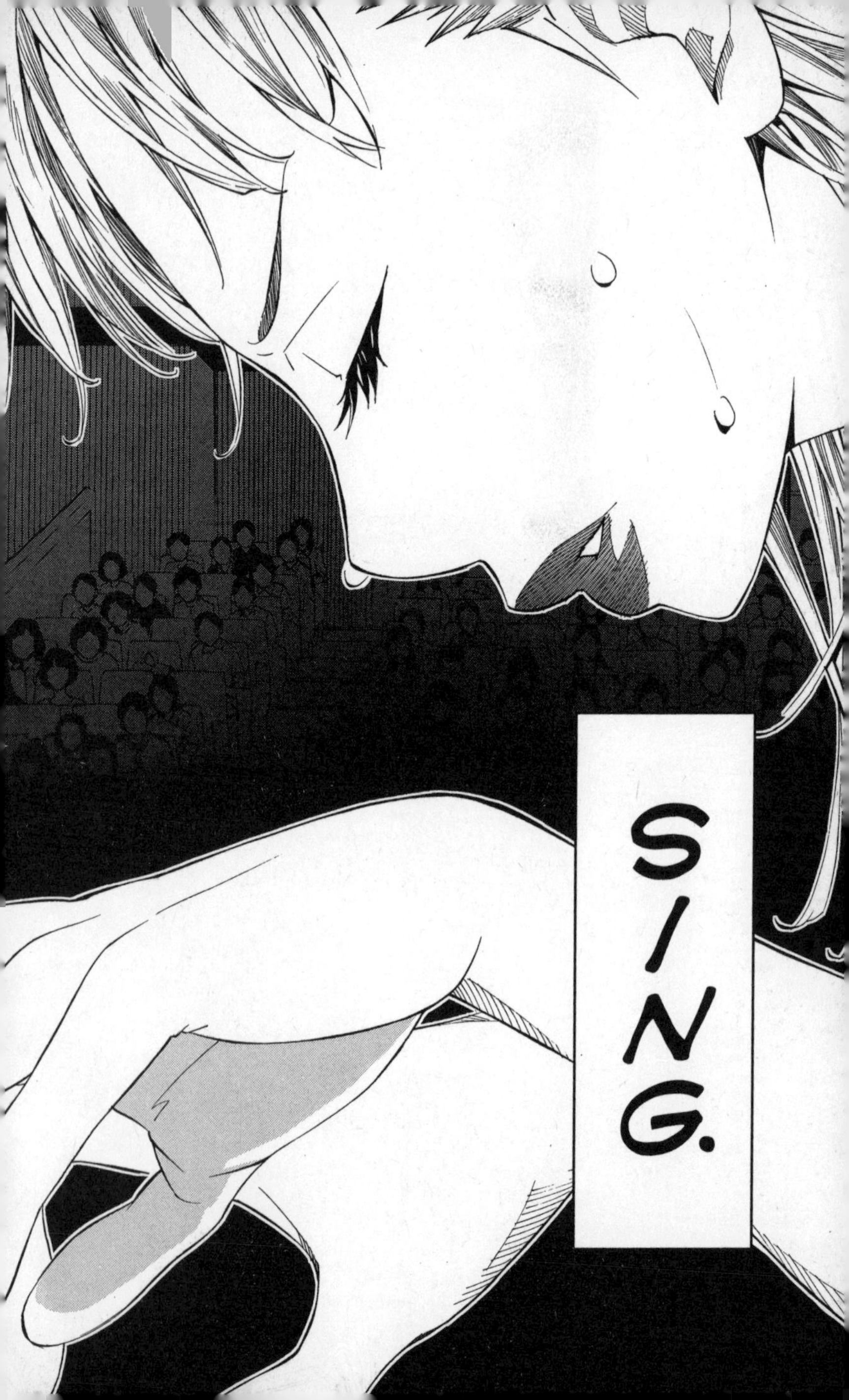
SING.

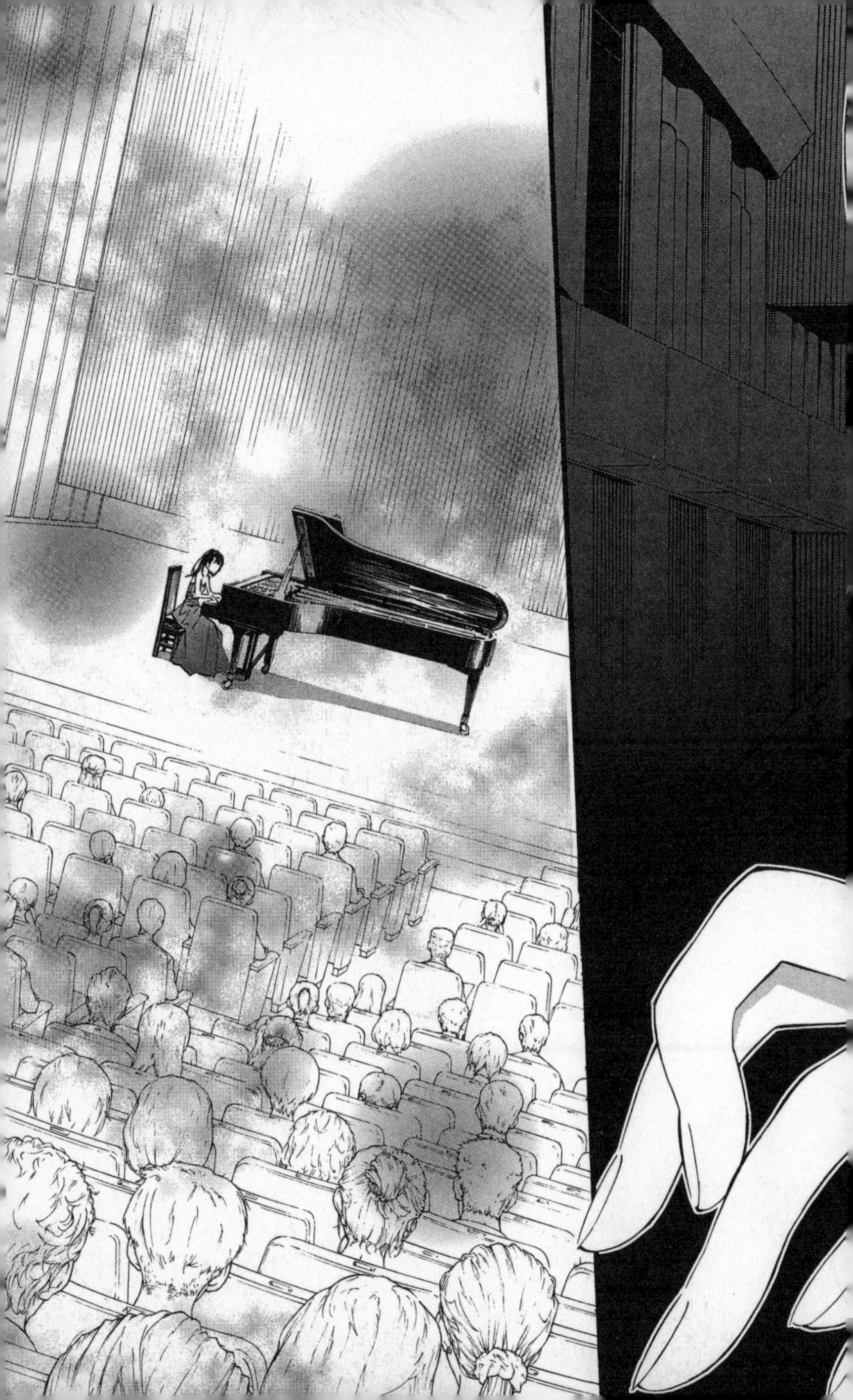

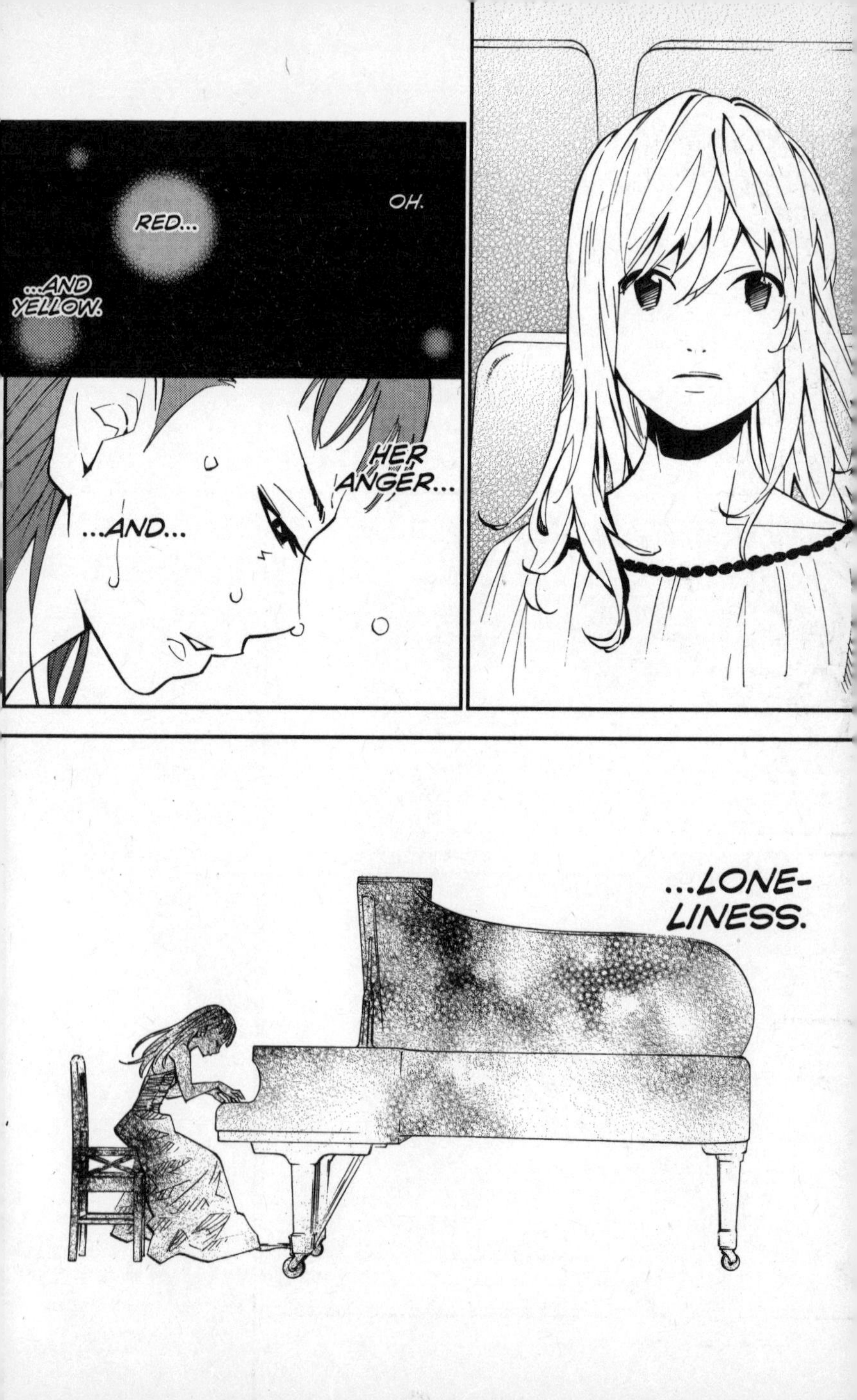
OH.
RED...
...AND YELLOW.
HER ANGER...
...AND...
...LONE-LINESS.

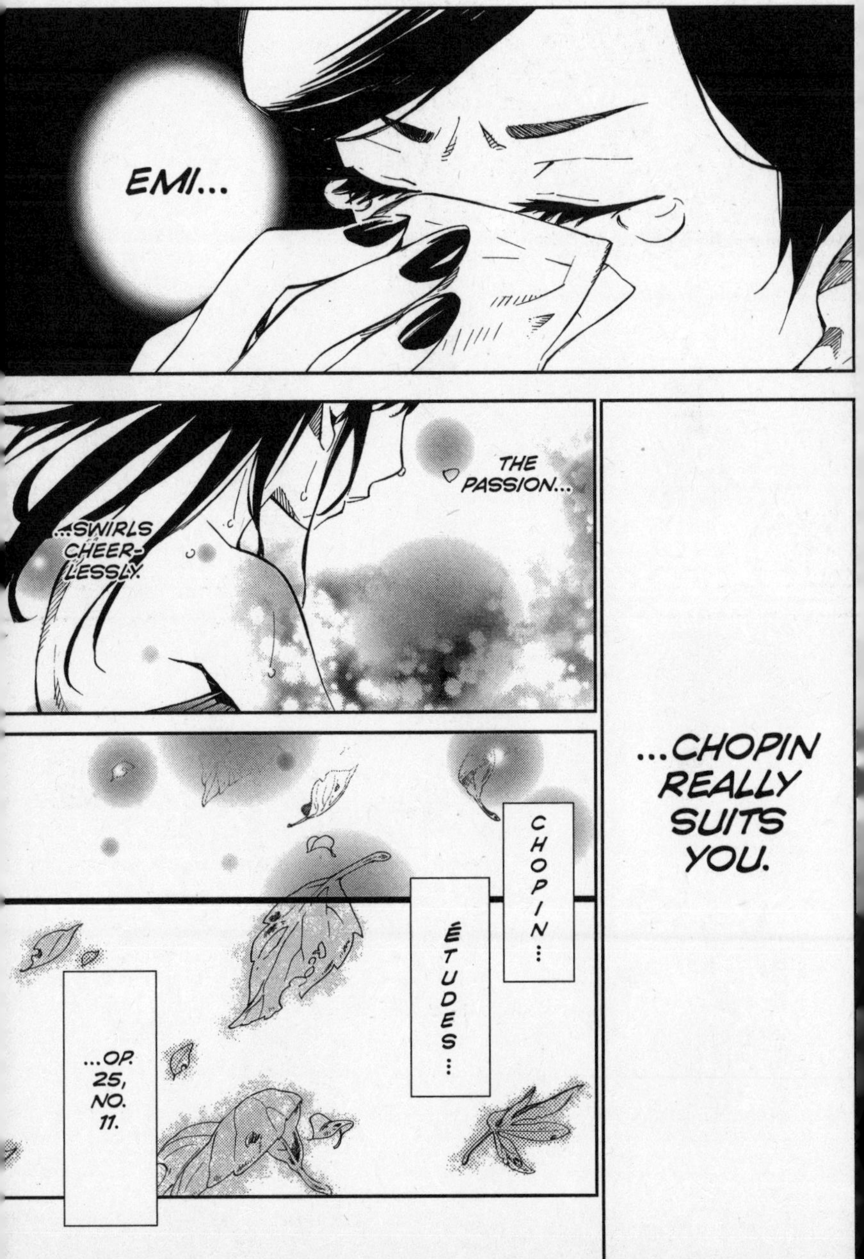
EMI...
...CHOPIN REALLY SUITS YOU.
THE PASSION...
...SWIRLS CHEERLESSLY.
CHOPIN...
ÉTUDES...
...OP. 25, NO. 11.

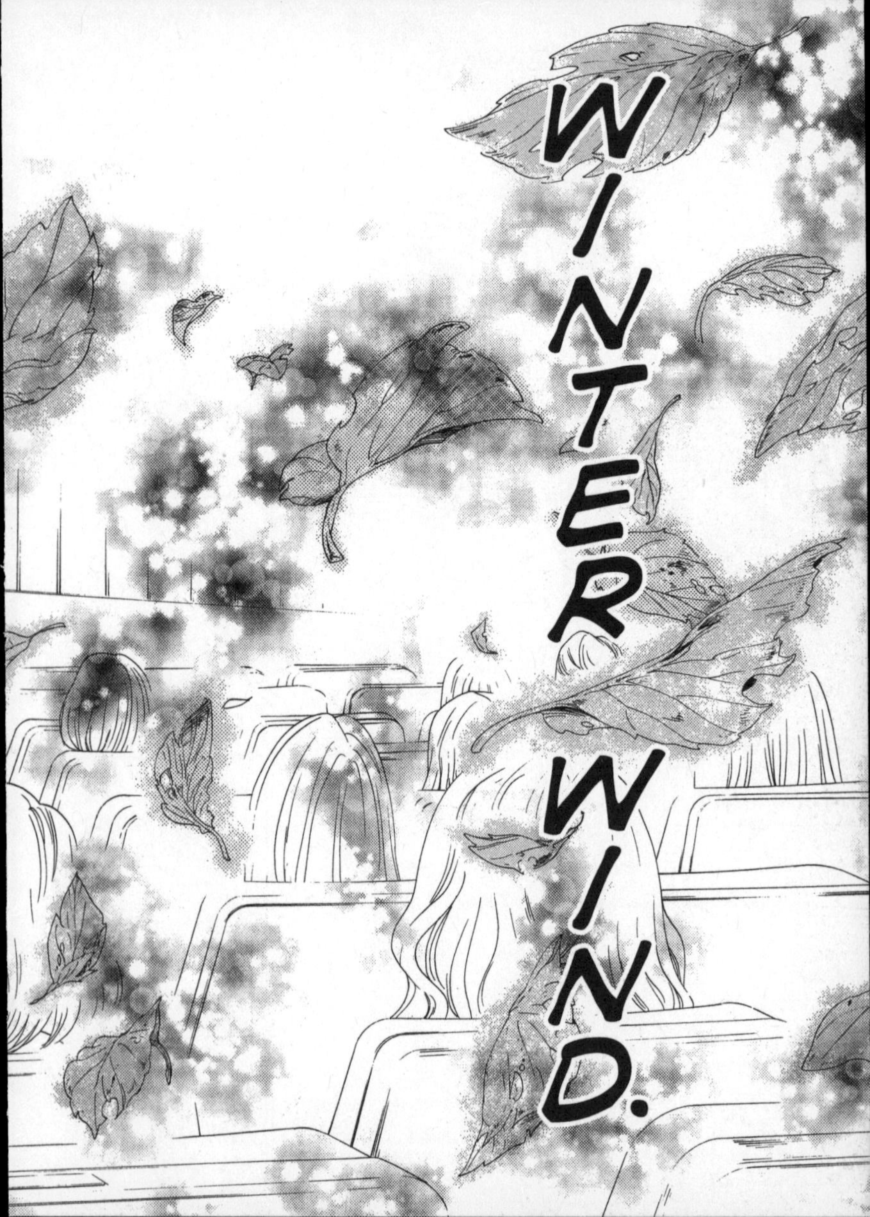
WINTER WIND.

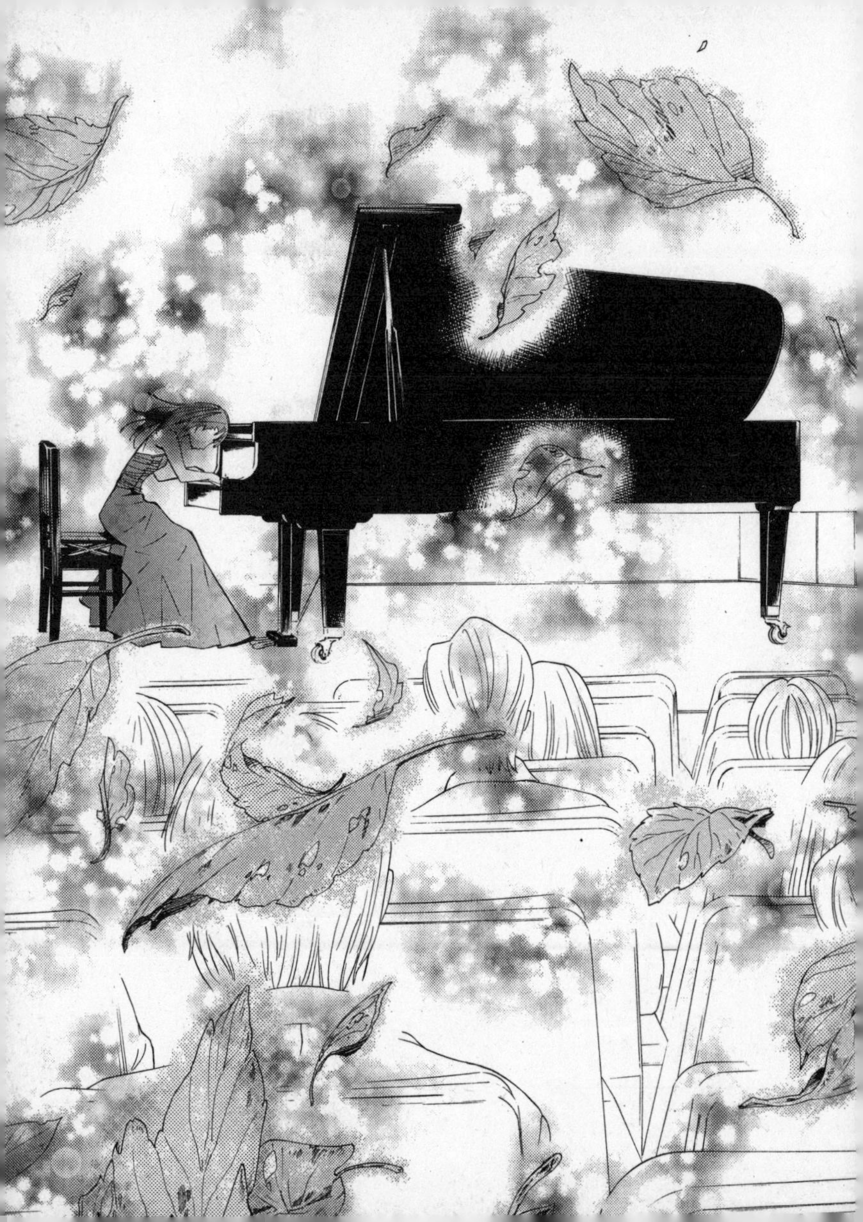

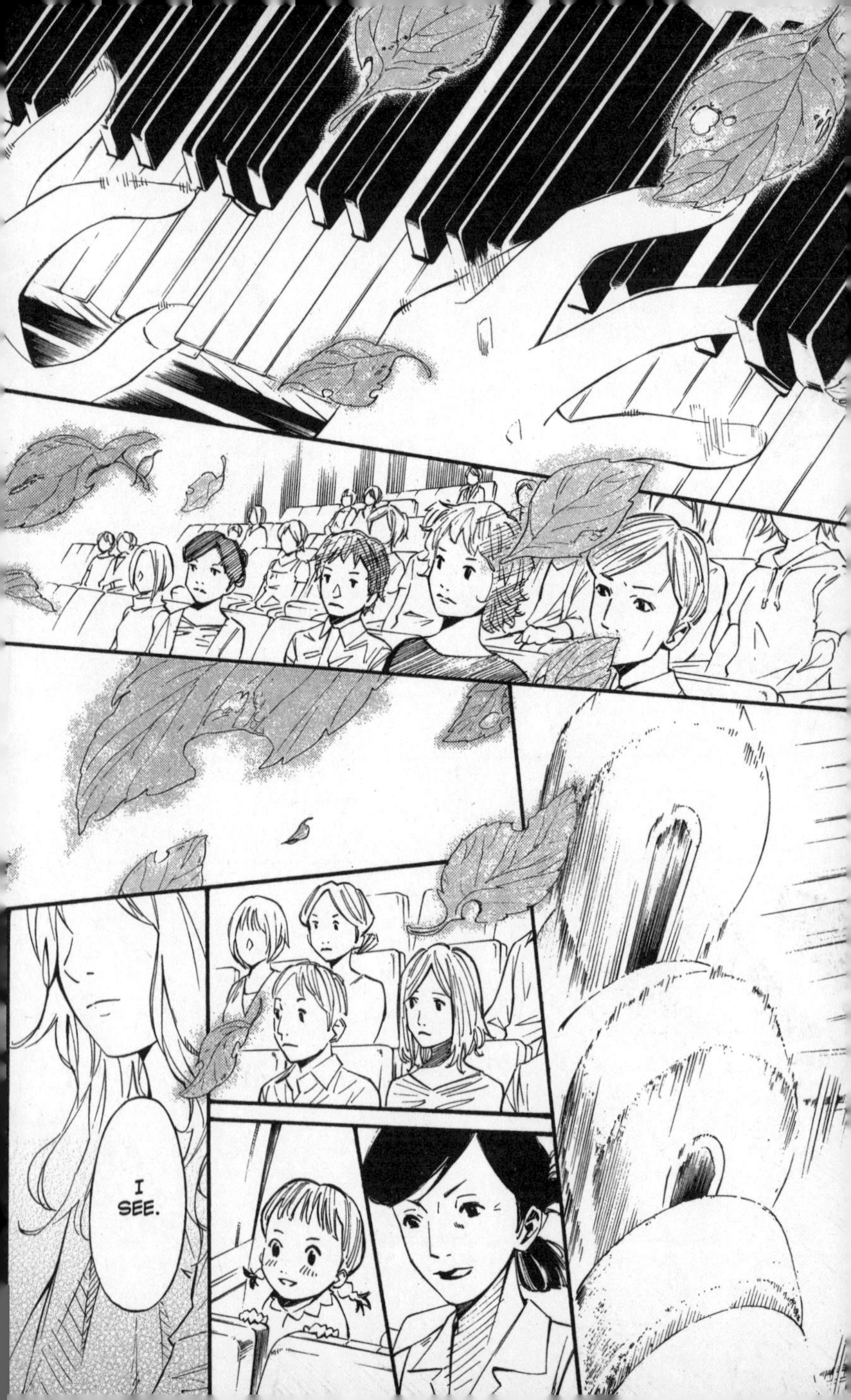
I SEE.

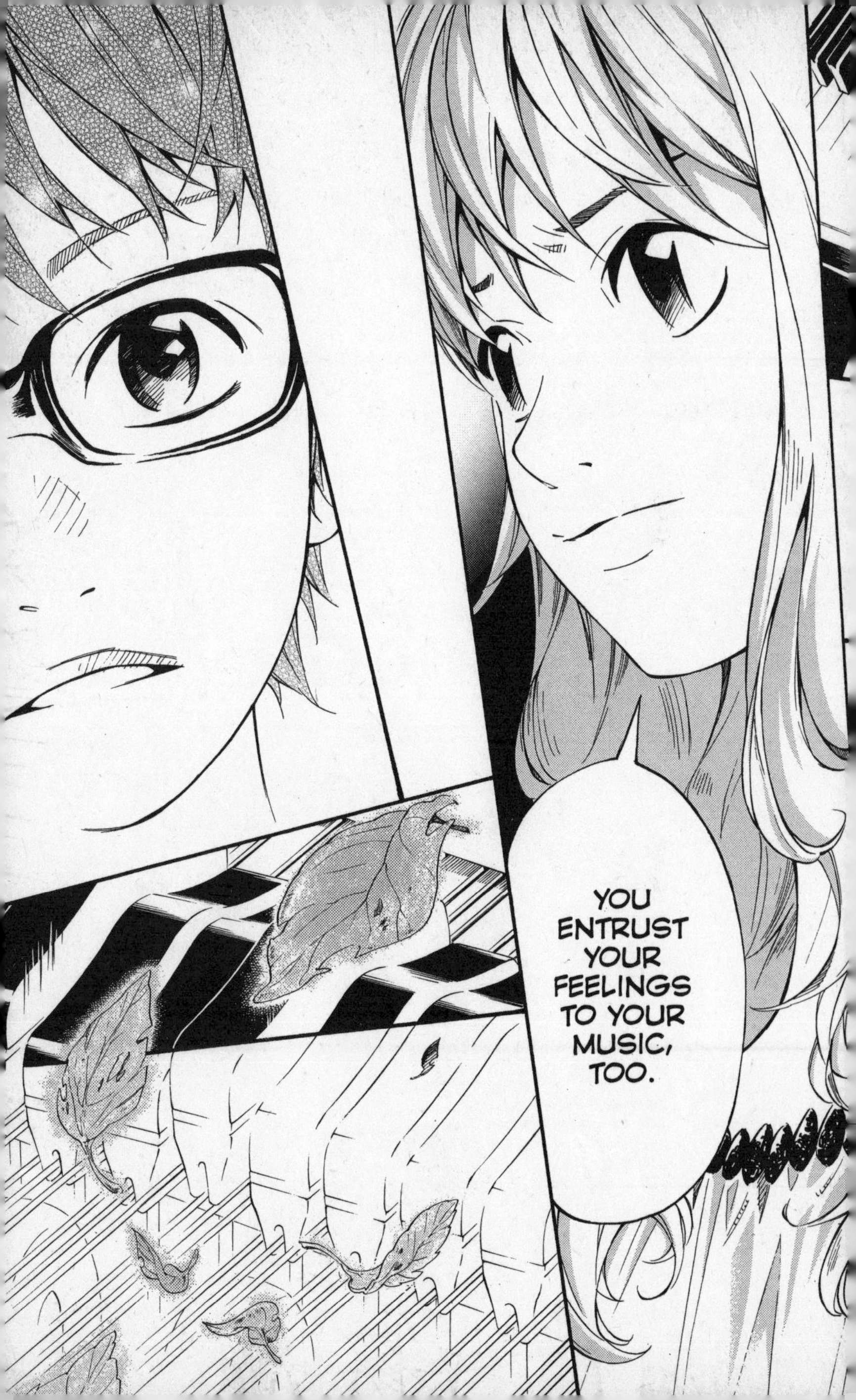
YOU ENTRUST YOUR FEELINGS TO YOUR MUSIC, TOO.

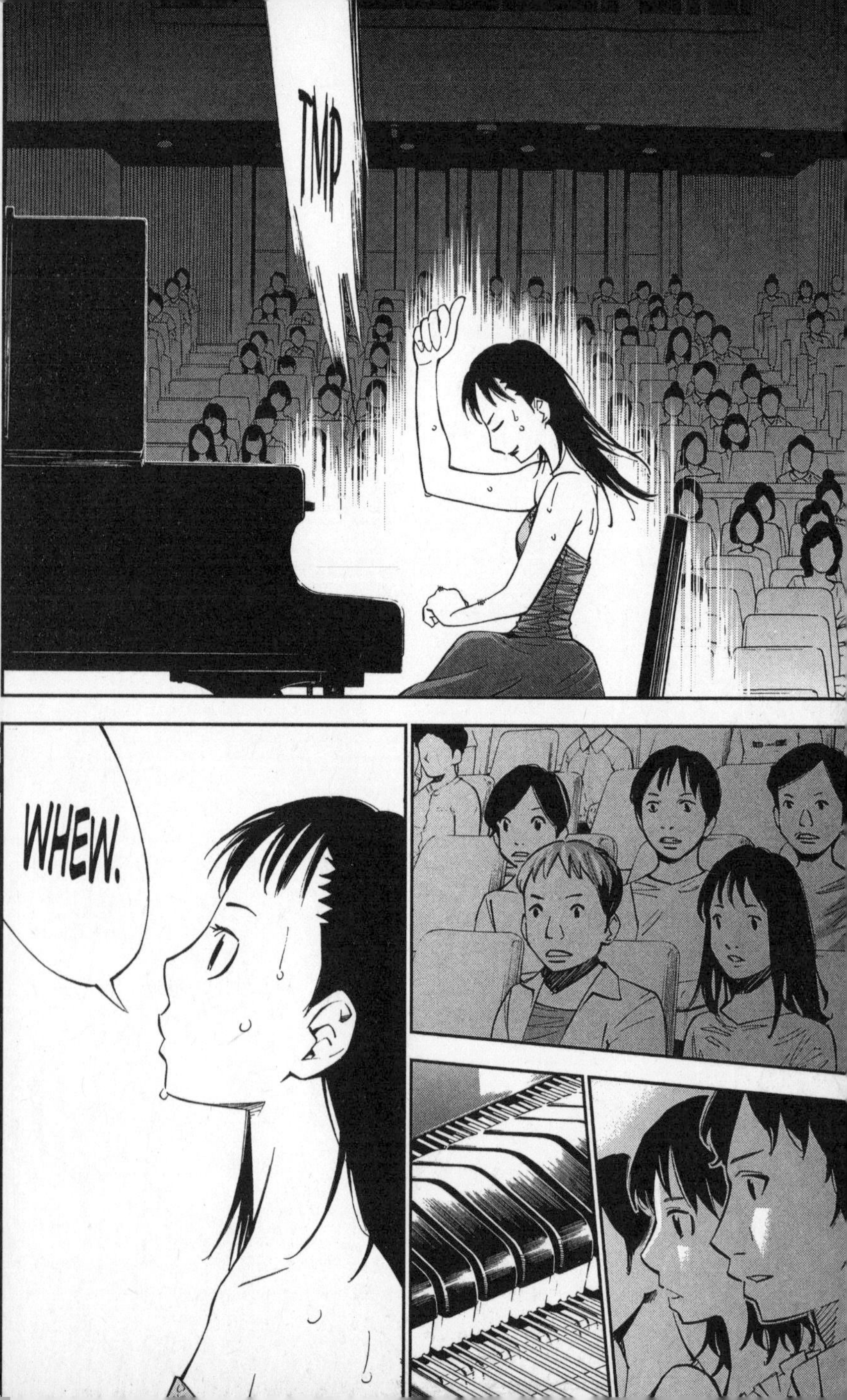
TMP
WHEW.

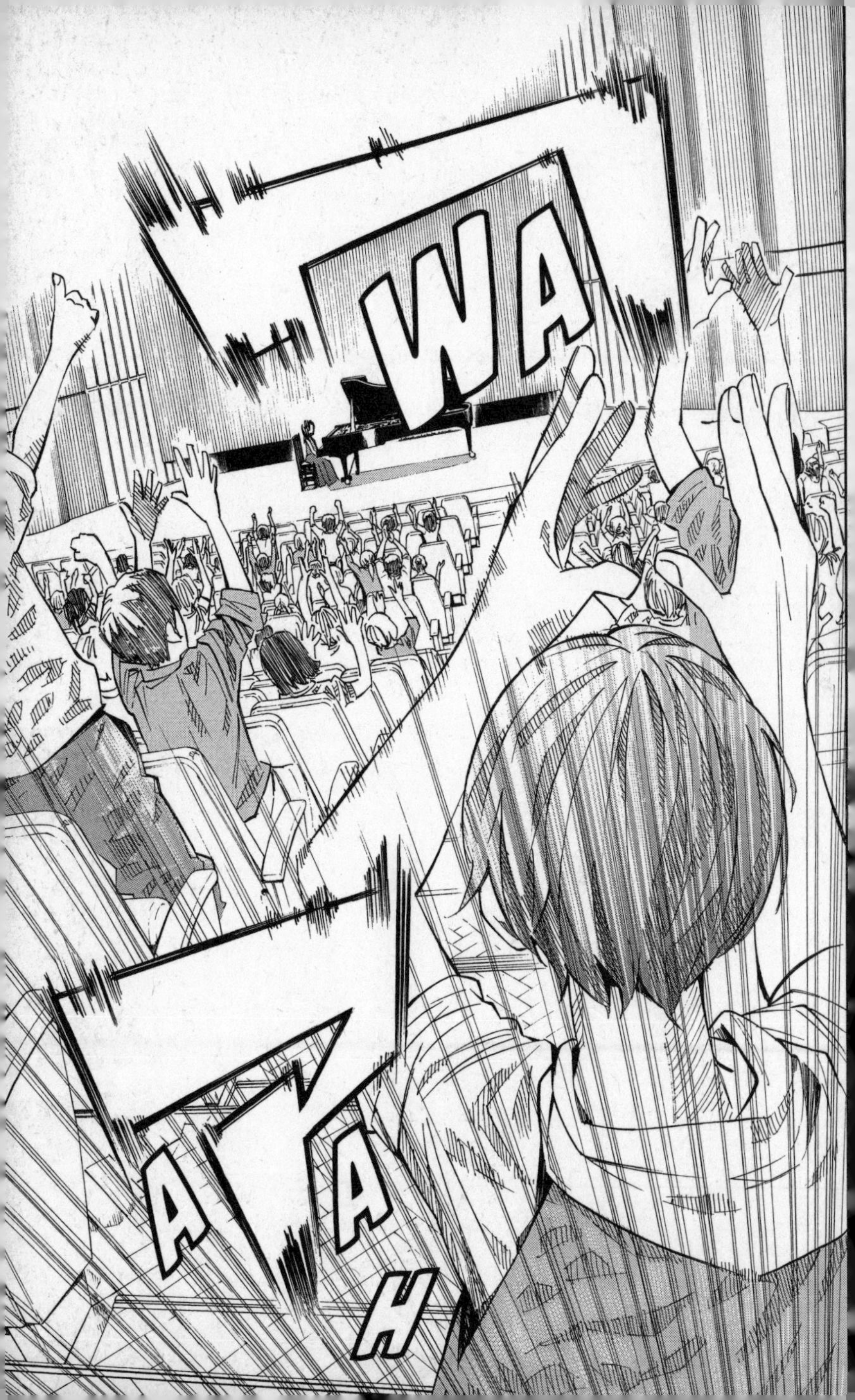
WA
AAH

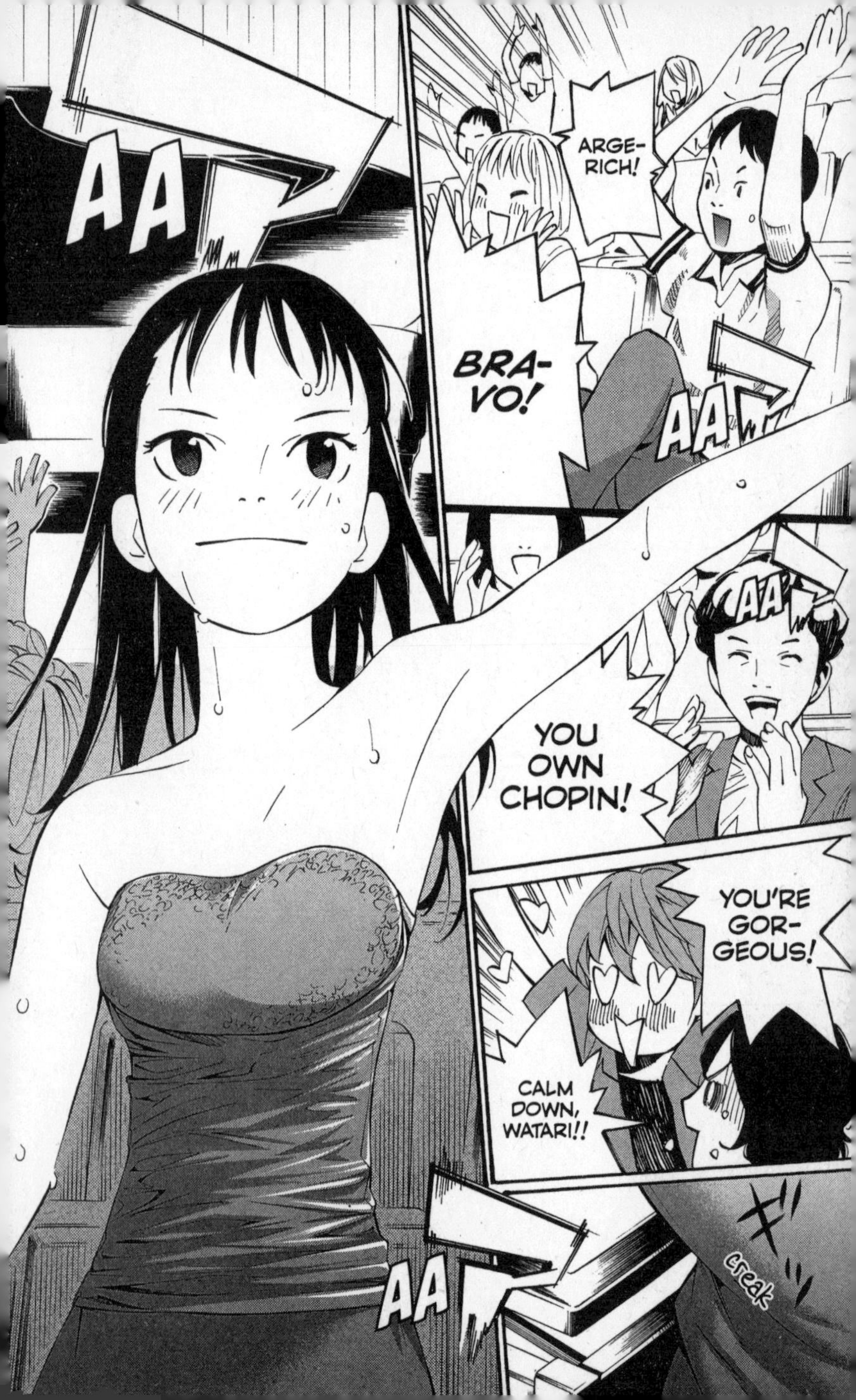
ARGE-RICH!
BRA-VO!
AA
AA
YOU OWN CHOPIN!
YOU'RE GOR-GEOUS!
CALM DOWN, WATARI!!
AA
creak
AA

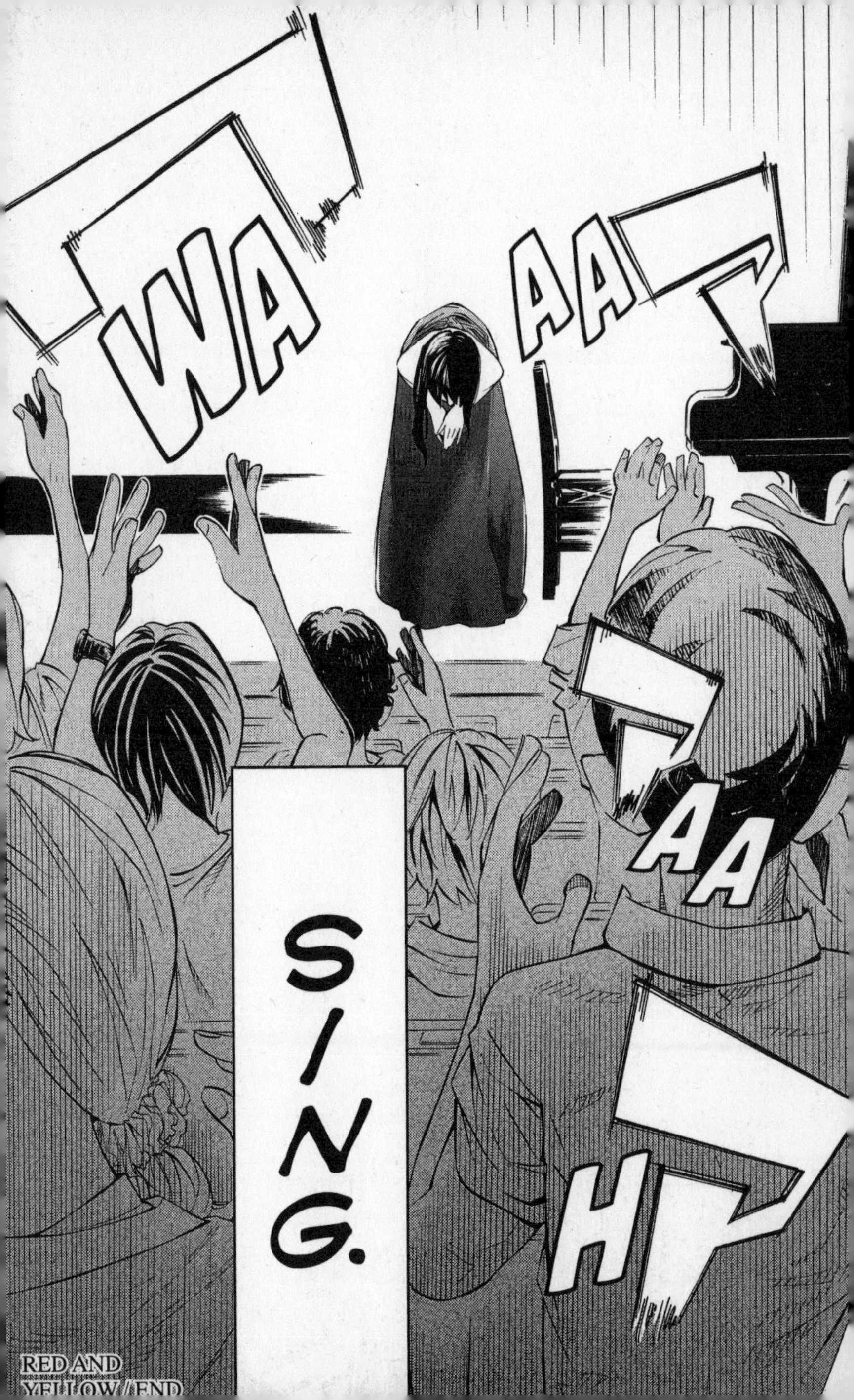
WAAAAAH
SING.
RED AND YELLOW / END

YOUR LIE IN APRIL FEATURED MUSIC

CHOPIN'S ÉTUDES OP. 25, NO. 11 IN A MINOR:
WINTER WIND

Because of its intensely expressive passages, this
famous piece is named lovingly after the winter wind
that causes dried leaves to dance. Overflowing with an
especially pianistic charm even among the études of
the poet of the piano, this piece was acclaimed by the
great German conductor and pianist Hans von Bülow
as perfect piano music.

The sounds created by the magnificent movements of
the right hand tend to steal the show, but the real key
when playing this piece is the sonorous melody played
by the left hand. An exquisite balance of superior
technique and emotional melody can make this gem of
a famous composition truly sparkle.

(Pianist Masanori Sugano, lecturer at Tokyo University
of the Arts and Musashino Academia Musicae)

Watch it on YouTube (Search "Monthly Shonen Magazine
Your Lie in April Featured Music")

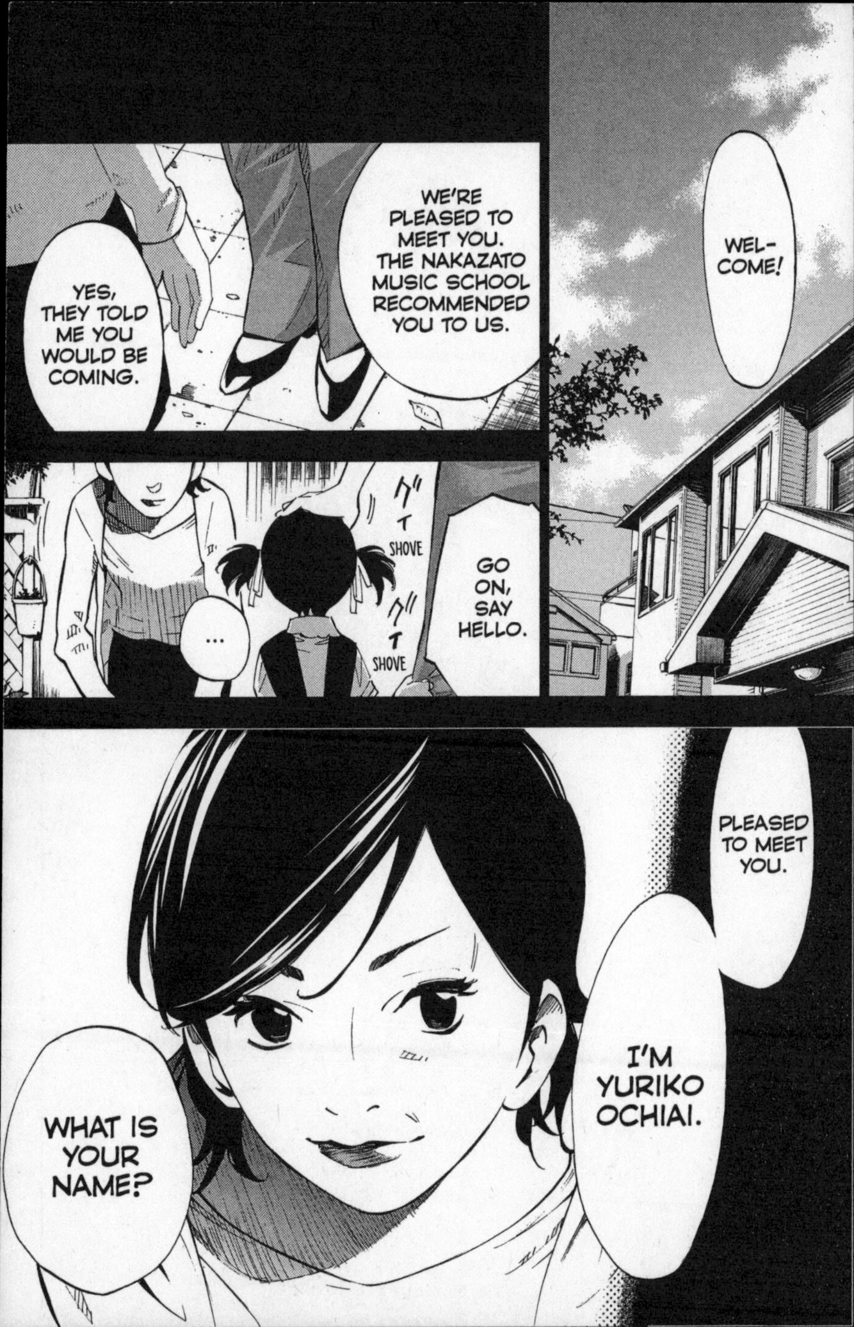
WEL-COME!
WE'RE PLEASED TO MEET YOU. THE NAKAZATO MUSIC SCHOOL RECOMMENDED YOU TO US.
YES, THEY TOLD ME YOU WOULD BE COMING.
GO ON, SAY HELLO.
SHOVE
SHOVE
...
PLEASED TO MEET YOU.
I'M YURIKO OCHIAI.
WHAT IS YOUR NAME?

Chapter 15: Resonance

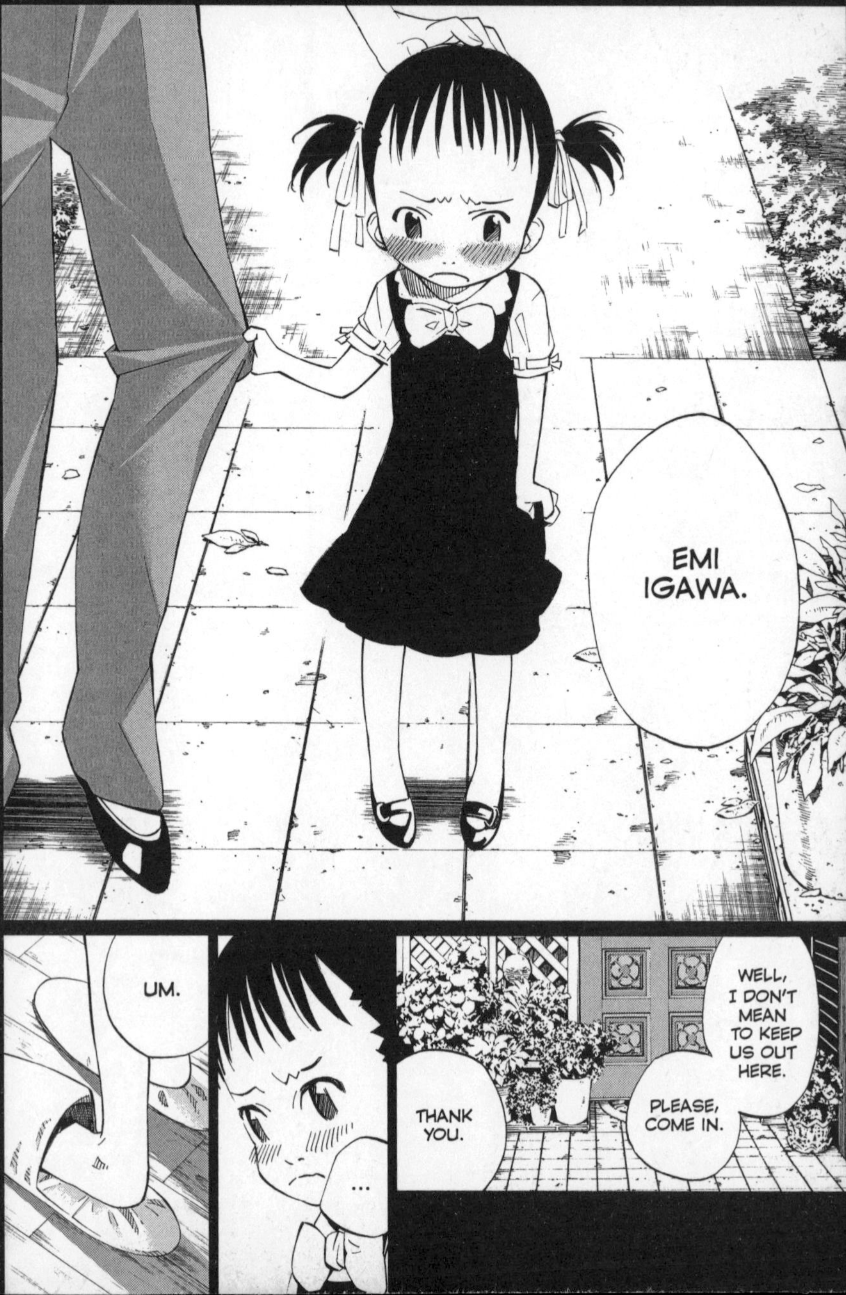
EMI IGAWA.
WELL, I DON'T MEAN TO KEEP US OUT HERE.
PLEASE, COME IN.
THANK YOU.
...
UM.

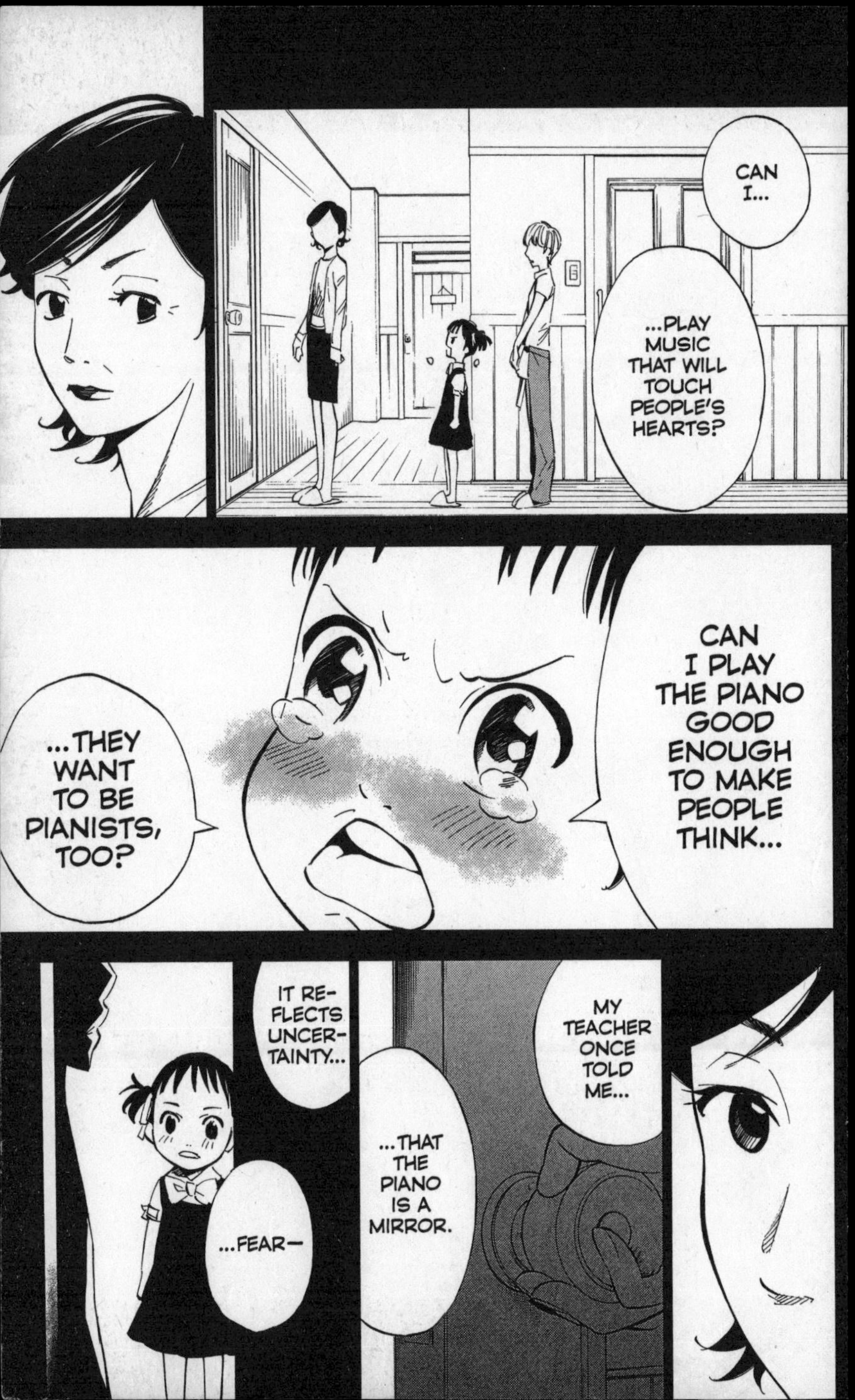
CAN I...
...PLAY MUSIC THAT WILL TOUCH PEOPLE'S HEARTS?
CAN I PLAY THE PIANO GOOD ENOUGH TO MAKE PEOPLE THINK...
...THEY WANT TO BE PIANISTS, TOO?
MY TEACHER ONCE TOLD ME...
...THAT THE PIANO IS A MIRROR.
IT RE-FLECTS UNCER-TAINTY...
...FEAR—

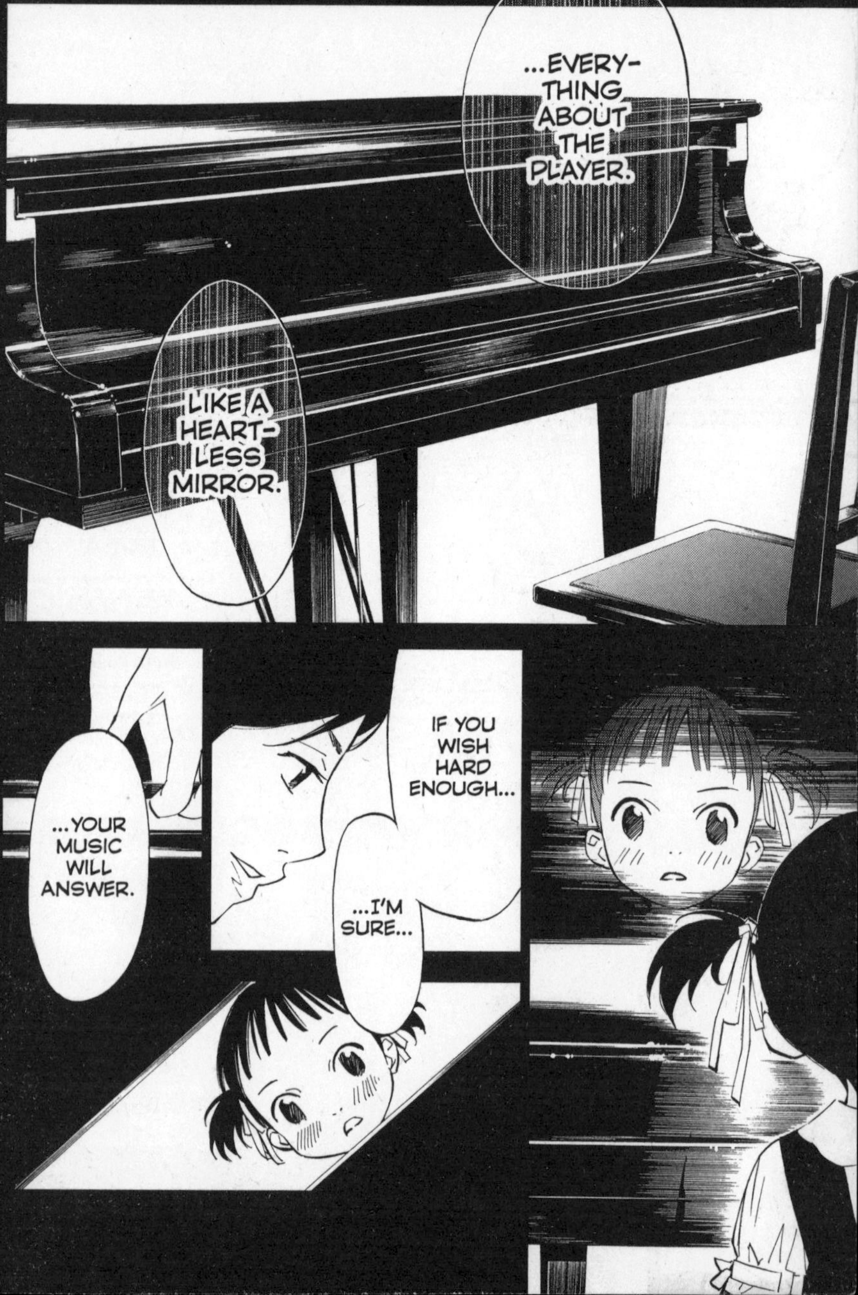
...EVERY-THING ABOUT THE PLAYER.
LIKE A HEART-LESS MIRROR.
IF YOU WISH HARD ENOUGH...
...I'M SURE...
...YOUR MUSIC WILL ANSWER.

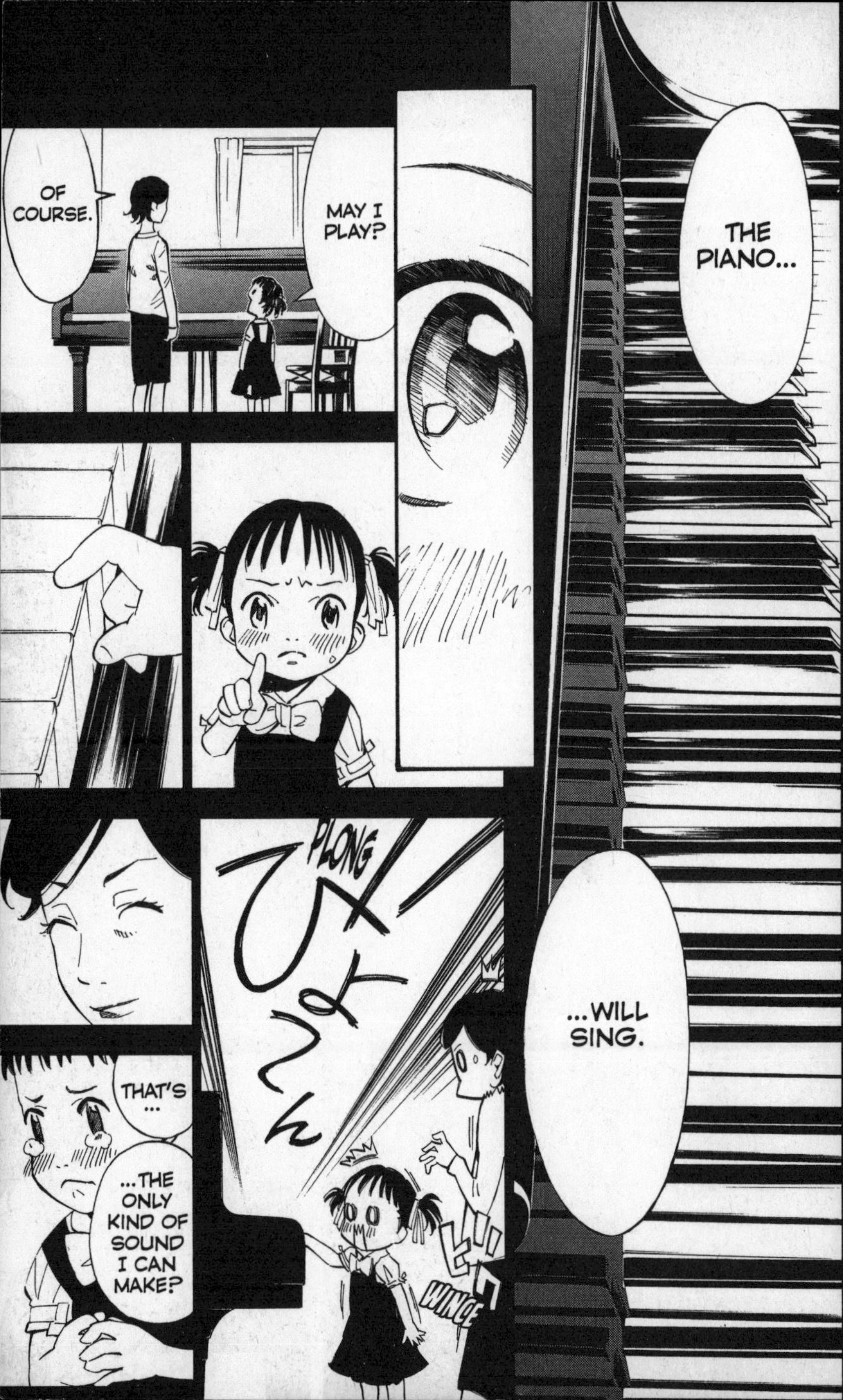

THE PIANO...
...WILL SING.
MAY I PLAY?
OF COURSE.
PLONG
WINCE
THAT'S...
...THE ONLY KIND OF SOUND I CAN MAKE?

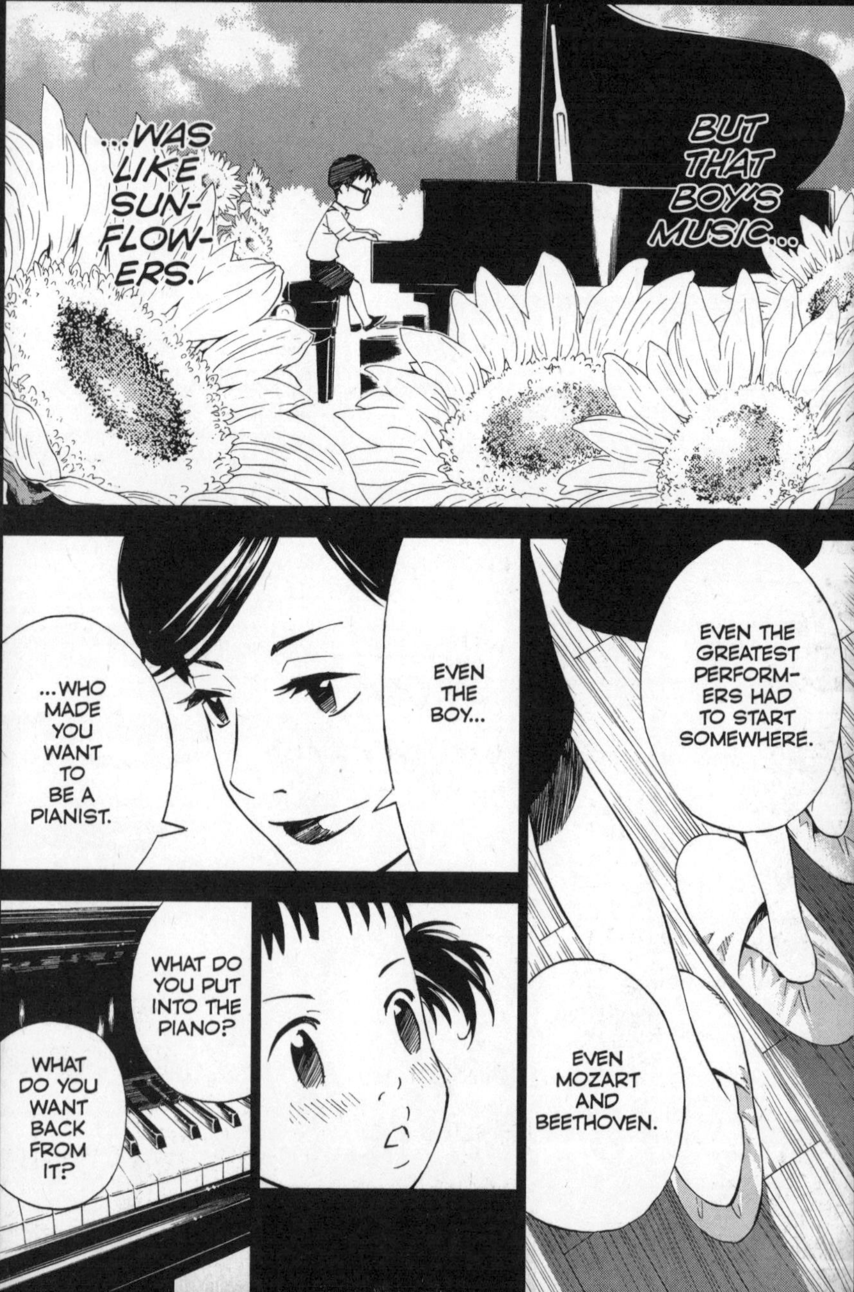
BUT THAT BOY'S MUSIC...
...WAS LIKE SUN-FLOWERS.
EVEN THE GREATEST PERFORMERS HAD TO START SOMEWHERE.
EVEN MOZART AND BEETHOVEN.
EVEN THE BOY...
...WHO MADE YOU WANT TO BE A PIANIST.
WHAT DO YOU PUT INTO THE PIANO?
WHAT DO YOU WANT BACK FROM IT?

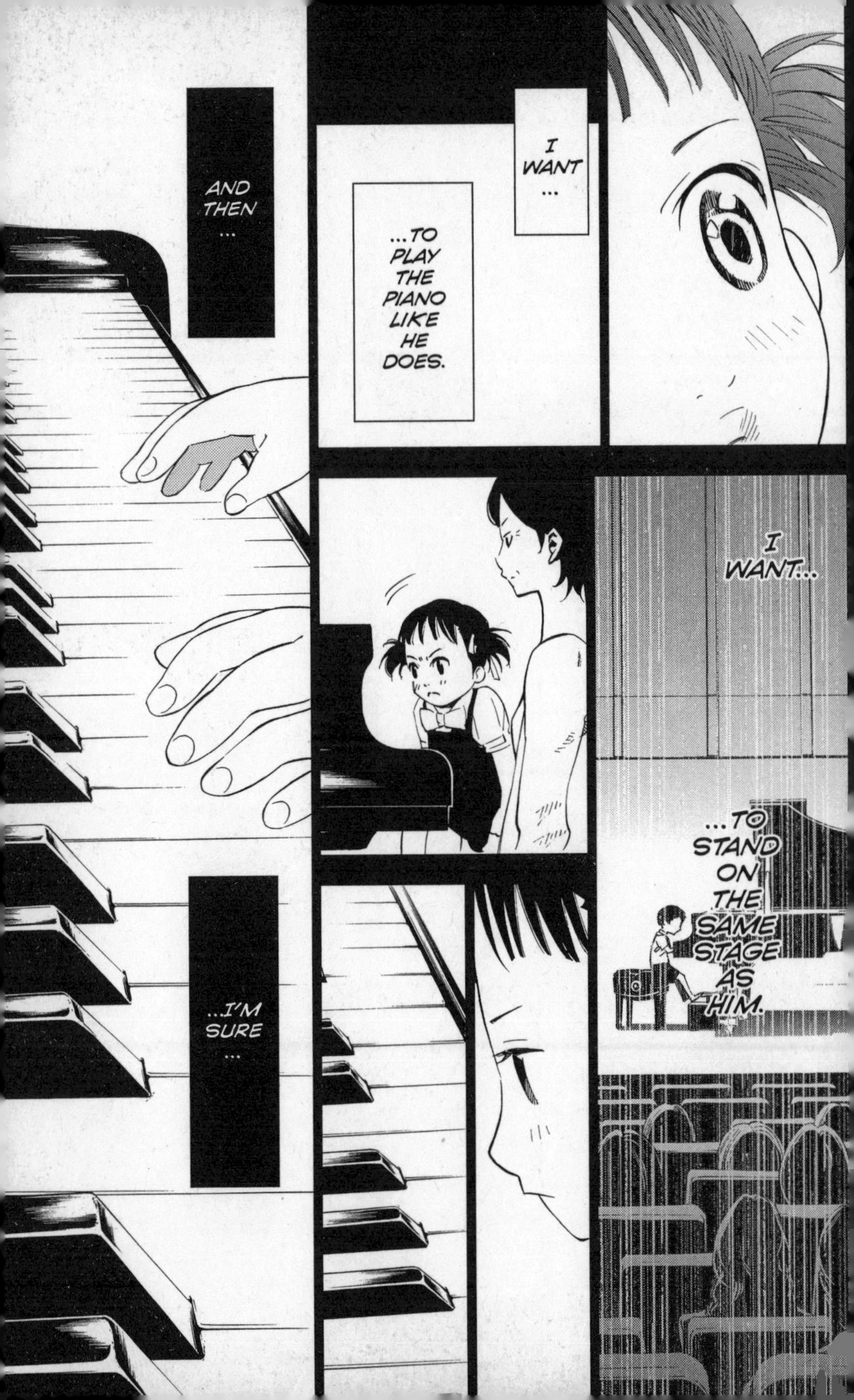
I WANT...
...TO PLAY THE PIANO LIKE HE DOES.
I WANT...
...TO STAND ON THE SAME STAGE AS HIM.
AND THEN...
...I'M SURE...

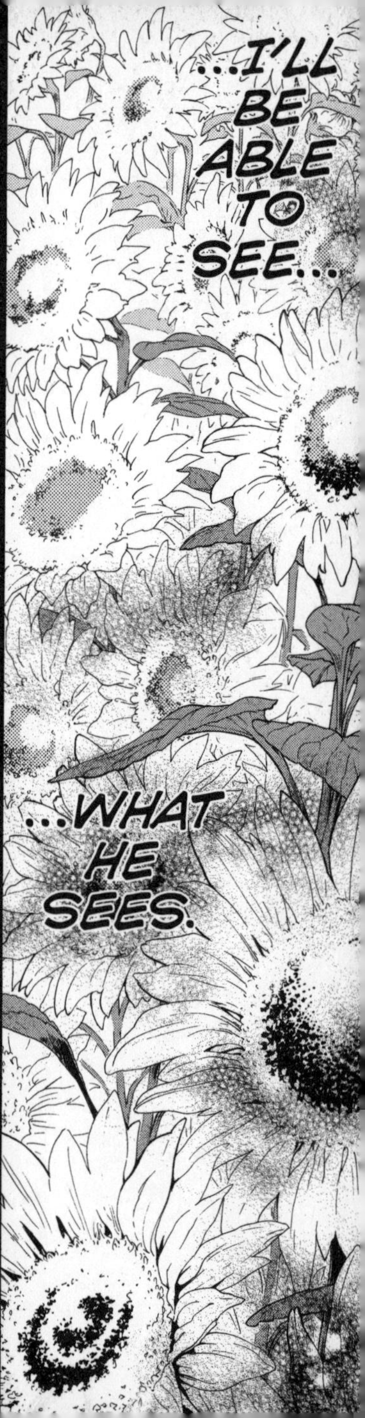
...I'LL BE ABLE TO SEE...
...WHAT HE SEES.
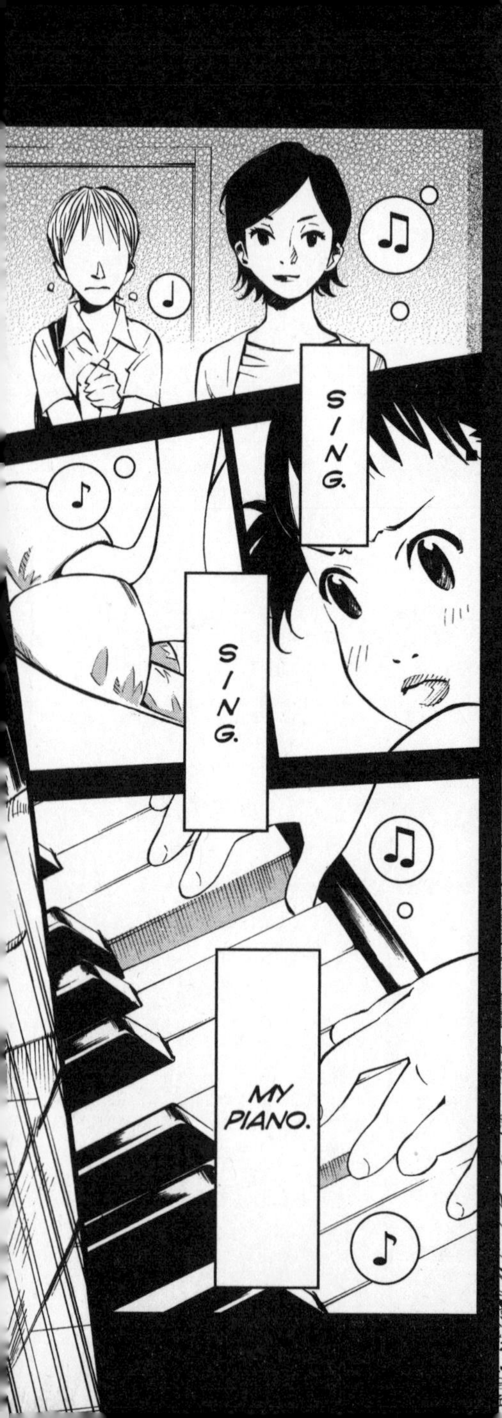
SING.
SING.
MY PIANO.

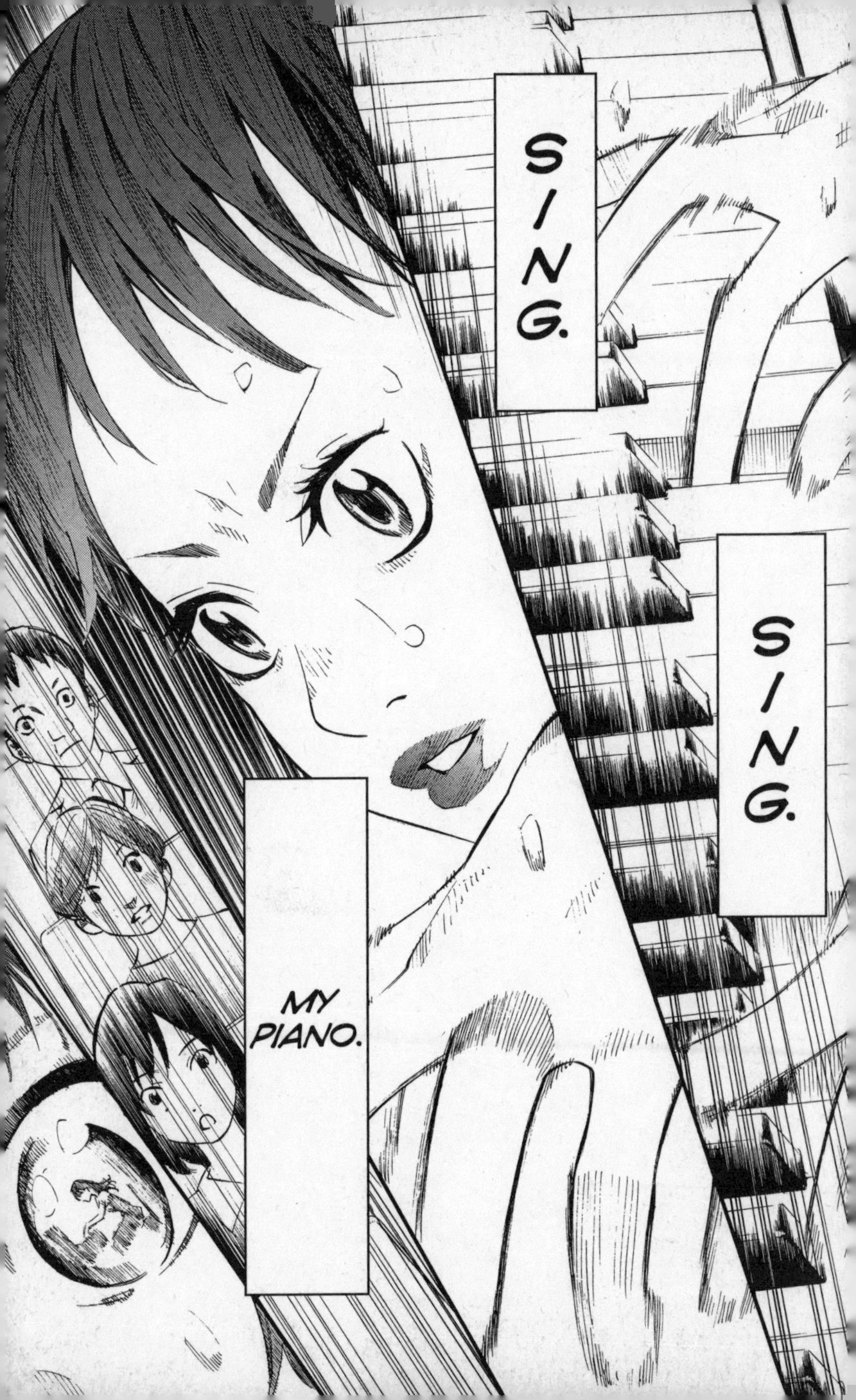
SING.
SING.
MY PIANO.

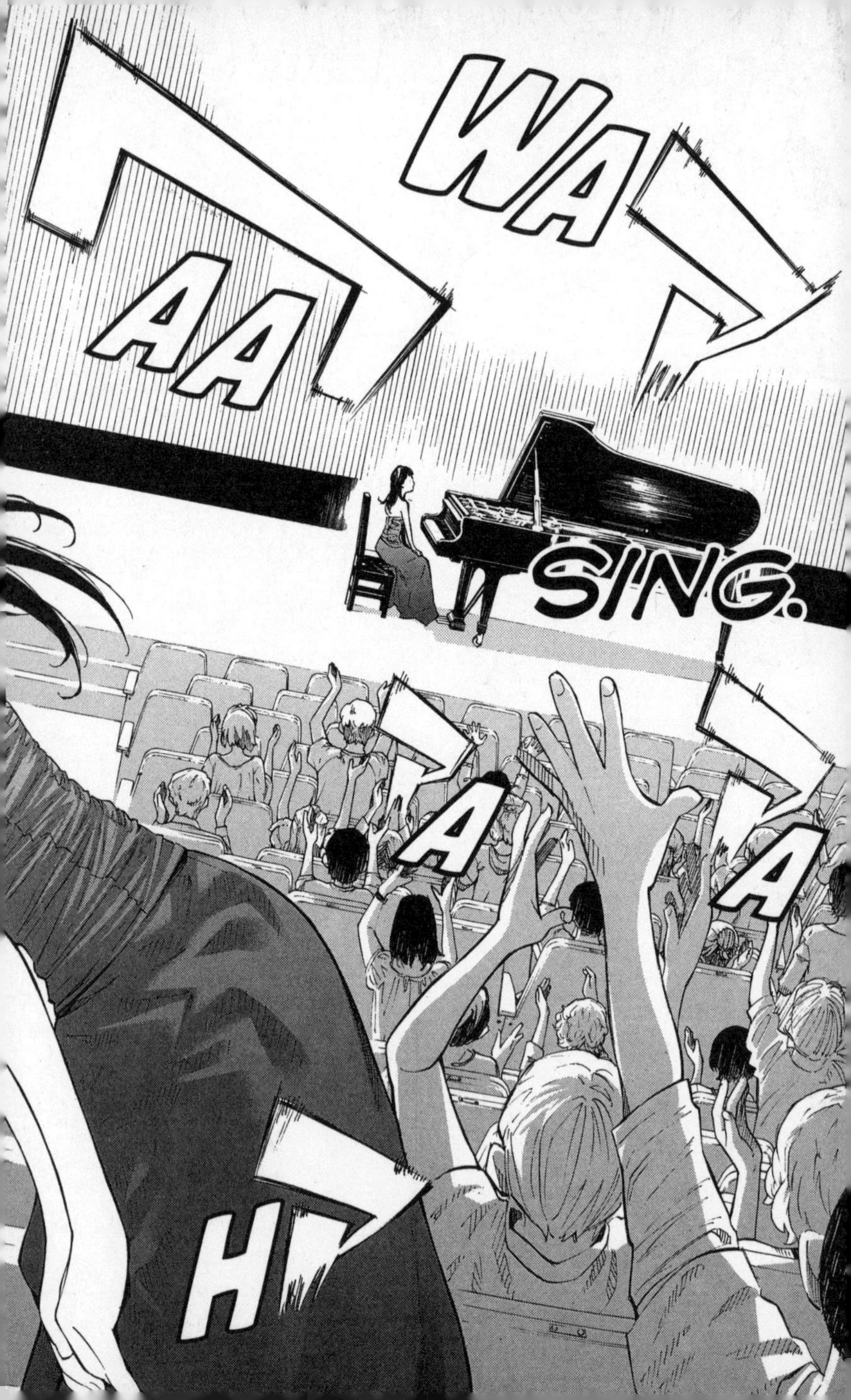

WA
AA
SING.
A
A
H

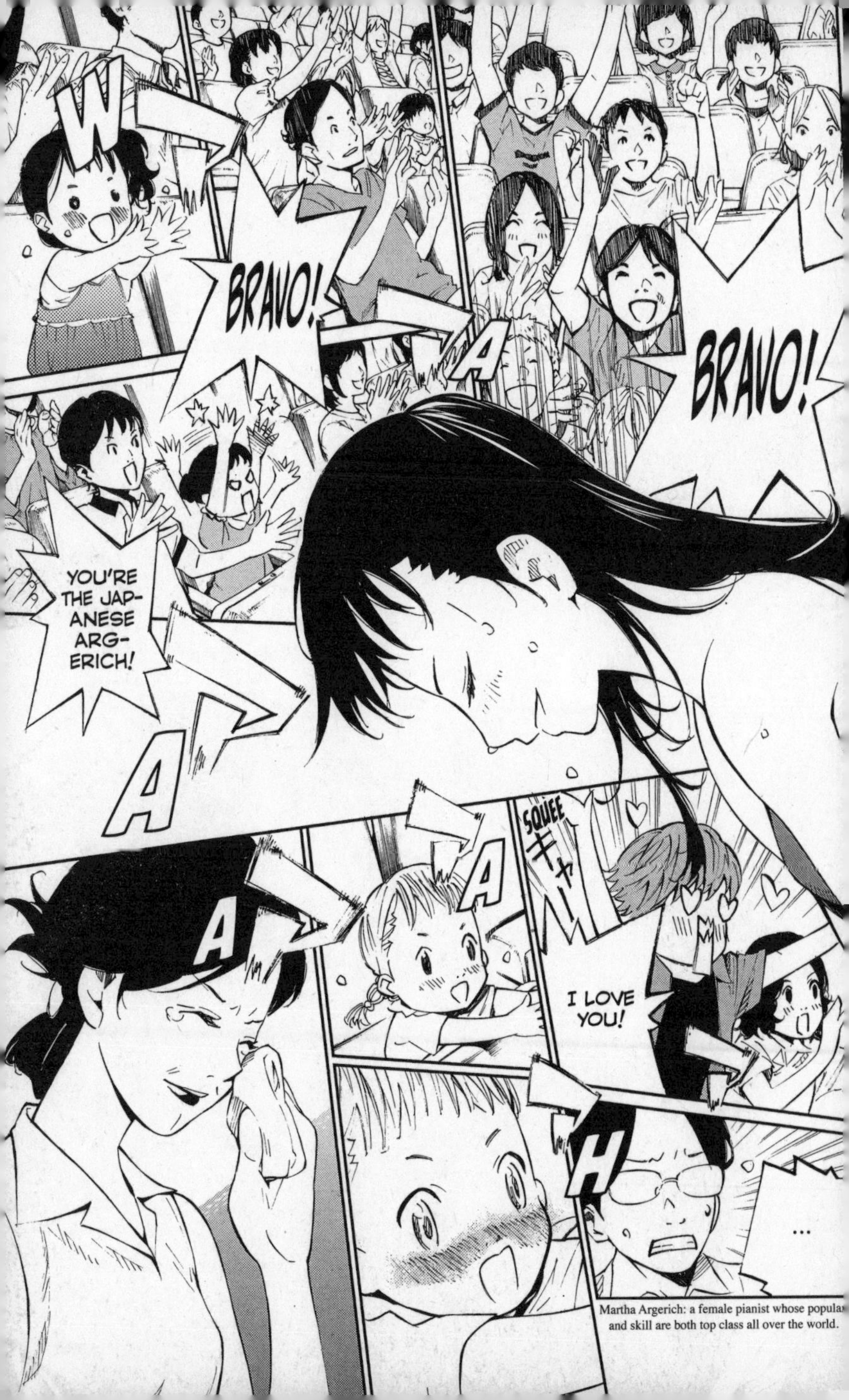
BRAVO!
W
BRAVO!
A
YOU'RE THE JAP- ANESE ARG- ERICH!
A
SQUEE
キャー
I LOVE YOU!
A
A
...
H

Martha Argerich: a female pianist whose popular and skill are both top class all over the world.

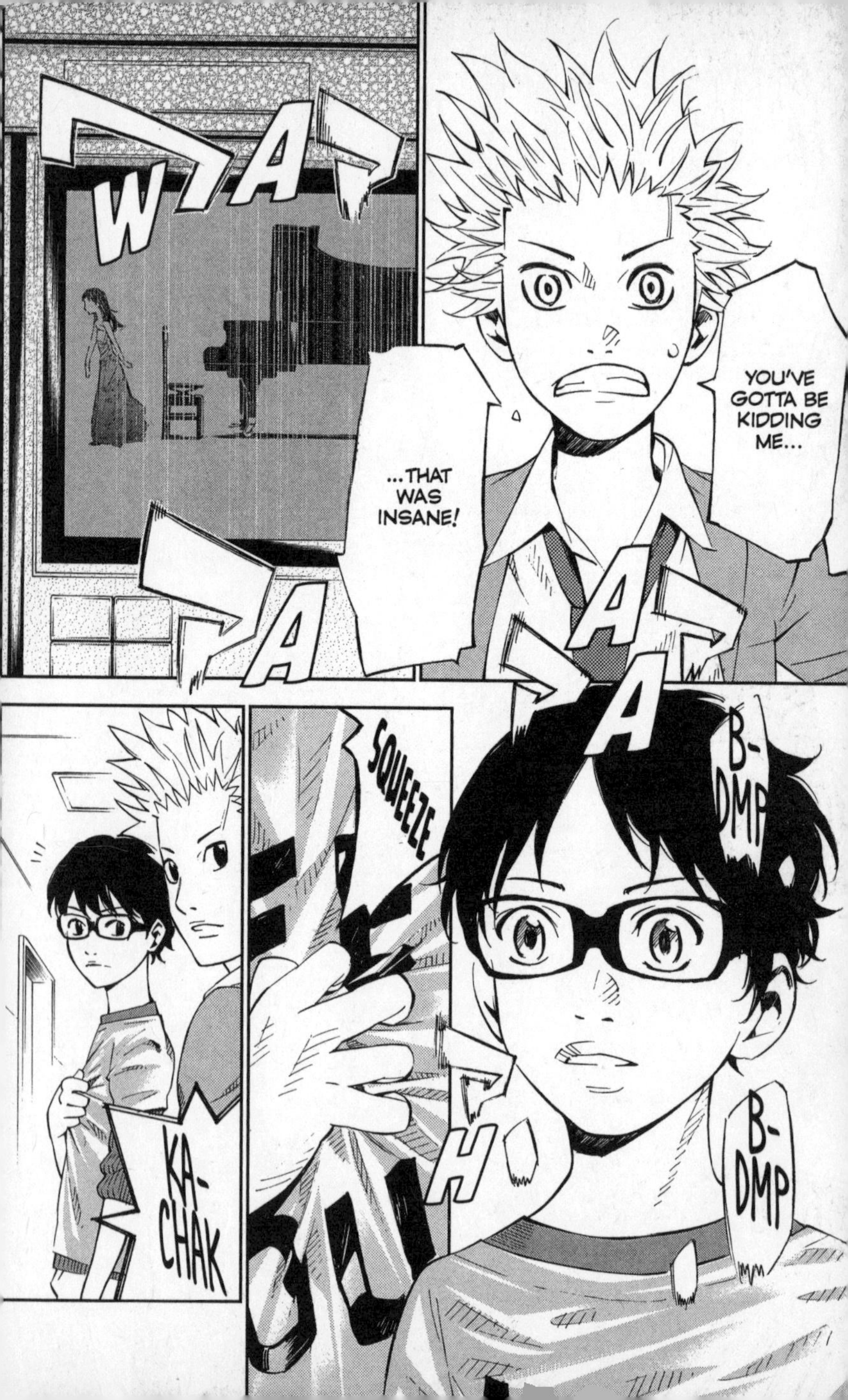

YOU'VE GOTTA BE KIDDING ME...
...THAT WAS INSANE!
WAAAAAAH
B-DMP
B-DMP
SQUEEZE
KA-CHAK

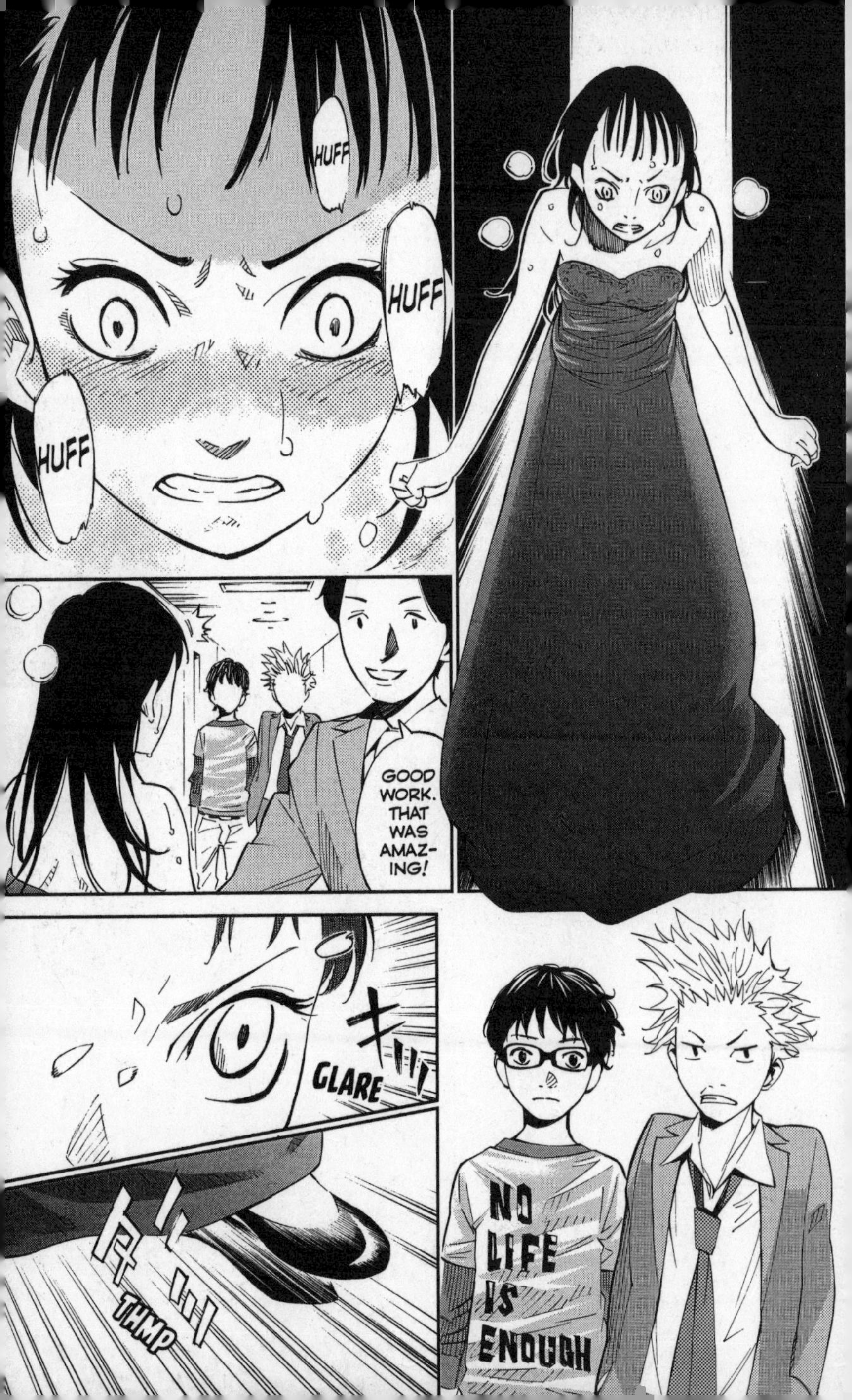
HUFF
HUFF
HUFF
GOOD WORK. THAT WAS AMAZ-ING!
NO LIFE IS ENOUGH
GLARE
THMP

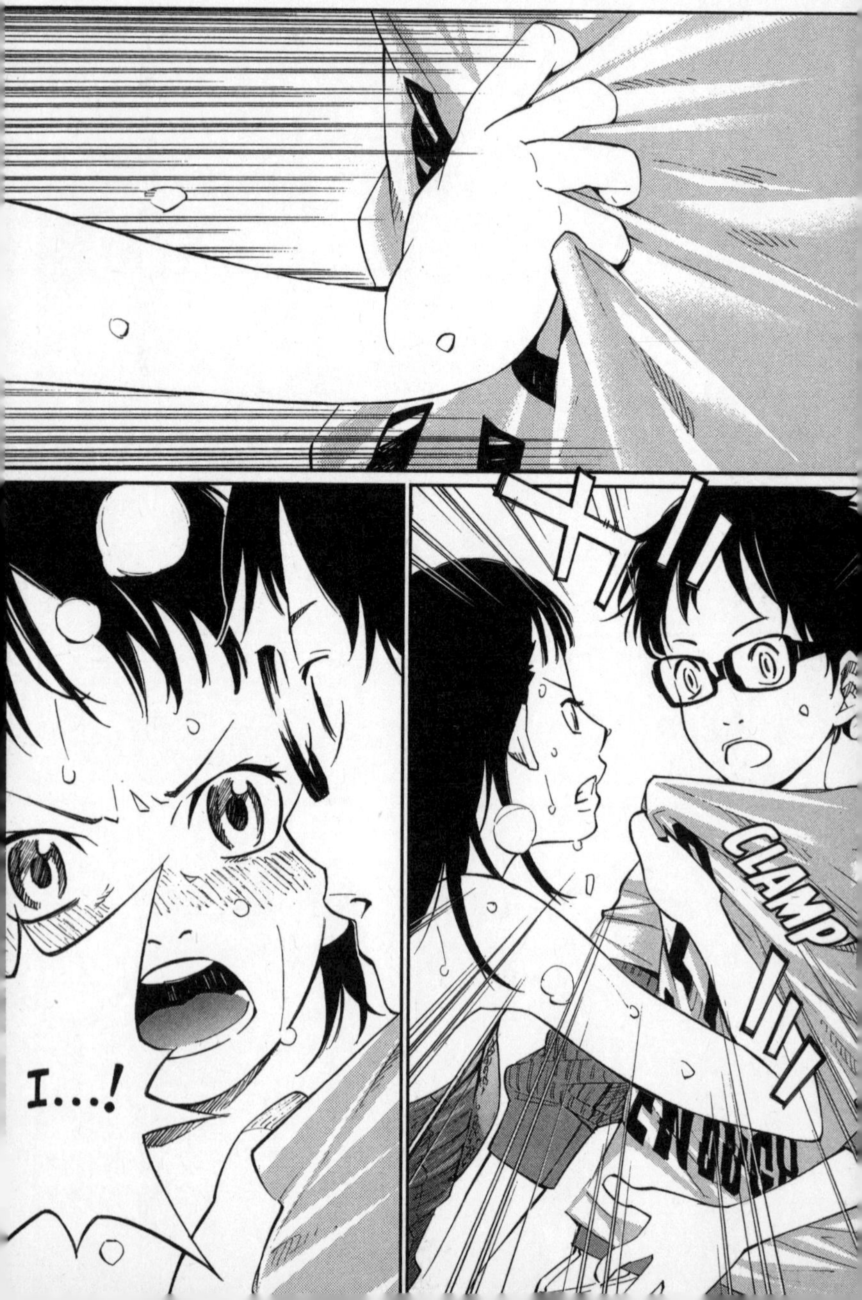
CLAMP
I...!

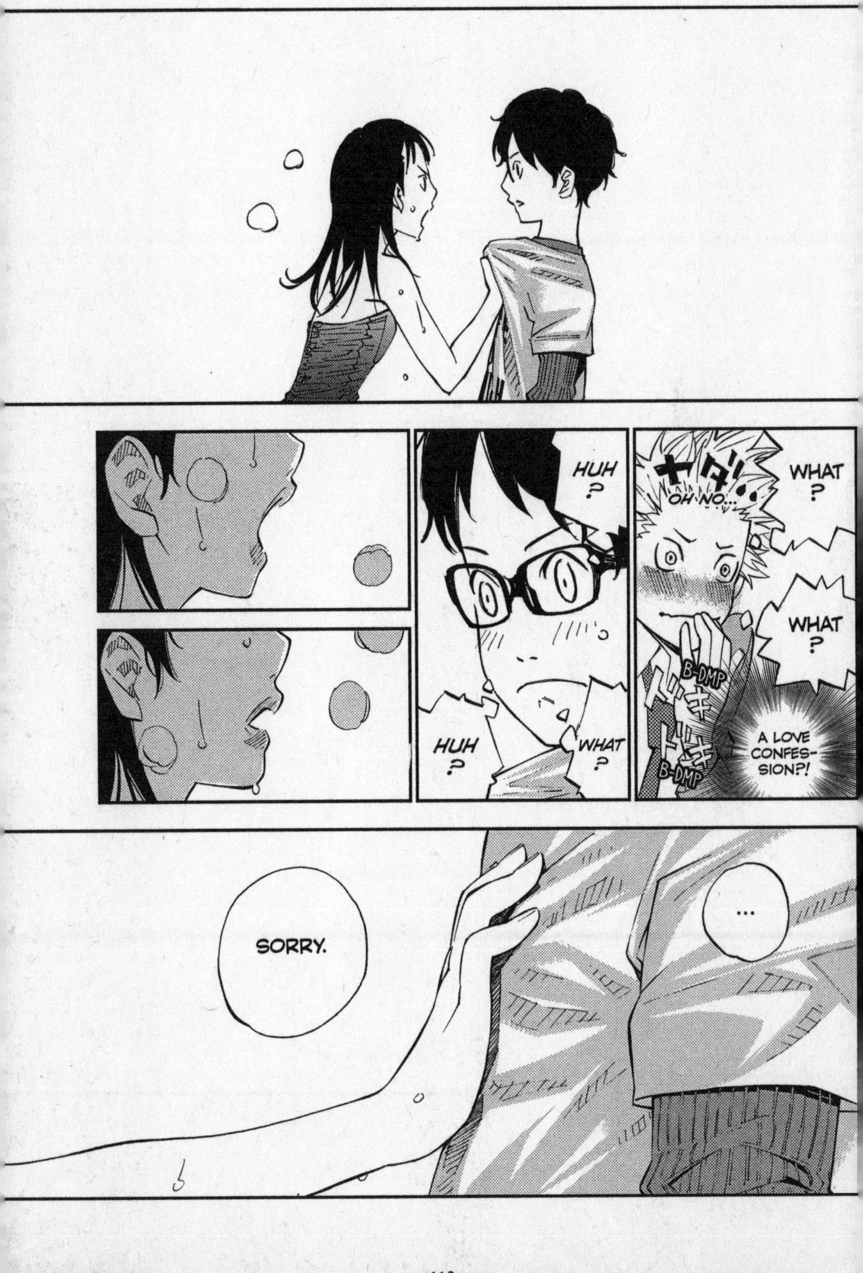
ヤダ!
OH NO...
WHAT?
WHAT?
ドキドキ
B-DMP
B-DMP
A LOVE CONFESSION?!
HUH?
HUH?
WHAT?
...
SORRY.

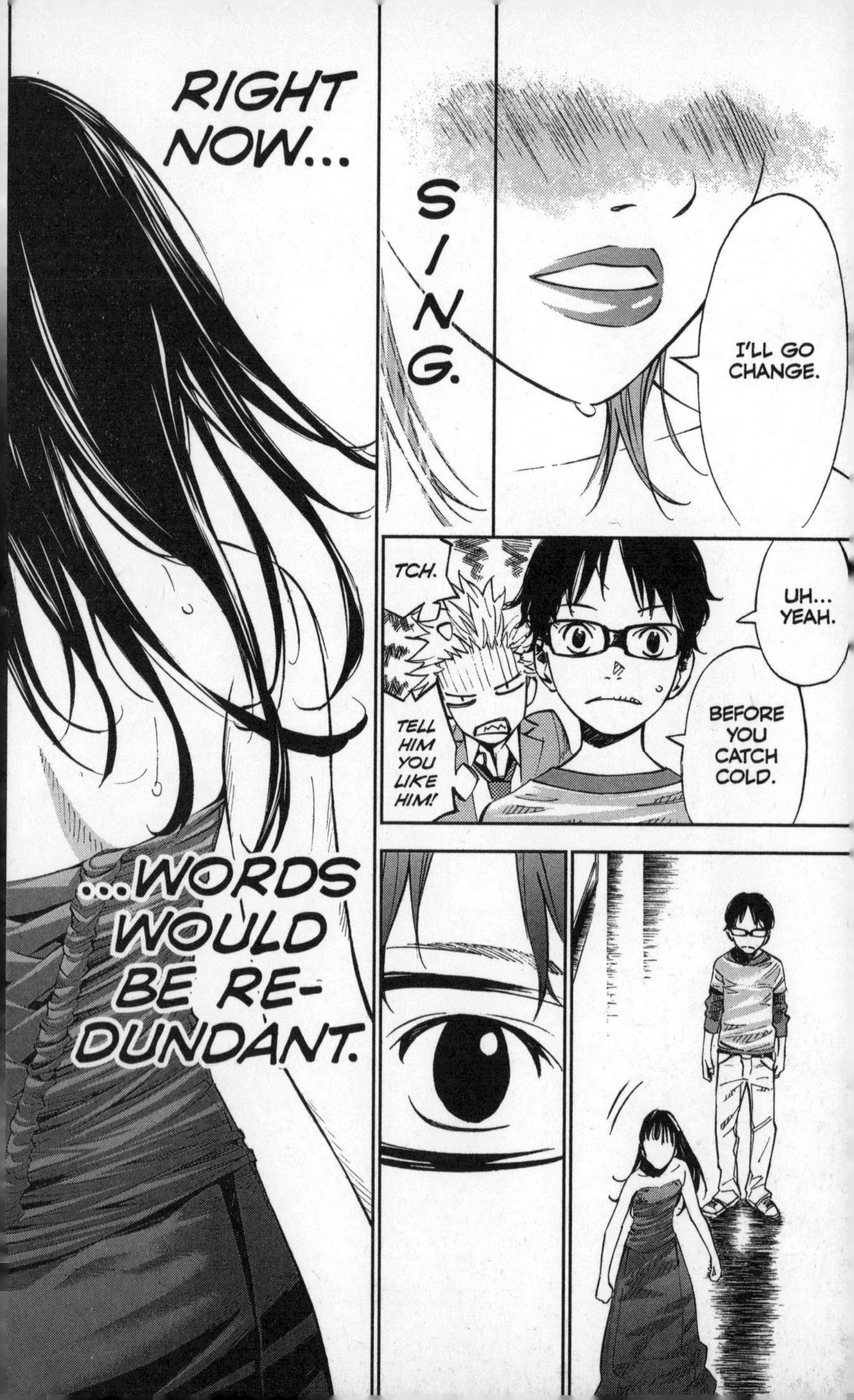
I'LL GO CHANGE.
SING.
UH... YEAH.
BEFORE YOU CATCH COLD.
TCH.
TELL HIM YOU LIKE HIM!
RIGHT NOW...
...WORDS WOULD BE RE-DUNDANT.

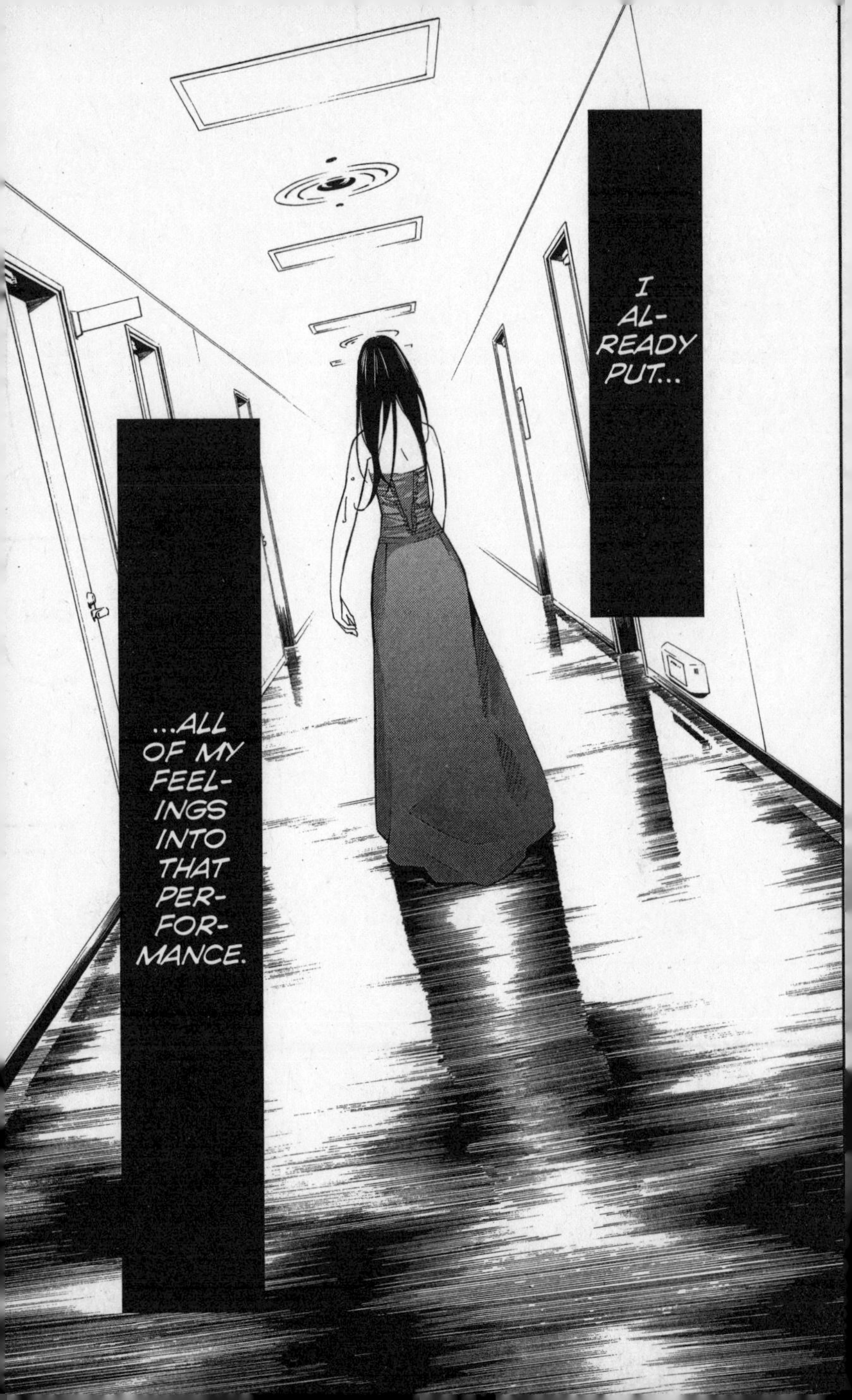
I AL-READY PUT...
...ALL OF MY FEEL-INGS INTO THAT PER-FOR-MANCE.

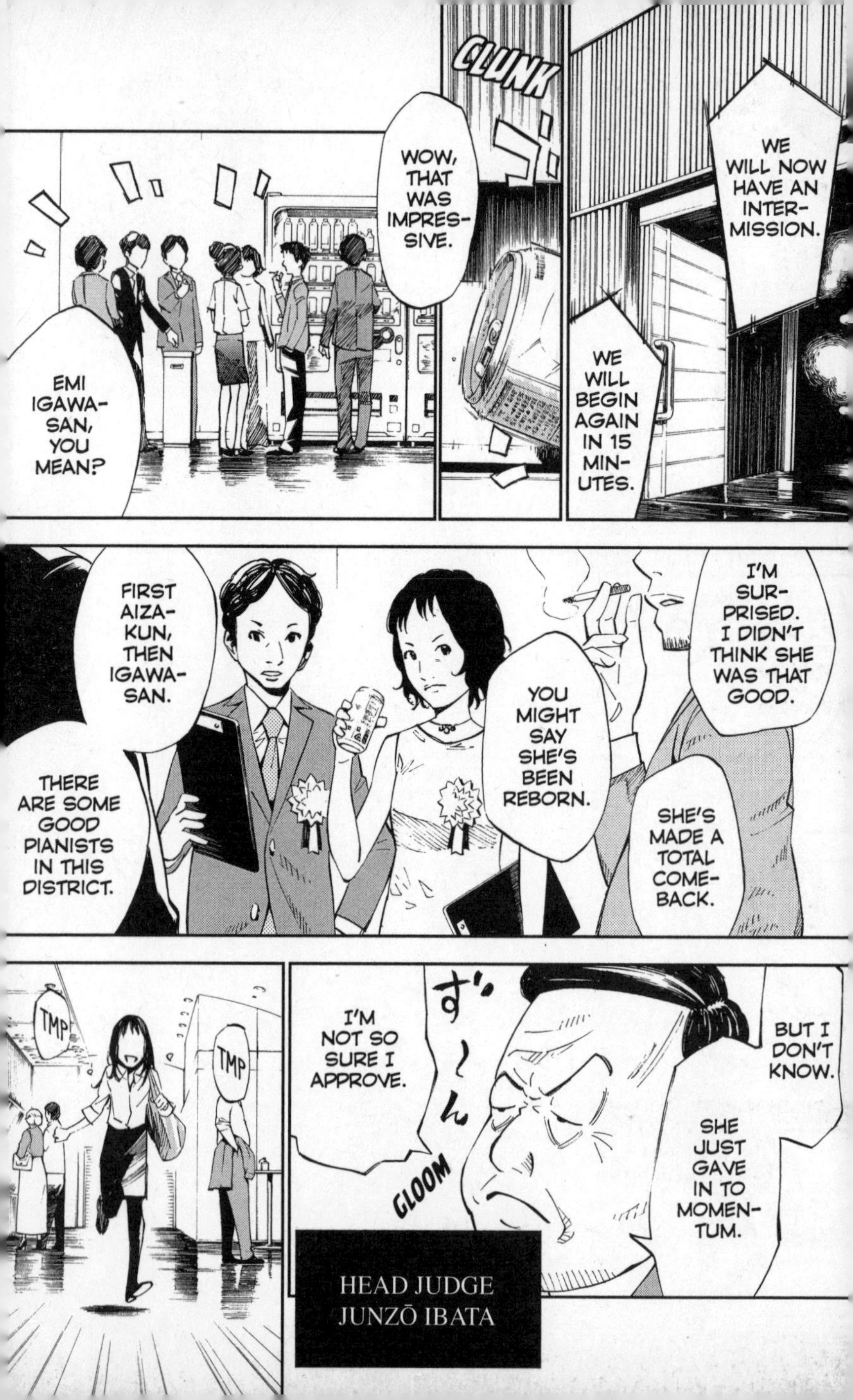
CLUNK
WE WILL NOW HAVE AN INTERMISSION.
WE WILL BEGIN AGAIN IN 15 MINUTES.
WOW, THAT WAS IMPRESSIVE.
EMI IGAWA-SAN, YOU MEAN?
I'M SURPRISED. I DIDN'T THINK SHE WAS THAT GOOD.
YOU MIGHT SAY SHE'S BEEN REBORN.
SHE'S MADE A TOTAL COMEBACK.
FIRST AIZA-KUN, THEN IGAWA-SAN.
THERE ARE SOME GOOD PIANISTS IN THIS DISTRICT.
BUT I DON'T KNOW.
SHE JUST GAVE IN TO MOMENTUM.
ずーん
GLOOM
I'M NOT SO SURE I APPROVE.
HEAD JUDGE JUNZŌ IBATA
TMP
TMP

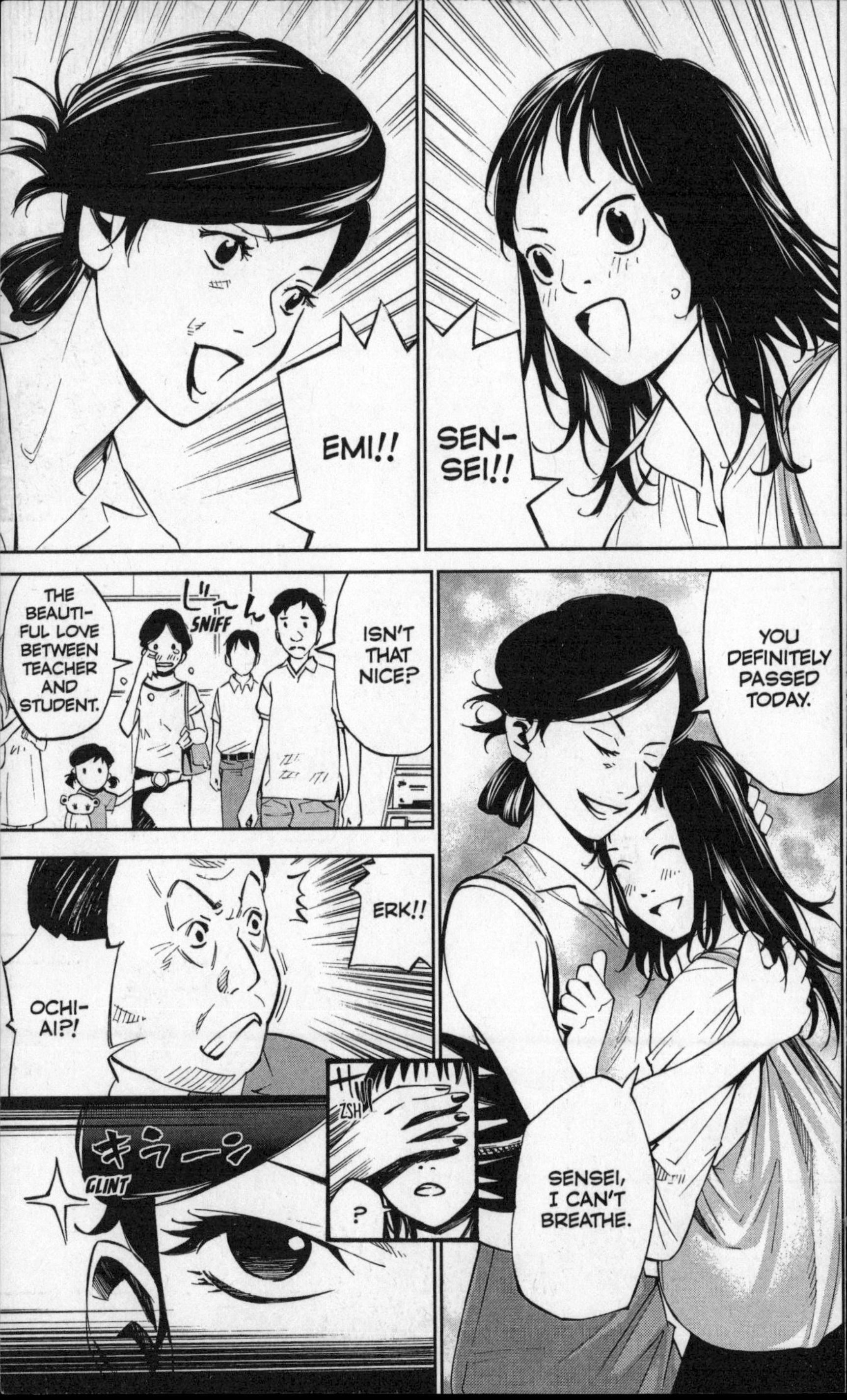
SEN-SEI!!
EMI!!
YOU DEFINITELY PASSED TODAY.
SENSEI, I CAN'T BREATHE.
ISN'T THAT NICE?
じ〜ん
SNIFF
THE BEAUTIFUL LOVE BETWEEN TEACHER AND STUDENT.
ERK!!
OCHI-AI?!
ZSH
?
キラーン
GLINT

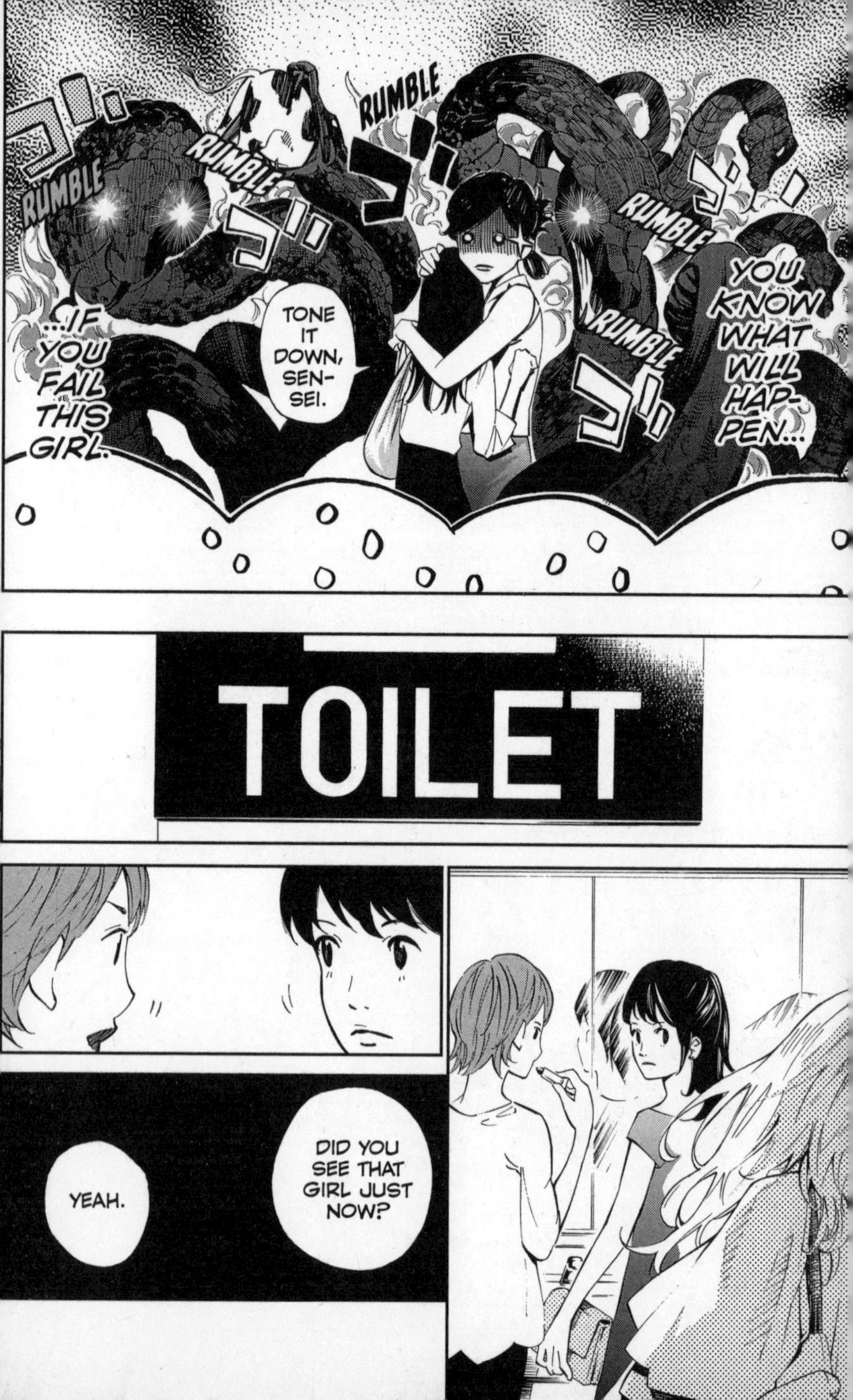
RUMBLE
RUMBLE
RUMBLE
RUMBLE
RUMBLE
RUMBLE
YOU KNOW WHAT WILL HAPPEN...
...IF YOU FAIL THIS GIRL.
TONE IT DOWN, SENSEI.
TOILET
DID YOU SEE THAT GIRL JUST NOW?
YEAH.

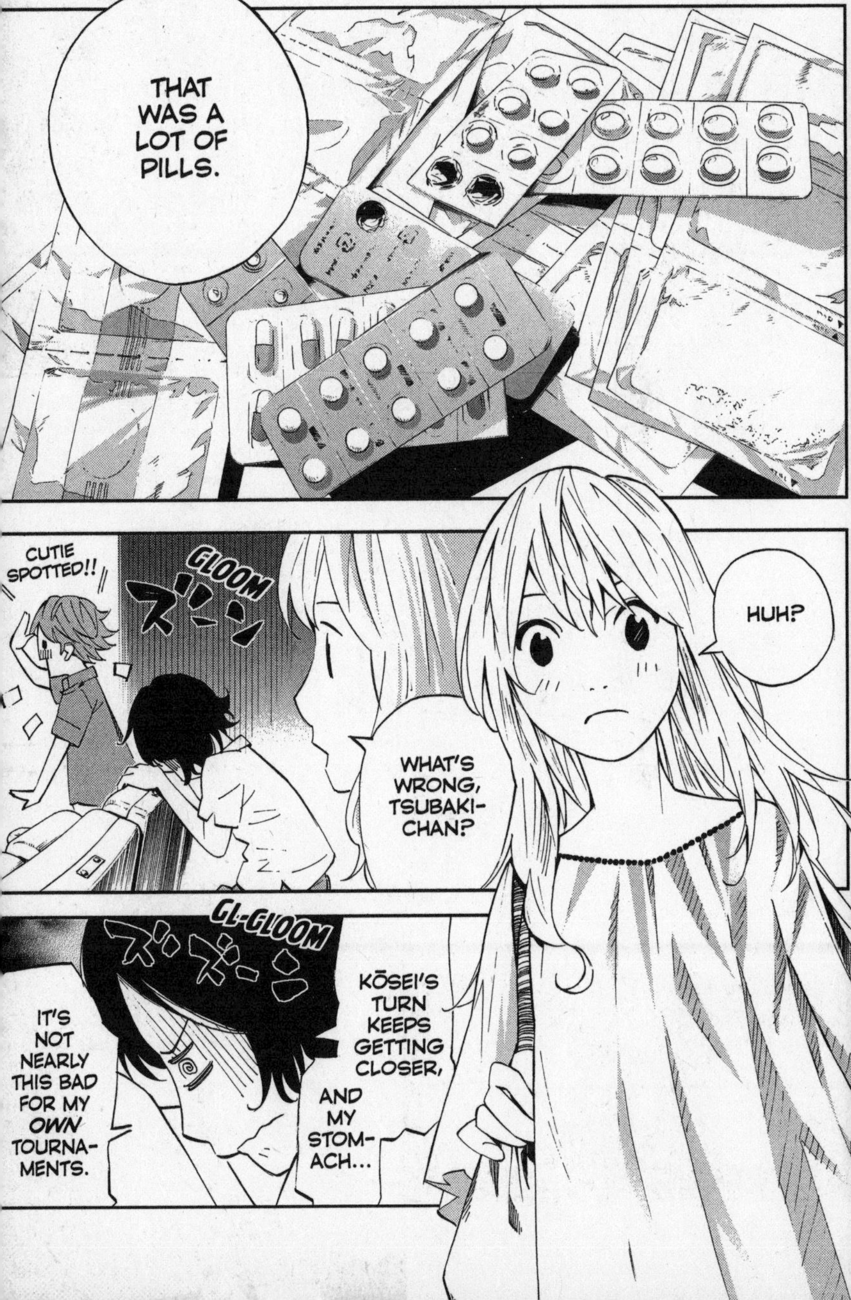
THAT WAS A LOT OF PILLS.
HUH?
WHAT'S WRONG, TSUBAKI-CHAN?
GLOOM
CUTIE SPOTTED!!
GL-GLOOM
KŌSEI'S TURN KEEPS GETTING CLOSER,
AND MY STOMACH...
IT'S NOT NEARLY THIS BAD FOR MY *OWN* TOURNAMENTS.

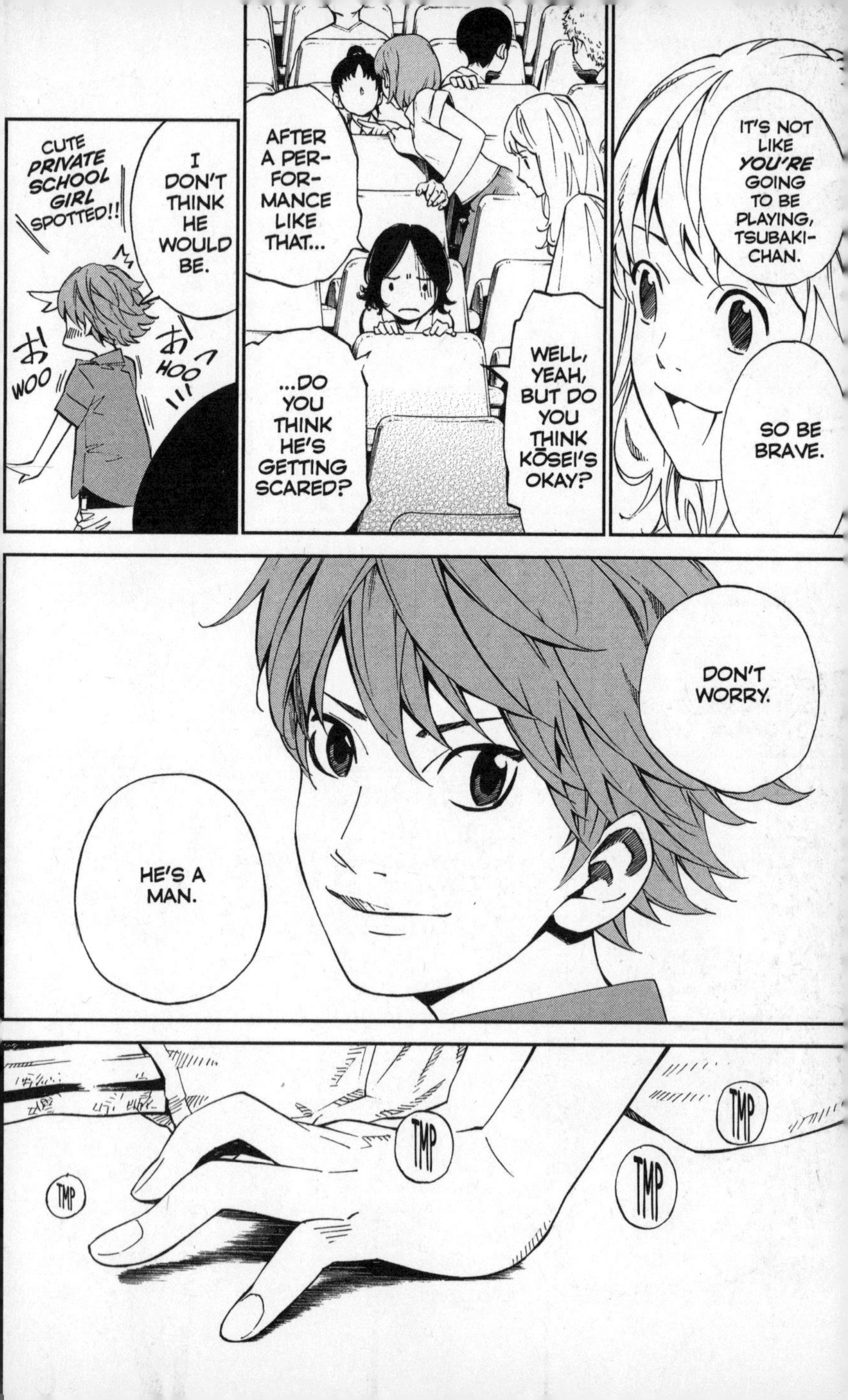
IT'S NOT LIKE *YOU'RE* GOING TO BE PLAYING, TSUBAKI-CHAN.
SO BE BRAVE.
WELL, YEAH, BUT DO YOU THINK KŌSEI'S OKAY?
AFTER A PERFORMANCE LIKE THAT...
...DO YOU THINK HE'S GETTING SCARED?
I DON'T THINK HE WOULD BE.
CUTE *PRIVATE SCHOOL GIRL* SPOTTED!!
HOO
WOO
DON'T WORRY.
HE'S A MAN.
TMP
TMP
TMP
TMP

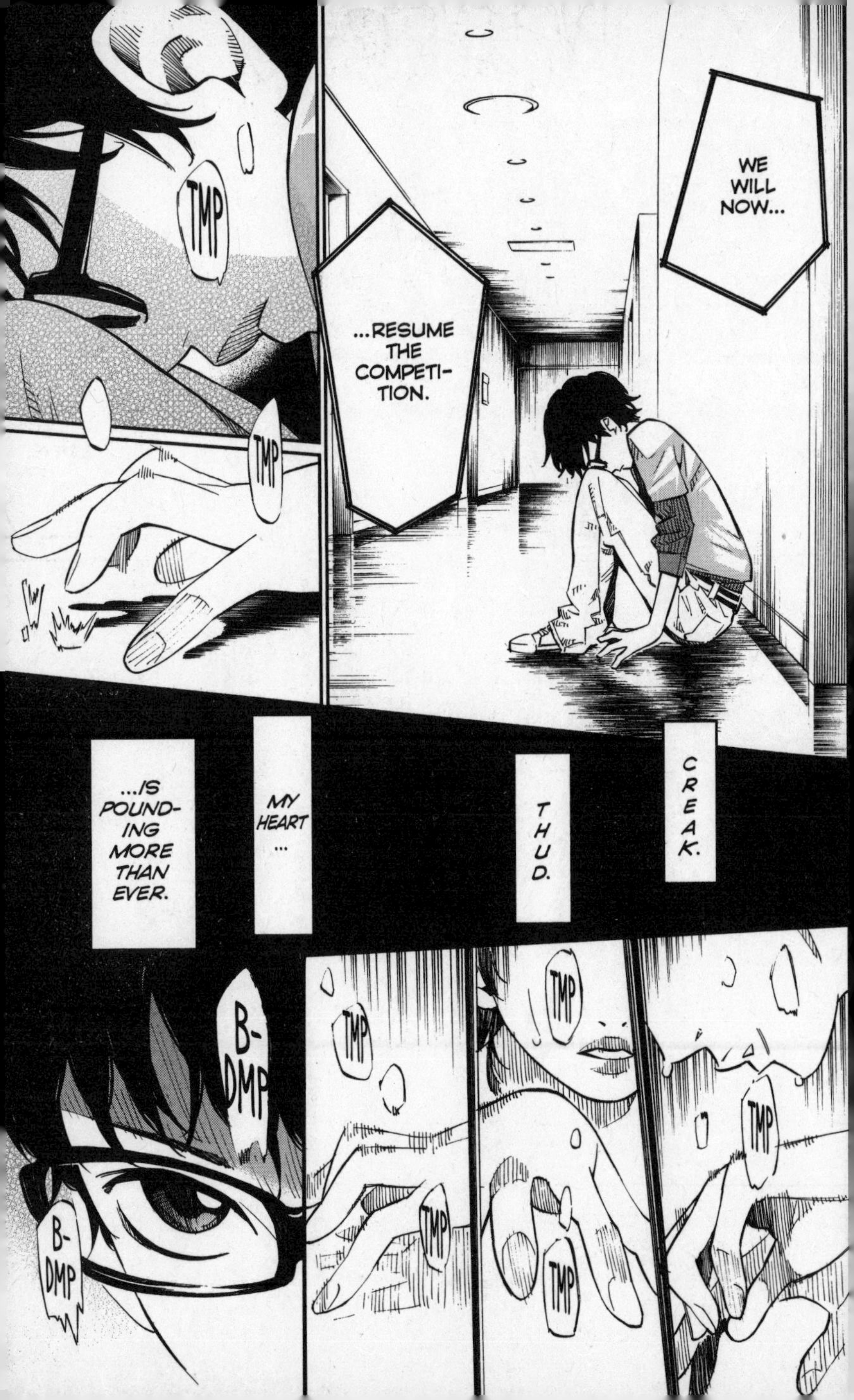
WE WILL NOW...
...RESUME THE COMPETITION.
TMP
TMP
CREAK.
THUD.
MY HEART...
...IS POUNDING MORE THAN EVER.
TMP
TMP
TMP
TMP
TMP
B-DMP
B-DMP

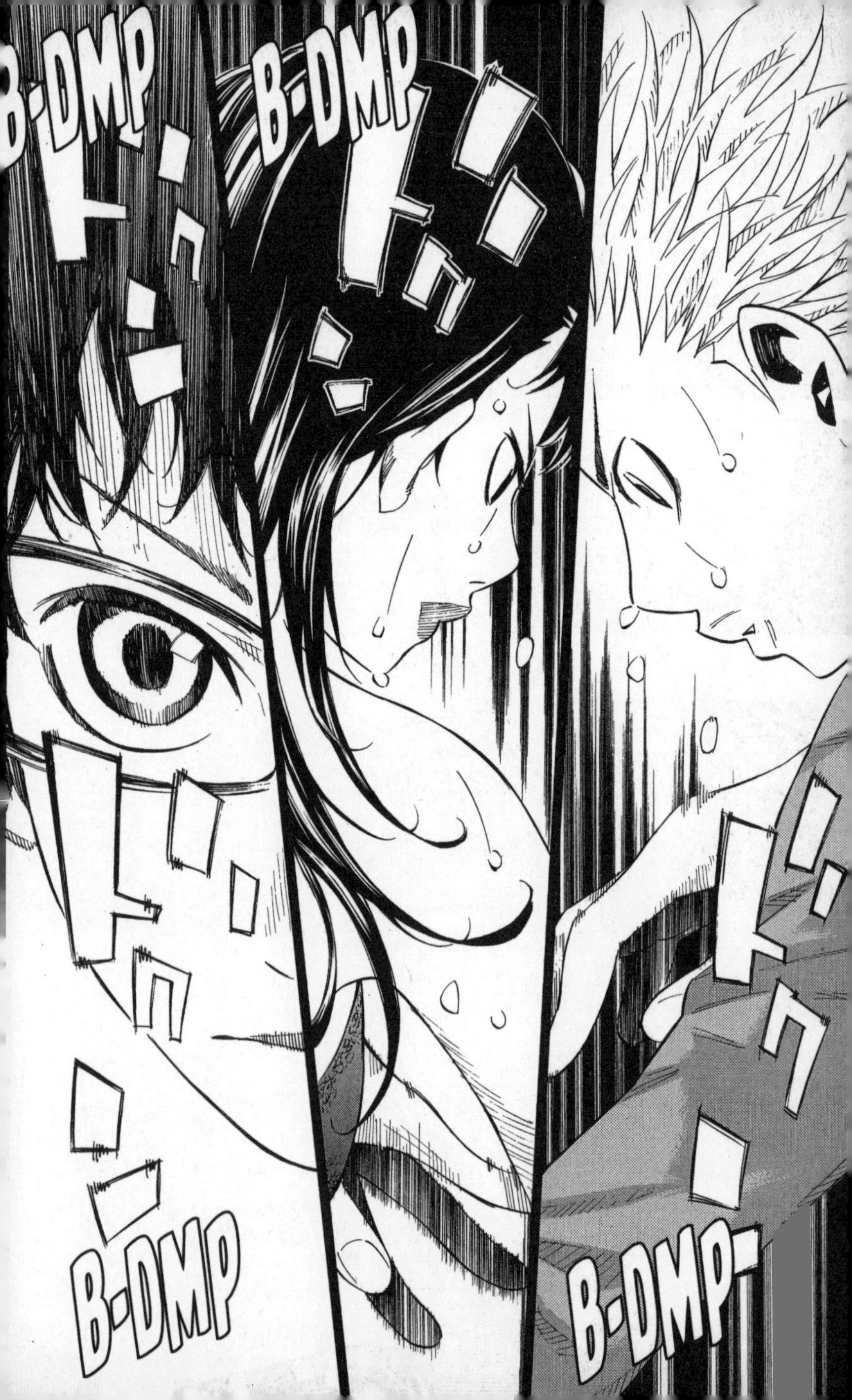
B-DMP-
B-DMP
B-DMP
B-DMP

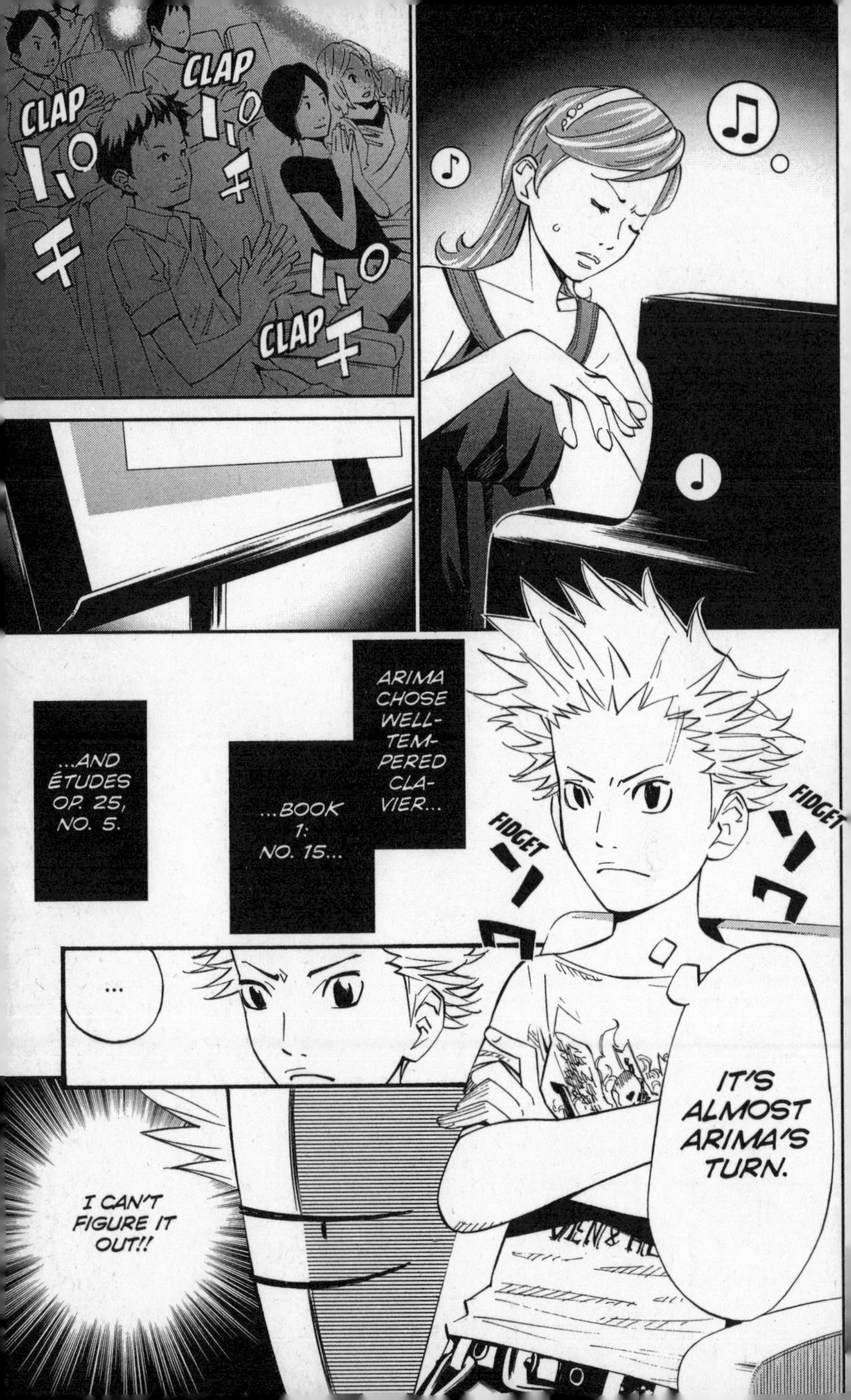
CLAP
CLAP
CLAP
ARIMA CHOSE WELL-TEMPERED CLAVIER...
...BOOK 1: NO. 15...
...AND ÉTUDES OP. 25, NO. 5.
FIDGET
FIDGET
...
IT'S ALMOST ARIMA'S TURN.
I CAN'T FIGURE IT OUT!!

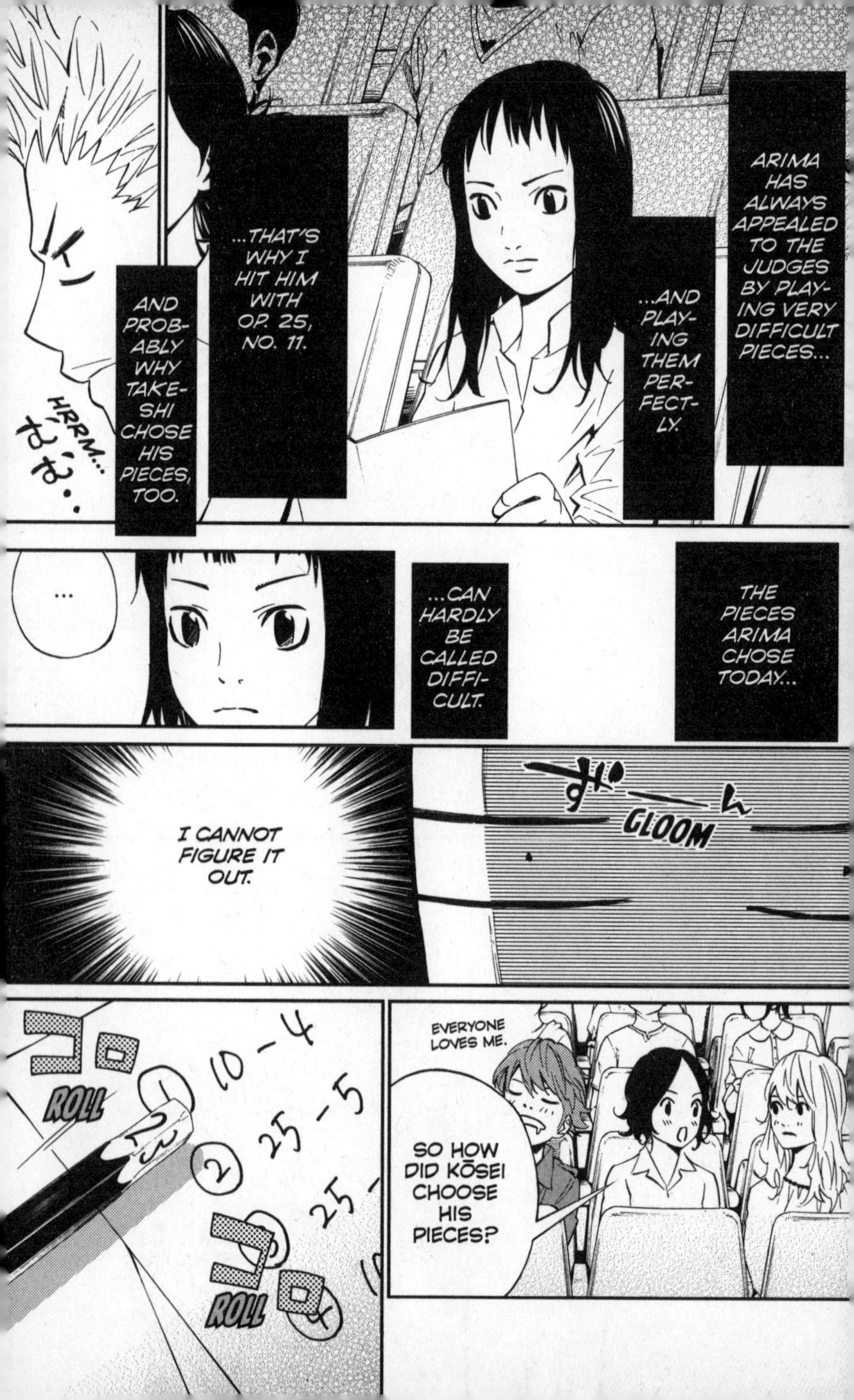
ARIMA HAS ALWAYS APPEALED TO THE JUDGES BY PLAYING VERY DIFFICULT PIECES...
...AND PLAYING THEM PERFECTLY.
...THAT'S WHY I HIT HIM WITH OP. 25, NO. 11.
AND PROBABLY WHY TAKESHI CHOSE HIS PIECES, TOO.
むむ・・
HRRM...
THE PIECES ARIMA CHOSE TODAY...
...CAN HARDLY BE CALLED DIFFICULT.
...
ずーーん
GLOOM
I CANNOT FIGURE IT OUT.
EVERYONE LOVES ME.
SO HOW DID KŌSEI CHOOSE HIS PIECES?
コロ
ROLL
10-4
25-5
25-
コロ
ROLL

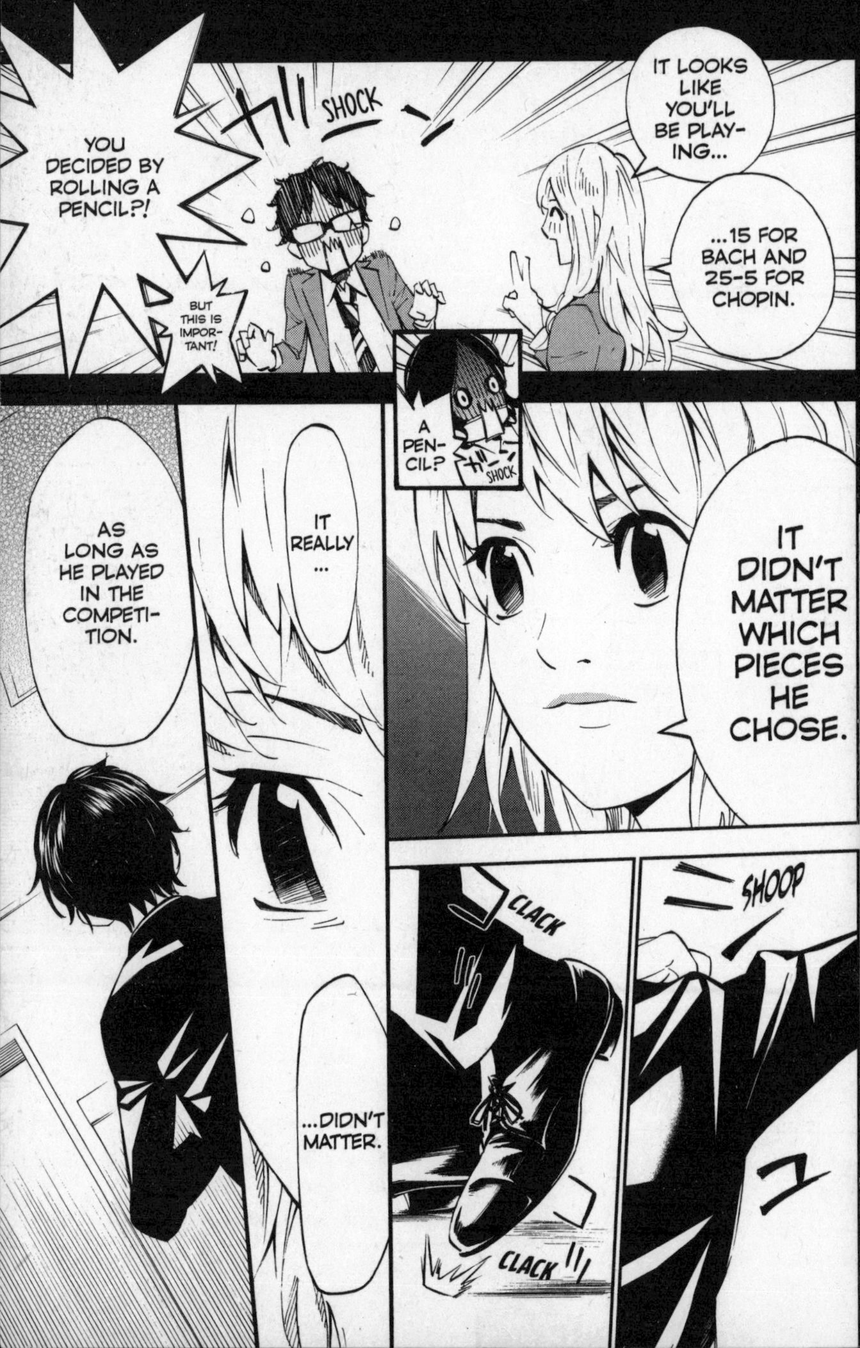
IT LOOKS LIKE YOU'LL BE PLAY-ING...
...15 FOR BACH AND 25-5 FOR CHOPIN.
SHOCK
YOU DECIDED BY ROLLING A PENCIL?!
BUT THIS IS IMPOR-TANT!
A PEN-CIL?
SHOCK
IT DIDN'T MATTER WHICH PIECES HE CHOSE.
SHOOP
CLACK
CLACK
IT REALLY ...
AS LONG AS HE PLAYED IN THE COMPETI-TION.
...DIDN'T MATTER.

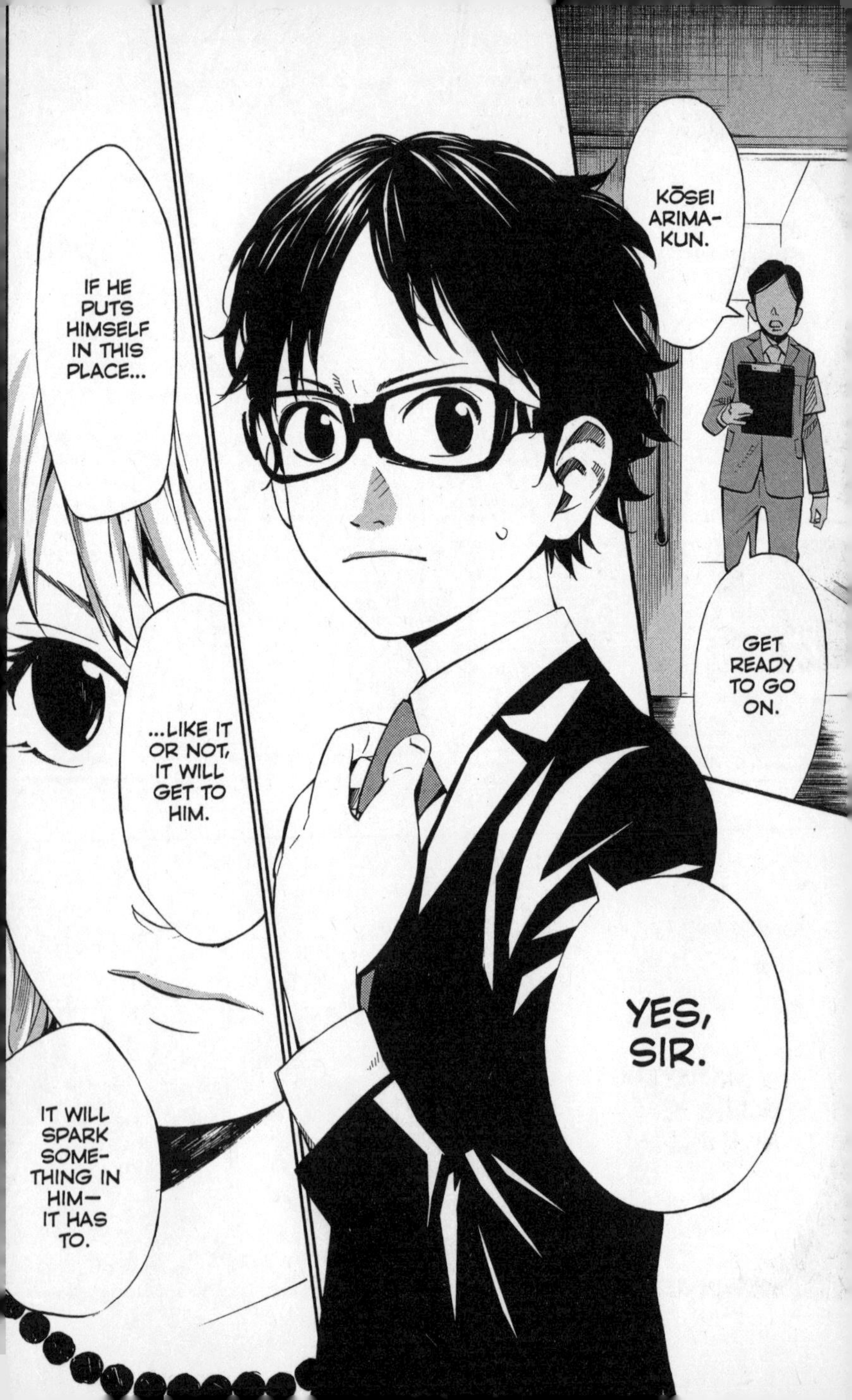
KŌSEI ARIMA-KUN.
GET READY TO GO ON.
YES, SIR.
IF HE PUTS HIMSELF IN THIS PLACE...
...LIKE IT OR NOT, IT WILL GET TO HIM.
IT WILL SPARK SOME-THING IN HIM—IT HAS TO.

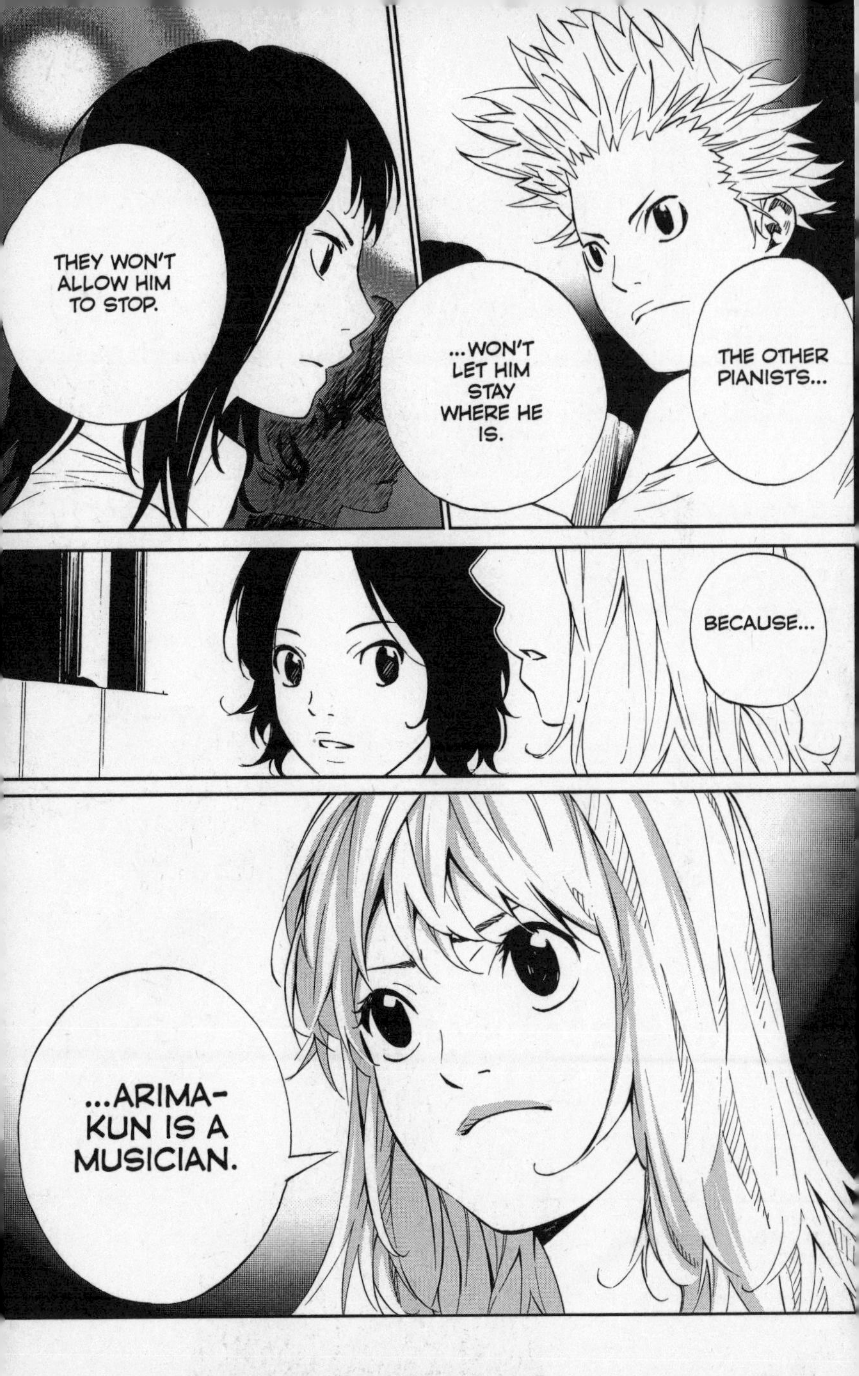
THE OTHER PIANISTS...
...WON'T LET HIM STAY WHERE HE IS.
THEY WON'T ALLOW HIM TO STOP.
BECAUSE...
...ARIMA-KUN IS A MUSICIAN.

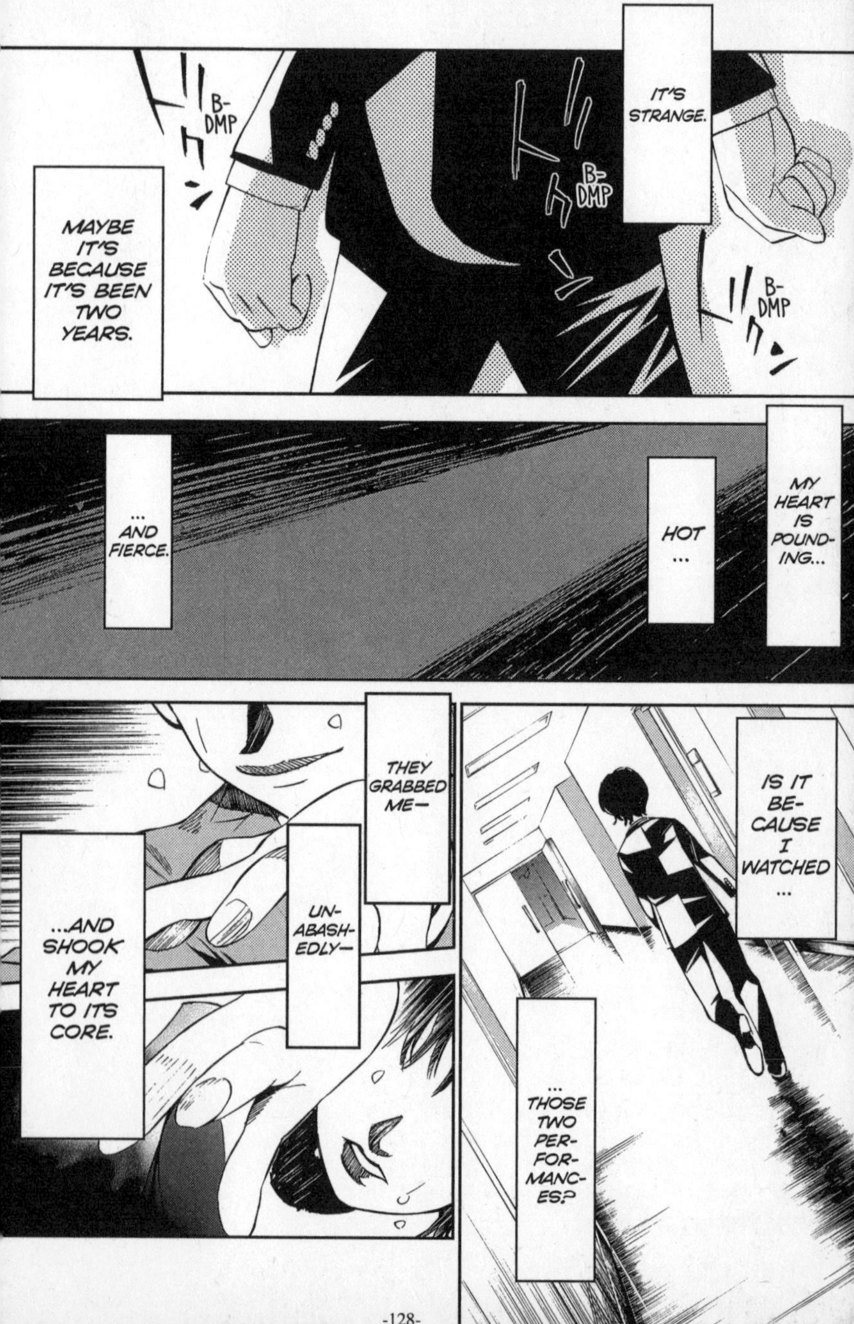
IT'S STRANGE.
B-DMP
B-DMP
B-DMP
MAYBE IT'S BECAUSE IT'S BEEN TWO YEARS.
MY HEART IS POUNDING...
HOT ...
... AND FIERCE.
IS IT BECAUSE I WATCHED ...
... THOSE TWO PERFORMANCES?
THEY GRABBED ME—
UNABASHEDLY—
...AND SHOOK MY HEART TO ITS CORE.

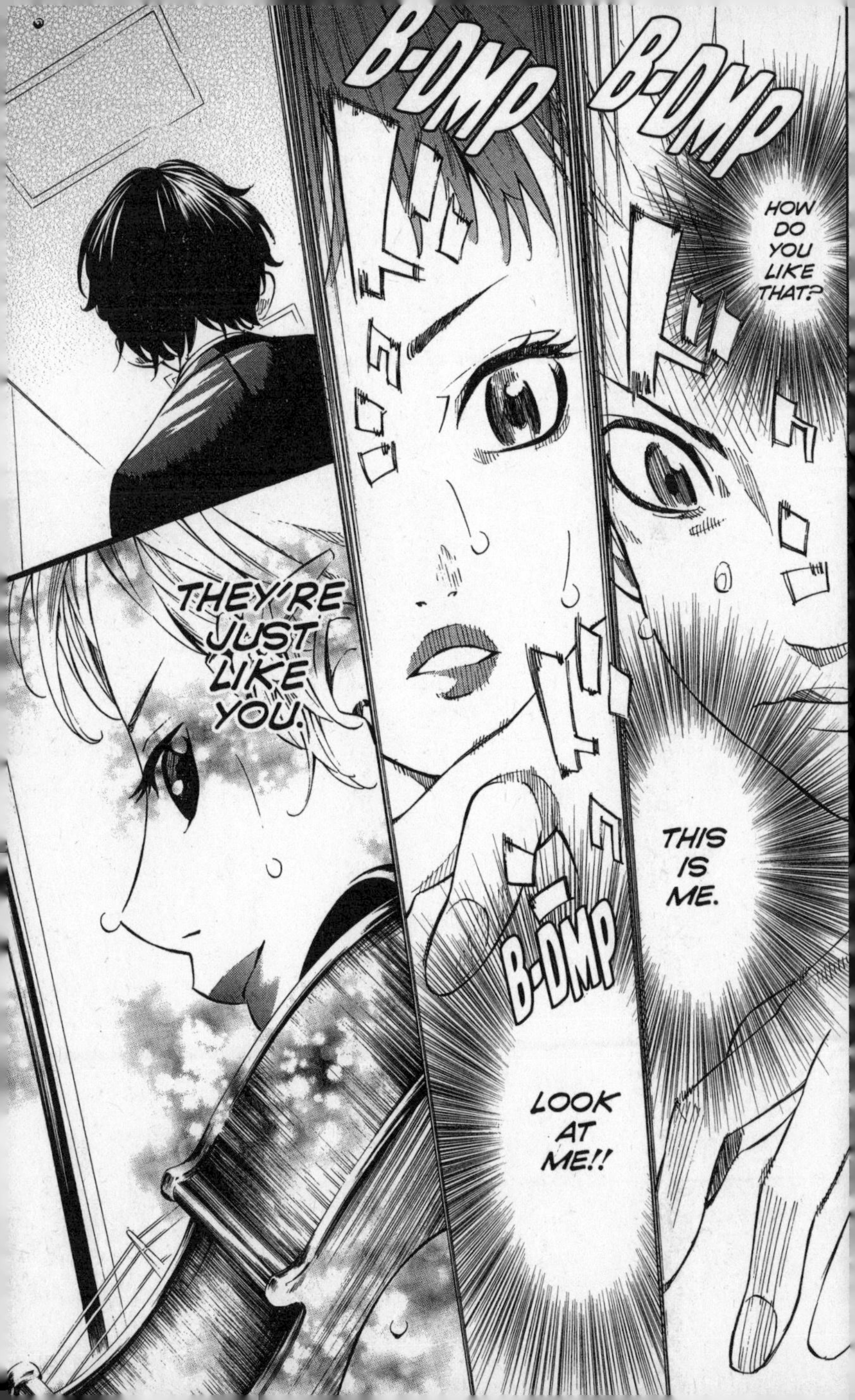

B-DMP B-DMP
HOW DO YOU LIKE THAT?
THIS IS ME.
LOOK AT ME!!
B-DMP
THEY'RE JUST LIKE YOU.

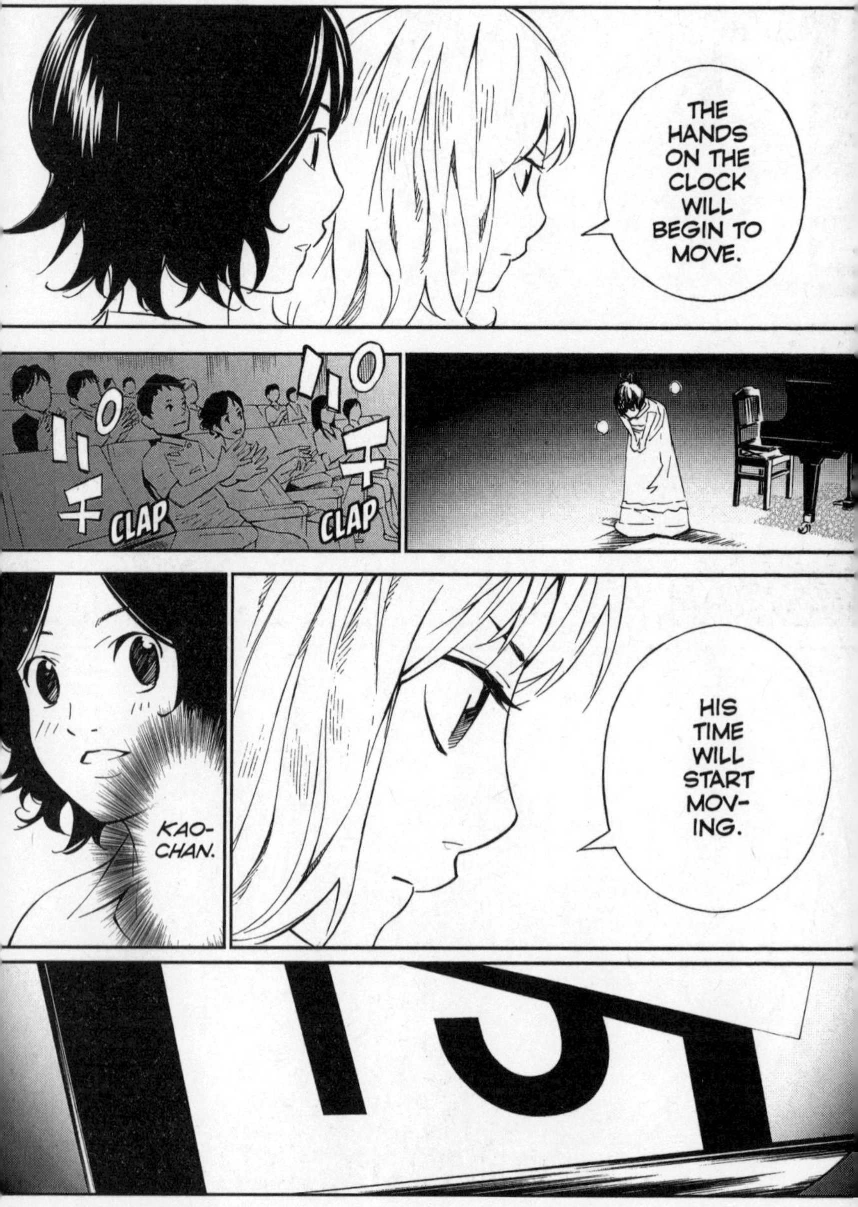
THE HANDS ON THE CLOCK WILL BEGIN TO MOVE.
CLAP
CLAP
HIS TIME WILL START MOV-ING.
KAO-CHAN.

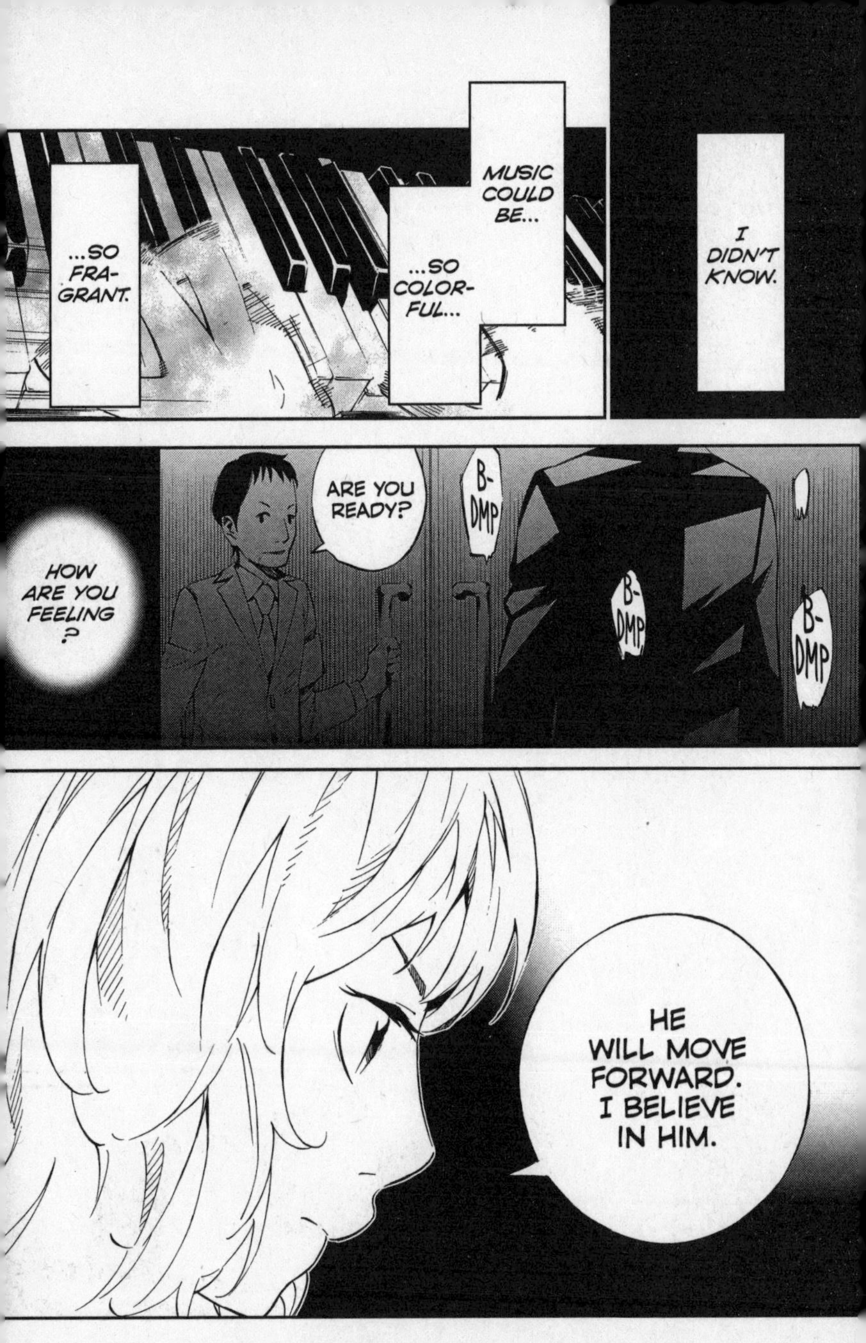
I DIDN'T KNOW.
MUSIC COULD BE...
...SO COLORFUL...
...SO FRAGRANT.
B-DMP
B-DMP
ARE YOU READY?
B-DMP
HOW ARE YOU FEELING?
HE WILL MOVE FORWARD. I BELIEVE IN HIM.

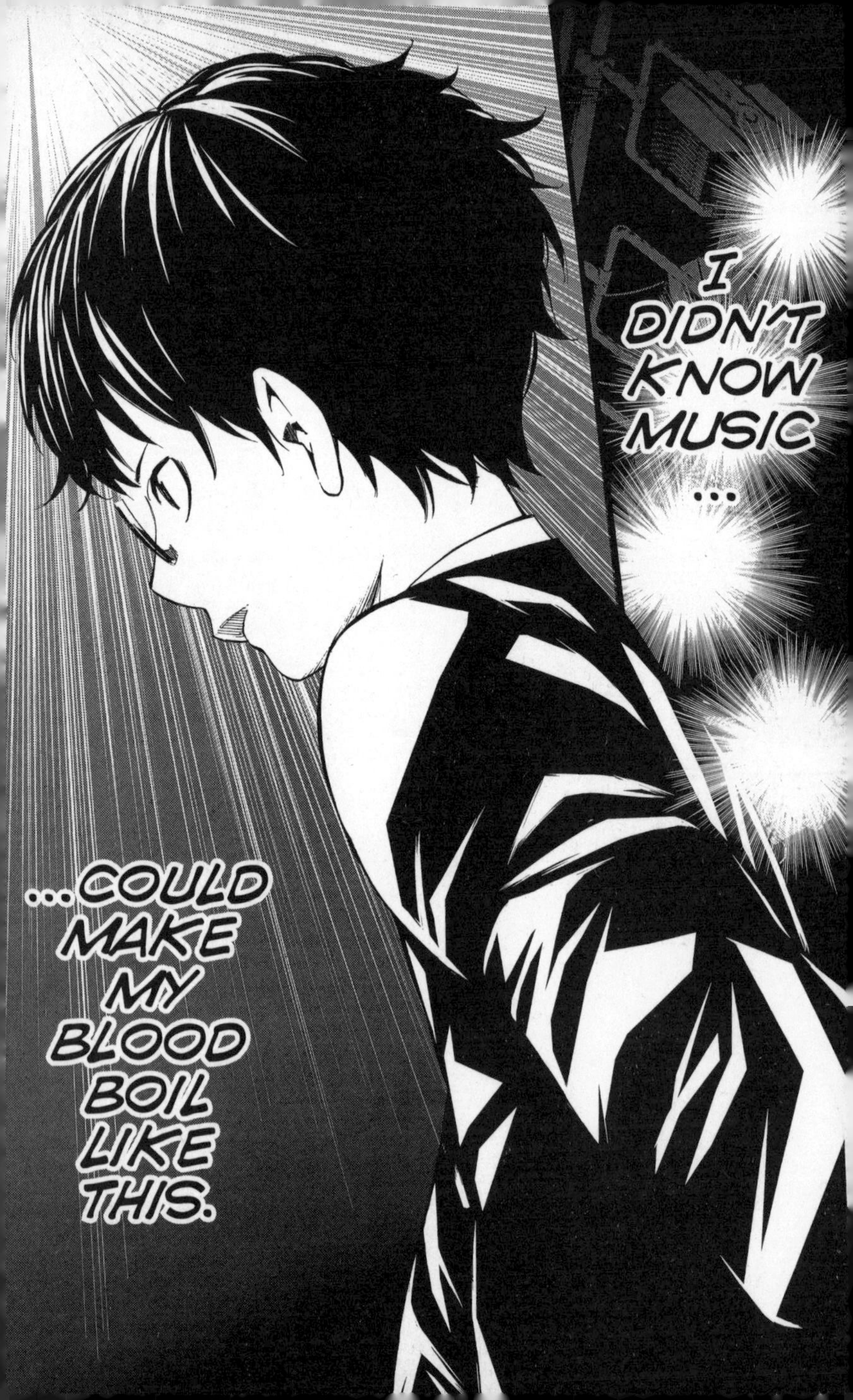
I DIDN'T KNOW MUSIC...
...COULD MAKE MY BLOOD BOIL LIKE THIS.

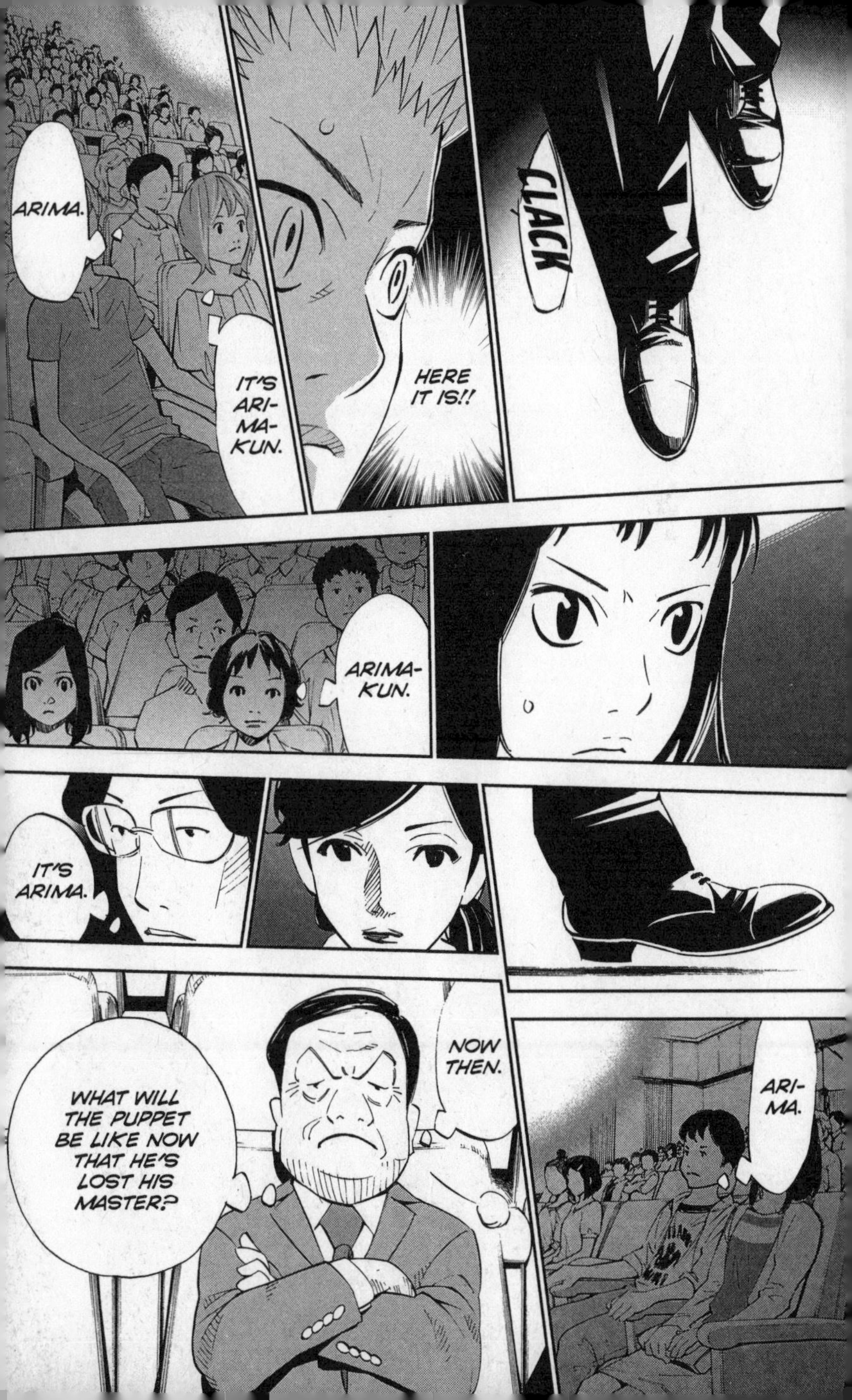
CLACK
HERE IT IS!!
IT'S ARI-MA-KUN.
ARIMA.
ARIMA-KUN.
IT'S ARIMA.
ARI-MA.
NOW THEN.
WHAT WILL THE PUPPET BE LIKE NOW THAT HE'S LOST HIS MASTER?

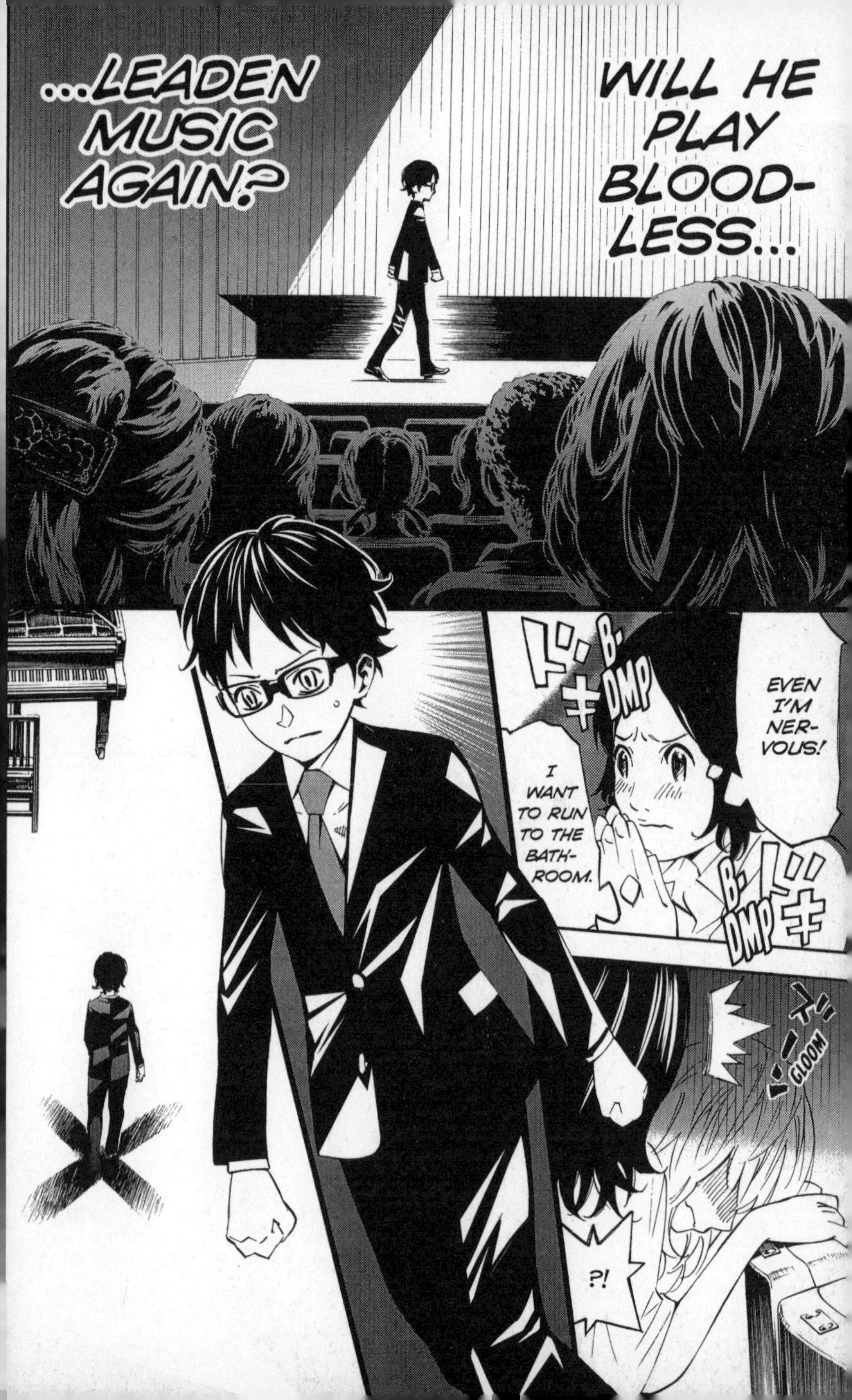
WILL HE PLAY BLOOD-LESS...
...LEADEN MUSIC AGAIN?
B-DMP
EVEN I'M NER-VOUS!
I WANT TO RUN TO THE BATH-ROOM.
B-DMP
GLOOM
?!

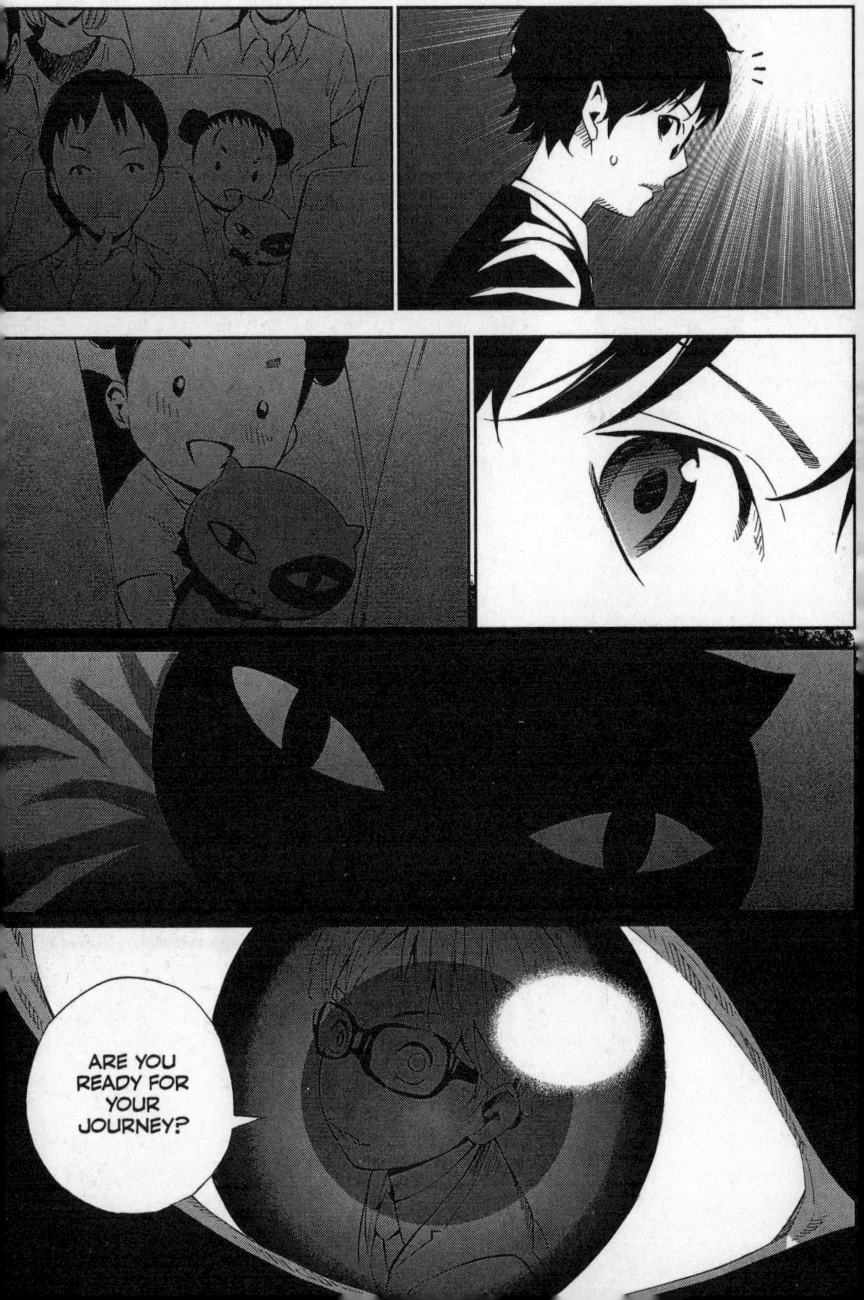
ARE YOU READY FOR YOUR JOURNEY?

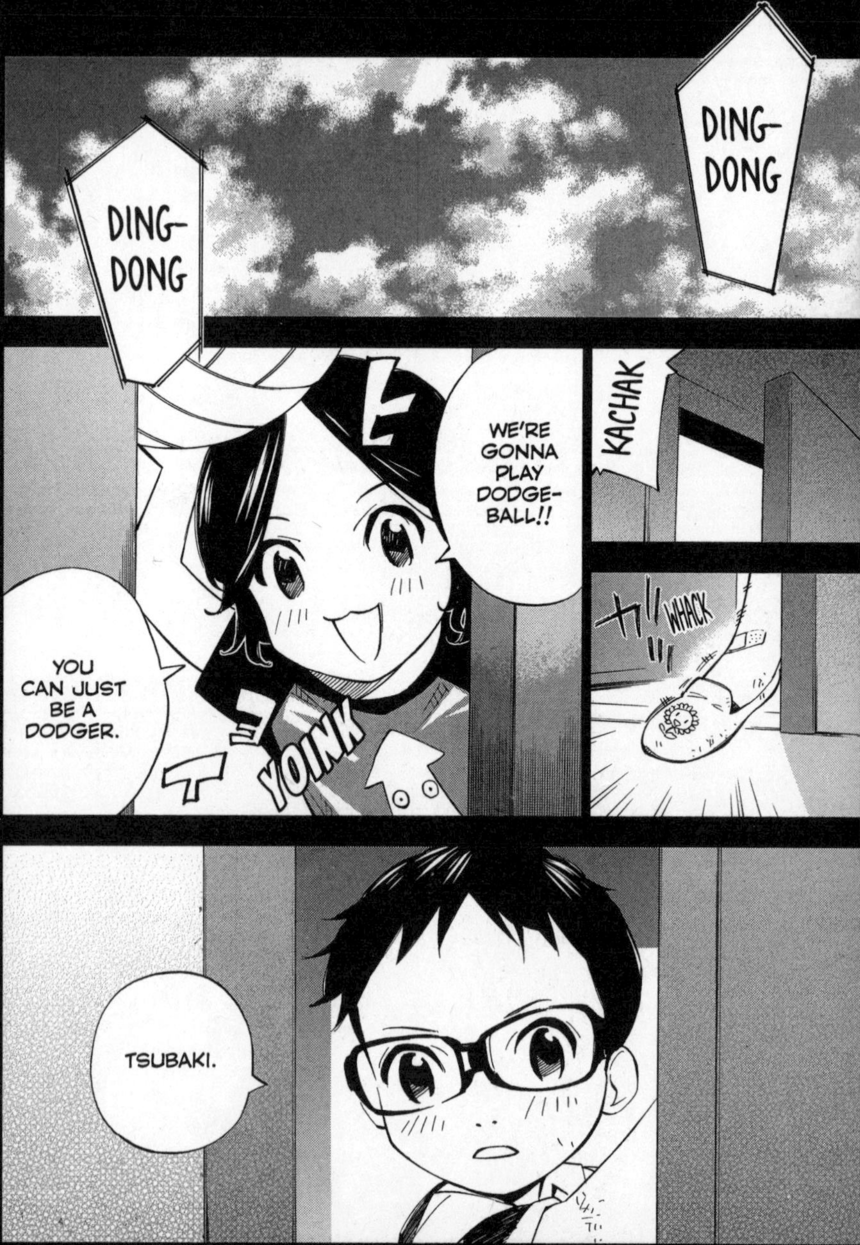
DING-DONG
DING-DONG
KACHAK
WHACK
WE'RE GONNA PLAY DODGE-BALL!!
YOINK
YOU CAN JUST BE A DODGER.
TSUBAKI.

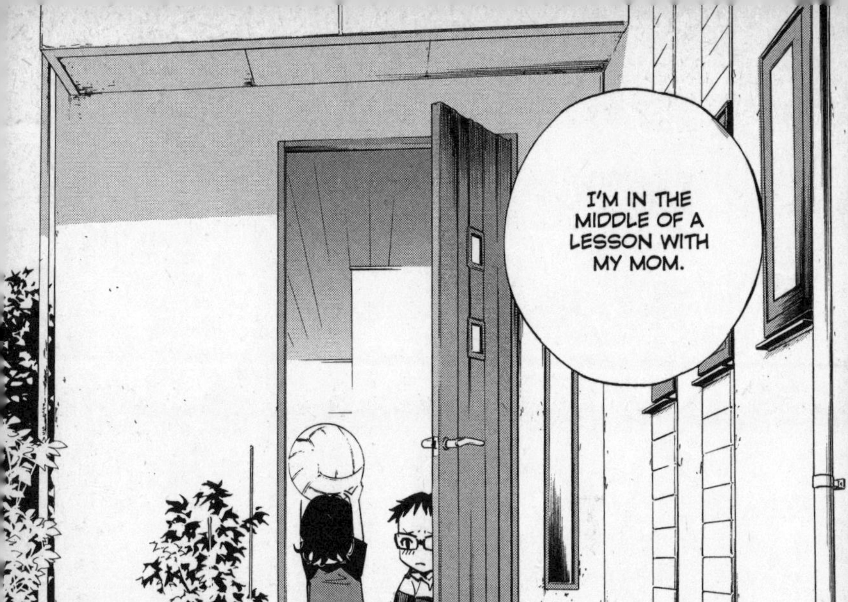
I'M IN THE MIDDLE OF A LESSON WITH MY MOM.

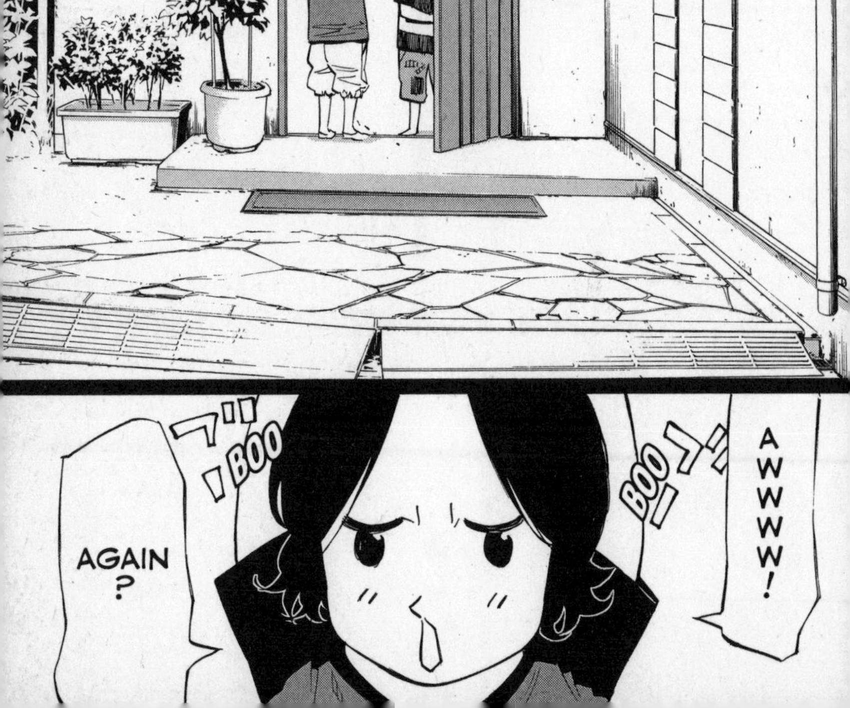
AWWWW!
BOO
BOO
AGAIN?

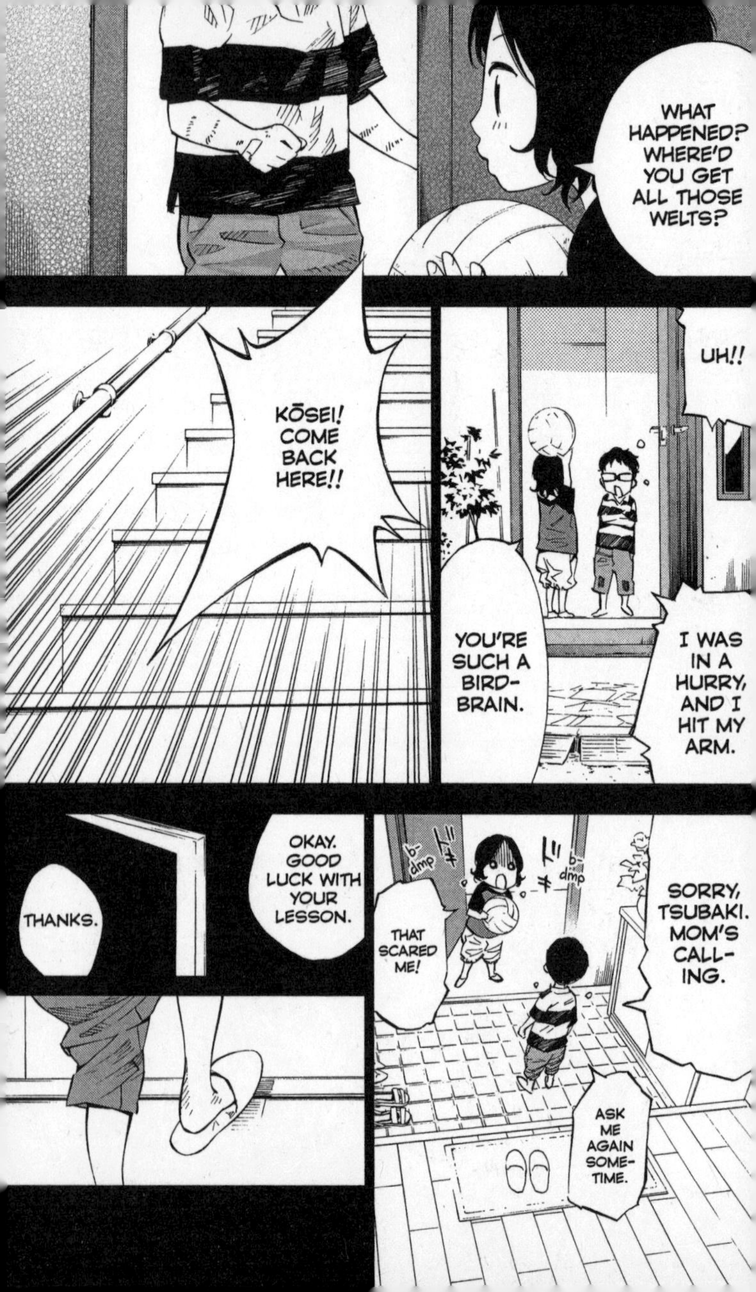
WHAT HAPPENED? WHERE'D YOU GET ALL THOSE WELTS?
UH!!
I WAS IN A HURRY, AND I HIT MY ARM.
YOU'RE SUCH A BIRD-BRAIN.
KŌSEI! COME BACK HERE!!
SORRY, TSUBAKI. MOM'S CALL-ING.
ASK ME AGAIN SOME-TIME.
b-dmp
b-dmp
THAT SCARED ME!
OKAY. GOOD LUCK WITH YOUR LESSON.
THANKS.

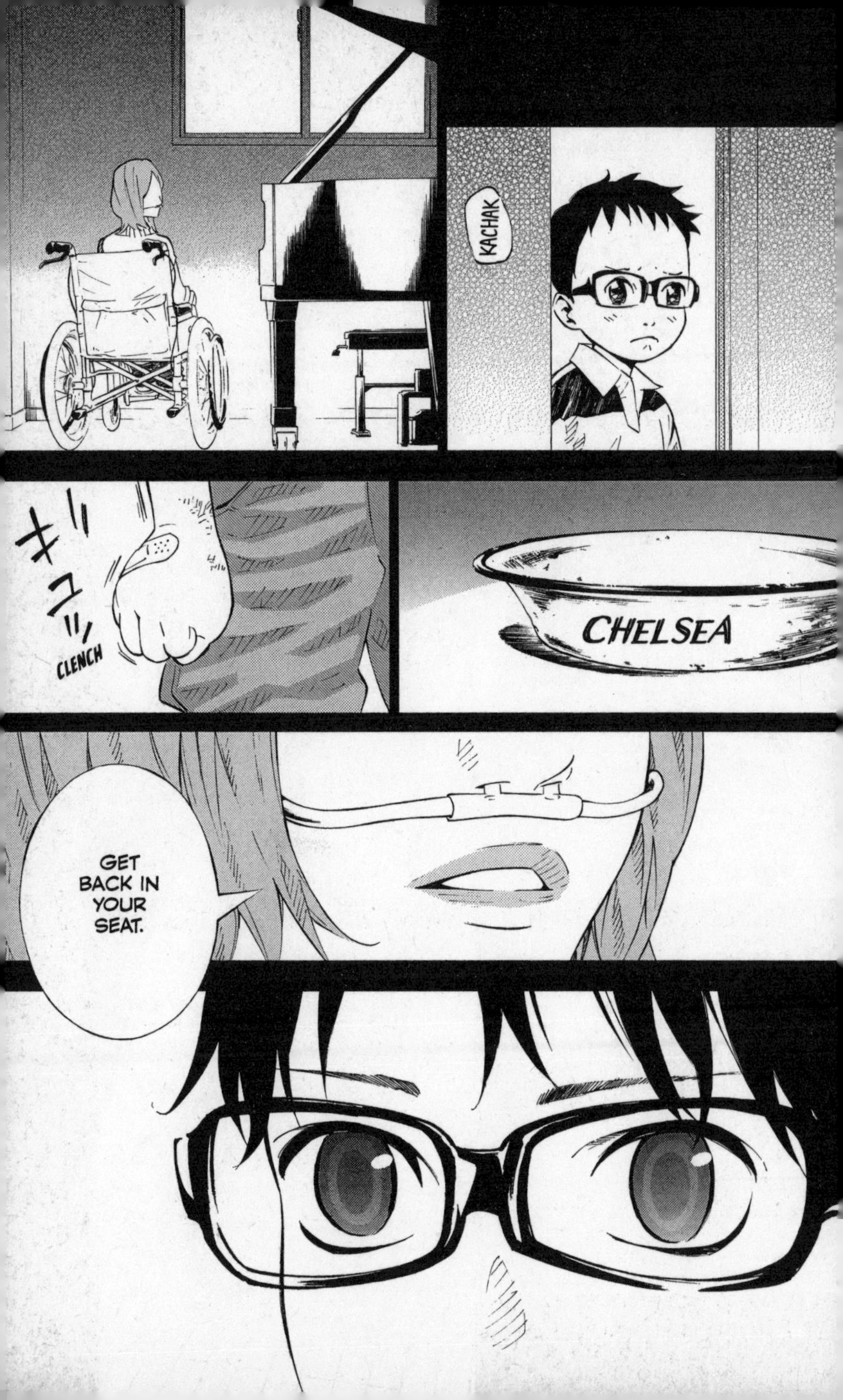
KACHAK
CHELSEA
キュッ
CLENCH
GET BACK IN YOUR SEAT.

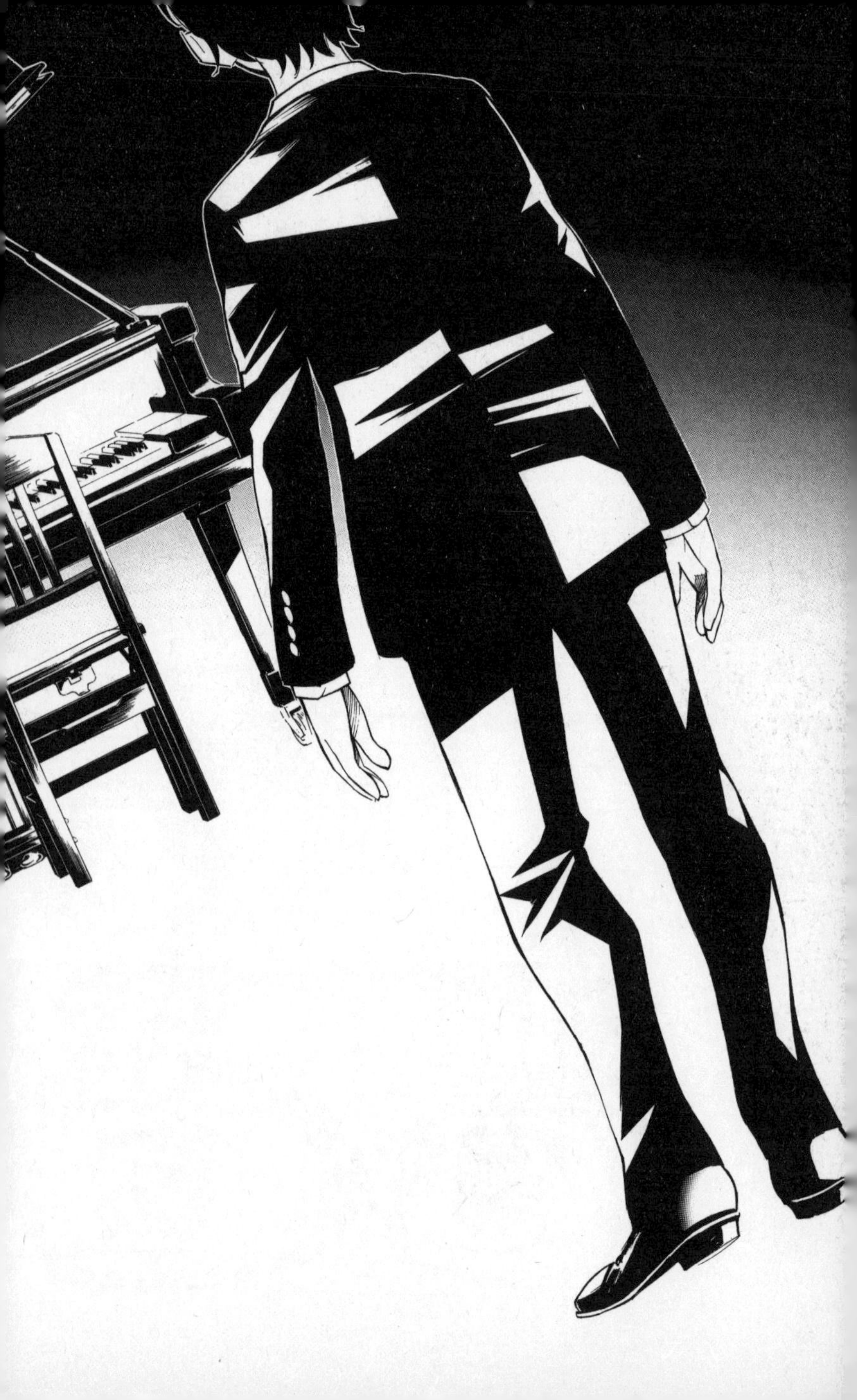

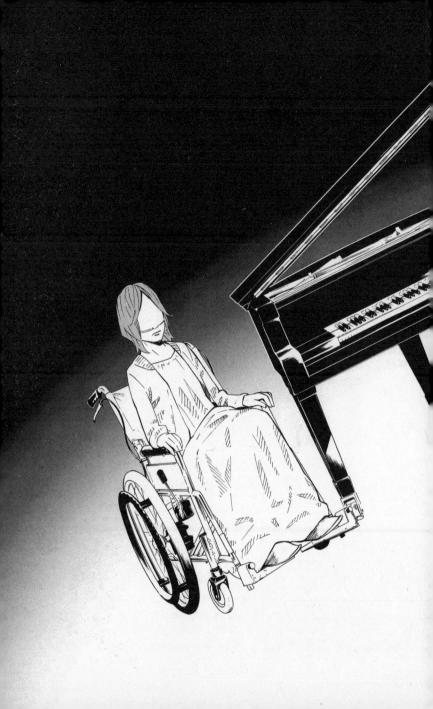

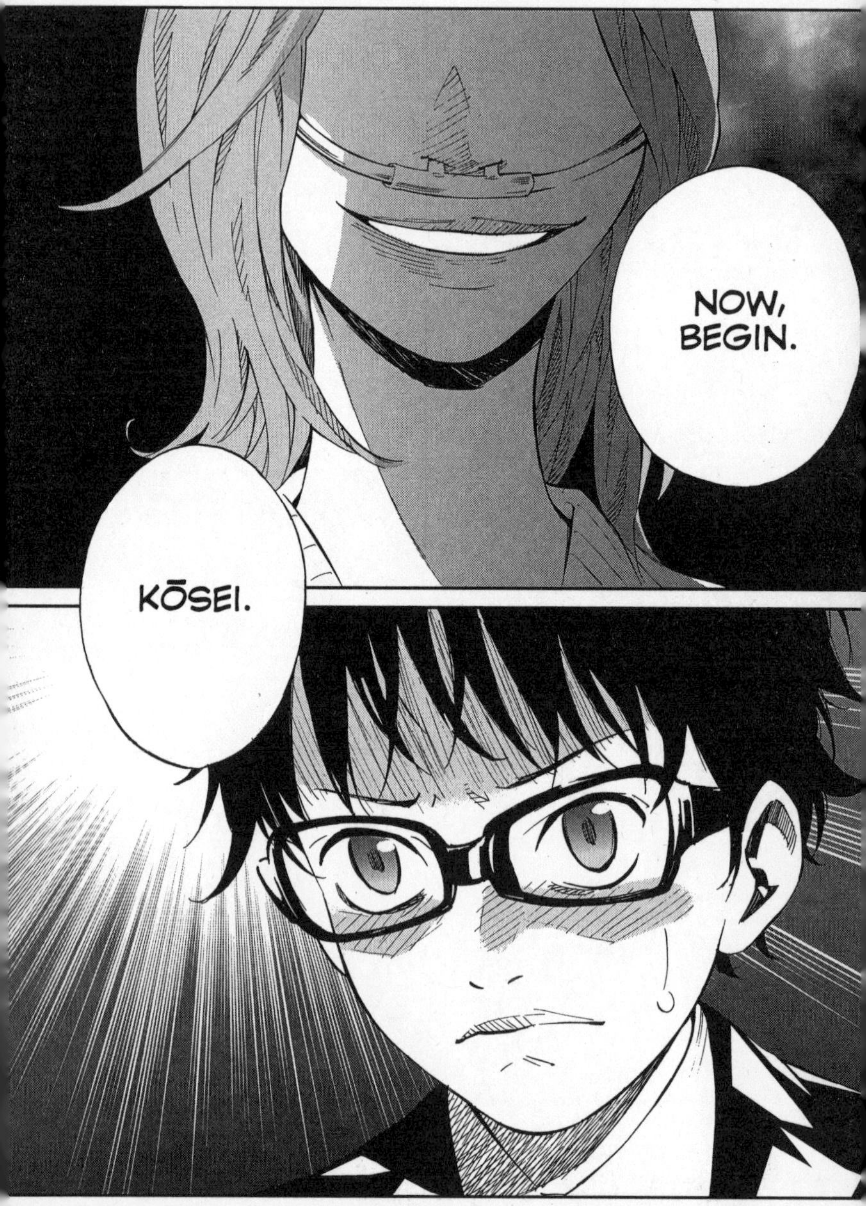
NOW, BEGIN.
KŌSEI.

RESONANCE / END

Your Lie in April

I met the girl under full-bloomed cherry blossoms, and my fate has begun to change.

Your Lie in April

I met the girl under full-bloomed cherry blossoms, and my fate has begun to change.

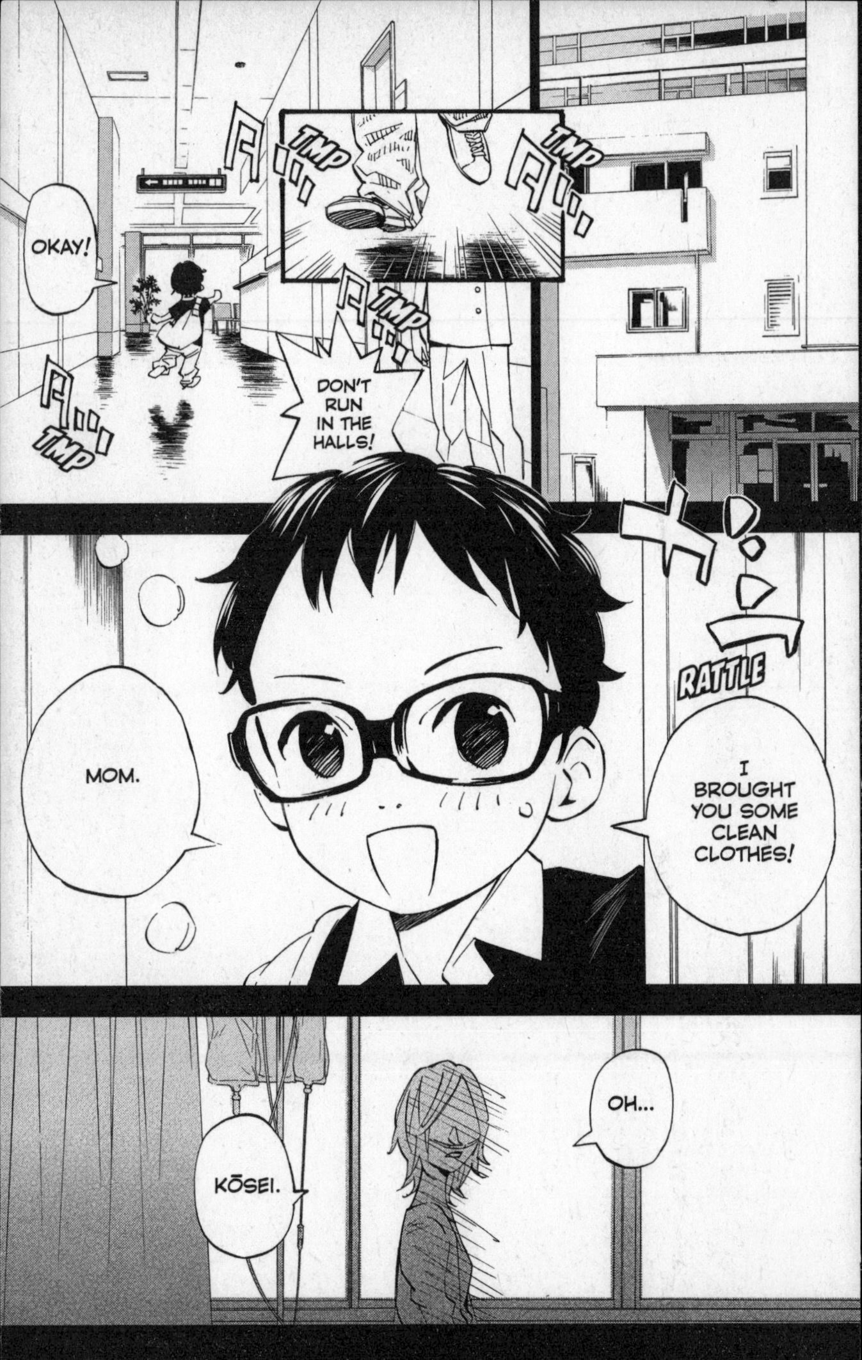
TMP
TMP
TMP
DON'T RUN IN THE HALLS!
OKAY!
TMP
RATTLE
I BROUGHT YOU SOME CLEAN CLOTHES!
MOM.
OH...
KŌSEI.

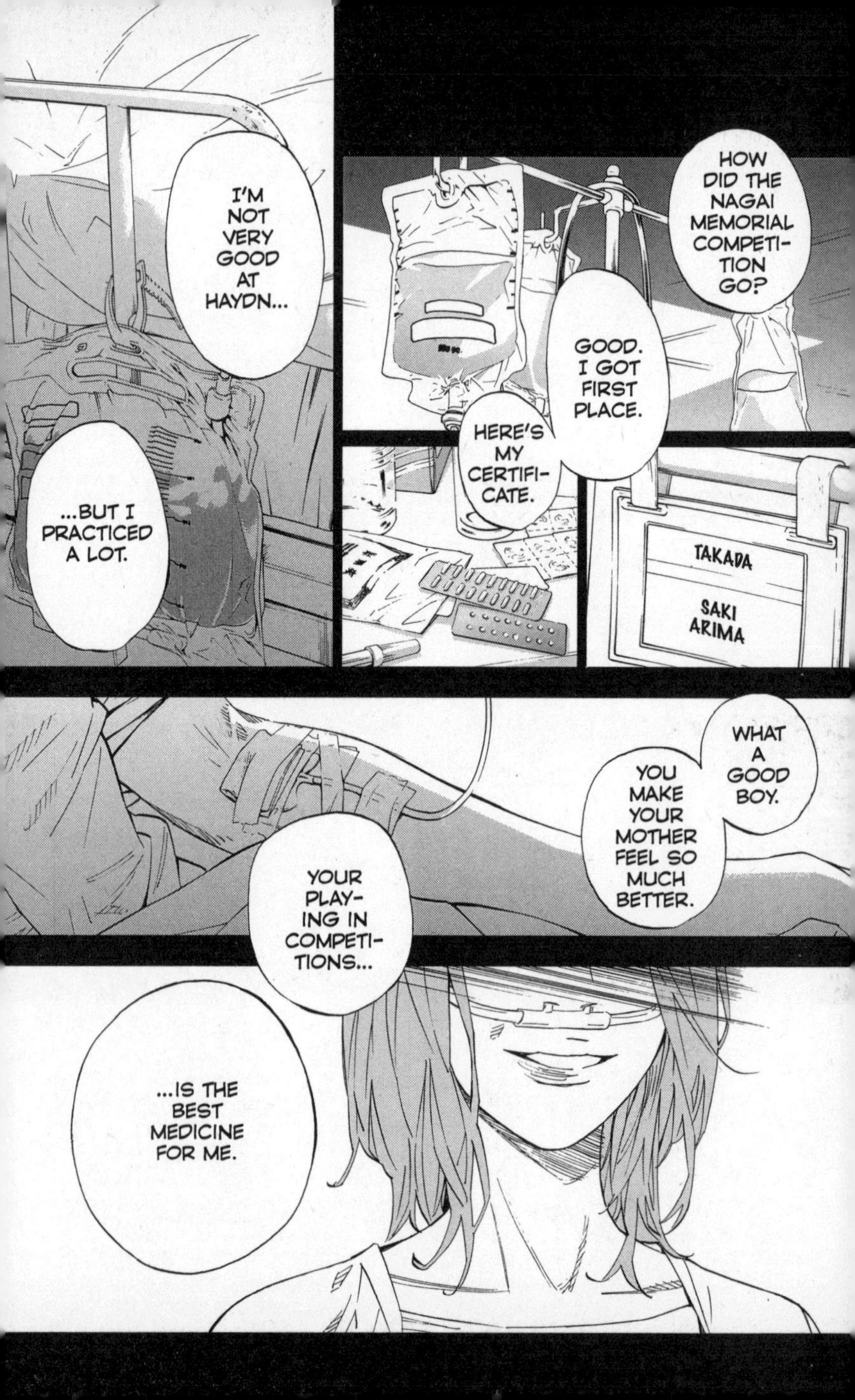
HOW DID THE NAGAI MEMORIAL COMPETITION GO?
GOOD. I GOT FIRST PLACE.
TAKADA
SAKI ARIMA
HERE'S MY CERTIFICATE.
I'M NOT VERY GOOD AT HAYDN...
...BUT I PRACTICED A LOT.
WHAT A GOOD BOY.
YOU MAKE YOUR MOTHER FEEL SO MUCH BETTER.
YOUR PLAYING IN COMPETITIONS...
...IS THE BEST MEDICINE FOR ME.

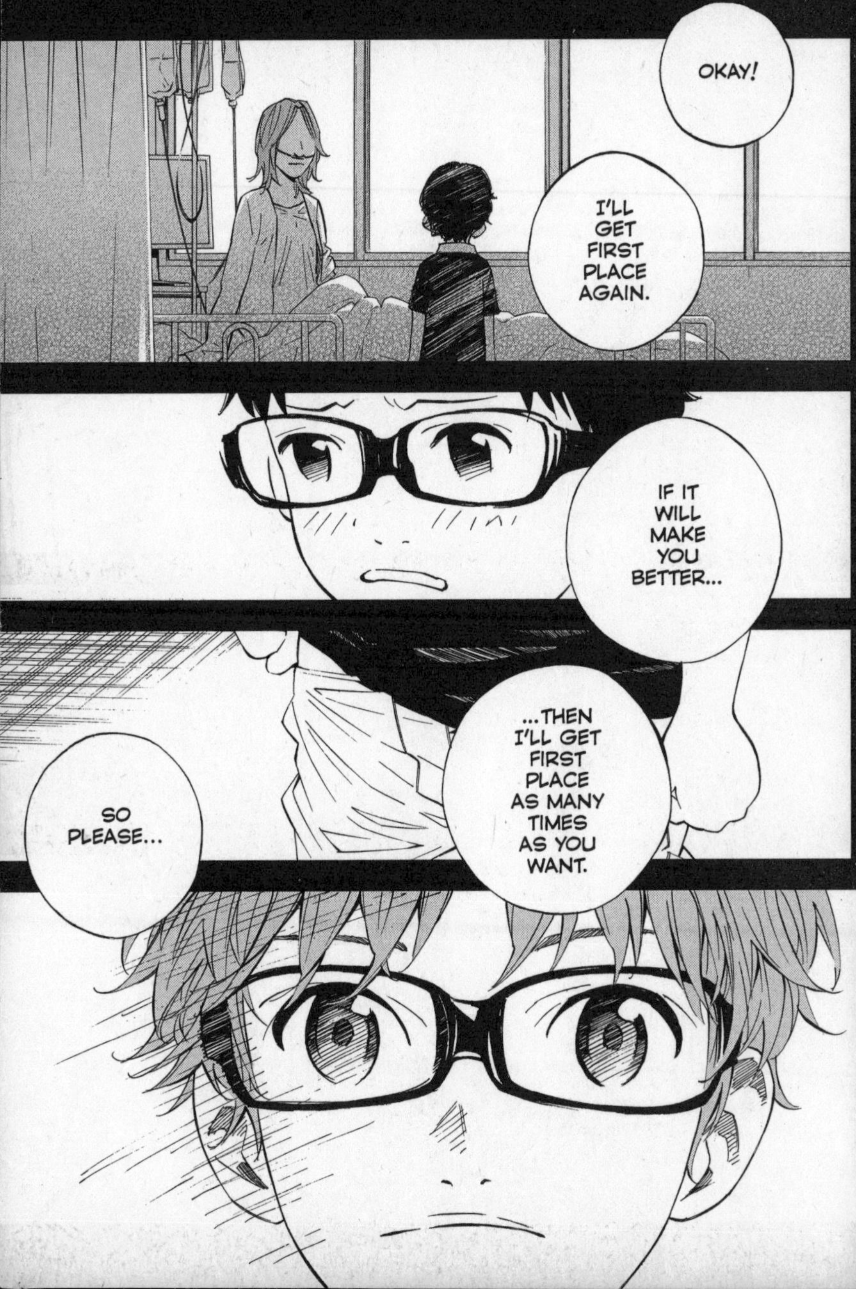
OKAY!
I'LL GET FIRST PLACE AGAIN.
IF IT WILL MAKE YOU BETTER...
...THEN I'LL GET FIRST PLACE AS MANY TIMES AS YOU WANT.
SO PLEASE...

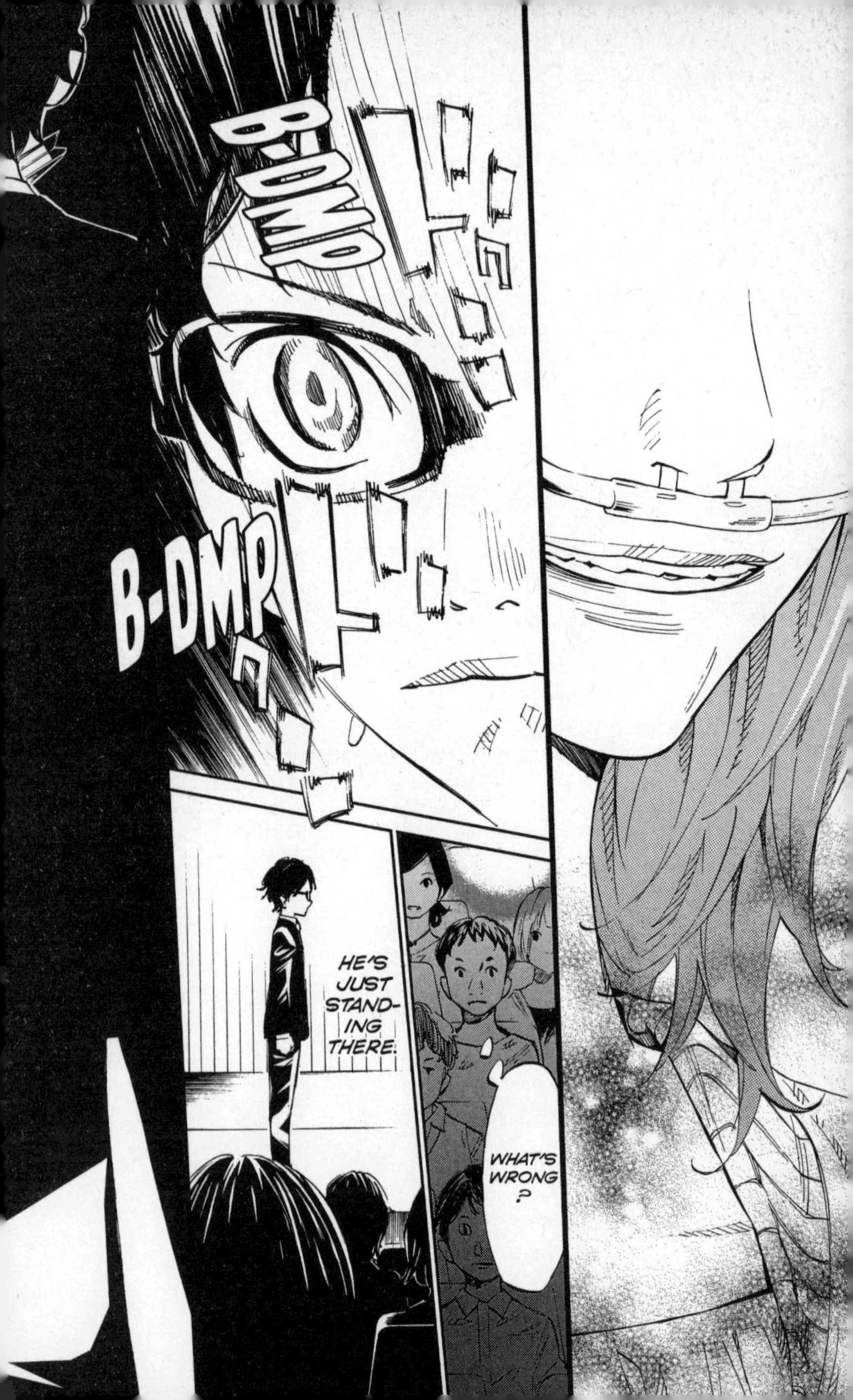
B-DMP
B-DMP
HE'S JUST STANDING THERE.
WHAT'S WRONG?

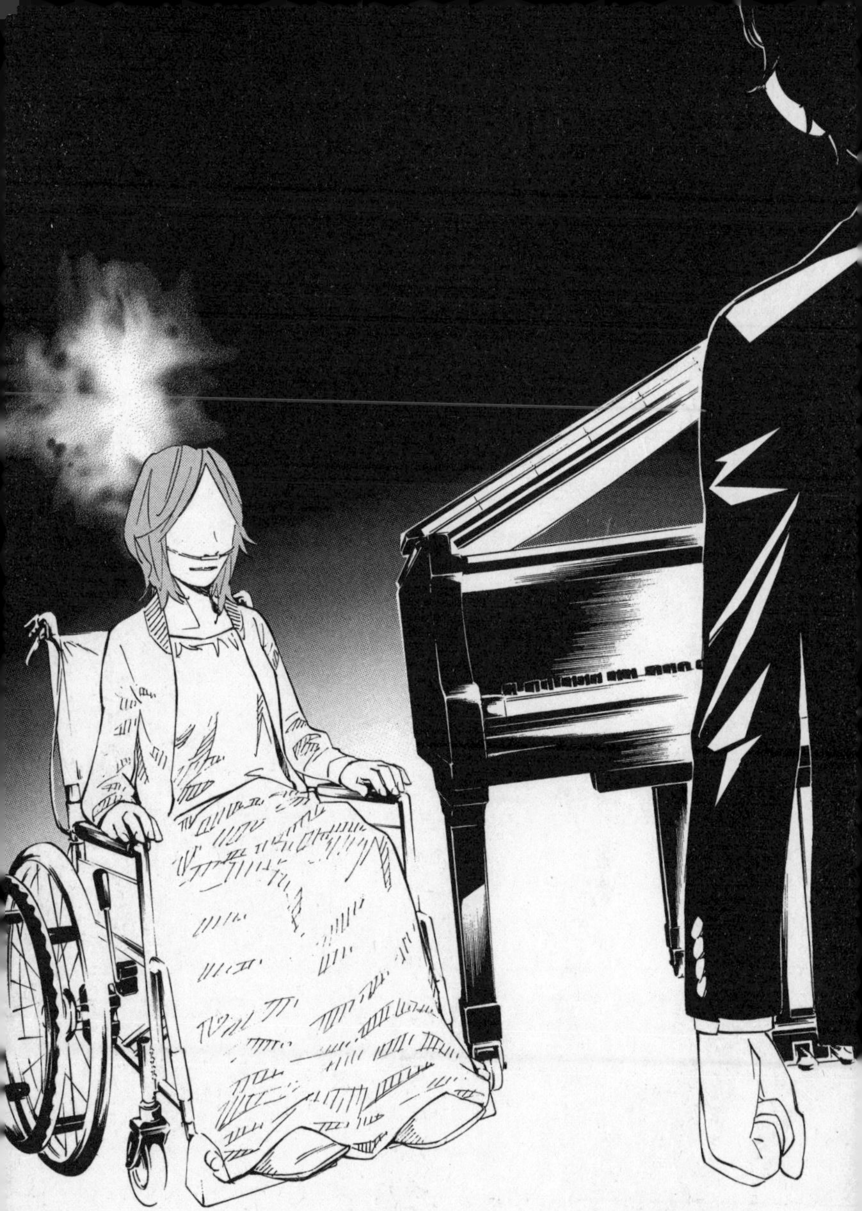

Chapter 16: Listen, Mama!

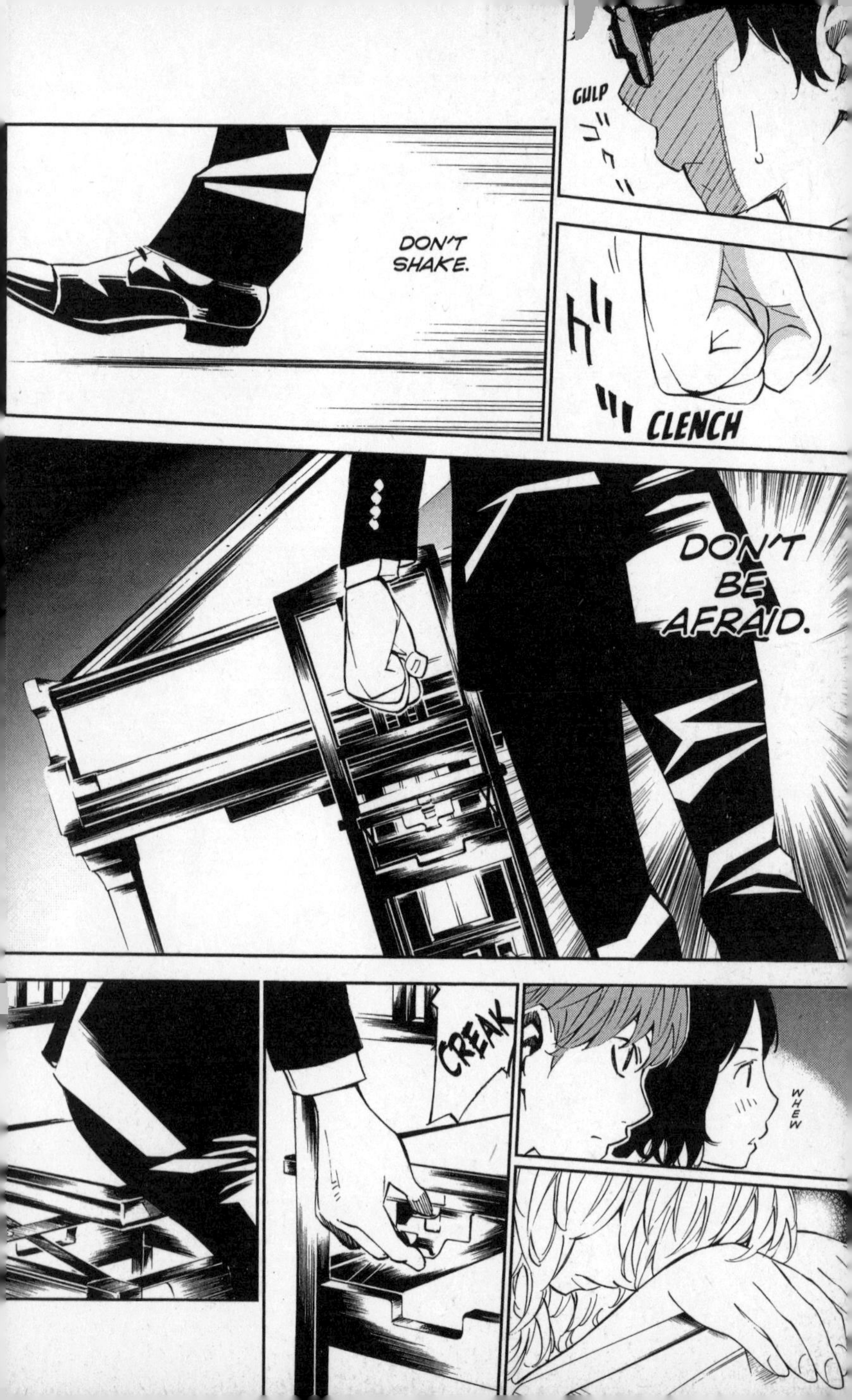
GULP
CLENCH
DON'T SHAKE.
DON'T BE AFRAID.
WHEW
CREAK

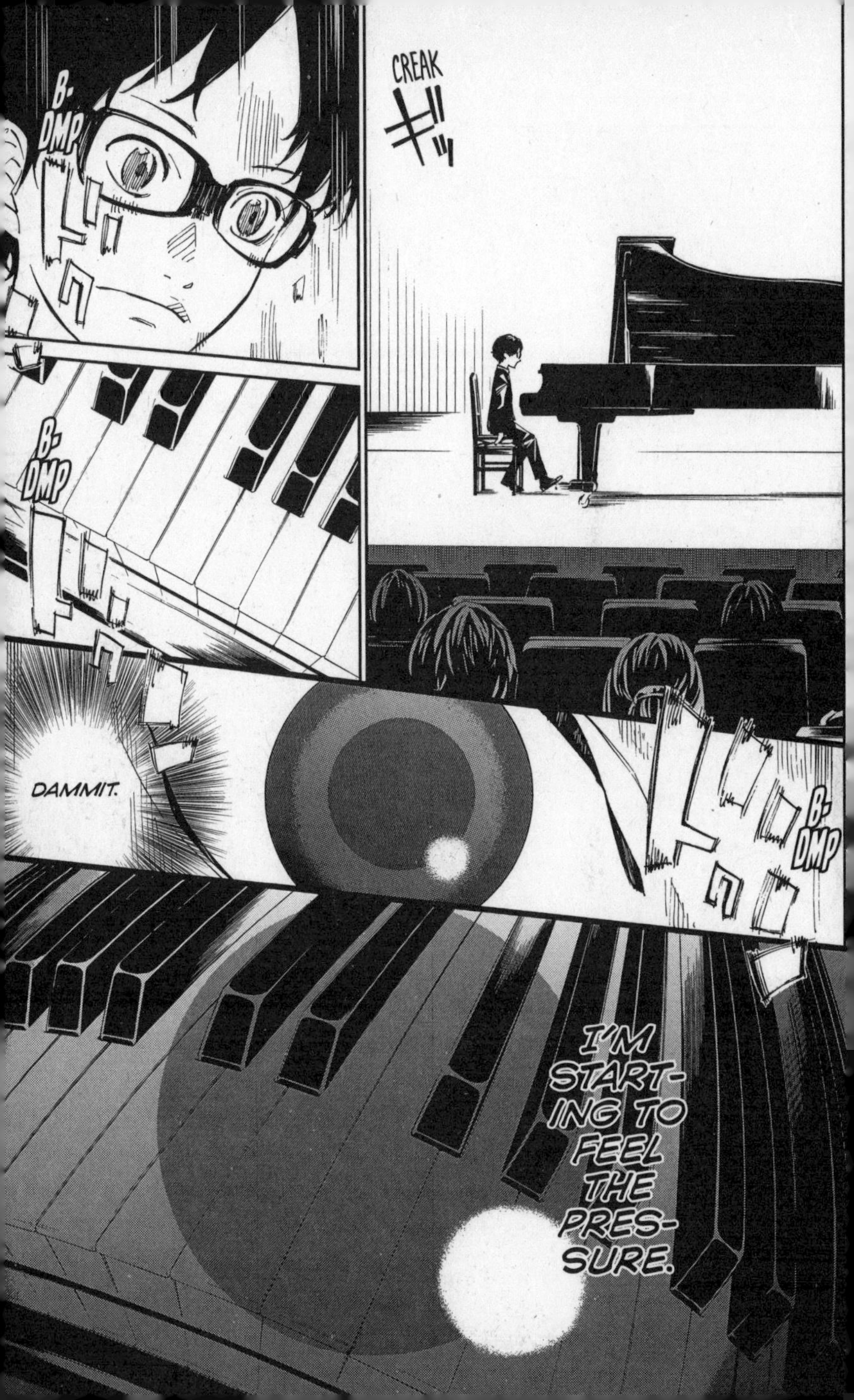
CREAK
ギッ
B-DMP
B-DMP
B-DMP
DAMMIT.
I'M STARTING TO FEEL THE PRESSURE.

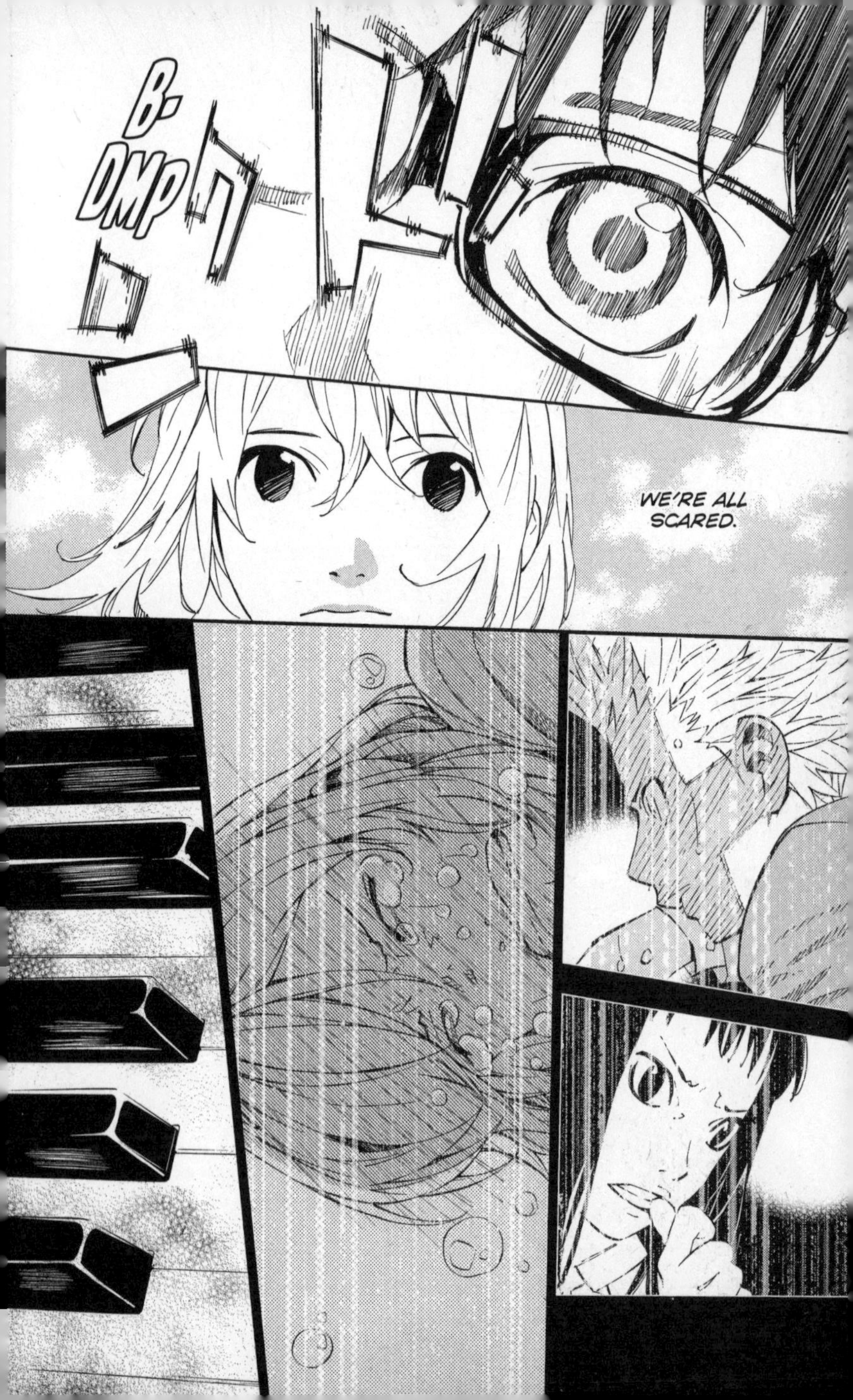
B-DMP
WE'RE ALL SCARED.

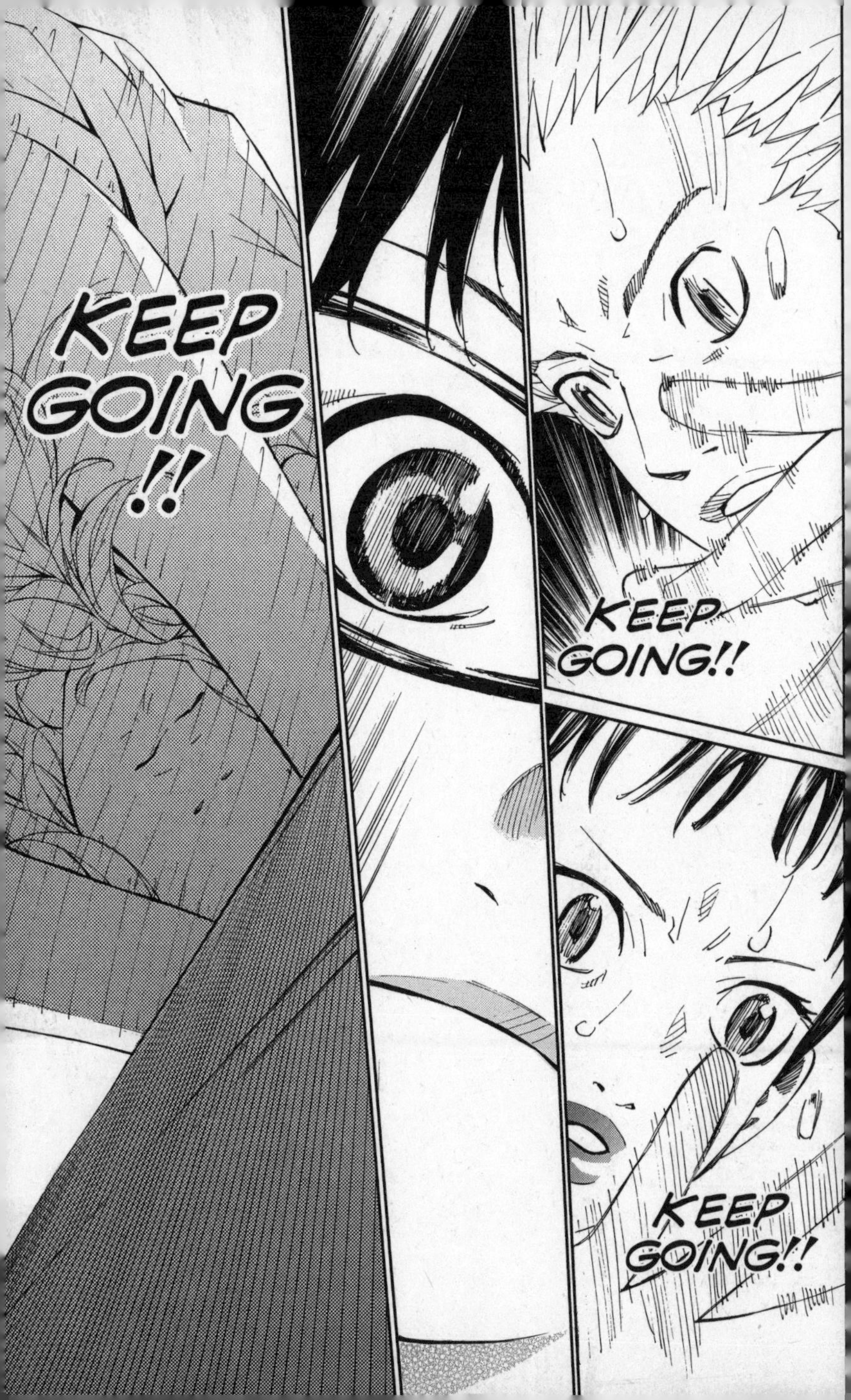
KEEP GOING!!
KEEP GOING!!
KEEP GOING!!

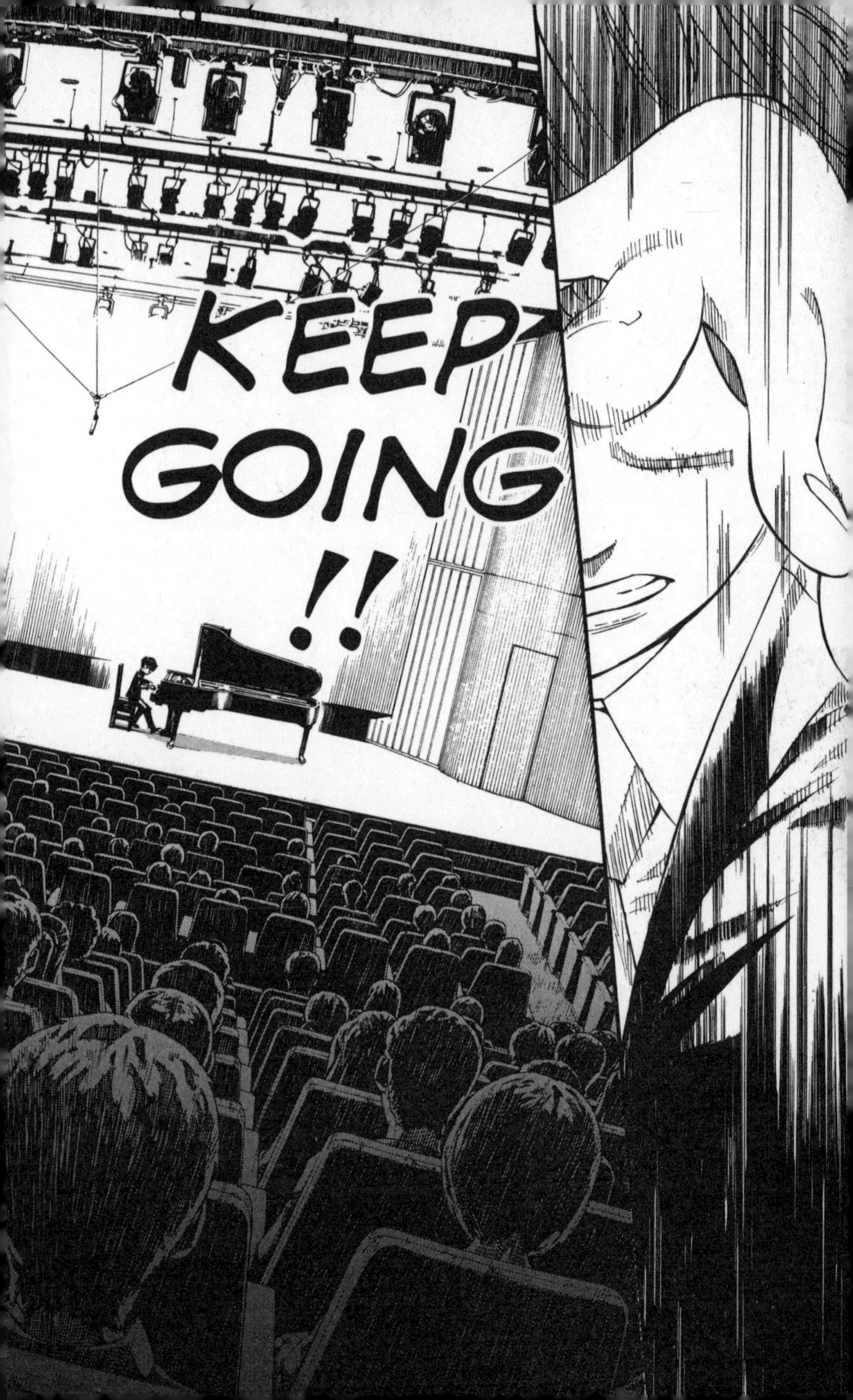
KEEP GOING !!

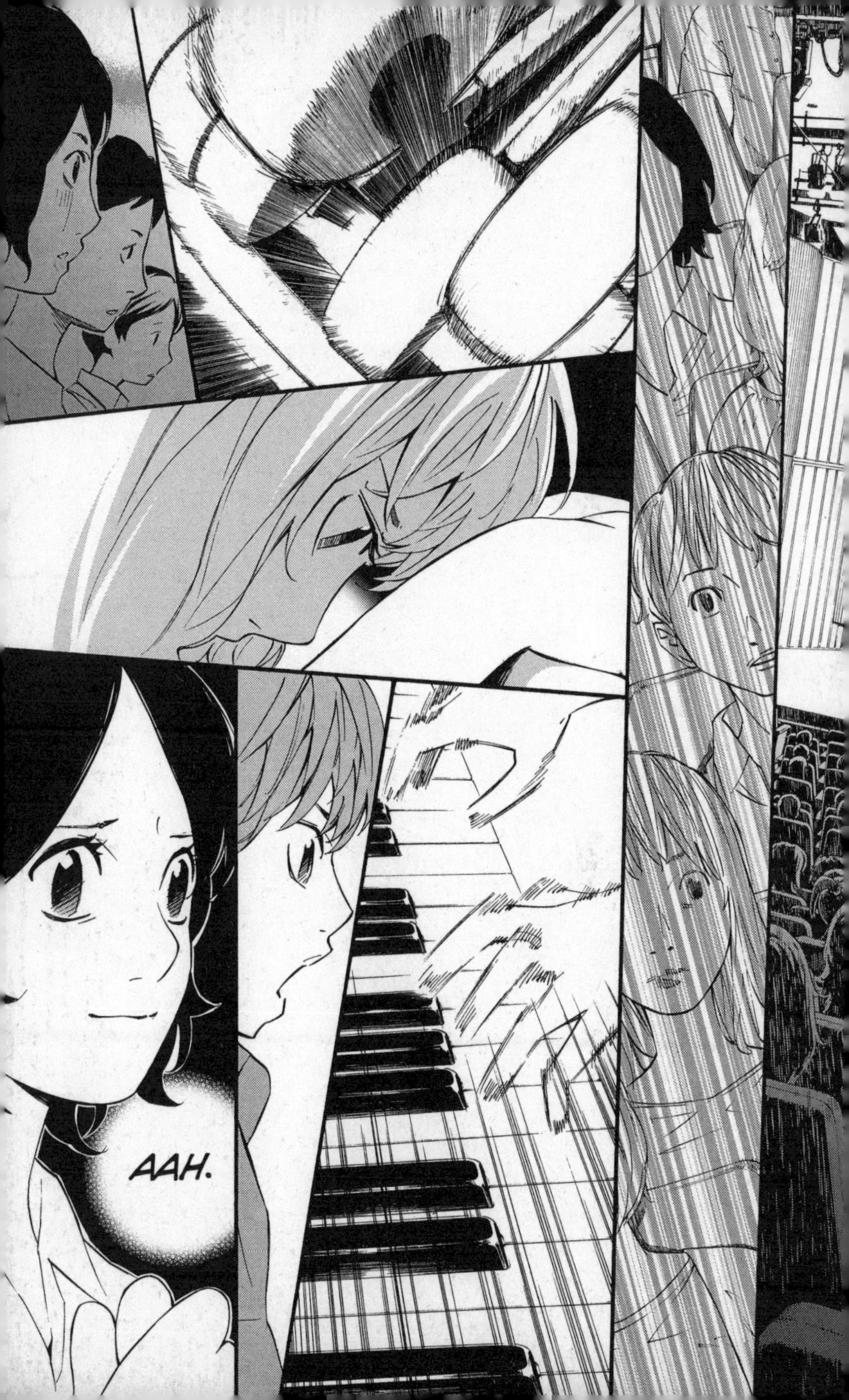
AAH.

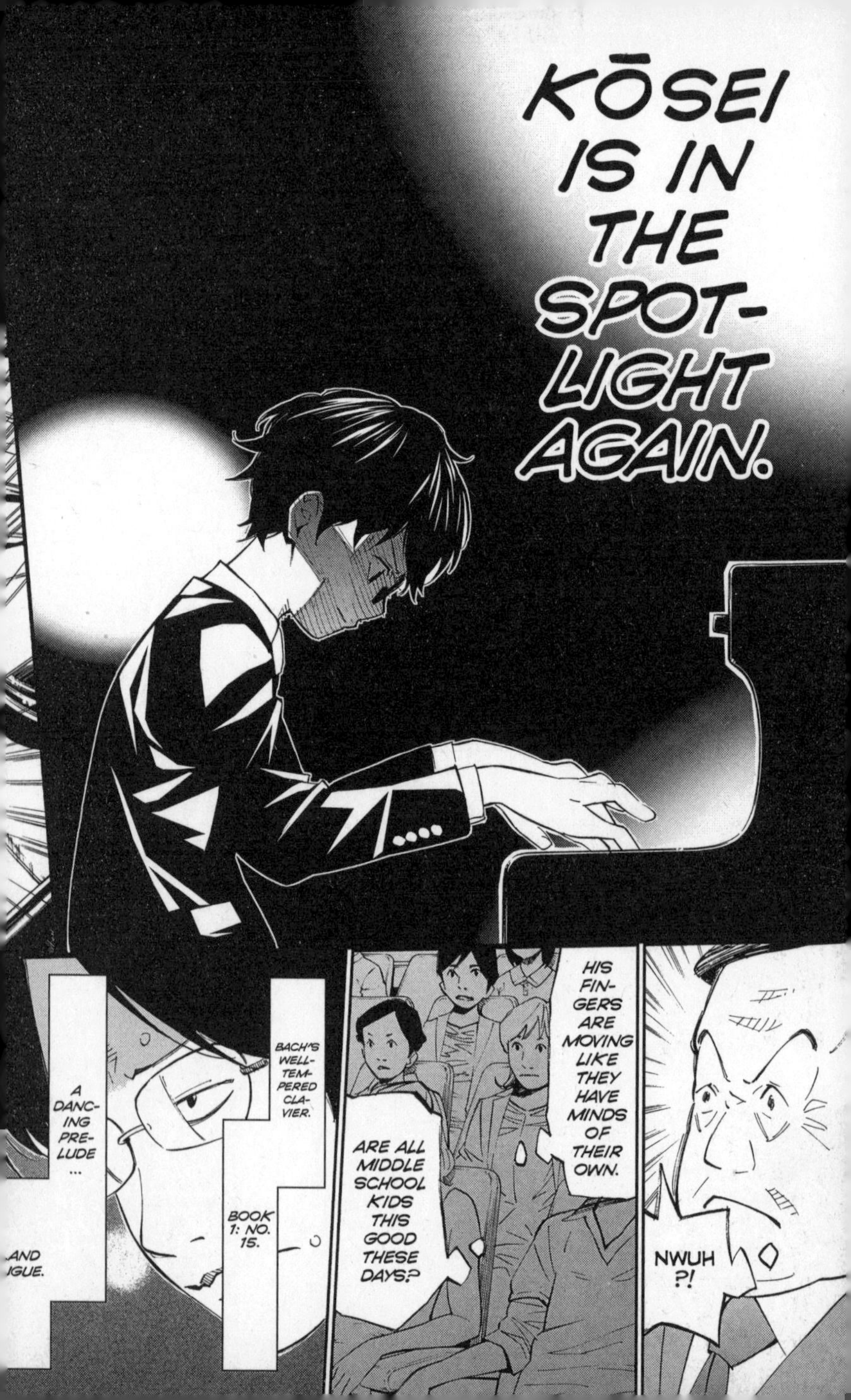
KŌSEI IS IN THE SPOT-LIGHT AGAIN.
NWUH ?!
HIS FINGERS ARE MOVING LIKE THEY HAVE MINDS OF THEIR OWN.
ARE ALL MIDDLE SCHOOL KIDS THIS GOOD THESE DAYS?
BACH'S WELL-TEMPERED CLAVIER.
BOOK 1: NO. 15.
A DANCING PRELUDE ...
AND IGUE.

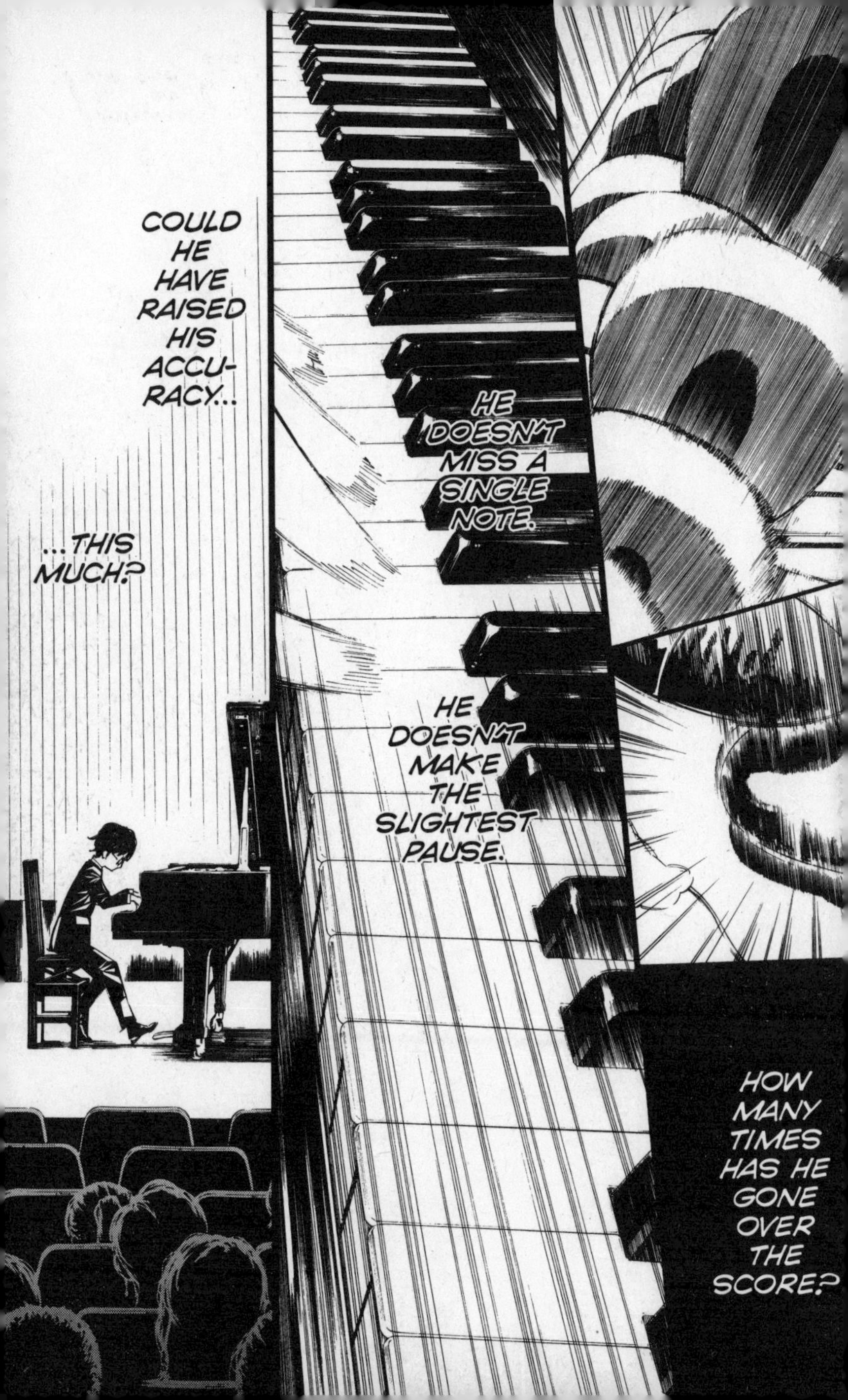
HOW MANY TIMES HAS HE GONE OVER THE SCORE?
HE DOESN'T MISS A SINGLE NOTE.
HE DOESN'T MAKE THE SLIGHTEST PAUSE.
COULD HE HAVE RAISED HIS ACCU-RACY...
...THIS MUCH?

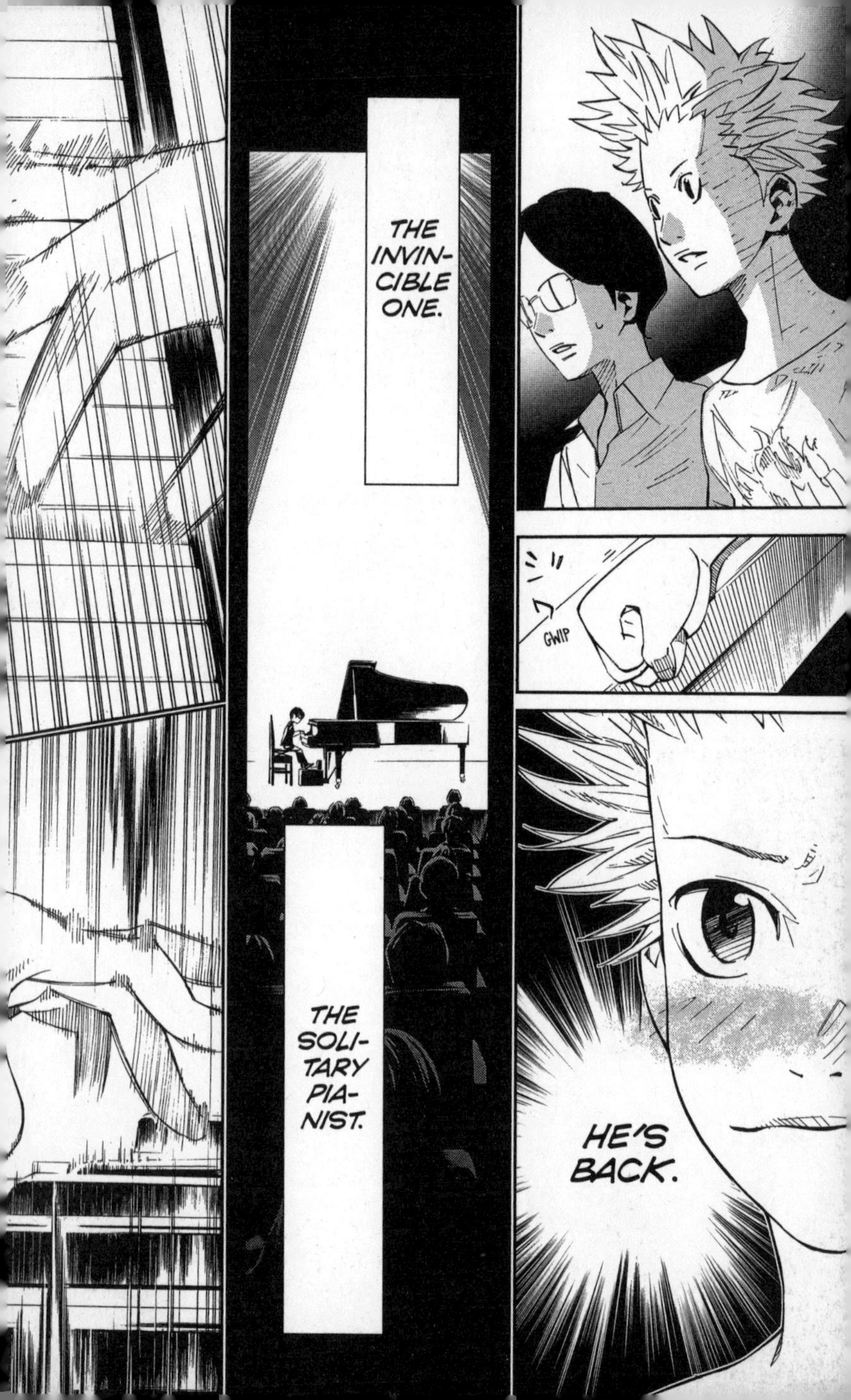
GWIP
HE'S BACK.
THE INVINCIBLE ONE.
THE SOLITARY PIANIST.

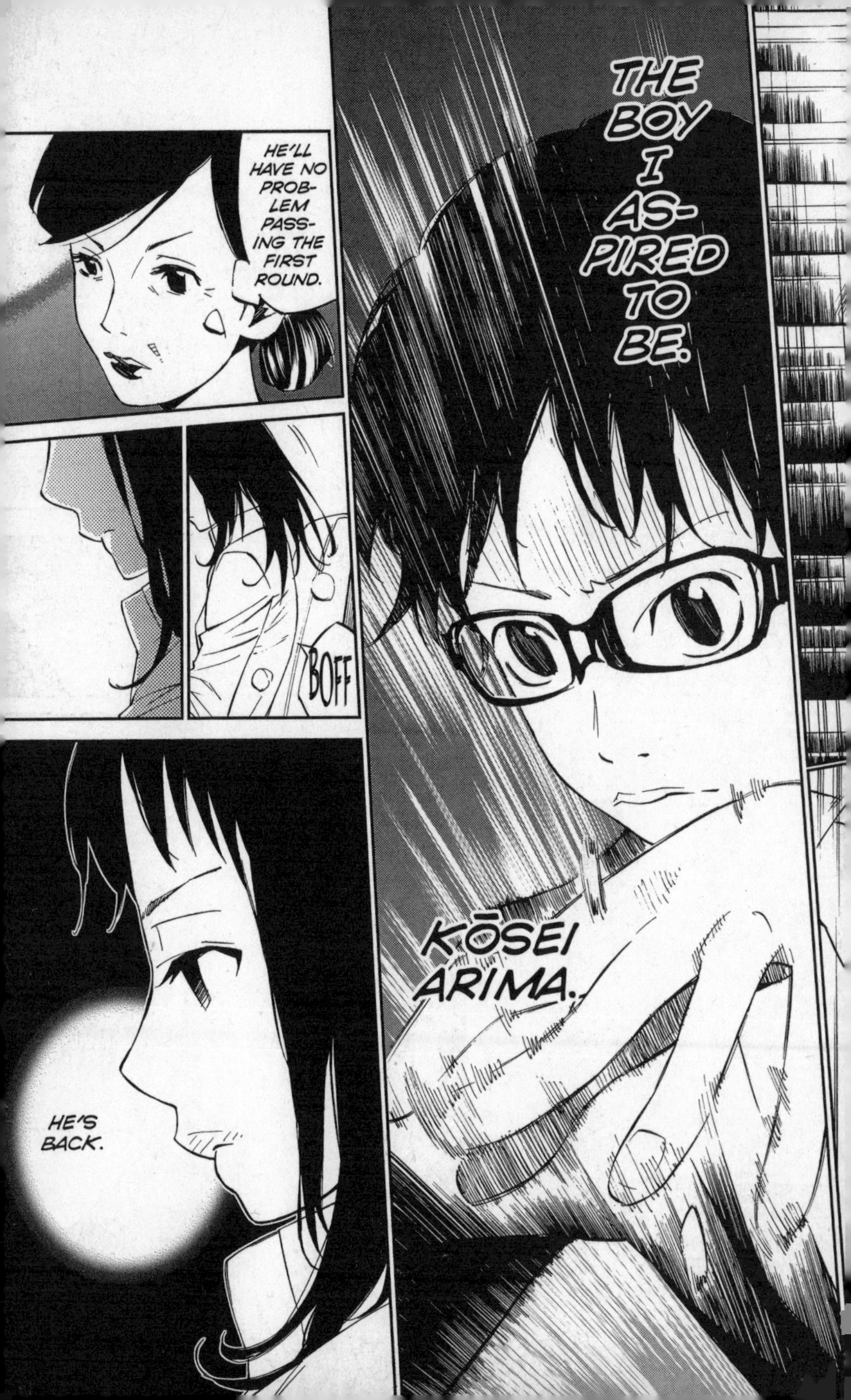
THE BOY I ASPIRED TO BE.
KŌSEI ARIMA...
HE'LL HAVE NO PROBLEM PASSING THE FIRST ROUND.
BOFF
HE'S BACK.

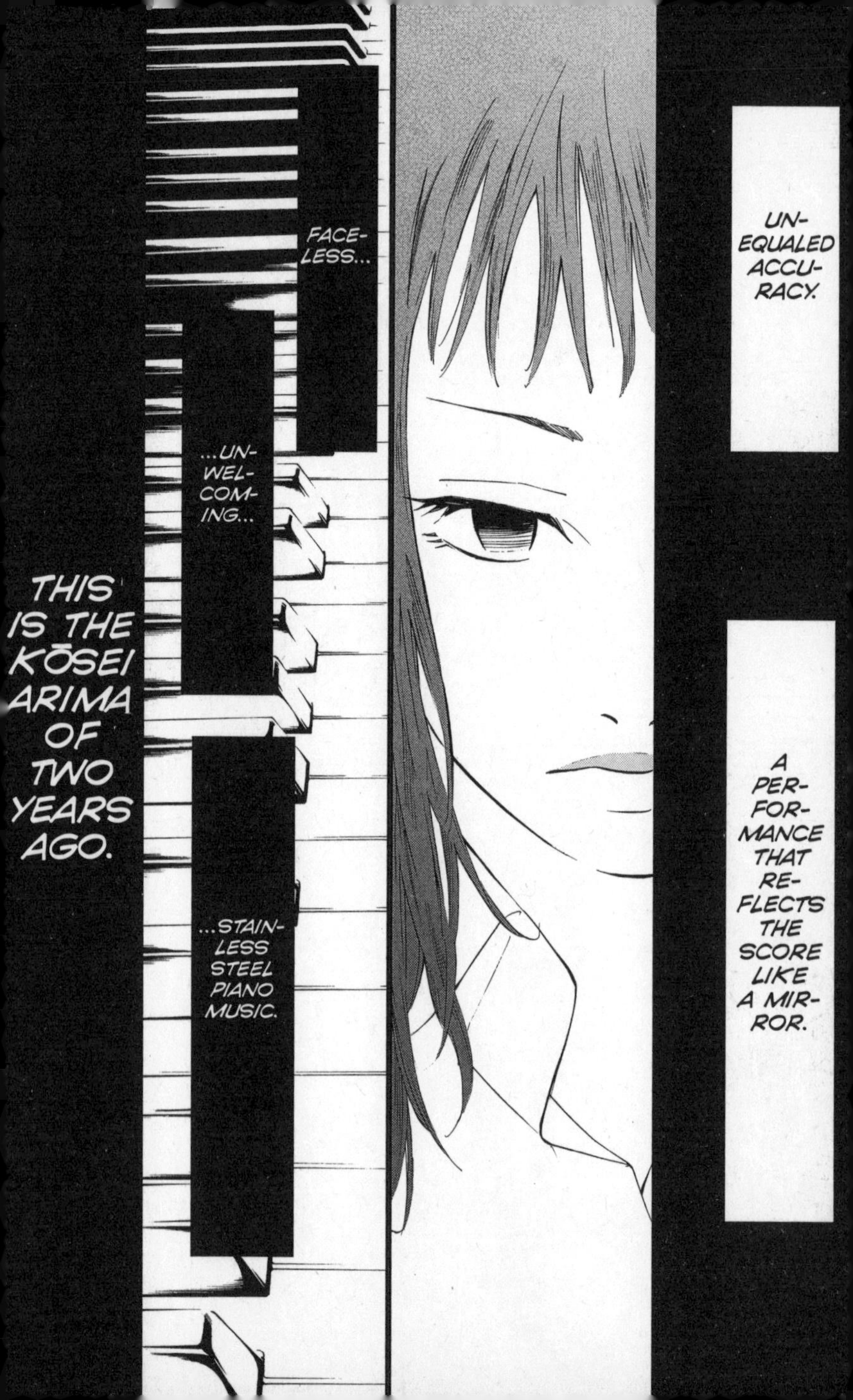
UNEQUALED ACCURACY.
A PERFORMANCE THAT REFLECTS THE SCORE LIKE A MIRROR.
FACELESS...
...UNWELCOMING...
...STAINLESS STEEL PIANO MUSIC.
THIS IS THE KŌSEI ARIMA OF TWO YEARS AGO.

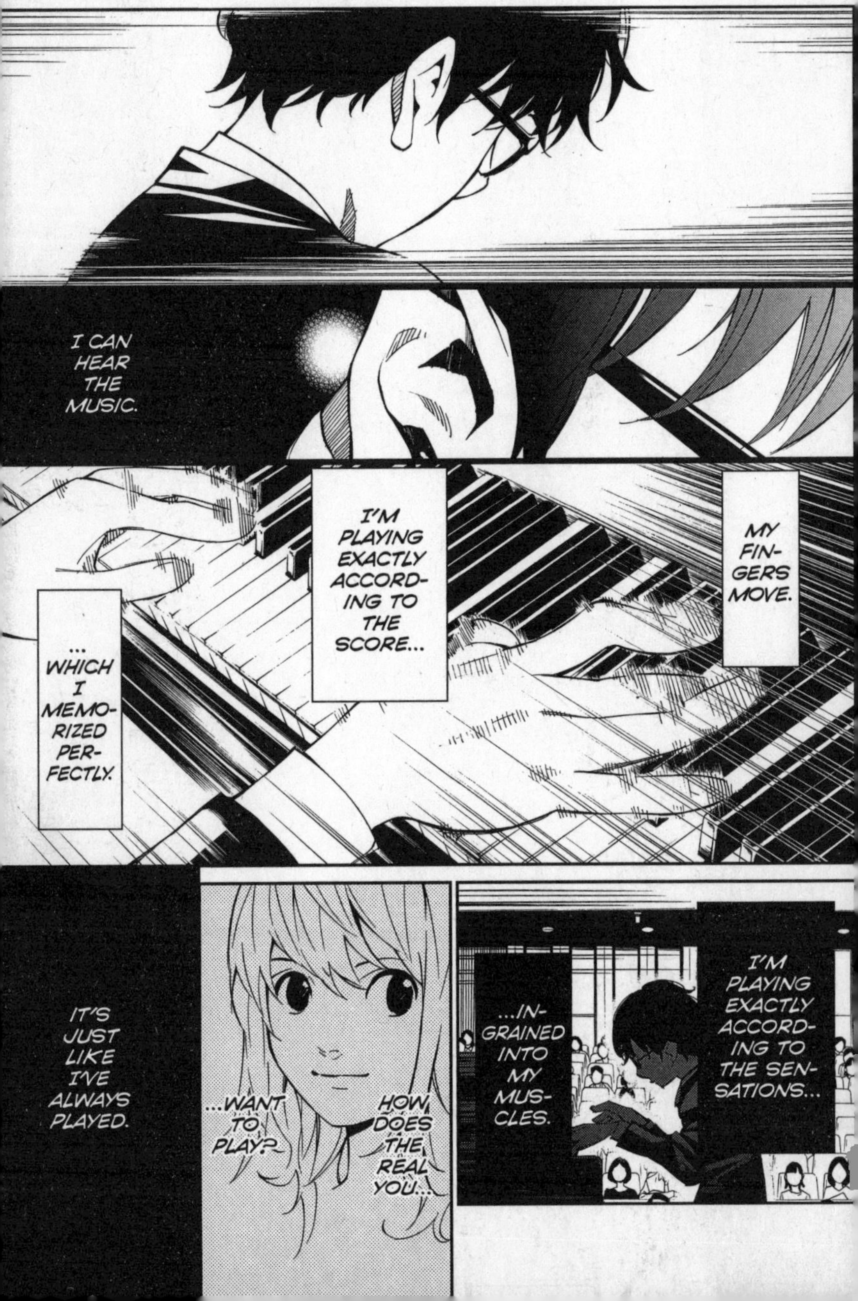
I CAN HEAR THE MUSIC.
MY FINGERS MOVE.
I'M PLAYING EXACTLY ACCORDING TO THE SCORE...
...WHICH I MEMORIZED PERFECTLY.
I'M PLAYING EXACTLY ACCORDING TO THE SENSATIONS...
...INGRAINED INTO MY MUSCLES.
HOW DOES THE REAL YOU...
...WANT TO PLAY?
IT'S JUST LIKE I'VE ALWAYS PLAYED.

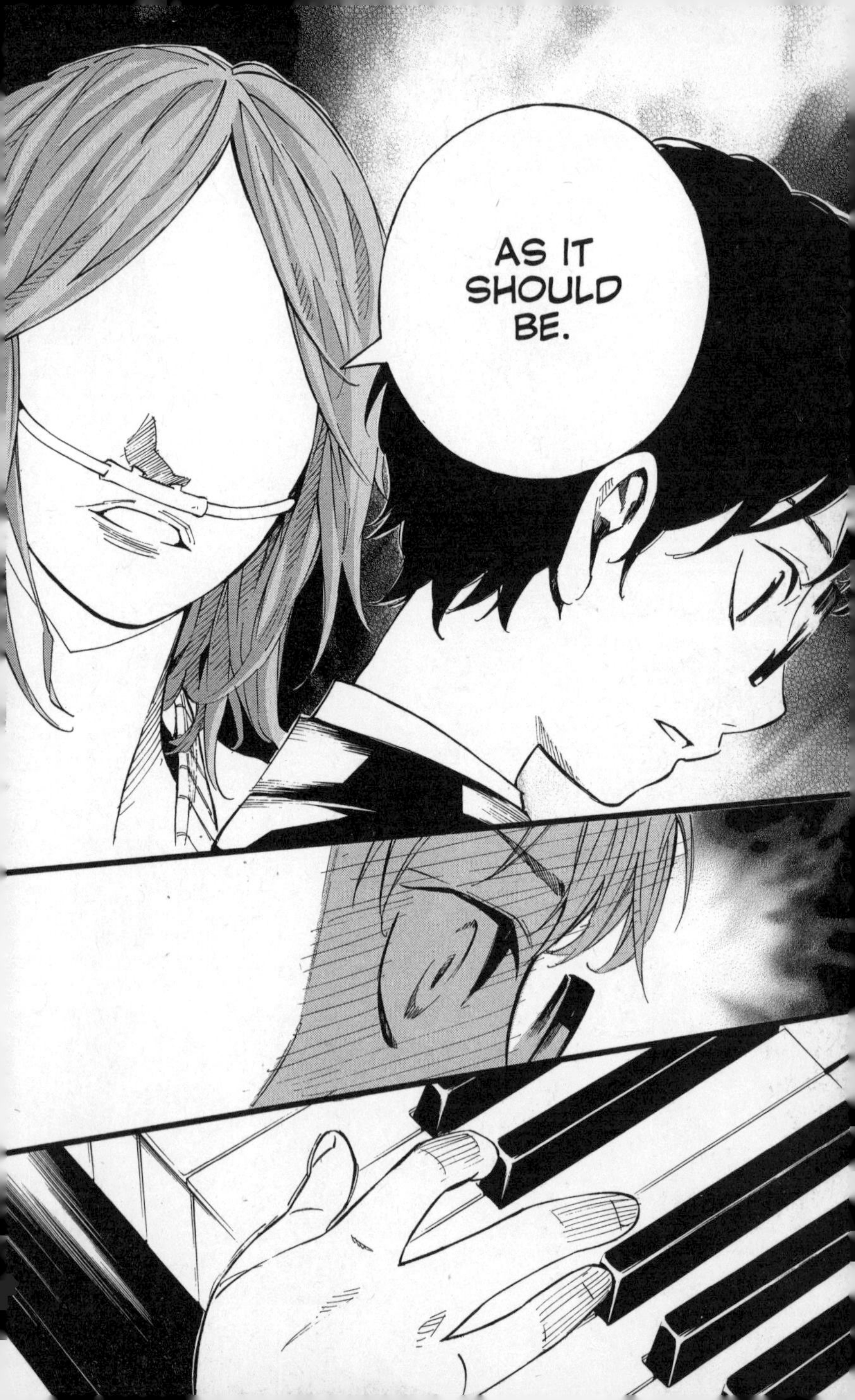
AS IT SHOULD BE.

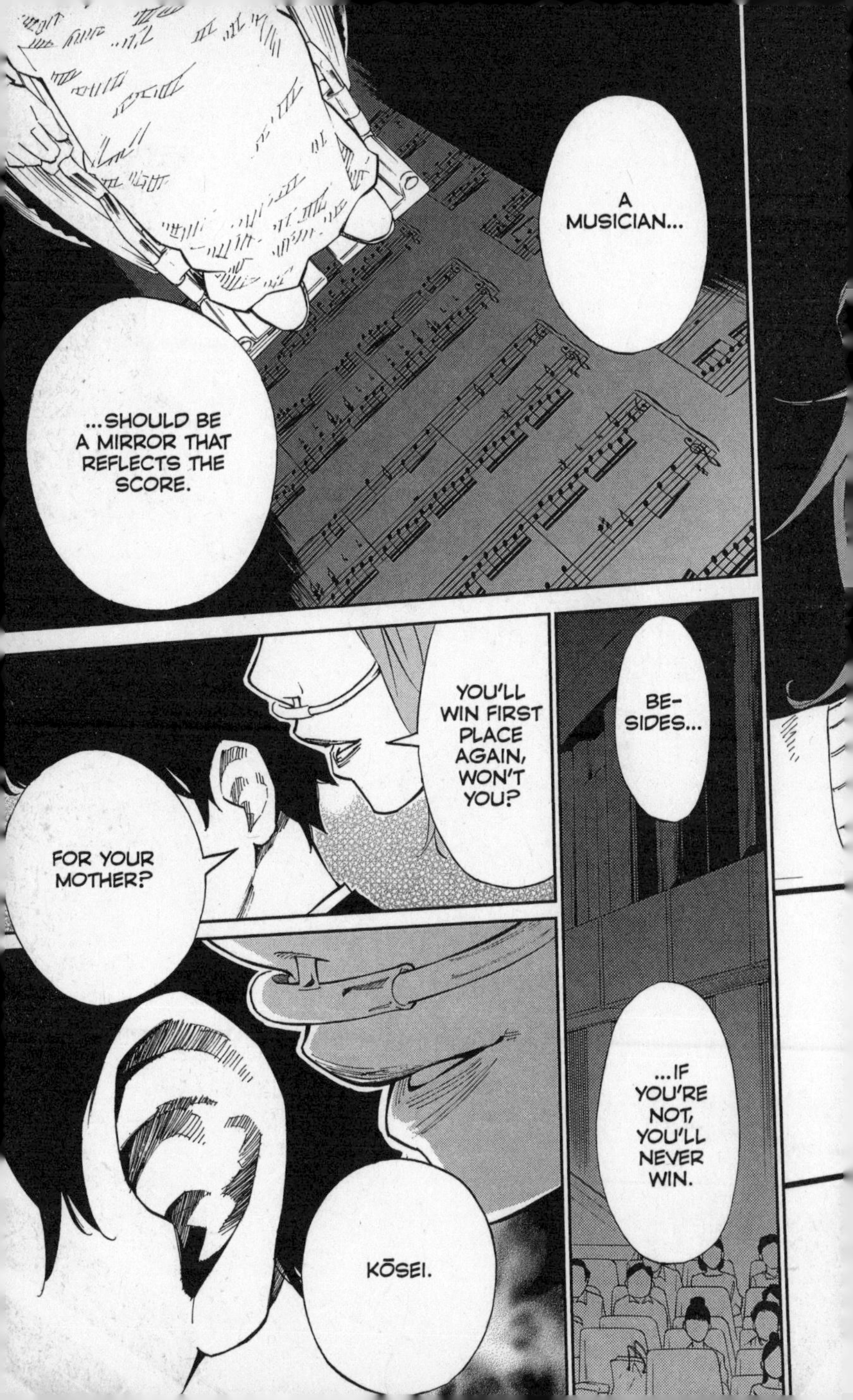
A MUSICIAN...
...SHOULD BE A MIRROR THAT REFLECTS THE SCORE.
BE-SIDES...
...IF YOU'RE NOT, YOU'LL NEVER WIN.
YOU'LL WIN FIRST PLACE AGAIN, WON'T YOU?
FOR YOUR MOTHER?
KŌSEI.

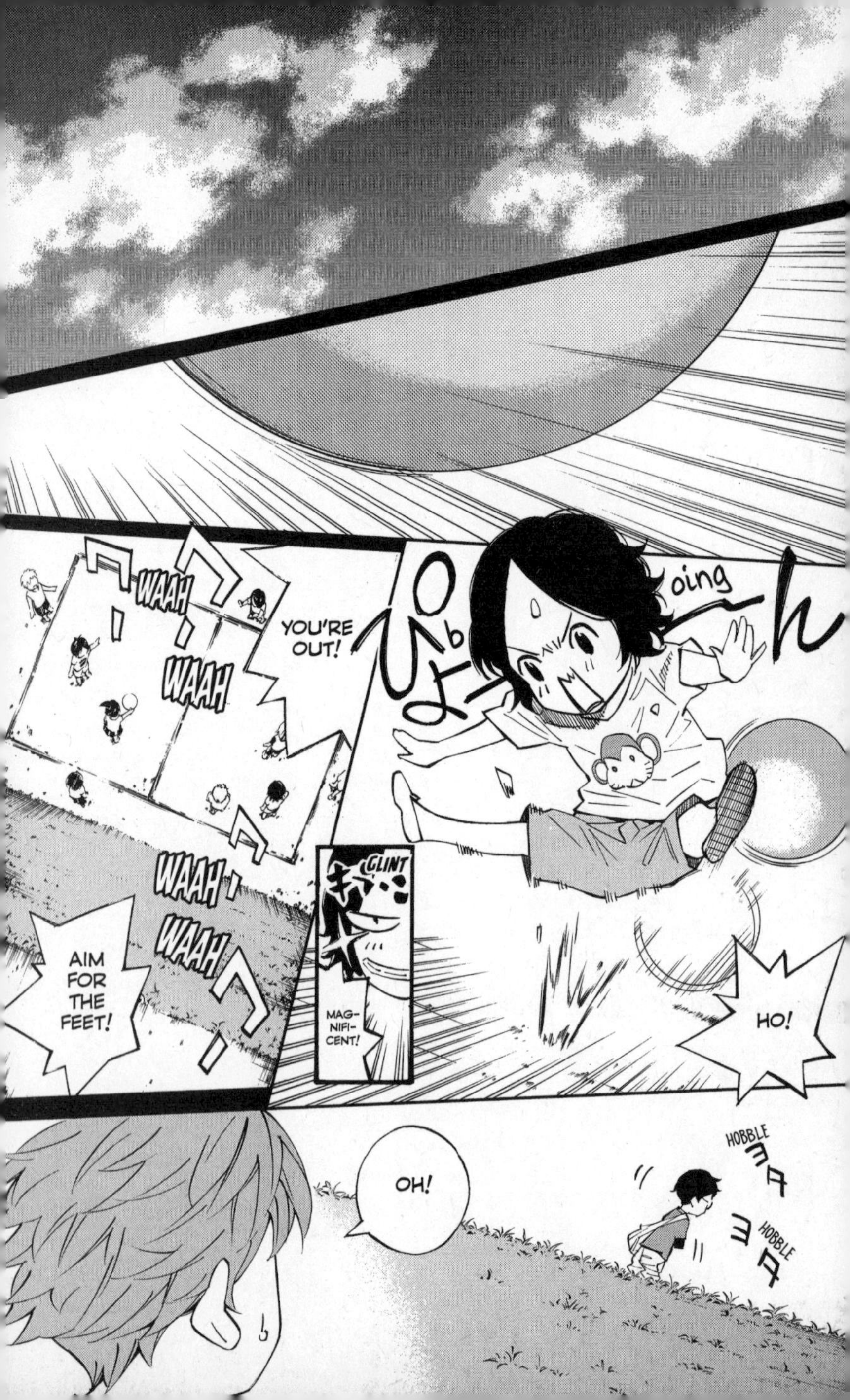

ひょ
O b oing h
HO!
CLINT
キ
MAG-NIFI-CENT!
YOU'RE OUT!
WAAH WAAH
WAAH WAAH
AIM FOR THE FEET!
HOBBLE ヨタ
HOBBLE ヨタ
OH!

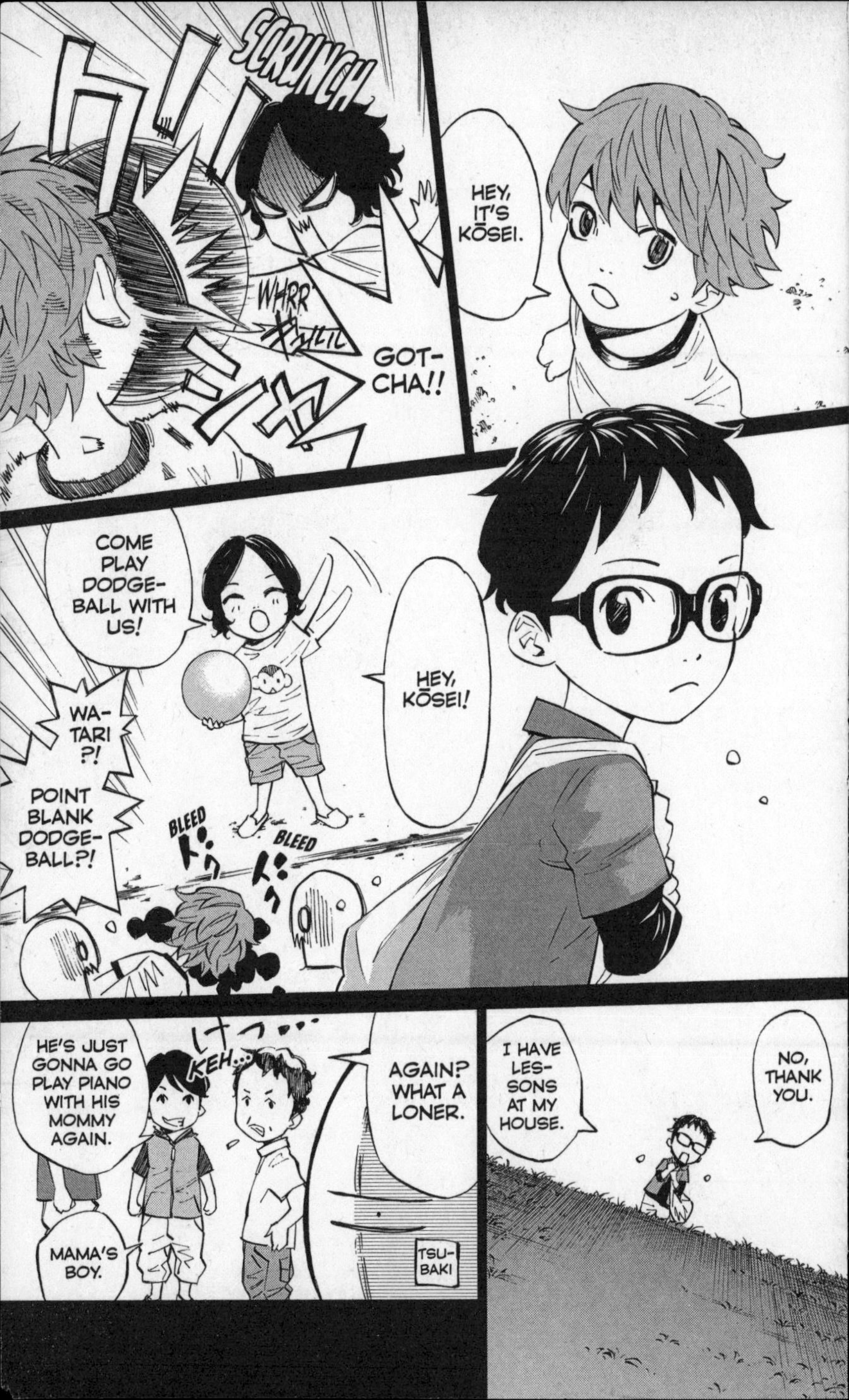
HEY, IT'S KŌSEI.
SCRUNCH
WHRR
GOT-CHA!!
HEY, KŌSEI!
COME PLAY DODGE-BALL WITH US!
WA-TARI?!
POINT BLANK DODGE-BALL?!
BLEED
BLEED
NO, THANK YOU.
I HAVE LES-SONS AT MY HOUSE.
AGAIN? WHAT A LONER.
KEH...
HE'S JUST GONNA GO PLAY PIANO WITH HIS MOMMY AGAIN.
TSU-BAKI
MAMA'S BOY.

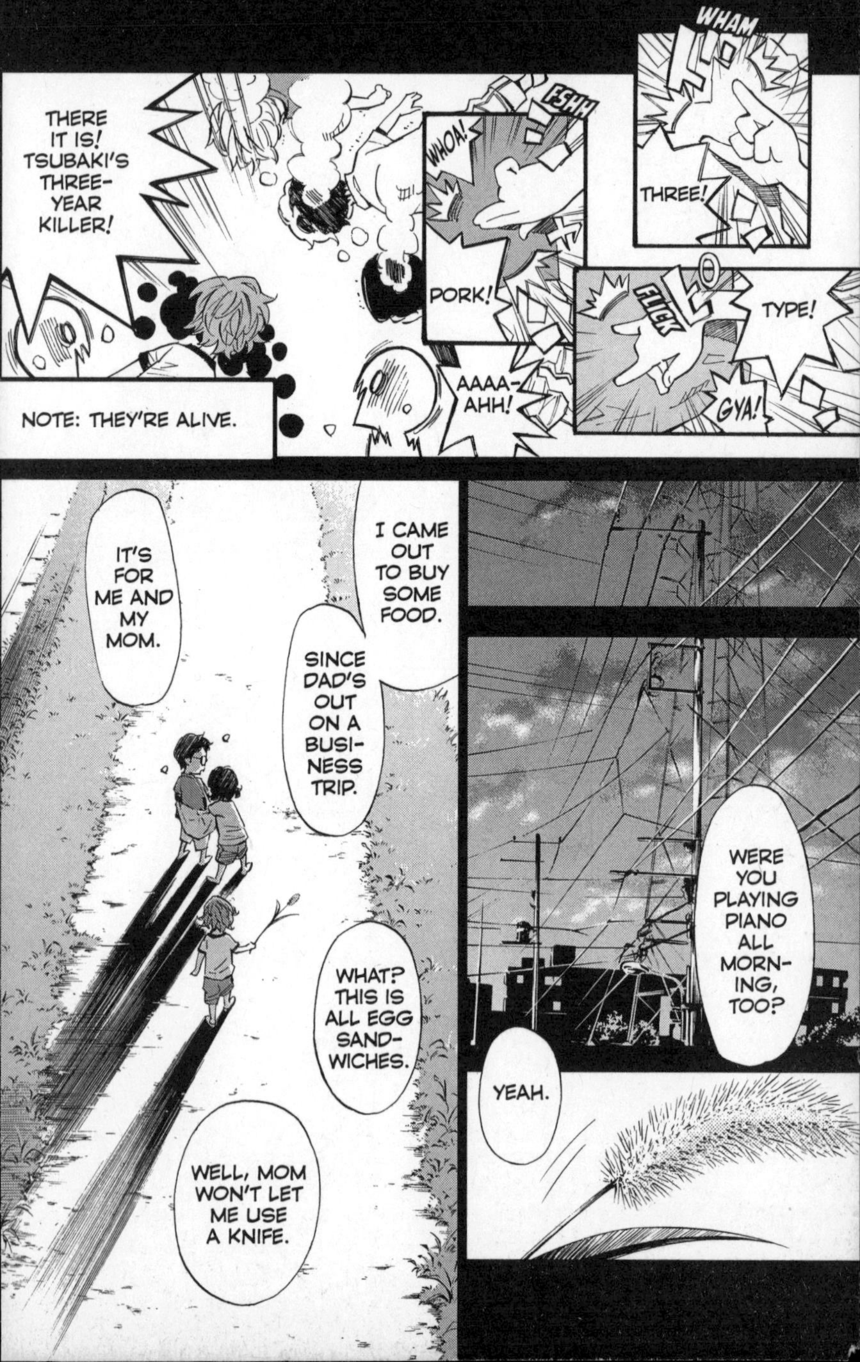
WHAM
THREE!
FLICK
TYPE!
GYA!
FSHH
WHOA!
PORK!
AAAA-AHH!
THERE IT IS! TSUBAKI'S THREE-YEAR KILLER!
NOTE: THEY'RE ALIVE.
WERE YOU PLAYING PIANO ALL MORNING, TOO?
YEAH.
I CAME OUT TO BUY SOME FOOD.
SINCE DAD'S OUT ON A BUSINESS TRIP.
IT'S FOR ME AND MY MOM.
WHAT? THIS IS ALL EGG SANDWICHES.
WELL, MOM WON'T LET ME USE A KNIFE.

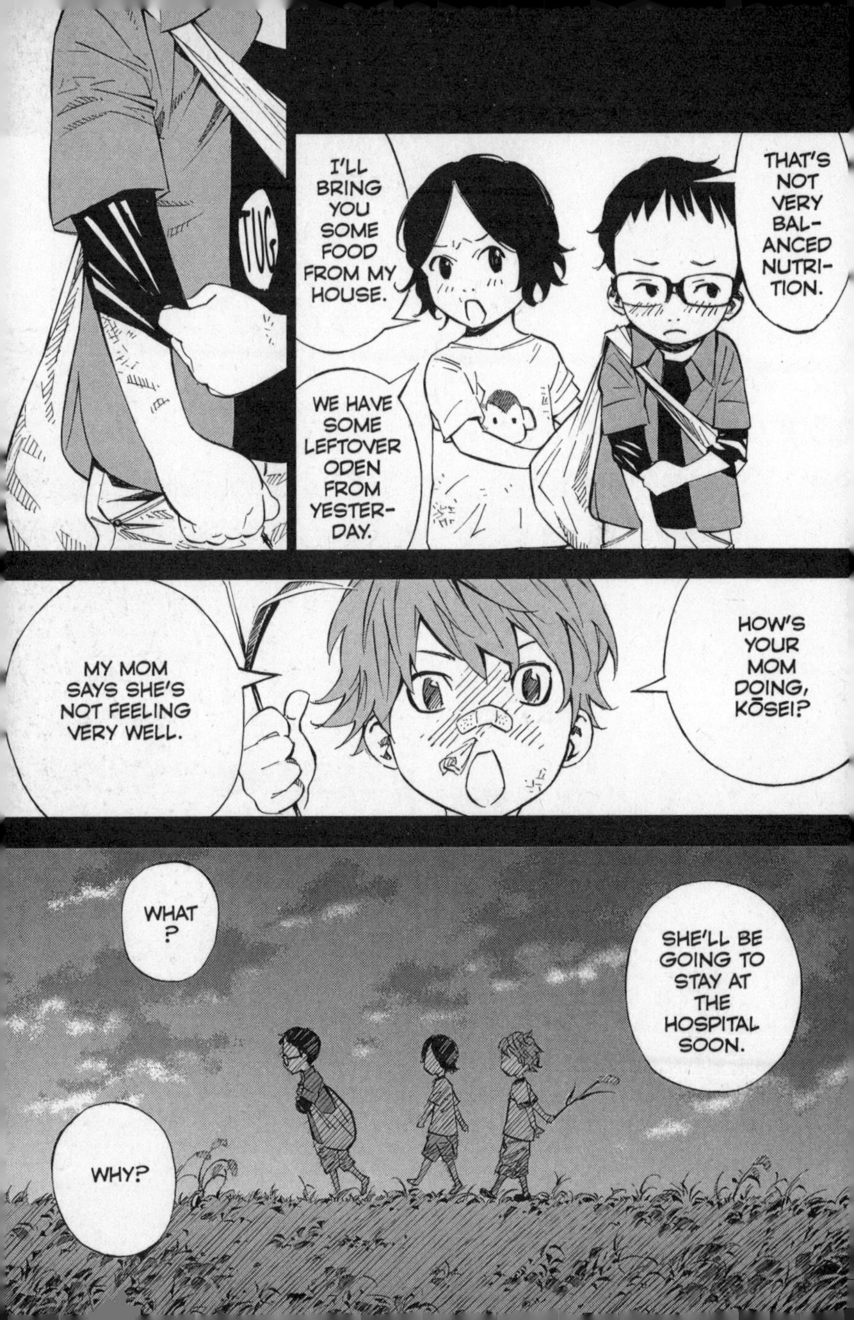
THAT'S NOT VERY BALANCED NUTRITION.
I'LL BRING YOU SOME FOOD FROM MY HOUSE.
WE HAVE SOME LEFTOVER ODEN FROM YESTERDAY.
TUG
HOW'S YOUR MOM DOING, KŌSEI?
MY MOM SAYS SHE'S NOT FEELING VERY WELL.
SHE'LL BE GOING TO STAY AT THE HOSPITAL SOON.
WHAT?
WHY?

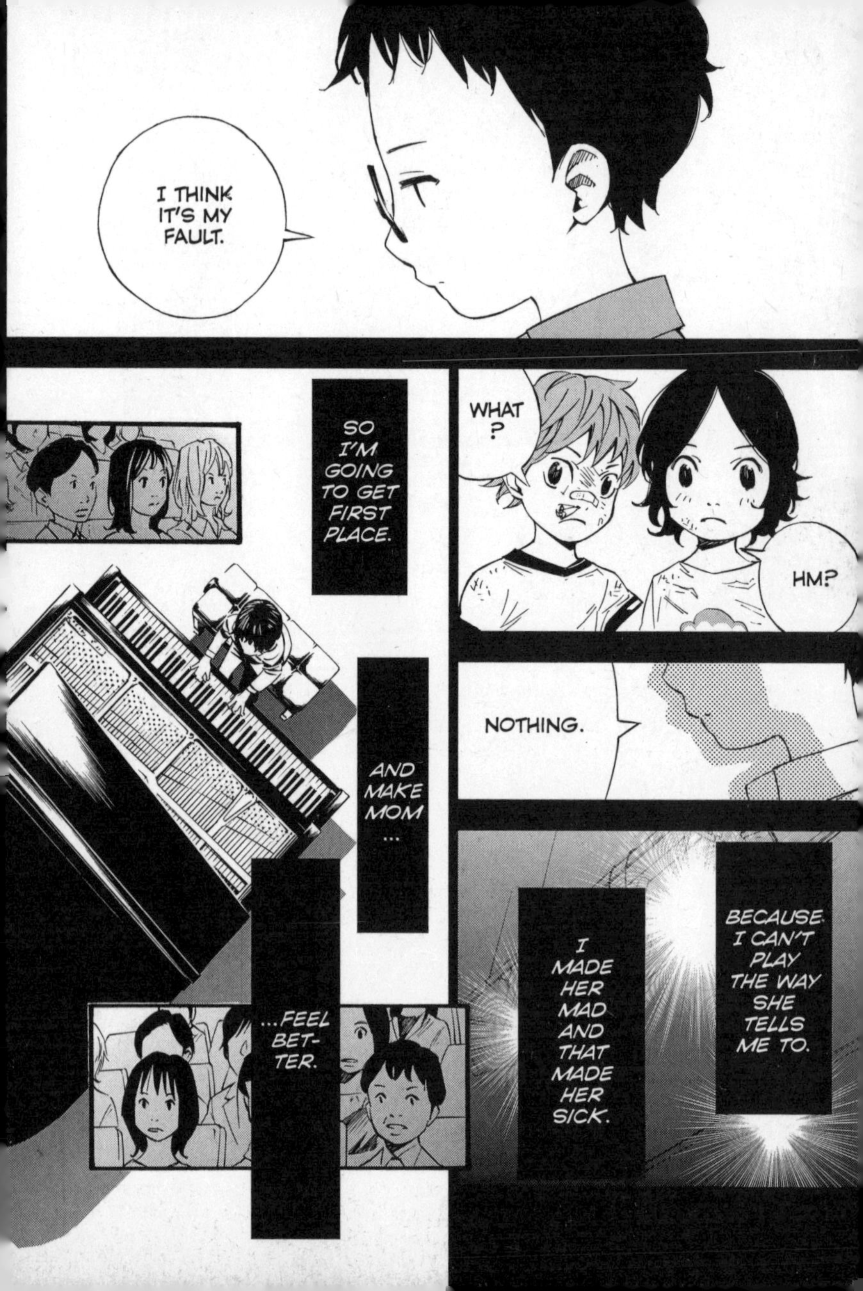
I THINK IT'S MY FAULT.
WHAT?
HM?
NOTHING.
BECAUSE I CAN'T PLAY THE WAY SHE TELLS ME TO.
I MADE HER MAD AND THAT MADE HER SICK.
SO I'M GOING TO GET FIRST PLACE.
AND MAKE MOM...
...FEEL BET-TER.

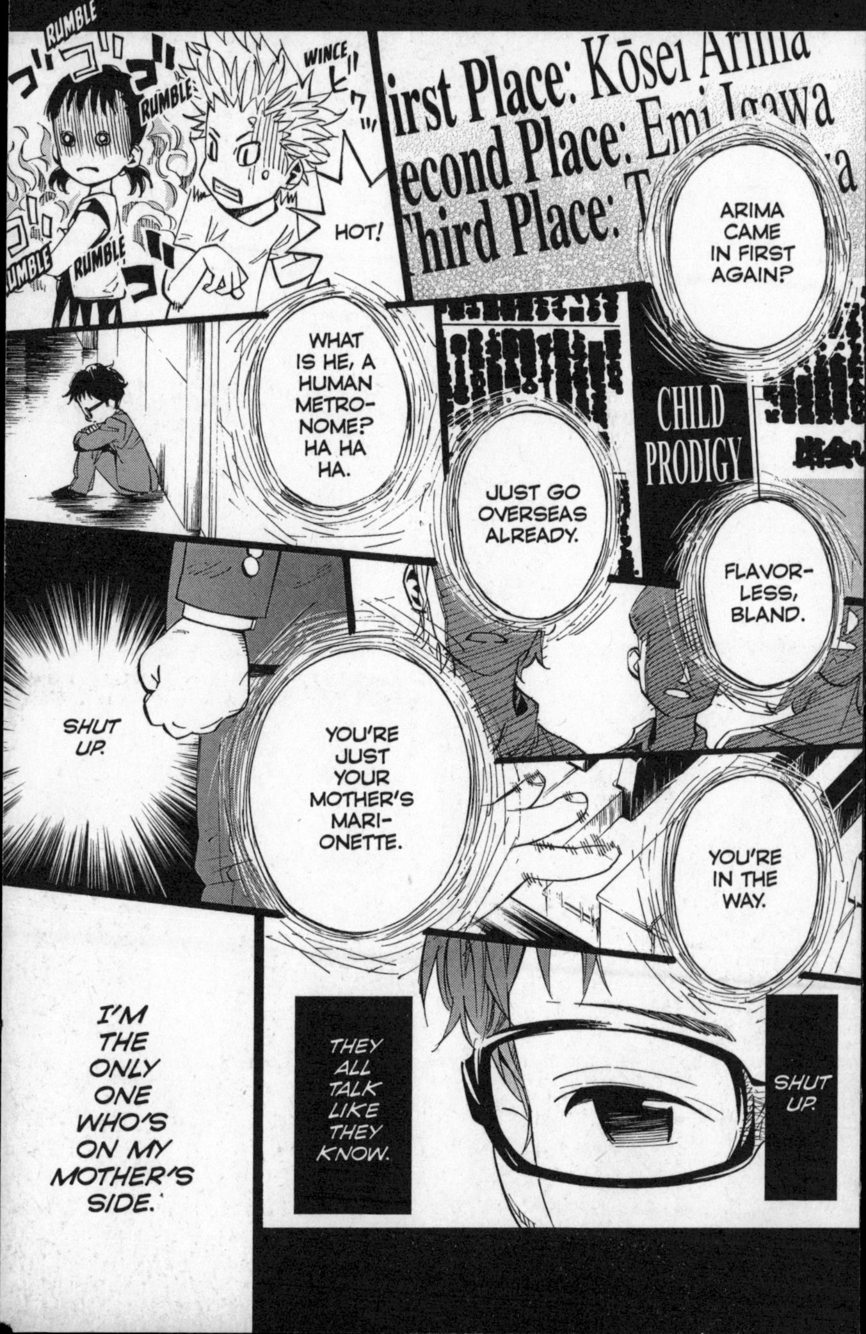
irst Place: Kōsei Arima
econd Place: Emi Igawa
hird Place: T
ARIMA CAME IN FIRST AGAIN?
WINCE
RUMBLE
RUMBLE
RUMBLE
RUMBLE
UMBLE
HOT!
CHILD PRODIGY
FLAVOR-LESS, BLAND.
JUST GO OVERSEAS ALREADY.
WHAT IS HE, A HUMAN METRO-NOME? HA HA HA.
YOU'RE IN THE WAY.
YOU'RE JUST YOUR MOTHER'S MARI-ONETTE.
SHUT UP.
SHUT UP.
THEY ALL TALK LIKE THEY KNOW.
I'M THE ONLY ONE WHO'S ON MY MOTHER'S SIDE.

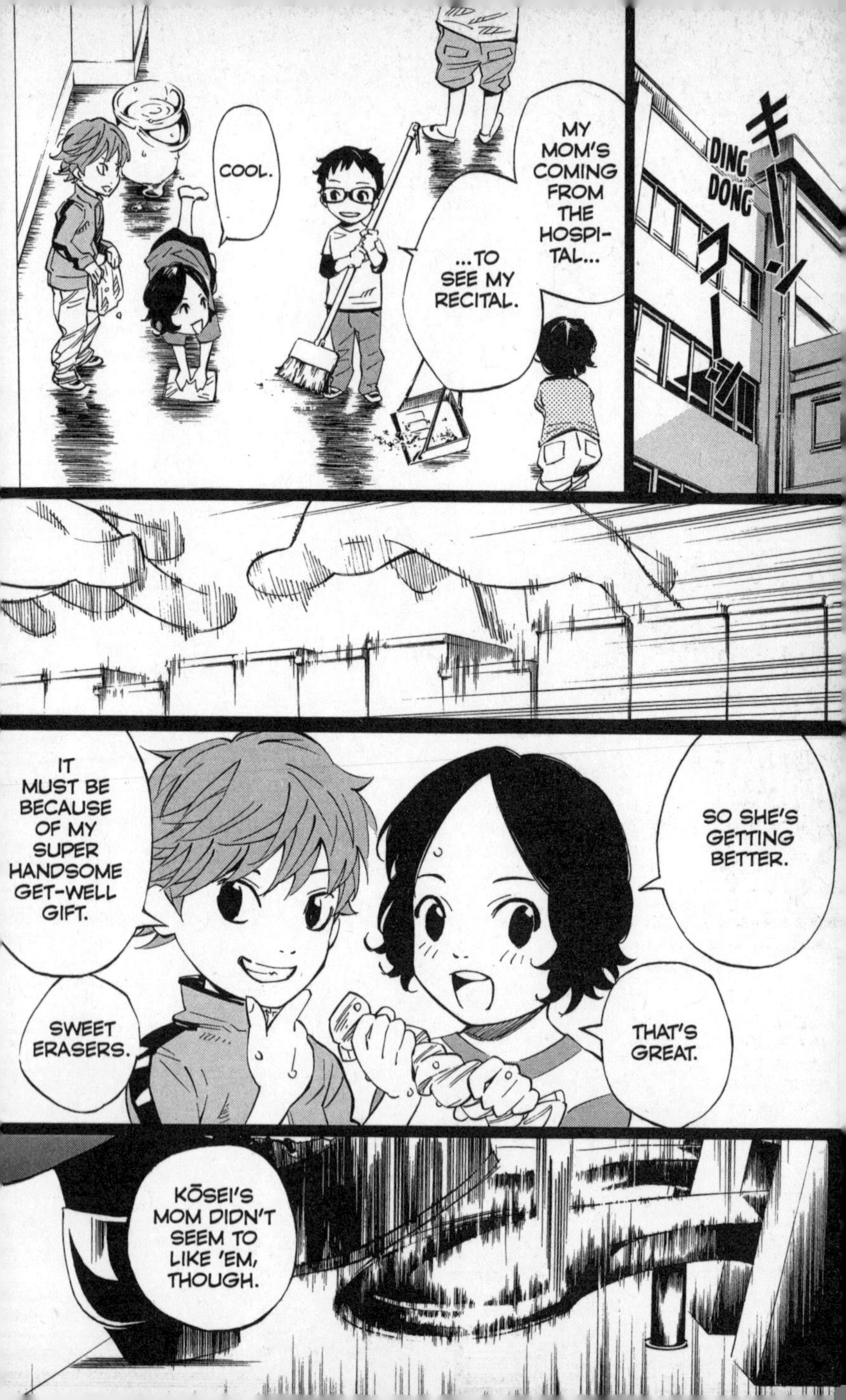
DING DONG
MY MOM'S COMING FROM THE HOSPITAL...
...TO SEE MY RECITAL.
COOL.
SO SHE'S GETTING BETTER.
THAT'S GREAT.
IT MUST BE BECAUSE OF MY SUPER HANDSOME GET-WELL GIFT.
SWEET ERASERS.
KŌSEI'S MOM DIDN'T SEEM TO LIKE 'EM, THOUGH.

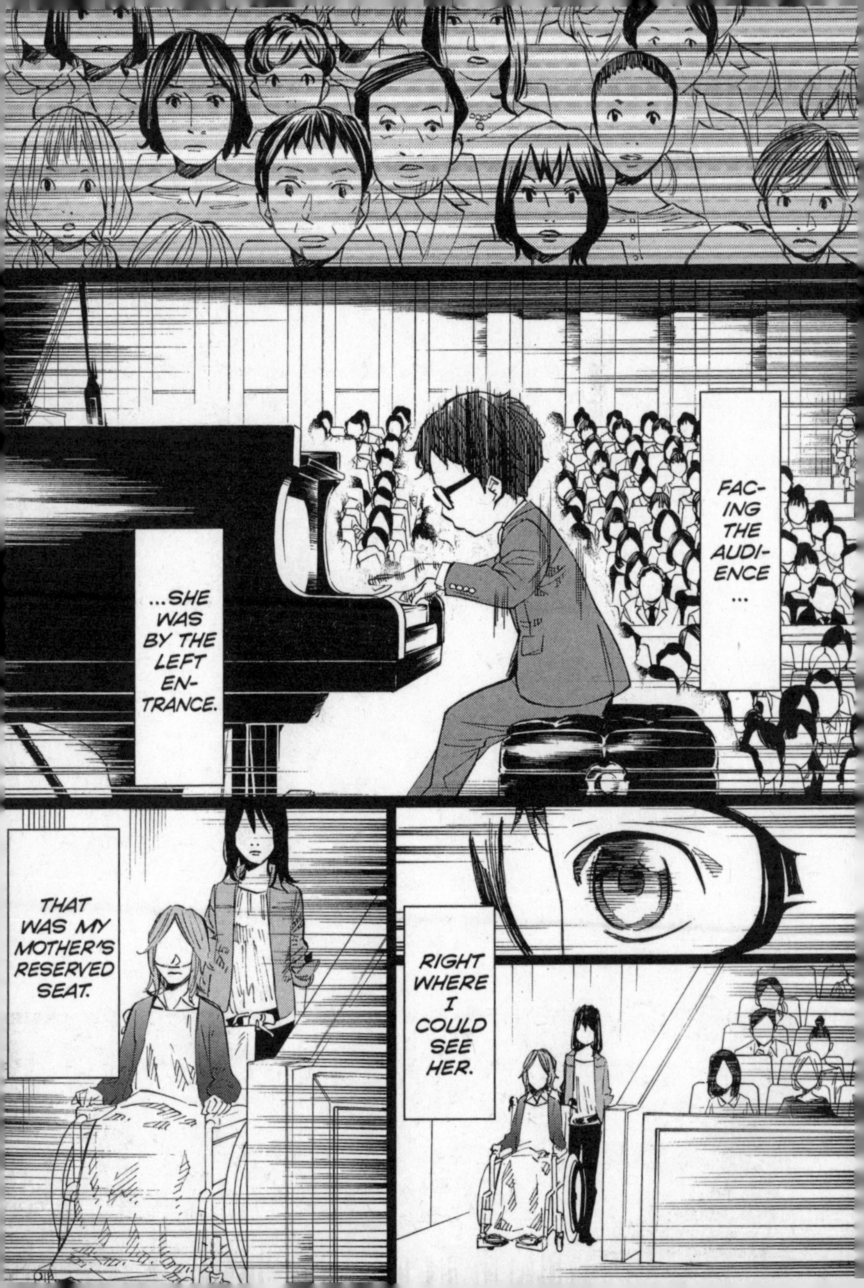
FACING THE AUDIENCE...
...SHE WAS BY THE LEFT ENTRANCE.
RIGHT WHERE I COULD SEE HER.
THAT WAS MY MOTHER'S RESERVED SEAT.

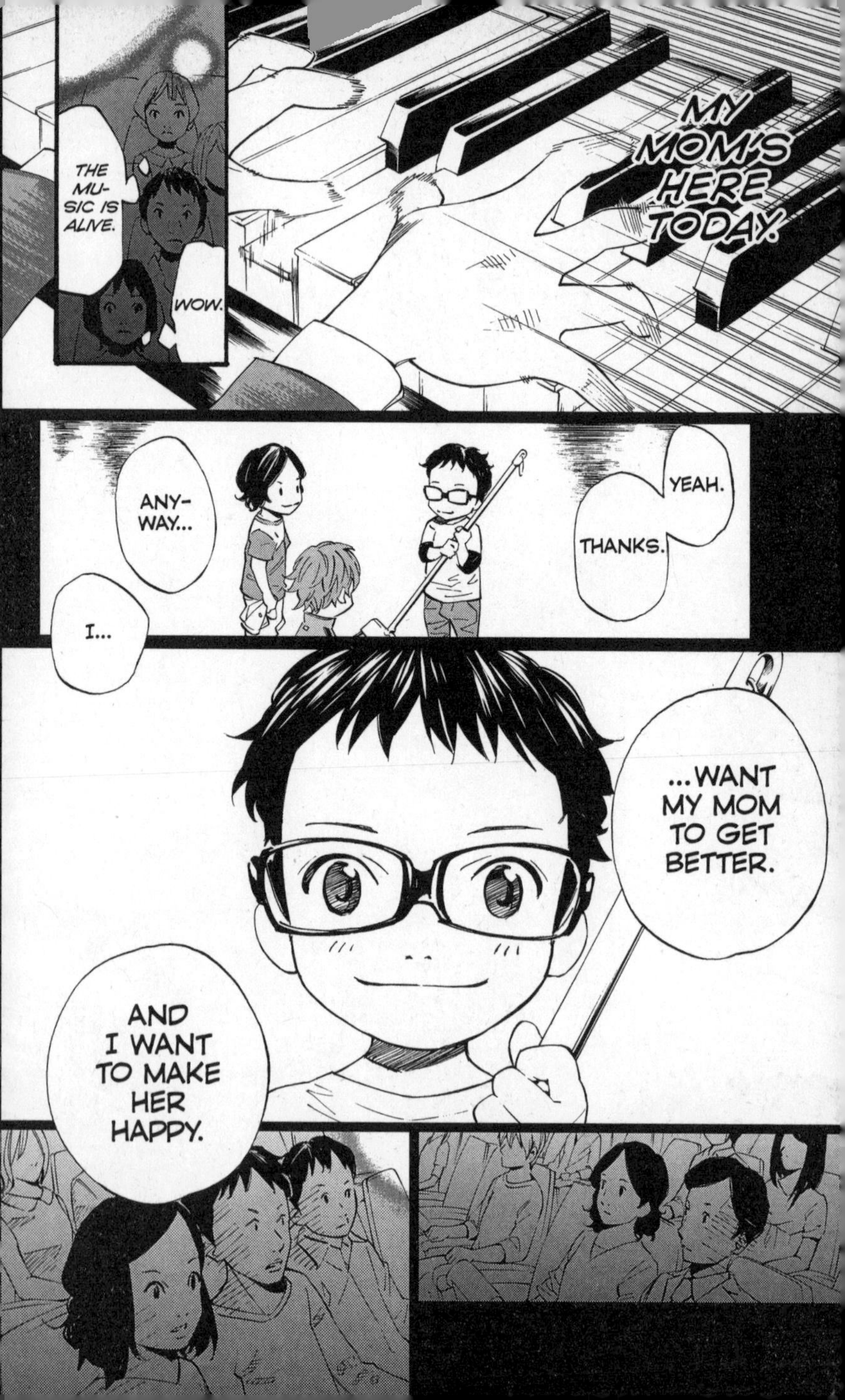
MY MOM'S HERE TODAY.
THE MU-SIC IS ALIVE.
WOW.
YEAH.
THANKS.
ANY-WAY...
I...
...WANT MY MOM TO GET BETTER.
AND I WANT TO MAKE HER HAPPY.

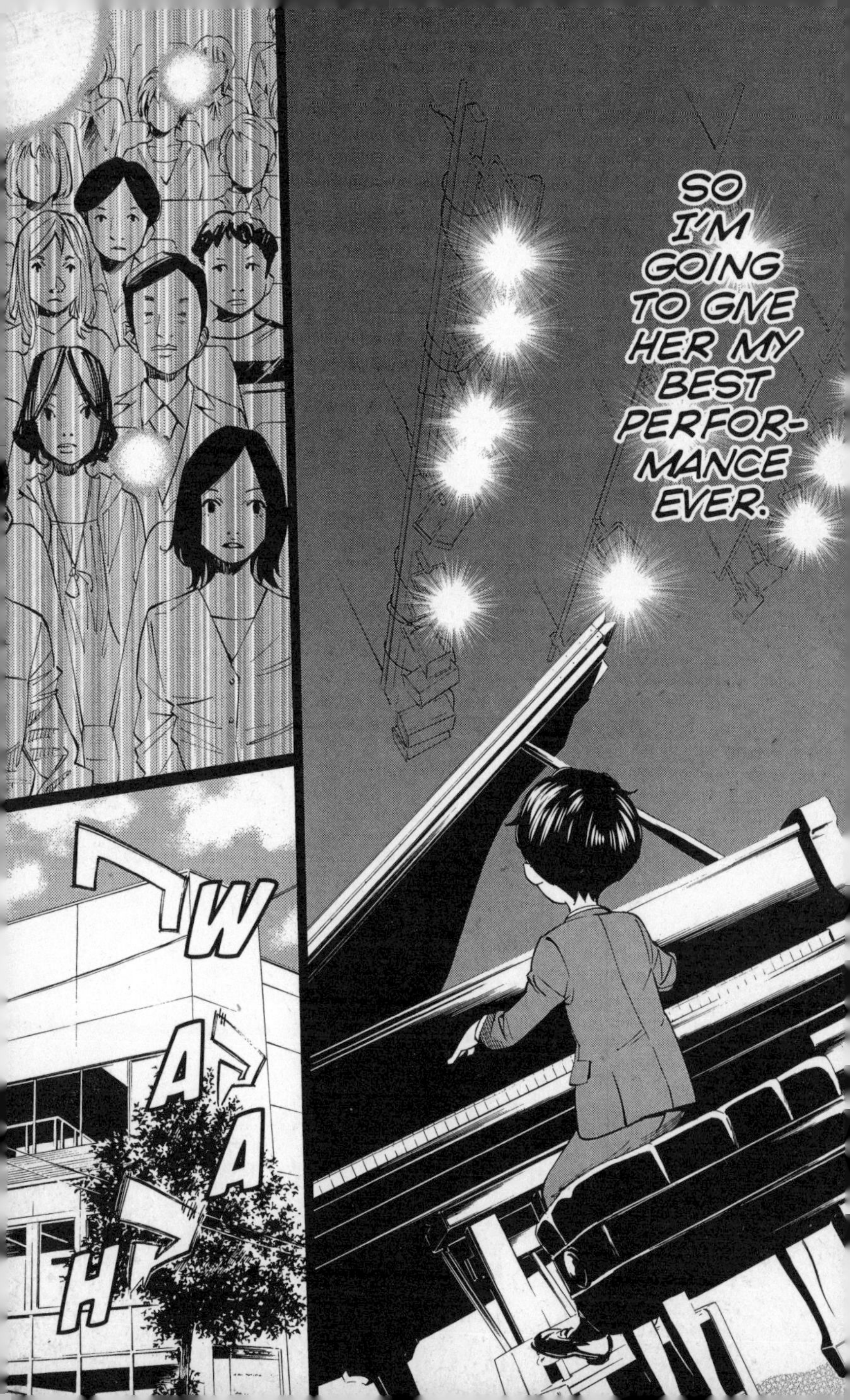
SO I'M GOING TO GIVE HER MY BEST PERFORMANCE EVER.
WAAH

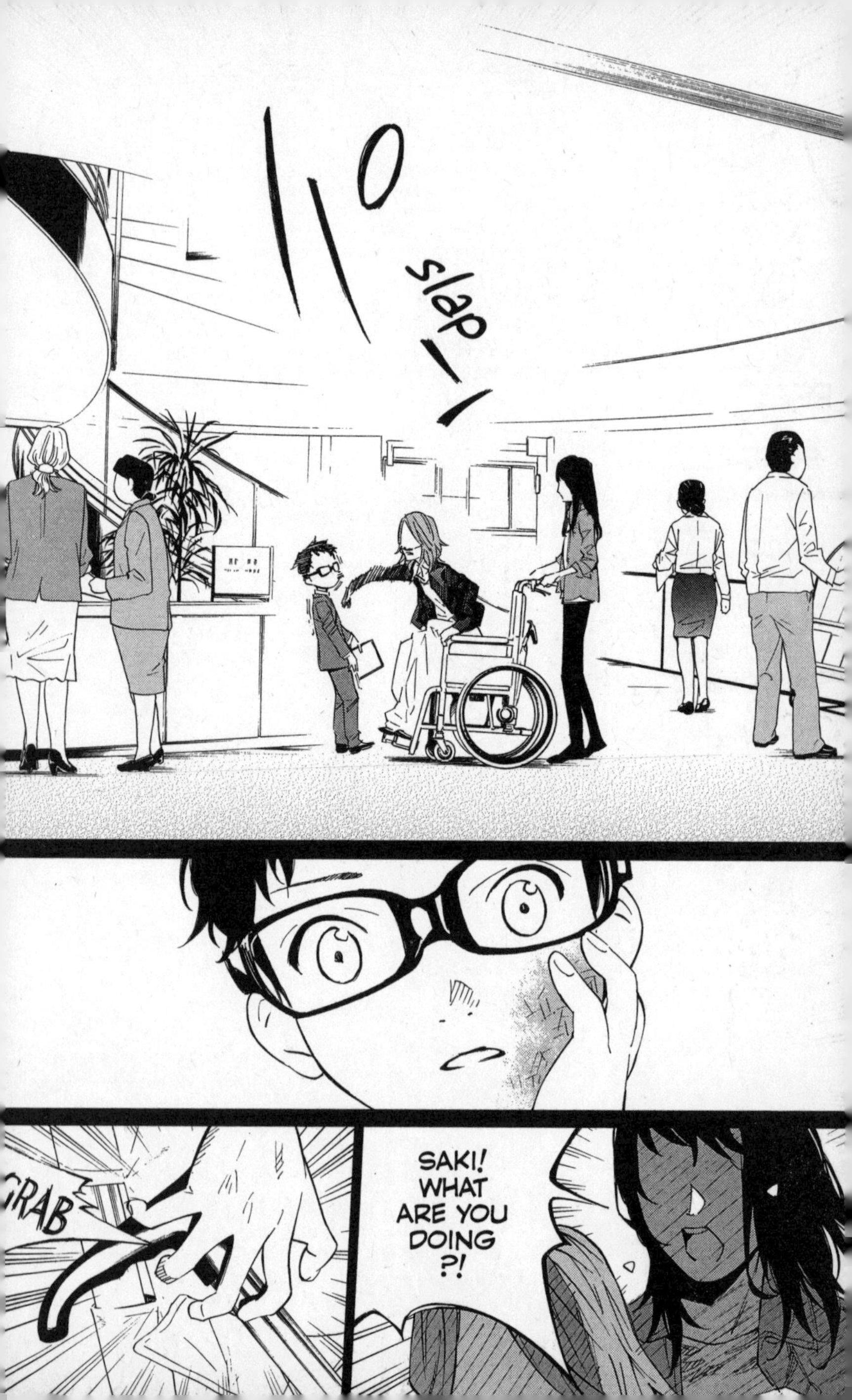
slap
SAKI! WHAT ARE YOU DOING ?!
GRAB

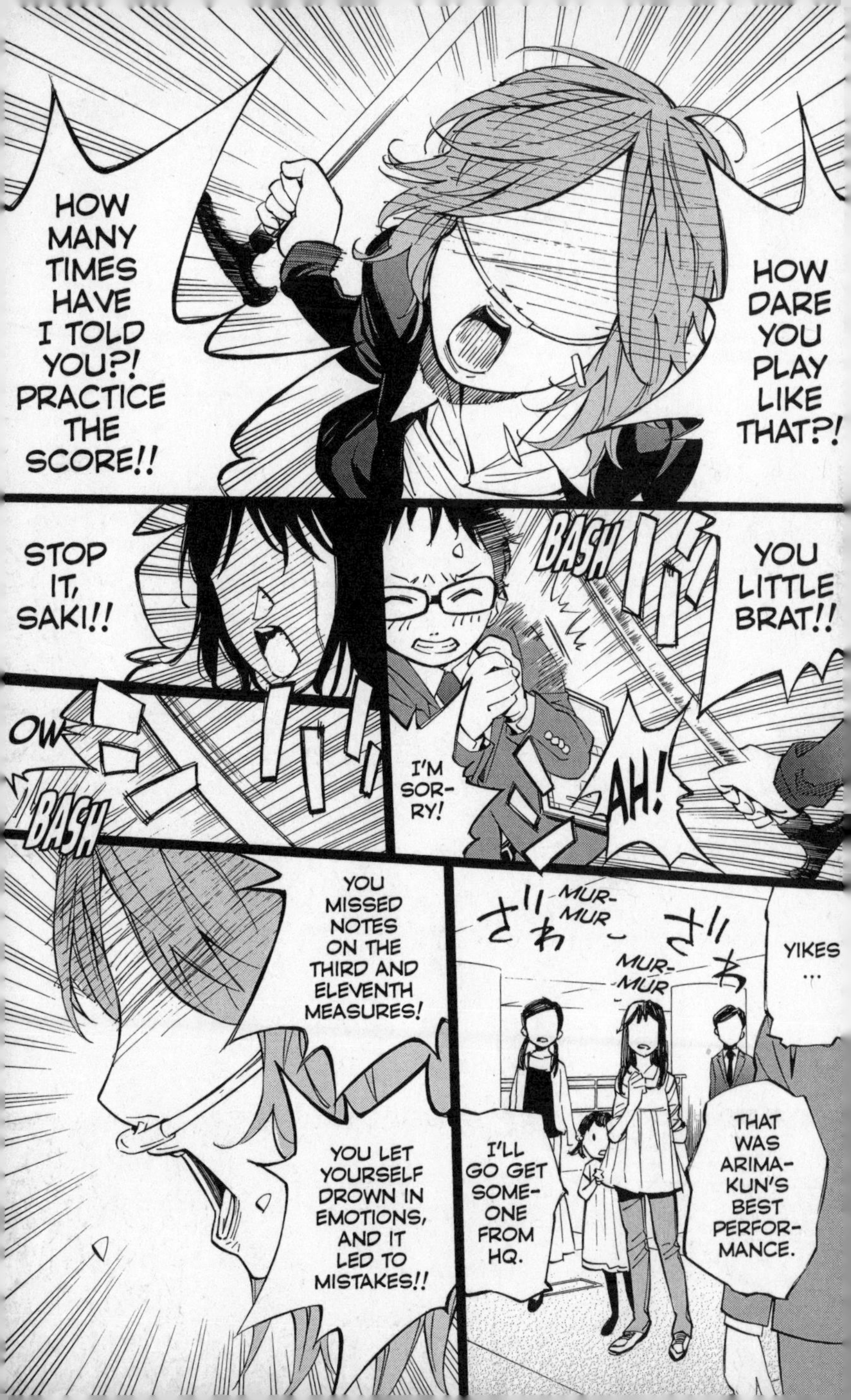
HOW DARE YOU PLAY LIKE THAT?!
HOW MANY TIMES HAVE I TOLD YOU?! PRACTICE THE SCORE!!
YOU LITTLE BRAT!!
BASH
AH!
I'M SOR-RY!
STOP IT, SAKI!!
OW
BASH
YIKES ...
ざわ ざわ
MUR-MUR
MUR-MUR
THAT WAS ARIMA-KUN'S BEST PERFOR-MANCE.
I'LL GO GET SOME-ONE FROM HQ.
YOU MISSED NOTES ON THE THIRD AND ELEVENTH MEASURES!
YOU LET YOURSELF DROWN IN EMOTIONS, AND IT LED TO MISTAKES!!

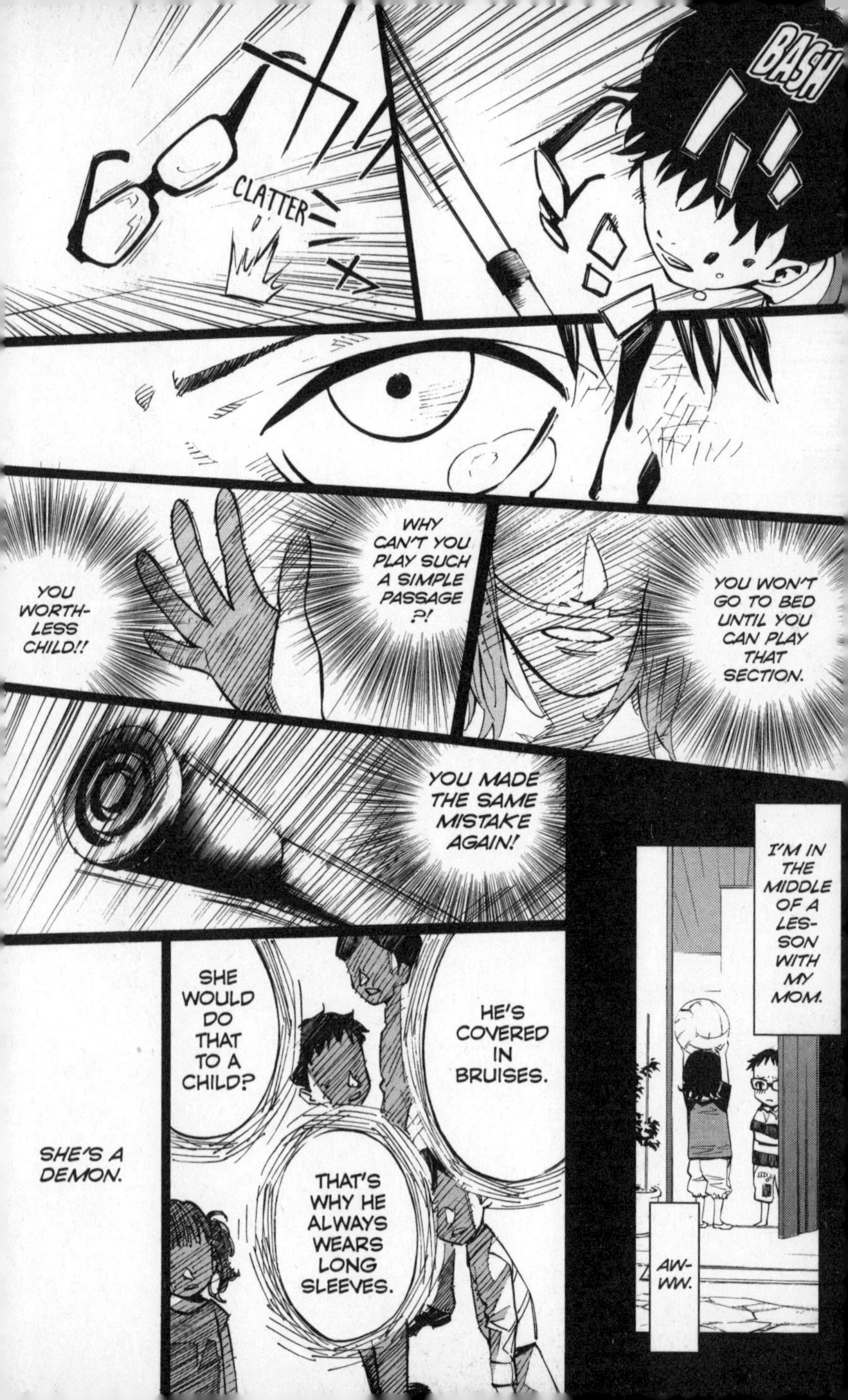
BASH
CLATTER
YOU WON'T GO TO BED UNTIL YOU CAN PLAY THAT SECTION.
WHY CAN'T YOU PLAY SUCH A SIMPLE PASSAGE?!
YOU WORTH-LESS CHILD!!
I'M IN THE MIDDLE OF A LES-SON WITH MY MOM.
AW-WW.
YOU MADE THE SAME MISTAKE AGAIN!
HE'S COVERED IN BRUISES.
SHE WOULD DO THAT TO A CHILD?
THAT'S WHY HE ALWAYS WEARS LONG SLEEVES.
SHE'S A DEMON.

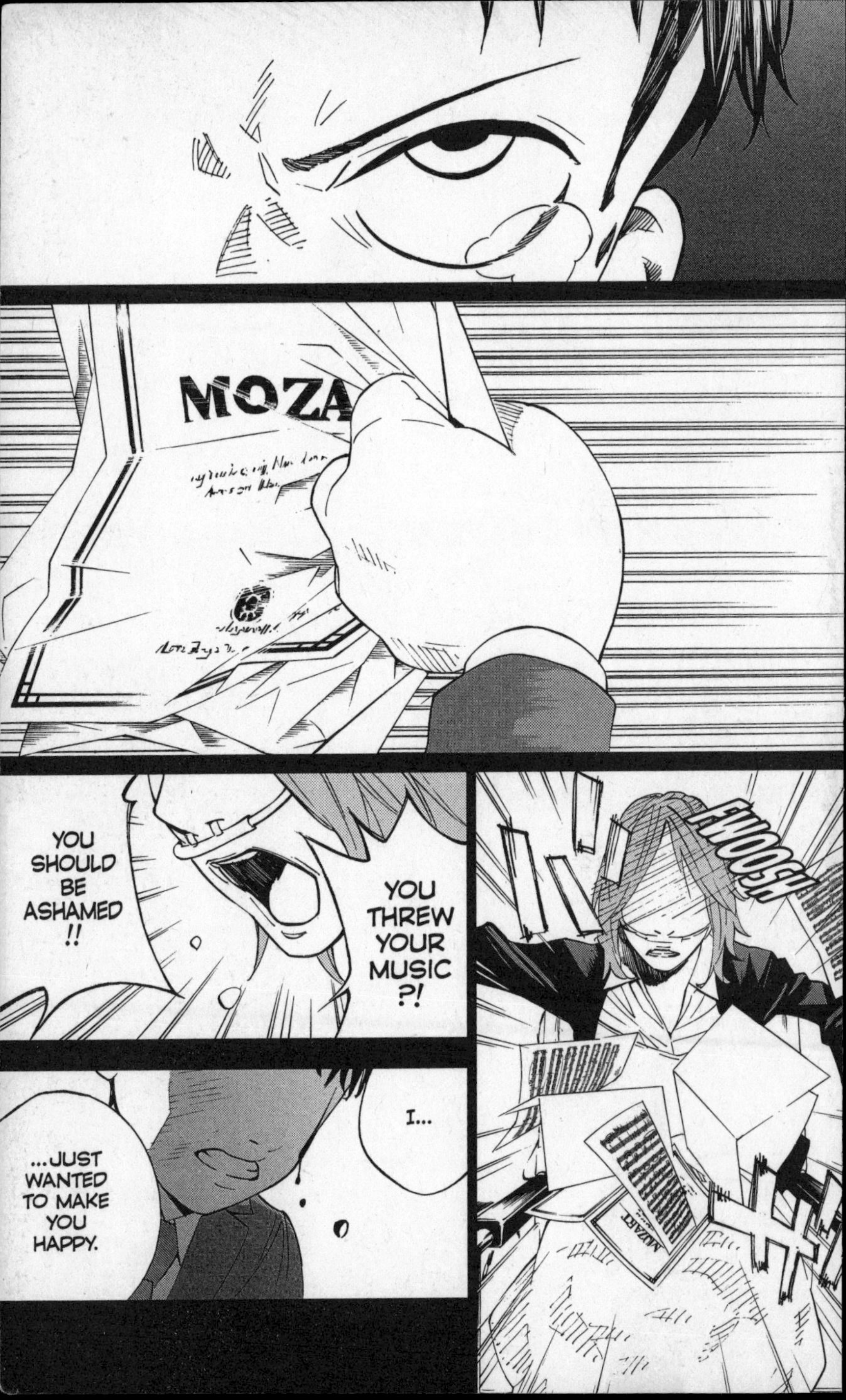
MOZA
WHOOSH!
YOU THREW YOUR MUSIC ?!
YOU SHOULD BE ASHAMED !!
I...
...JUST WANTED TO MAKE YOU HAPPY.

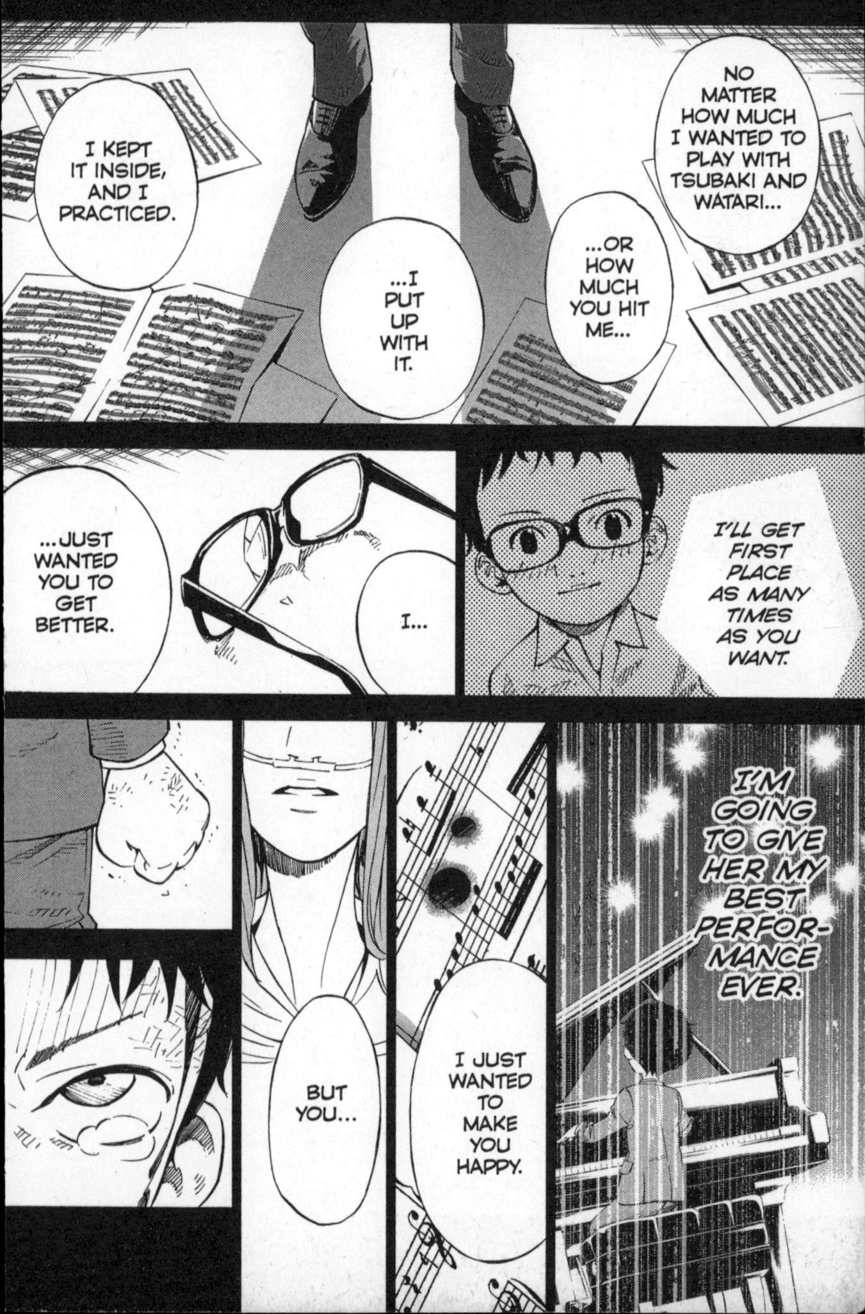
NO MATTER HOW MUCH I WANTED TO PLAY WITH TSUBAKI AND WATARI...
...OR HOW MUCH YOU HIT ME...
...I PUT UP WITH IT.
I KEPT IT INSIDE, AND I PRACTICED.
I'LL GET FIRST PLACE AS MANY TIMES AS YOU WANT.
I...
...JUST WANTED YOU TO GET BETTER.
I'M GOING TO GIVE HER MY BEST PERFORMANCE EVER.
I JUST WANTED TO MAKE YOU HAPPY.
BUT YOU...

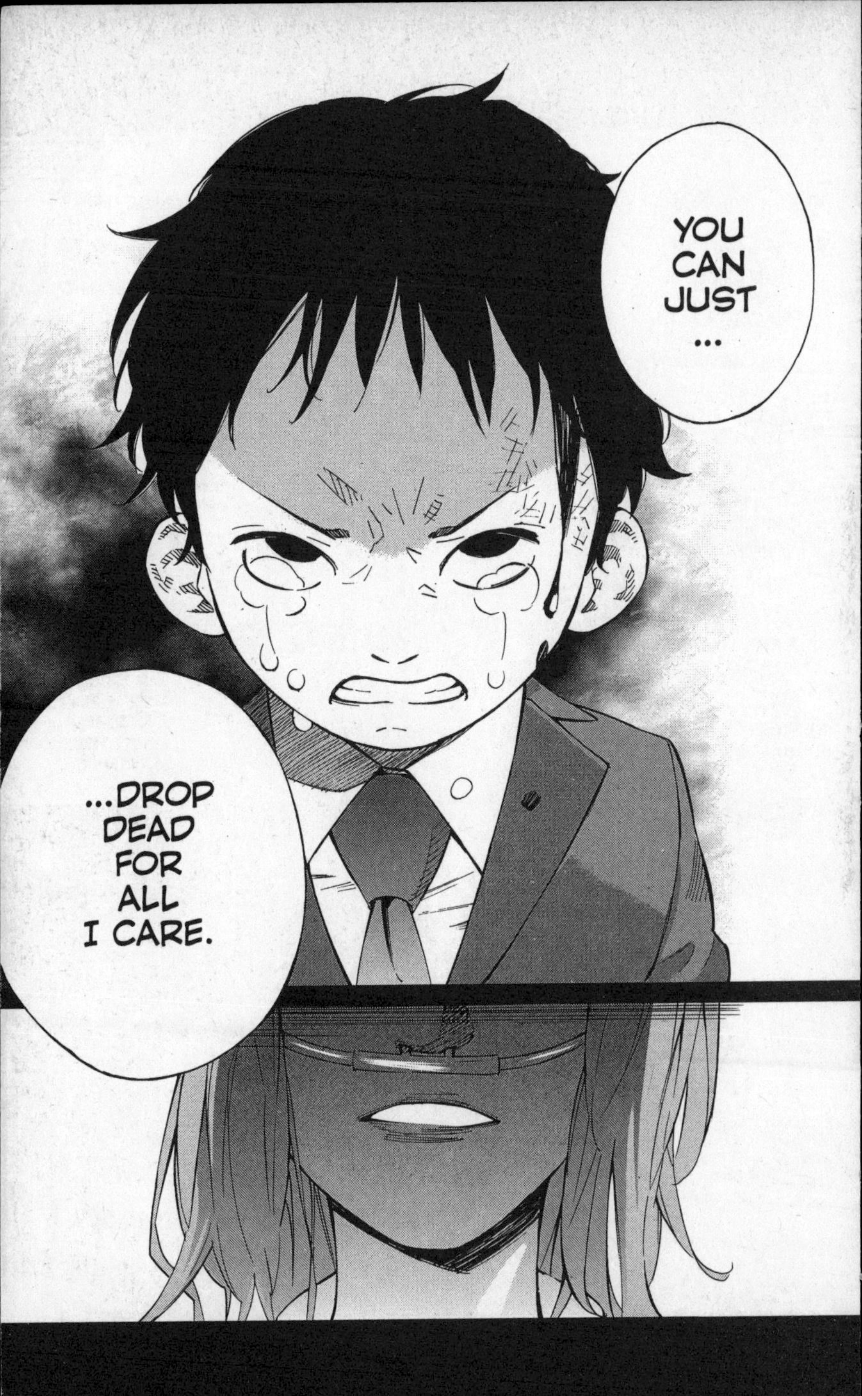
YOU CAN JUST ...
...DROP DEAD FOR ALL I CARE.

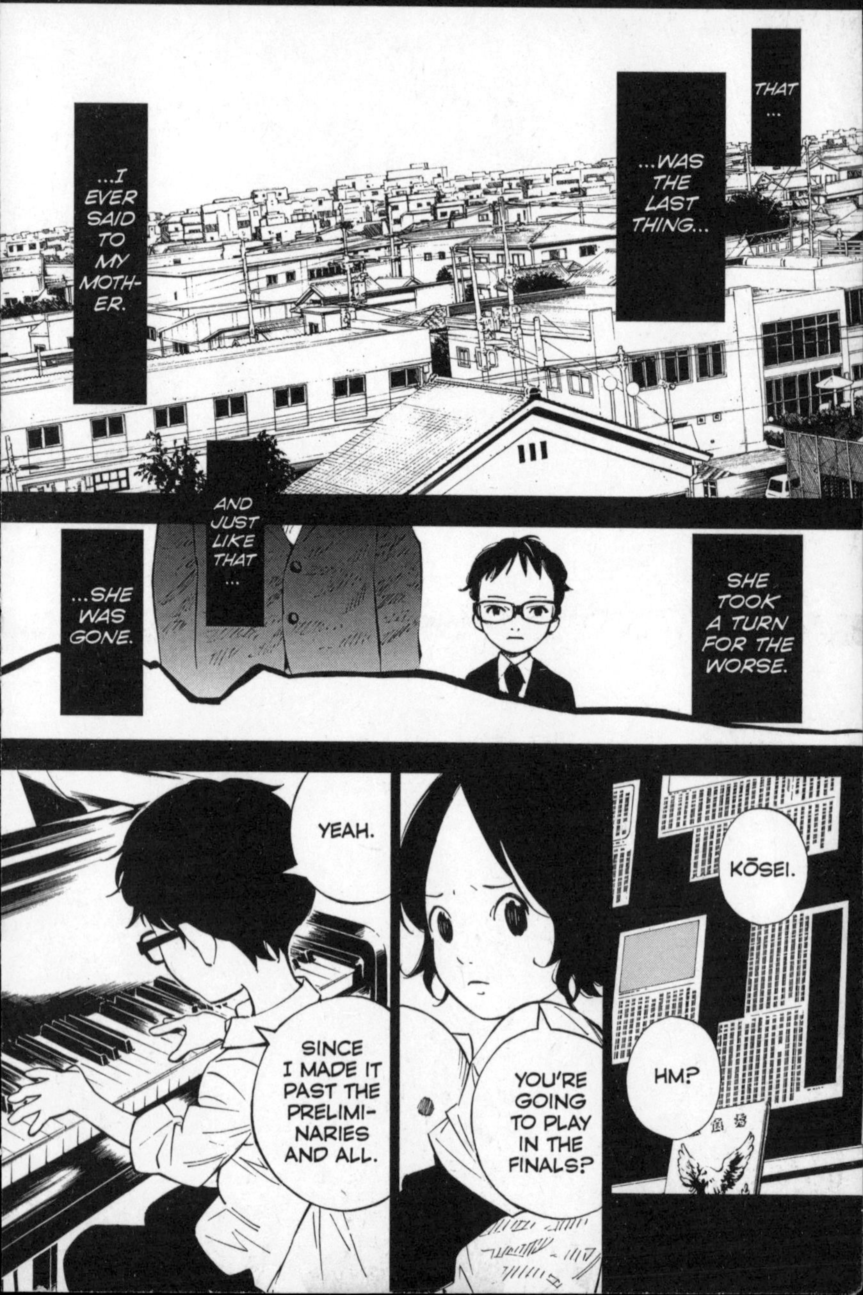
THAT...
...WAS THE LAST THING...
...I EVER SAID TO MY MOTHER.
SHE TOOK A TURN FOR THE WORSE.
AND JUST LIKE THAT...
...SHE WAS GONE.
KŌSEI.
HM?
YOU'RE GOING TO PLAY IN THE FINALS?
YEAH.
SINCE I MADE IT PAST THE PRELIMINARIES AND ALL.

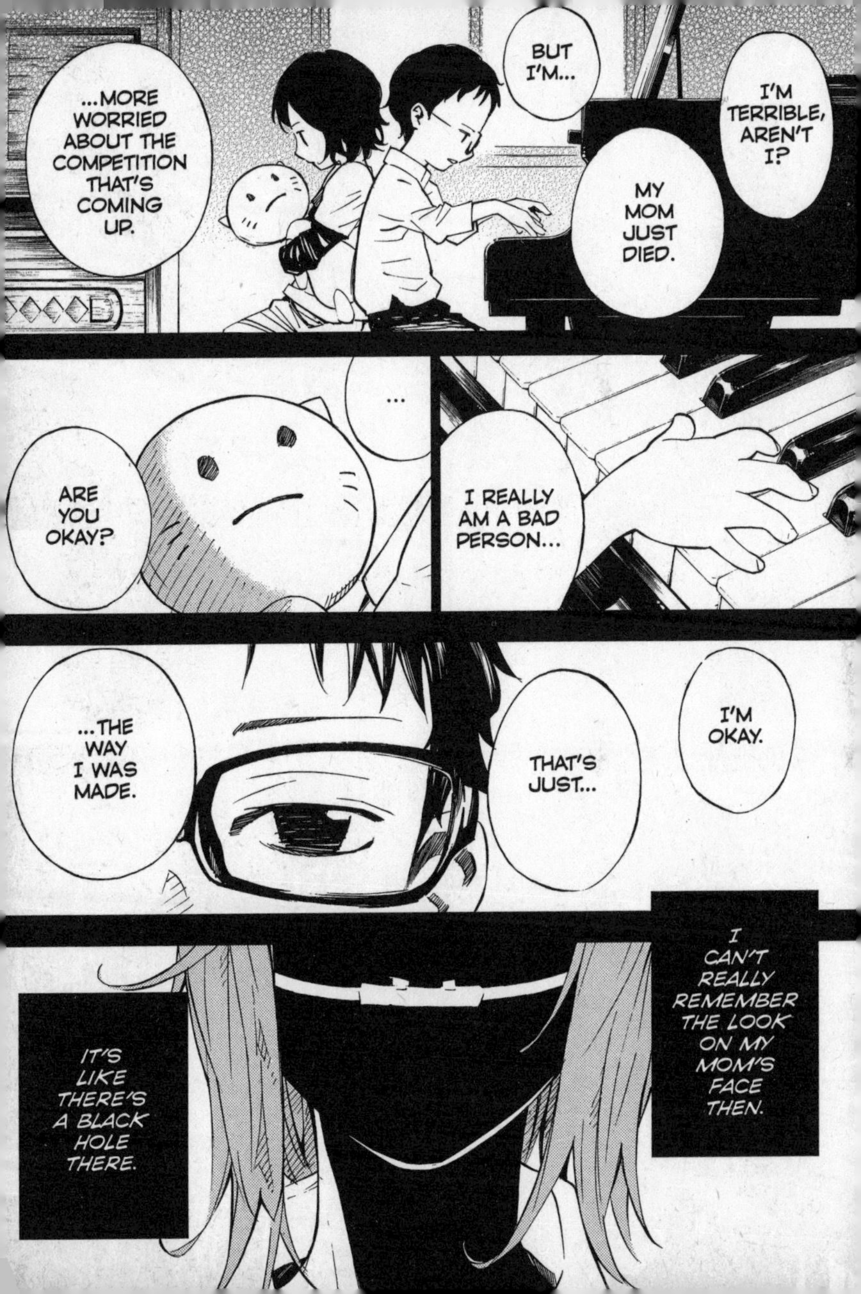
I'M TERRIBLE, AREN'T I?
MY MOM JUST DIED.
BUT I'M...
...MORE WORRIED ABOUT THE COMPETITION THAT'S COMING UP.
I REALLY AM A BAD PERSON...
...
ARE YOU OKAY?
I'M OKAY.
THAT'S JUST...
...THE WAY I WAS MADE.
I CAN'T REALLY REMEMBER THE LOOK ON MY MOM'S FACE THEN.
IT'S LIKE THERE'S A BLACK HOLE THERE.

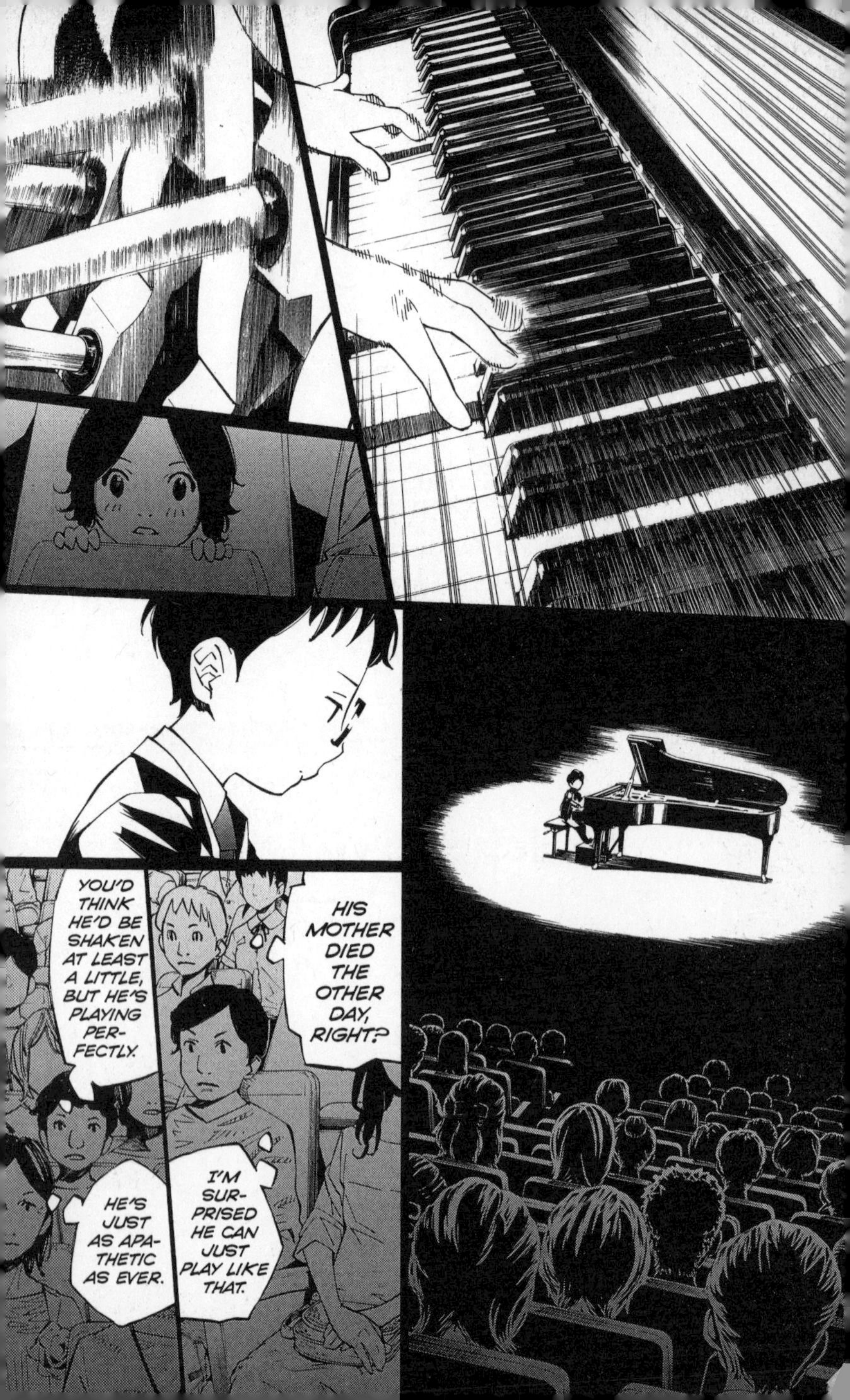
HIS MOTHER DIED THE OTHER DAY, RIGHT?
YOU'D THINK HE'D BE SHAKEN AT LEAST A LITTLE, BUT HE'S PLAYING PER-FECTLY.
I'M SUR-PRISED HE CAN JUST PLAY LIKE THAT.
HE'S JUST AS APA-THETIC AS EVER.

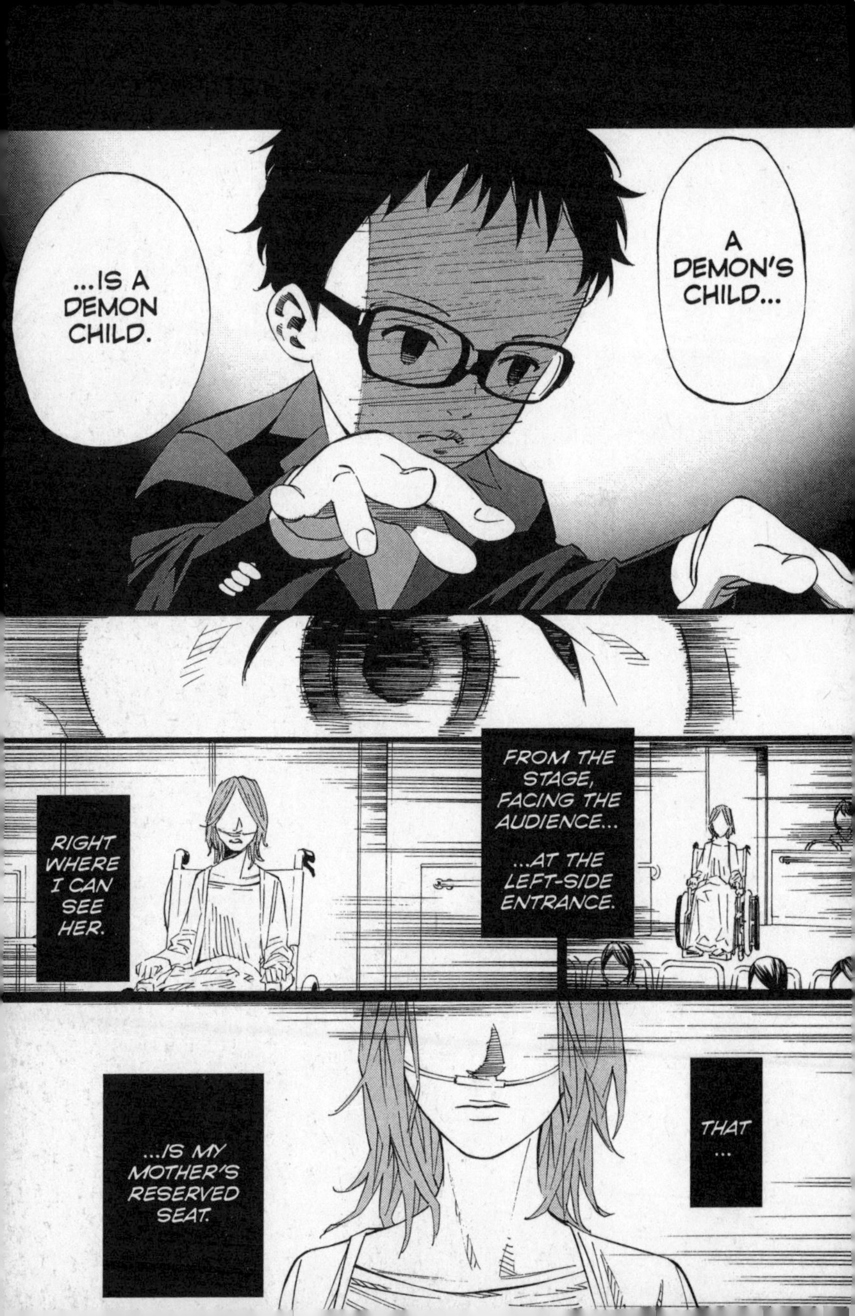
A DEMON'S CHILD...
...IS A DEMON CHILD.
FROM THE STAGE, FACING THE AUDIENCE...
...AT THE LEFT-SIDE ENTRANCE.
RIGHT WHERE I CAN SEE HER.
THAT...
...IS MY MOTHER'S RESERVED SEAT.

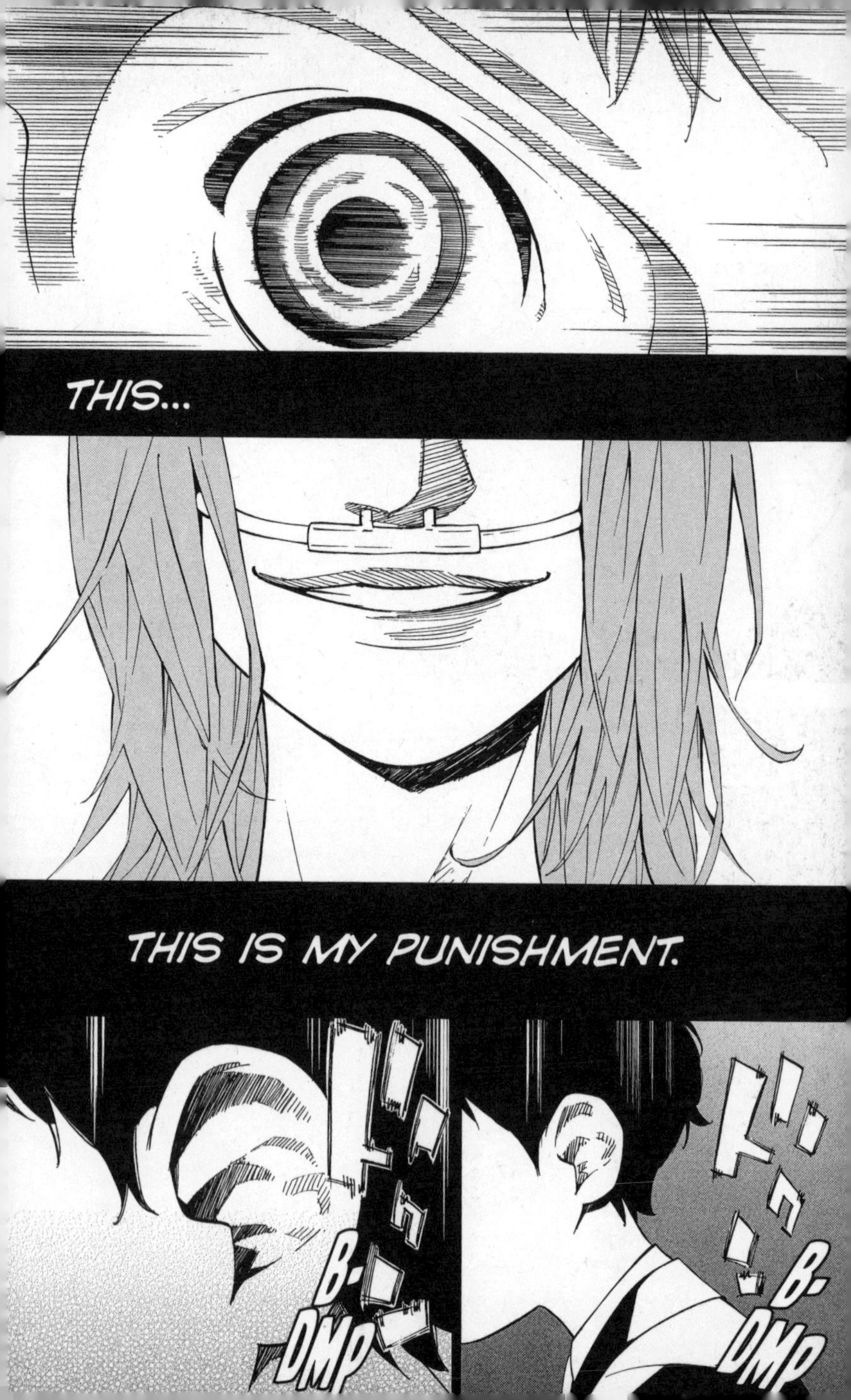
THIS...
THIS IS MY PUNISHMENT.
B-DMP
B-DMP

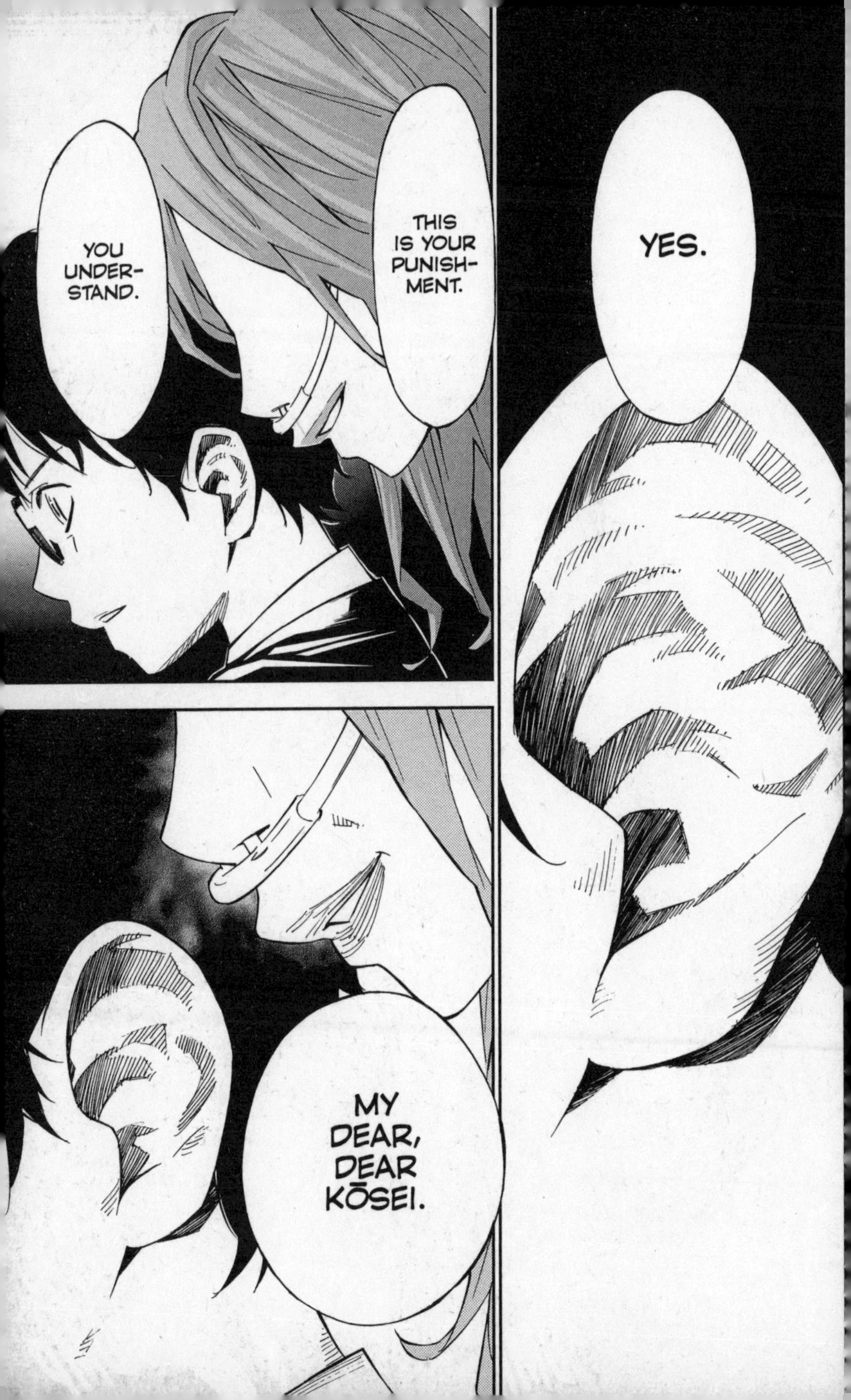
YES.
THIS IS YOUR PUNISHMENT.
YOU UNDERSTAND.
MY DEAR, DEAR KŌSEI.

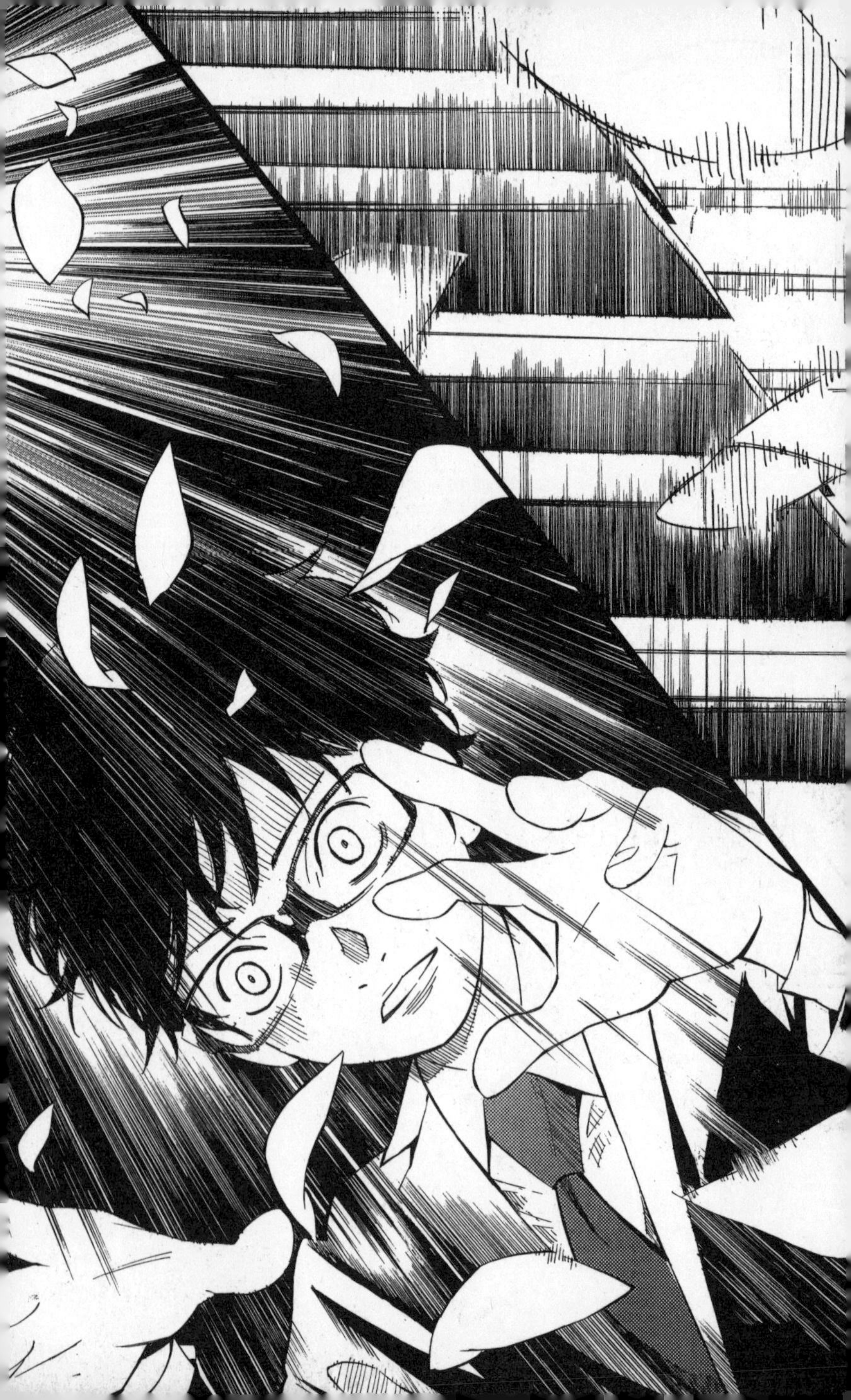

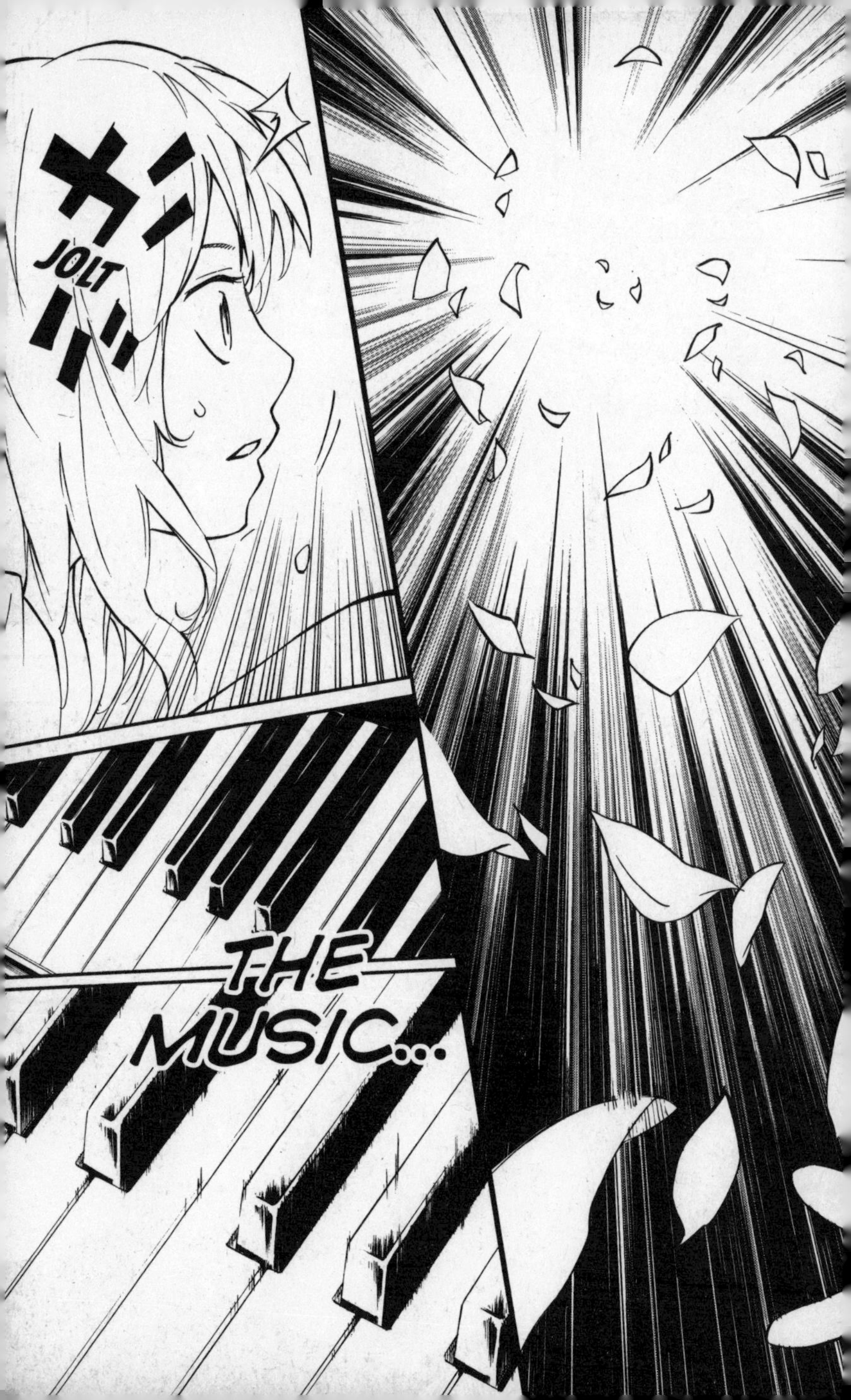
JOLT
THE MUSIC...

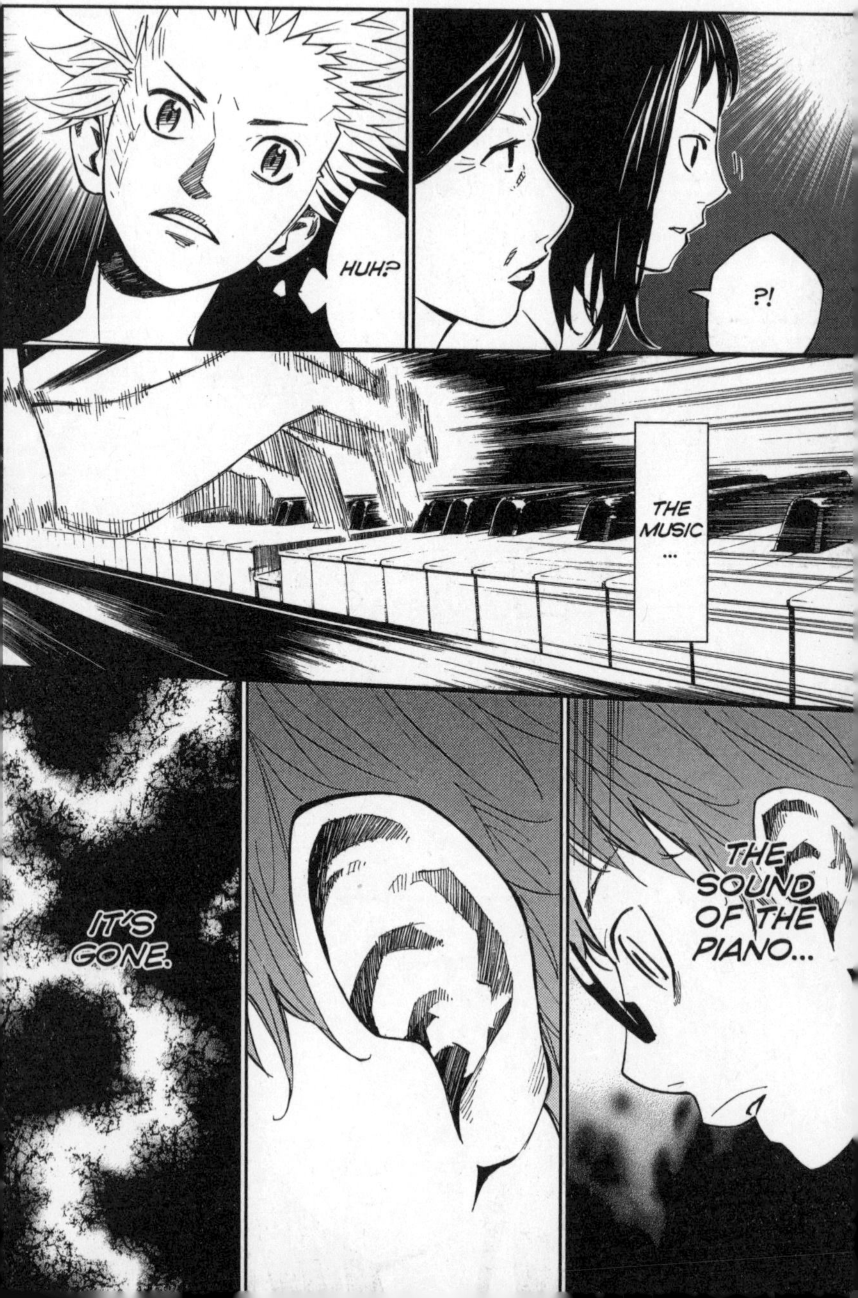
?!
HUH?
THE MUSIC ...
THE SOUND OF THE PIANO...
IT'S GONE.

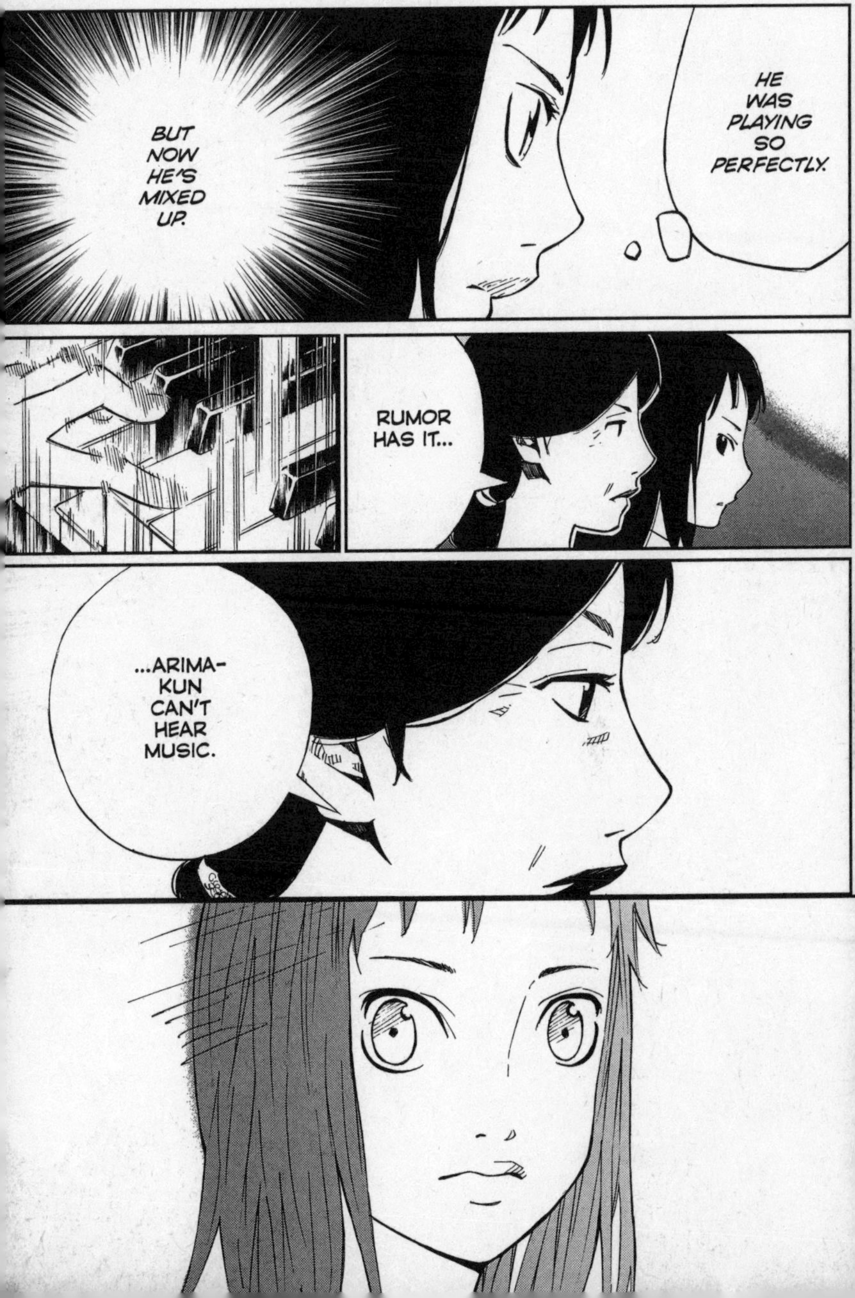
HE WAS PLAYING SO PERFECTLY.
BUT NOW HE'S MIXED UP.
RUMOR HAS IT...
...ARIMA-KUN CAN'T HEAR MUSIC.

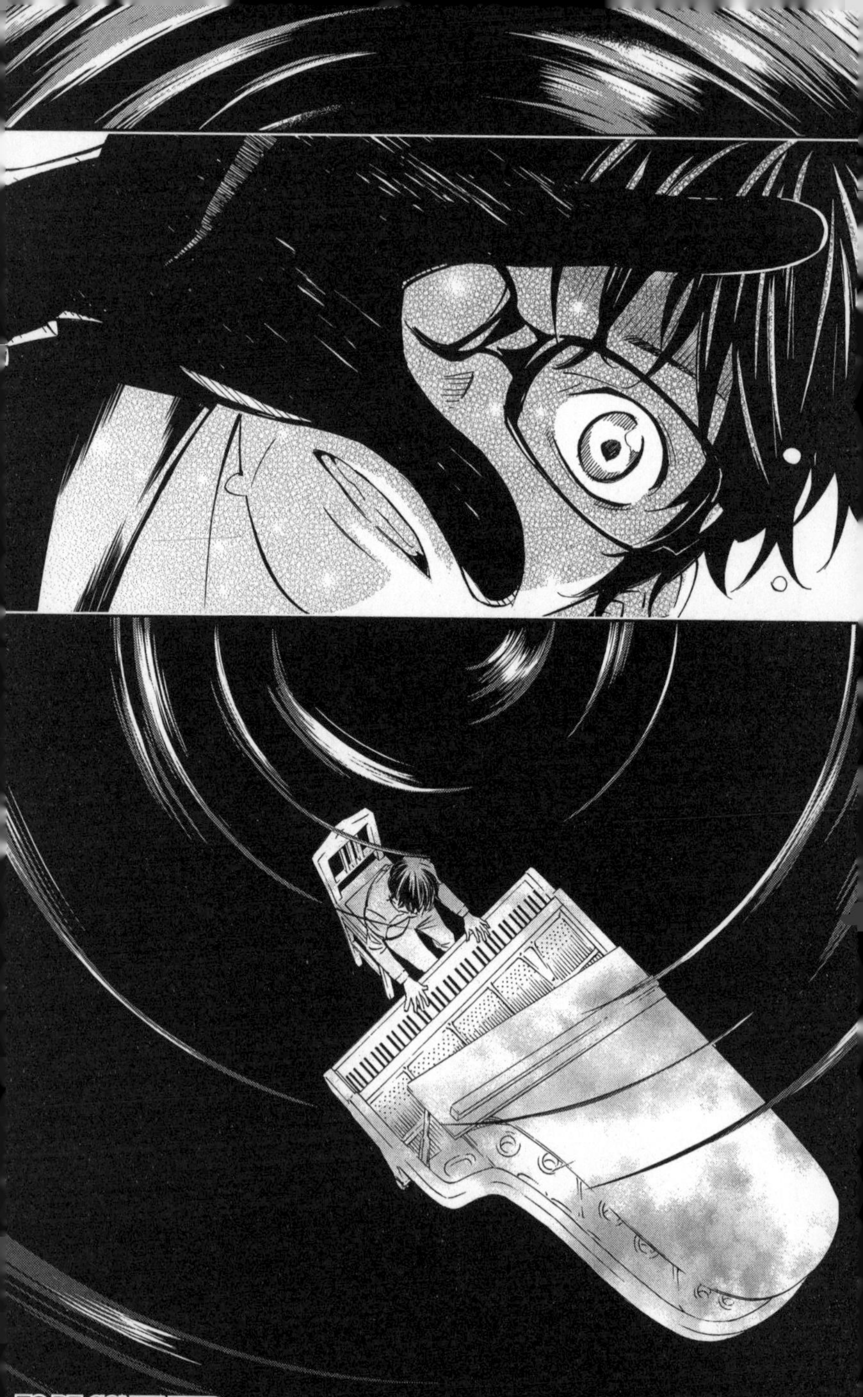

TO BE CONTINUED

YOUR LIE IN APRIL FEATURED MUSIC

JOHANN SEBASTIAN BACH'S WELL-TEMPERED CLAVIER, BOOK 1: PRELUDE AND FUGUE NO. 15 IN G MAJOR BWV 860

The prelude contains a passage where both the right and left hands are playing 16th notes quickly, and you get a strong sense that this piece requires technical practice. This prelude may seem somewhat monotonous, but it enhances the radiance of the fugue, which is packed with musicality.

The melody of the fugue is played at a relaxed pace, and then it overlaps, as the musical patterns invert between the right and left hands. This forms a complex puzzle world, that has even the experts debating which part of it is the main melody. The performer must find his own answer and express it in this very mature composition.

(Pianist Masanori Sugano, lecturer at Tokyo University of the Arts and Musashino Academia Musicae)

Watch it on YouTube (Search "Monthly Shonen Magazine Your Lie In April Featured Music")

Special Thanks:

AKINORI ŌSAWA

MASANORI SUGANO

RIEKO IKEDA

KAORI YAMAZAKI

Translation Notes

Magnifique, page 53

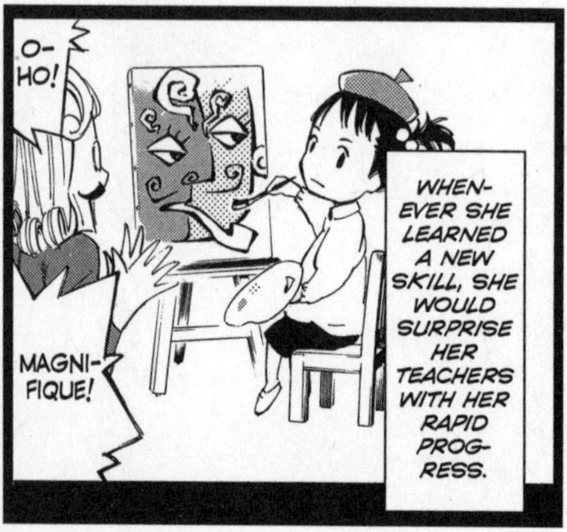
WHEN-EVER SHE LEARNED A NEW SKILL, SHE WOULD SURPRISE HER TEACHERS WITH HER RAPID PROG-RESS.
O-HO!
MAGNI-FIQUE!

If you guessed that this teacher didn't speak French in the original Japanese text, you guessed right! The teacher actually used the Russian word "khorosho," which means "good" and has been adopted into the Japanese language. The translators chose to use the French "magnifique" instead, because it's more commonly used in English and hopefully wouldn't slow the readers down as much.

Deciding with a pencil, page 125

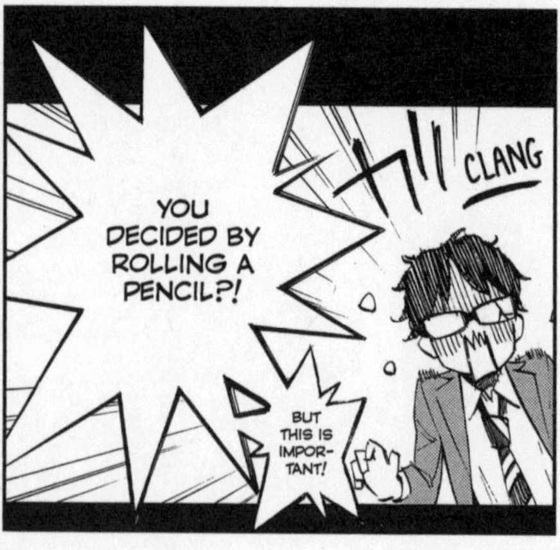
CLANG
YOU DECIDED BY ROLLING A PENCIL?!
BUT THIS IS IMPOR-TANT!

For a little more detail, Kaori chose Kōsei's pieces for the competition by using a pencil like dice. As you can see, she carved a number into each side of the pencil, and assigned a number to each of the possible pieces. Then she rolled the pencil, and chose the piece based on which number was on top when the pencil stopped.

Three-year killer/three-type pork, page 166

WHAM
THREE
FLICK
TYPE
GYA!
FSHH
WHOA!
PORK.
AAAA-AHH!

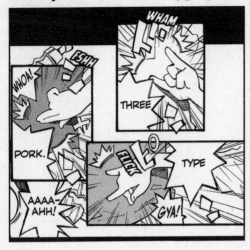

Tsubaki's killer move, *sangenton*, is either named after a favorite food—it means "three-type pork", and comes from three-way cross-bred pigs—or was the first thing Tsubaki could come up with that started with the word "three" and had three parts to it. Her friends call it a three-year killer, indicating that its victims will die in three years from its harmful effects.

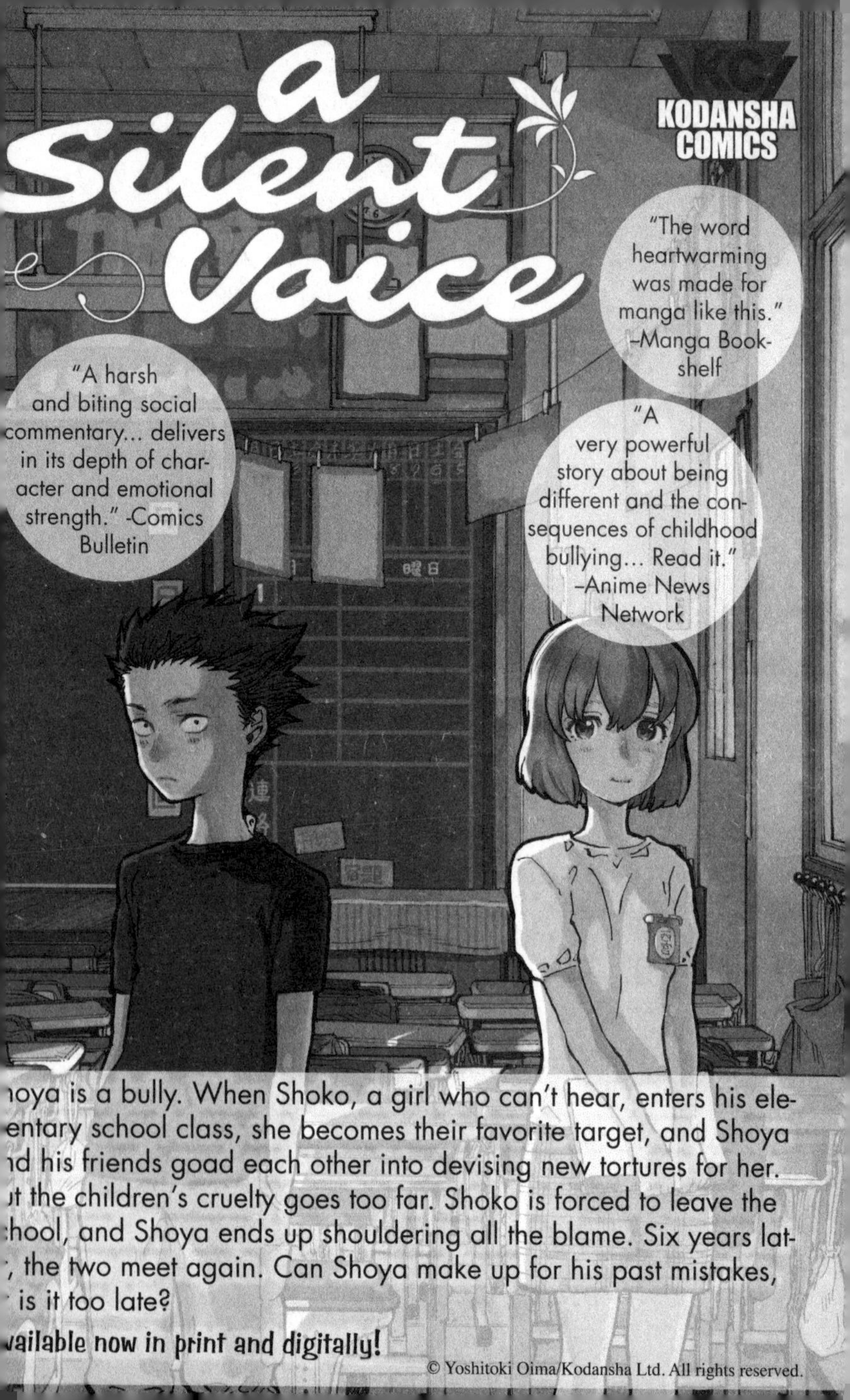
a Silent Voice
KODANSHA COMICS
"The word heartwarming was made for manga like this." –Manga Bookshelf
"A harsh and biting social commentary... delivers in its depth of character and emotional strength." -Comics Bulletin
"A very powerful story about being different and the consequences of childhood bullying... Read it." –Anime News Network
oya is a bully. When Shoko, a girl who can't hear, enters his ele-
entary school class, she becomes their favorite target, and Shoya
d his friends goad each other into devising new tortures for her.
t the children's cruelty goes too far. Shoko is forced to leave the
hool, and Shoya ends up shouldering all the blame. Six years lat-
, the two meet again. Can Shoya make up for his past mistakes,
is it too late?
vailable now in print and digitally!
© Yoshitoki Oima/Kodansha Ltd. All rights reserved.

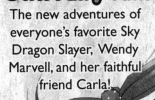

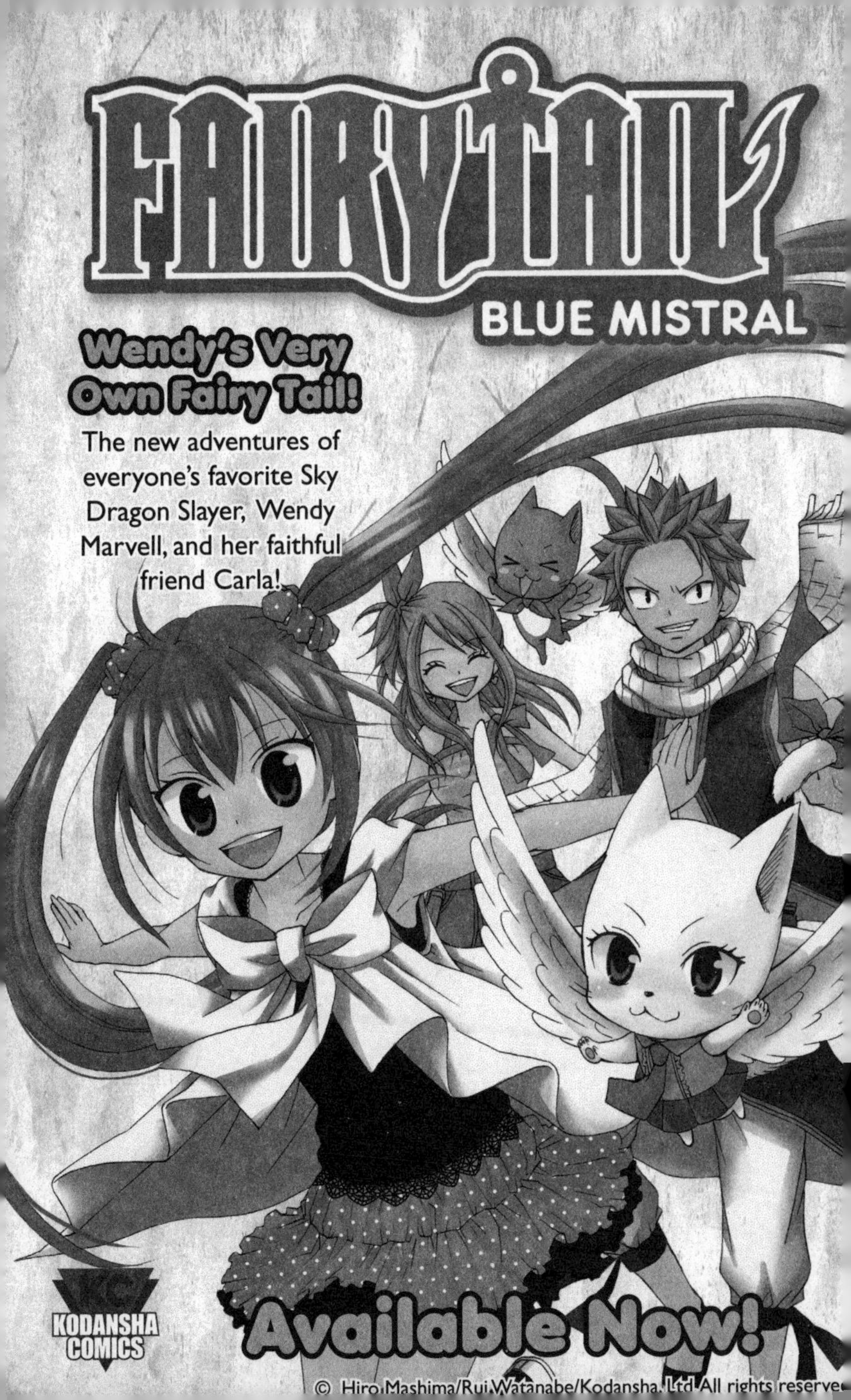

FAIRY TAIL
BLUE MISTRAL

Wendy's Very Own Fairy Tail!

The new adventures of everyone's favorite Sky Dragon Slayer, Wendy Marvell, and her faithful friend Carla!

KODANSHA COMICS

Available Now!

© Hiro Mashima/Rui Watanabe/Kodansha Ltd. All rights reserved.

KC
ODANSHA
COMICS

THE HEROIC LEGEND OF
ARSLAN

READ THE NEW SERIES FROM THE CREATOR OF
FULLMETAL ALCHEMIST, HIROMU ARAKAWA!
NOW A HIT TV SERIES!

"Arakawa proves to be more than up to the task of adapting Tanaka's fantasy novels and fans of historical or epic fantasy will be quite pleased with the resulting book."
-Anime News Network

ECBATANA IS BURNING!

Arslan is the young and curious prince of Pars who, despite his best efforts doesn't seem to have what it takes to be a proper king like his father. At the age of 14, Arslan goes to his first battle and loses everything as the blood-soaked mist of war gives way to scorching flames, bringing him to face the demise of his once glorious kingdom. However, it is Arslan's destiny to be a ruler, and despite the trials that face him, he must now embark on a journey to reclaim his fallen kingdom.

Available now in print and digitally!

© Hiromu Arakawa/Yoshiki Tanaka/Kodansha Ltd. All rights reserved.

Yamada-kun AND THE Seven Witches

KG
KODANSHA COMICS

"A very funny manga with a lot of heart and character."
—Adventures in Poor Taste

SWAPPED WITH A KISS?!

Class troublemaker Ryu Yamada is already having a bad day when he stumbles down a staircase along with star student Urara Shiraishi. When he wakes up, he realizes they have switched bodies—and that Ryu has the power to trade places with anyone just by kissing them! Ryu and Urara take full advantage of the situation to improve their lives, but with such an oddly amazing power, just how long will they be able to keep their secret under wraps?

Available now in print and digitally!

© Miki Yoshikawa/Kodansha Ltd. All rights reserved.

Maria
THE VIRGIN WITCH

"Maria's brand of righteous justice, passion and plain talking make for one of the freshest manga series of 2015. I dare any other book to top it."
—UK Anime Network

PURITY AND POWER

As a war to determine the rightful ruler of medieval France ravages the land, the witch Maria decides she will not stand idly by as men kill each other in the name of God and glory. Using her powerful magic, she summons various beasts and demons —even going as far as using a succubus to seduce soldiers into submission under the veil of night— all to stop the needless slaughter. However, after the Archangel Michael puts an end to her meddling, he curses her to lose her powers if she ever gives up her virginity. Will she forgo the forbidden fruit of adulthood in order to bring an end to the merciless machine of war?

Available now in print and digitally!

KODANSHA COMICS

©Mayasuki Ishikawa /Kodansha. Ltd. All rights reserved.

INUYASHIKI

A superhero like none you've ever seen, from the creator of "Gantz"!

ICHIRO INUYASHIKI IS DOWN ON HIS LUCK. HE LOOKS MUCH OLDER THAN HIS 58 YEARS, HIS CHILDREN DESPISE HIM, AND HIS WIFE THINKS HE'S A USELESS COWARD. SO WHEN HE'S DIAGNOSED WITH STOMACH CANCER AND GIVEN THREE MONTHS TO LIVE, IT SEEMS THE ONLY ONE WHO'LL MISS HIM IS HIS DOG.

THEN A BLINDING LIGHT FILLS THE SKY, AND THE OLD MAN IS KILLED... ONLY TO WAKE UP LATER IN A BODY HE ALMOST RECOGNIZES AS HIS OWN. CAN IT BE THAT ICHIRO INUYASHIKI IS NO LONGER HUMAN?

COMES IN EXTRA-LARGE EDITIONS WITH COLOR PAGES!

KODANSHA COMICS

Inuyashiki © Hiroya Oku/Kodansha Ltd. All rights reserved.

FINALLY, A LOWER-COST OMNIBUS EDITION OF FAIRY TAIL! CONTAINS VOLUMES 1-5. ONLY $39.99!

- NEARLY 1,000 PAGES!
- EXTRA LARGE 7"x10.5" TRIM SIZE!
- HIGH-QUALITY PAPER!

KC
KODANSHA COMICS

Fairy Tail takes place in a world filled with magic. 17-year-old Lucy is a wizard-in-training who wants to join a magic guild so that she can become a full-fledged wizard. She dreams of joining the most famous guild, known as Fairy Tail. One day she meets Natsu, a boy raised by a dragon which vanished when he was young. Natsu has devoted his life to finding his dragon father. When Natsu helps Lucy out of a tricky situation, she discovers that he is a member of Fairy Tail, and our heroes' adventure together begins.

FAIRY TAIL

MASTER'S EDITION

Hiro Mashima/Kodansha Ltd. All rights reserved.

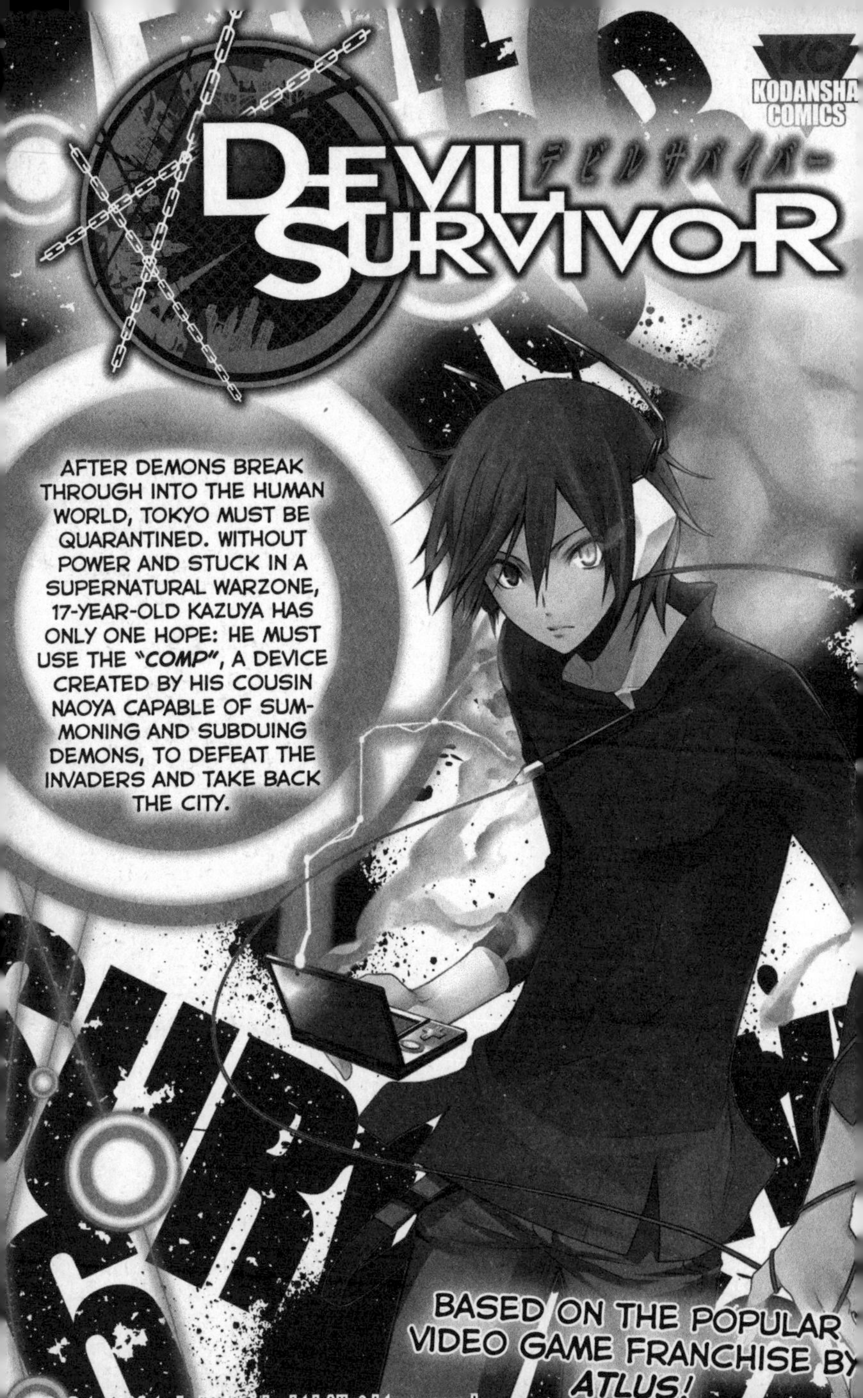
KODANSHA COMICS
DEVIL SURVIVOR
デビルサバイバー
AFTER DEMONS BREAK THROUGH INTO THE HUMAN WORLD, TOKYO MUST BE QUARANTINED. WITHOUT POWER AND STUCK IN A SUPERNATURAL WARZONE, 17-YEAR-OLD KAZUYA HAS ONLY ONE HOPE: HE MUST USE THE "COMP", A DEVICE CREATED BY HIS COUSIN NAOYA CAPABLE OF SUM-MONING AND SUBDUING DEMONS, TO DEFEAT THE INVADERS AND TAKE BACK THE CITY.
BASED ON THE POPULAR VIDEO GAME FRANCHISE BY ATLUS!

DON'T MISS THE MOST ACCLAIMED ACTION MANGA OF 2013!

"Gripping doesn't begin to describe Vinland Saga. __ stars."
—ICv2

"Deeply engrossing... If you have any interest at all in Vikings, the Medieval period, or pirates, this __ not a series you want to miss."
—Anime News Network

"The art is gorgeous, a combination of beautiful cartooning and realistic backgrounds. Yukimura is also a master of pacing, both in frenetic battle scenes and charged emotional moments."
—Faith Erin Hicks, *Friends With Boys*

"For those who love Berserk, you'll love this too... Worth the long wait."
—A Case Suitable for Treatment

"It will be impossible to stop watching this story unfold."
—Japan Media Arts Awards jury

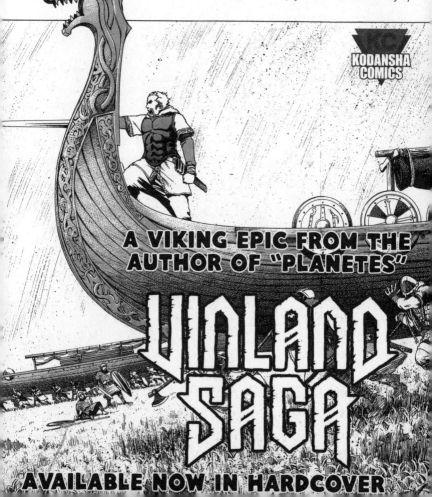

KODANSHA COMICS

A VIKING EPIC FROM THE AUTHOR OF "PLANETES"

VINLAND SAGA

AVAILABLE NOW IN HARDCOVER

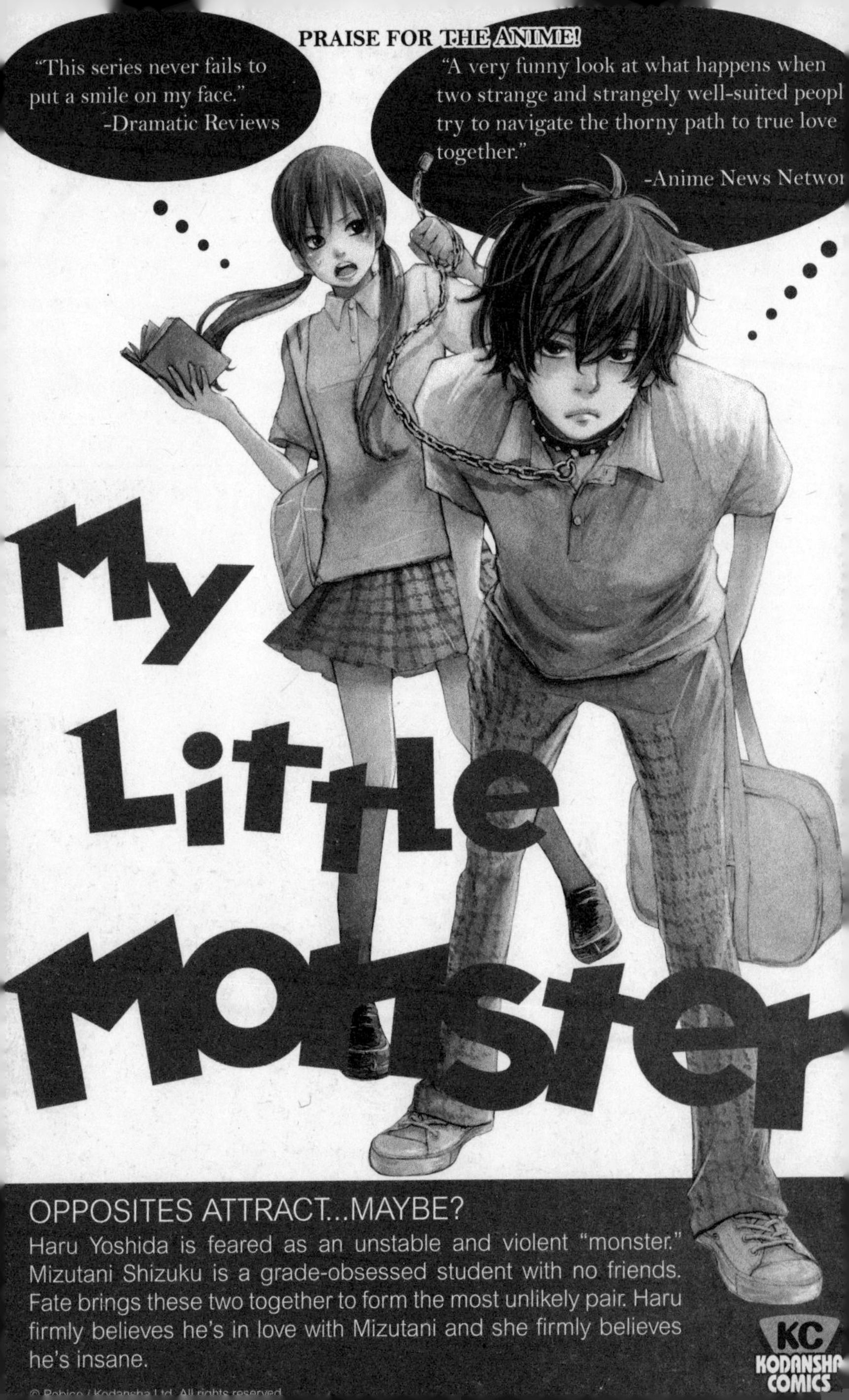
PRAISE FOR THE ANIME!
"This series never fails to put a smile on my face."
-Dramatic Reviews
"A very funny look at what happens when two strange and strangely well-suited peopl try to navigate the thorny path to true love together."
-Anime News Networ
My Little Monster
OPPOSITES ATTRACT...MAYBE?
Haru Yoshida is feared as an unstable and violent "monster." Mizutani Shizuku is a grade-obsessed student with no friends. Fate brings these two together to form the most unlikely pair. Haru firmly believes he's in love with Mizutani and she firmly believes he's insane.
KC KODANSHA COMICS
© Robico / Kodansha Ltd. All rights reserved.

Praise for the anime:

"The show provides a pleasant window on the highs and lows of young love with two young people who are first timers at the real thing."

-The Fandom Post

"Always it is smarter, more poetic, more touching, just plain better than you think it is going to be."

-Anime News Network

Say I Love You.

KC
KODANSHA COMICS

Mei Tachibana has no friends — and says she doesn't need them! But everything changes when she accidentally roundhouse kicks the most popular boy in school! However, Yamato Kurosawa isn't angry in the slightest— in fact, he thinks his ordinary life could use an unusual girl like Mei. But winning Mei's trust will be a tough task. How long will she refuse to say, "I love you"?

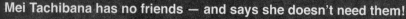

© Kanae Hazuki / Kodansha Ltd. All rights reserved.

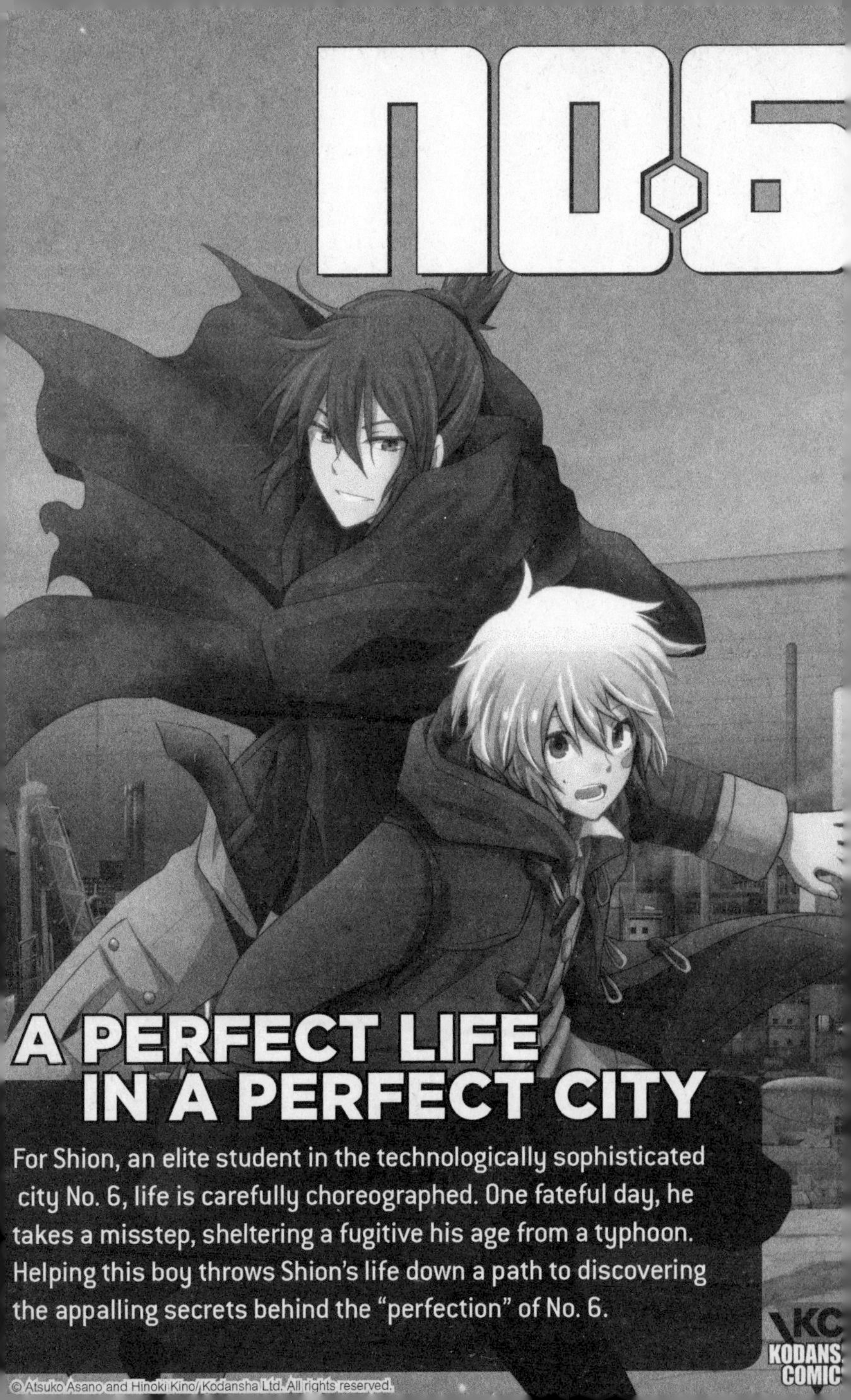
NO.6
A PERFECT LIFE IN A PERFECT CITY
For Shion, an elite student in the technologically sophisticated city No. 6, life is carefully choreographed. One fateful day, he takes a misstep, sheltering a fugitive his age from a typhoon. Helping this boy throws Shion's life down a path to discovering the appalling secrets behind the "perfection" of No. 6.
KC KODANSHA COMICS
© Atsuko Asano and Hinoki Kino / Kodansha Ltd. All rights reserved.

SHERLOCK BONES

KC/ KODANSHA COMICS

DEDUCTIVE DOG DETECTIVE

When Takeru adopts a new pet, he's in for a surprise—the dog is none other than the reincarnation of Sherlock Holmes. With no one else able to communicate with Holmes, Takeru is roped into becoming Sherdog's assistant, John Watson. Using his sleuthing skills, Holmes uncovers clues to solve the trickiest crimes. 🐾

© Yuma Ando and Yuki Sato / Kodansha Ltd. All rights reserved.

Your Lie in April volume 4 is a work of fiction. Names, characters, places, and incidents are the products of the author's imagination or are used fictitiously. Any resemblance to actual events, locales, or persons, living or dead, is entirely coincidental.

A Kodansha Comics Trade Paperback Original
Your Lie in April volume 4 copyright © 2012 Naoshi Arakawa
English translation copyright © 2015 Naoshi Arakawa

All rights reserved.

Published in the United States by Kodansha Comics, an imprint of Kodansha USA Publishing, LLC, New York.

Publication rights for this English edition arranged through Kodansha Ltd, Tokyo.

ISBN 978-1-63236-174-5

Special thanks:
Akinori Osawa, Rieko Ikeda, and Kaori Yamazaki

Printed in the United States of America.

www.kodanshacomics.com

9 8 7 6 5 4 3 2 1
Translation: Alethea and Athena Nibley
Lettering: Scott Brown
Editing: Haruko Hashimoto and Ben Applegate
Kodansha Comics edition cover design by Phil Balsman

TOMARE!
STOP

You're going the wrong way!

Manga is a completely different type of reading experience.

To start at the beginning, Go to the end!

That's right! Authentic manga is read the traditional Japanese way—from right to left, exactly the opposite of how American books are read. It's easy to follow: Just go to the other end of the book and read each page—and each panel—from right side to left side, starting at the top right. Now you're experiencing manga as it was meant to be!